Russia after Lenin

Following the Russian Revolution, the cultural and political landscape of Russia was strewn with contradictions. The dictatorship, censorship and repression of the Communist Party existed alongside private enterprise, the black market and open debates on socialism. In *Russia after Lenin*, Vladimir Brovkin offers a comprehensive cultural, political, economic and social history of developments in Russia in the 1920s.

By examining the contrast between Bolshevik propaganda claims and social reality, the author explains how Communist ideas were variously received, resisted and acted upon by workers, peasants, students, women, teachers and party officials. He presents a picture of cultural diversity and rejection of Communist constraints through many means including unauthorized protest, religion, jazz music and poetry.

In *Russia after Lenin*, Brovkin argues that these trends, if left unchecked, endangered the Communist Party's monopoly on political power. The Stalinist revolution and terror can thus be seen as a pre-emptive strike against this independent and vibrant society, as well as a product of Stalin's personality and Communist ideology.

Vladimir Brovkin is NATO Research Fellow and Adjunct Professor at the American University, in Washington DC.

Russia after Lenin

Politics, Culture and Society, 1921–1929

Vladimir Brovkin

London and New York

First published 1998
by Routledge
11 New Fetter Lane, London EC4P 4EE

Transferred to Digital Printing 2004

Simultaneously published in the USA and Canada
by Routledge
29 West 35th Street, New York, NY 10001

Typeset in Times by
Ponting–Green Publishing Services, Chesham,
Buckinghamshire

British Library Cataloguing in Publication Data
A catalogue record for this book is available from the
British Library

Library of Congress Cataloging in Publication Data
Brovkin, Vladimir N.
    Russia after Lenin: Politics, Culture and Society,
1921–1929 / Vladimir Brovkin.
        p.   cm.
    Includes bibliographical references and index.
    1. Soviet Union – Politics and government – 1917–1936.
2. Soviet Union – Civilization.   3. Soviet Union – Social
conditions – 1917–1945.   I. Title.
    DK266.5.B76   1998
947.084'2–dc21   97–39751
    CIP

ISBN   0–415–17991–2 (hbk)
ISBN   0–415–17992–0 (pbk)

FOR MY DEAR WIFE, ALYONA

Contents

Illustrations

Abbreviations

Agitprop	Agitation and Propaganda Department of the Central Committee
CC	Central Committee
CEC	Central Executive Committee
CheKa	Chesvychainaya Kommissiya – Extraordinary Commission
Chon	Chasti Osobogo Naznacheniya – Special Purpose Units
Comintern	Communist International
CP	Communist Party
EC	Executive Committee
GK	Gorodskoi Komitet – City Committee
GPU	Glavnoe Politicheskoe Upravlenia – Main Political Directorate
Gubkom	Gubernskii Komitet – Province Committee
Glavlit	Glavnyi Literaturnyi Komitet – Main Literature Committee
Gublit	Gubernskii Literaturnyi Komitet – Province Literature section
KA	Komsomol archive
Komsomol	KSM Kommunisticheskii Soyuz Molodezhi – Communist Youth League
LK	Leningradskii Komitet – Leningrad Party Committee
MK	Moskovskii Komitet – Moscow Party Committee
MRC	Main Repertoire Committee – Glavrepertkom
NS	Narodnye Sotsialisty – People's Socialists
Orgraspred	– CC Cadres Department
PSR	Party of Socialist Revolutionaries
Proletkult	Proletarskaya Kultura – Proletarian Culture
RCP(b)	Russian Communist Party of Bolsheviks – RKP(b)
SR	Socialist Revolutionary
VKP(b)	Vsesoyuznaya Kommunisticheskaya Partiya Bolshevikov – All-Union Communist Party of the Bolsheviks
VLKSM	All Russian Leninist Komsomol
VTsSNKh	Vrerossiiskii Tsentralnyi Sovet Narodnogo Khoziaistva – All-Russian Central Council of People's Economy

Acknowledgments

I always wanted to write a book on politics and culture in the 1920s that would be a sequel to Rene Füllop Miller's path-breaking *The Mind and Face of Bolshevism* (1926). In 1991 I was much influenced by my then colleague Simon Schama's discussion of culture and politics during the French Revolution in his *Citizens*. I was fascinated by the works of Robert Darnton and Roger Chartier on mentalities and representations. I owe an intellectual debt to many colleagues who had worked on the history of culture and politics in Russia, particularly Leonard Schapiro, Adam Ulam, Robert Tucker, Stephen Cohen, Richard Stites, Katerina Clark, Martin Malia, Robert Conquest, Peter Kenez, and Wladimir Berelovitch, to name only a few. I learned a great deal from Sheila Fitzpatrick, William Rosenberg, and Diane Koenker on the social history of the 1920s. I gained insight on youth culture and history of women from the works of Anne Gorsuch, Isabel Tirado, and Wendy Goldman.

Among my colleagues I owe deep gratitude to Richard Pipes who was the first reader of this book and gave me valuable suggestions. I also want to thank Caroline Ford who literally guided me through the literature on culture, mentalities, and representations. Above all I want to thank David Brandenberger who helped me translate some verses, edited the manuscript, and gave me valuable insights during our regular discussion sessions as the work progressed.

Research for this book has been made possible by the IREX Fellowship. I am grateful to IREX's Moscow staff who made my stay there fruitful and enjoyable. A generous grant from the John M. Olin Foundation enabled me to complete the manuscript and prepare it for publication.

Introduction
Revolutionary identity

The 1920s are popularly known as a Golden Age in Russia – eight short years after the end of the civil war and before Stalin's revolution from above. Much admired in both Soviet, post-Soviet Russian and Western historiography, the period of New Economic Policy has been seen as an alternative to Stalinism. The 1920s have been hailed as an example of at least one period in Soviet history which was a success, in economics, politics, and especially in terms of culture.

Soviet historians tended to represent the years of the NEP as a march forward towards socialism due to the wisdom of Lenin. From this perspective, the 1930s were the years of even more spectacular achievements but marred by what were called violations of socialist legality, a code name for the Great Terror. Most studies of political history of the 1920s have regarded the NEP years as an asset of the Bolsheviks and as proof that had it not been for Stalin a different kind of socialism could have emerged in Soviet Russia, socialism with a human face, displaying cultural diversity and private enterprise.[1]

The contemporary Russian intelligentsia raves about the 1920s as a period of unique creativity, when Russian culture was equal to what was evolving in Berlin and Vienna. It is a source of pride and accomplishment.[2] Russian intellectuals look back with admiration at the works of Eisenstein and Vertov in cinema, Mayerhold in theater, and Tatlin and Malevich in art as proof that, despite the ever stricter controls, artists sympathetic to the revolution continued to produce highly innovative and experimental works.[3]

Even though some non-Communist artists and writers remained, the terms of cultural discourse precluded production of explicitly anti-Soviet, apolitical and individually oriented works. All this was smashed to pieces as a bourgeois culture that had no place in Soviet society. After the banishing of all the anti-Communists and religious philosophers, those that remained appear to us to have constituted a rich society, especially when compared to the poverty that followed. When the 1920s are compared not with the totalitarian orthodoxy of the 1930s but with the period they followed, the teens, one receives a very different picture. These artists used to be only a small part of a much larger and richer whole. During the civil war years, not to mention the pre-Bolshevik experience, there was much more diversity in the world of ideas and culture than in the 1920s. The fact that the CP had not yet established complete control over the world of ideas and individual expression cannot be understood as testimony that it had no intention of doing so. It is hard to disagree with Nadezhda Mandelshtam who wrote:

> This hankering after the idyllic twenties is the result of a legend created by people who were then in their thirties and by their younger associates. But in reality it was the twenties in which all the foundations were laid for our future: the casuistical dialectic, the dismissal of older values, the longing for unanimity and self abasement.[4]

Russian culture of the 1920s has been primarily seen as high culture. There are many books on cinema, theater, art, and architecture but none on the culture of political discourse, or the history of mentalities, or popular attitudes. This is, of course, a great omission because the high culture of the time was explicitly political, conveying a message to the masses. In most cases, this message was produced or approved by the Department for Agitation and Propaganda of the Communist Party. The Bolsheviks tried to create and disseminate their own new culture, rituals, way of life, and morality. New cultural practices clashed with the traditional culture of workers and peasants. The result was a fascinating mixture of misunder-standings, misappropriation, distortion, and adaptation of the required behavior norms.

Indeed, the 1920s were full of contradictions – a period of relative openness in party debates on the meaning of socialism and yet strengthening of Stalin's personal dictatorship; creativity in artistic expression combined with the tightening of ideological controls; a period of the New Economic Policy – that is, individual family farming for market in agriculture combined with the rise of centralized planned economy in industry. It was a period when Communist orthodoxy in ideology, culture, behavioral norms, and cultural practices crystallized into a coherent whole.

The main problem in the scholarship on the 1920s is that the studies of culture and politics are disconnected. Strictly political histories of this age reconstruct political currents and struggles within the Communist Party without raising the question of why people thought the way they did. Why did Lenin choose to call NEP a "retreat," and not an age of prosperity, or an age of socialist democracy? Why did Stalin, Trotsky, and Bukharin – in fact all top Communists – define the construction of socialism as fighting on the industrial front? How did it happen that the idea of liberated labor transformed itself into a military campaign? This raises the questions: What did the top Bolsheviks actually mean when they were discussing the construction of socialism in Russia? Was there more than one level in their political vocabulary? How and why did it happen that an ideology inspired by positive utopian visions of creating a just society led to the establishment of a dictatorial regime? How can one explain the fact that NEP was ended so abruptly in 1929? The answers may lie in the Bolsheviks' background, experiences, and values that shaped their world-views.

The main purpose of this book, therefore, is to interpret political history of the 1920s in terms of a history of mentalities and to decode and unfold the meaning of political and cultural discourse. In this endeavor I am much influenced by the works of Robert Darnton and Simon Schama.[5] It is an attempt to follow what Roger Chartier called the process of amalgamation of cultures: the interaction of the officially projected values and the process of their absorption, incorporation, and assimilation into the pre-existing mental world of the Russian people.[6] The task is to explain the cultural content of the social and political trends of NEP Russia.

RUSSIAN SOCIALISM

The Bolshevik regime is customarily associated with Marxism.[7] The Bolsheviks were convinced that they were Marxists and never tired of repeating that the teaching of Karl Marx was their guide to action. Instead of accepting this claim at face value, it is essential to define its meaning in terms of culture. What was the cultural milieu of the Russian underground revolutionary parties? What kind of ethical norms did it nourish? What was the moral code of the Bolsheviks before they seized power? And finally, how had they themselves changed by 1921?[8]

When the idea of socialism captured the minds of the revolutionary intelligentsia in Russia at the end of the nineteenth century, it was a product not of analysis but of a dream.[9] No one produced a meaningful description of what society would be like under socialism. The perfect society of the future, where justice would be not for the privileged few but for all, remained a nebulous vision. To describe this society was contrary to their frame of mind at that stage. Socialism was the supreme goal and revolution a means to achieve it. The revolutionaries saw themselves as special people who possessed something denied to others, a special knowledge of laws of historical development.

For Russian revolutionaries, the idea of socialism was attractive because it foresaw the coming of social order better than capitalism. For Populists, socialism was primarily a protest against modernity associated with the rise of industry, social injustice, and Western materialism.[10] Populist socialism was a utopian vision of avoiding capitalist development in Russia. Populists idealized the peasant commune as an institution that could assure a just division of property and eliminate exploitation. Two key ideas stand out in the populist ideology: the people and the hero. The task of a critically thinking individual, the hero, was to serve the great Russian people. Salvation would

come through revolution and hence an individual had to be a revolutionary and lead the people.

Even though the revolutionary movement of the Russian intelligentsia was technically secular, it had a quasi-religious character. Men and women who had joined the movement were possessed by a zeal to spread the word among the masses. They felt they knew the way to salvation and were ready to sacrifice themselves for the cause. The very act of joining a revolutionary circle meant cutting off their links to normal everyday life and entering another culture, a brotherhood, a new family. Members of these circles saw themselves as missionaries sacrificing themselves for the people. They willingly faced certain arrest, imprisonment, and exile. Their sole task consisted of waking the people to their destiny by rising in revolution. Many revolutionaries saw themselves as moral people: honest, principled, and dedicated martyrs for the cause. They believed they were suffering privation and risking their lives for the people. To serve the cause was an escape from the reality they detested. This fostered a special identity of savior, martyr, and leader. But this identity was a self-delusion. They were in the movement not for the people but for themselves, seeking meaning in their lives, and fascinated by their own utopian visions. Joining a revolutionary circle was for many a way to reaffirm their superiority over the unenlightened masses.[11] Revolutionary struggle was a source of excitement, intellectual stimulation and human closeness that replaced the family.

Russian Marxism was in many ways much more an offshoot of populism than of Western Marxism despite the name. The formative stage of Plekhanov, Lenin, and other founders of Russian Marxism was in the populist milieu. Marxism was attractive because it claimed knowledge of the laws of history and a scientifically proven path that guaranteed the eventual coming of the revolution. The Marxists took over the populists' equation – the critically thinking individual + the people = revolution – and adapted it to a new equation: the Social Democratic Party + the working class = revolution. As they formed a Social Democratic Party in 1898, the Marxists found the working class rather than the peasantry to be the main vehicle of revolution.[12] The task of the SD was to engage in agitation and propaganda among the urban masses and wake them to the realization of their historic mission. All one had to do was develop the workers' revolutionary consciousness.

In the first years of the twentieth century Russian socialism crystallized into three distinct political parties: the Socialist Revolutionaries (SRs), the Mensheviks, and the Bolsheviks.[13] The SRs, the main party of Russian socialism, remained primarily preoccupied with the Russian peasantry.[14] Collective way of life and age-old village commune safeguarded Russian peasants from alien Western ethics of individual profit seeking. The SRs saw periodic redivision of land by the village commune as an innately socialist feature of peasant culture. At the same time Russian peasants were revolutionary in the sense that they craved all the land, including landlords' land, as God's gift to be divided equally among all.

The SRs are largely remembered for their terrorist activity.[15] In 1905–6 and after, SR terrorists assassinated hundreds of Tsarist officials. These terrorist plots were visible and dramatic events that captured public attention and shaped the party's reputation. Yet the vast majority of the SRs had nothing to do with terrorism. Tens of thousands of rural teachers, agronomists, statisticians, and midwives slowly integrated themselves into the local community. As soon as the old regime collapsed in February 1917, these people emerged as recognized and respected leaders. The PSR became a democratic party, although its rhetoric remained revolutionary and its reputation terrorist. Socialism was still on the books as the final goal, although in practical terms the SRs were much more concerned with the peasants' economic needs and democratic government. The proletarian revolution for the SRs was a Marxist heresy unsuited for Russia. By 1917 the SRs were the largest political party in Russia, claiming 1 million members, whereas their closest rivals, the Bolsheviks, had only 200,000 members on the eve of the October coup, as did the Mensheviks.

Just like the SRs, the Mensheviks were concerned with the well-being of the constituency they claimed to represent, the workers. When they argued that the working class should have its own party and strive for national representation, they really meant it. They immersed themselves in trade unions and mutual aid funds, and became a part of the national political scene. They differed from the Bolsheviks in that they did not replace workers' priorities with those of the party. They were willing to submit to the wishes of the majority. Socialism for the Mensheviks was impossible without democracy, the two concepts being inseparably linked in their minds.[16]

THE BOLSHEVIK VALUE SYSTEM

By 1917 the Mensheviks and SRs were well on the way of shaking off utopian visions and becoming political parties. Even though we conventionally refer to the Bolsheviks as a party, it never was a conventional political party. It was first and foremost a conspiratorial organization formed top-down and controlled by a small cohort. Hand-picked local committees of professional revolutionaries "elected" the Central Committee at party gatherings and a few around Lenin shaped party policy. This is not to say that Lenin had no challenges to his authority.[17] Several times he was outmaneuvered and his policies rejected. Yet he always managed to survive by using the few opportunities that offered themselves with more skill than his opponents. Lenin always preferred to split away with a few loyal supporters and preserve his independence of action. His political career up to 1917 is a history of endless intrigues about control over funds, newspapers, and representation at Bolshevik meetings.[18] His experience as a politician prior to 1917 was that of a master tactician who had succeeded time and again to outmaneuver his rivals. The game of politics for Lenin was essentially a process whereby he would place reliable comrades in charge. Compromises and deals with others were welcome and possible while they served the purpose of enlarging the domain of that which was under his control.

The essence of Marxism, as is well known, is a belief in class struggle as a moving force in history. Stages in history follow in sequence. Capitalism as a necessary stage of human development was to be replaced by socialism in due course after the capitalist mode of production exhausted its possibilities. Lenin's main contribution to Marxism, transforming it into Marxism–Leninism, is a profoundly un-Marxist idea that a revolutionary party could seize power and then create the necessary preconditions for the construction of socialism.[19] Marxist scientific laws of human development, he thought, could be altered from above by a revolutionary minority. Construction of socialism likewise is a concept alien to Marxism. Stages in history cannot be skipped or altered. The idea that the state could "build socialism" would have come across as absurd to Marx and Engels.

Marxism postulates a leading role of the working class in the replacement of capitalism with socialism. Lenin revised Marxism here as well. He believed that workers on their own would develop only trade union consciousness. It was the task of the party to fulfill the mission assigned to workers by Marx. On the one hand, Bolshevik official ideology always held that the working class was the main moving force of the revolution and later of the new order. On the other hand, it could not play that role while in the grip of "petty bourgeois consciousness." From here it followed that the party would act in the name of the working class as a whole. In the meantime, the workers had to be imbued with "true proletarian consciousness" and taught to follow the vanguard. The key here was a patronizing and utilitarian attitude towards workers. They were simply the means to an end. While in theory the well-being of the working class was the Bolsheviks' objective, in practice this well-being was understood as being guaranteed by the vanguard's seizure of power. Therefore, any voice in defense of workers' rights, collective or individual, was perceived as an assault on the prerogatives of the party, the true bearer of proletarian consciousness. What should a revolutionary party do if the people rejected socialism? The Bolsheviks would confront that question much later in 1921 and in 1928. Their revolutionary identity predisposed them to disregard the wishes of those they perceived as the backward masses because objectively it was the vanguard which possessed the supreme wisdom.

Before 1917 most Bolsheviks were well aware of the fact that they were not really the party of the working class but an organization of intellectuals trying to find contact with real workers. The vanguard identity was no more than a pleasant compliment that had little to do with reality. Yet as time went on, the Bolsheviks convinced themselves that they indeed were the vanguard of the proletariat. They needed that identity in order to justify in their minds their claim to power. Thus the real situation was substituted with the imaginary and idealized one.

Individual rights were a bourgeois concept for the Bolsheviks. They were preoccupied with the classes, supposedly the true makers of history. In the Bolshevik iconography, the mass replaced the man. What mattered was his social origin, class identity, and the level of acquired proletarian consciousness. The individual's life did not matter in comparison with the historic task of liberation of the whole of mankind. The idea of individual guilt or innocence was also thrown out by the Bolshevik ethics, as the well-being of the revolution and of the working class as a whole was superior to any rights of any one person. If an individual who belonged to the proletarian class deviated from the prescribed norms of political behavior by displaying bourgeois consciousness, he could be purged. Therefore, in Bolshevik usage, this unique property, proletarian consciousness, was nothing but a loyalty test, a required norm of obedience to the bearers of the supreme wisdom.

In the Marxian ethics, even though the class of workers was certainly preeminent over an individual, the ultimate goal remained in theory to better the life of individuals and to increase their rights. In the Russian peasant commune an individual did not have much of a voice. His being was subordinate to the well-being of the entire commune. An individual in a village was clearly subordinate but not altogether excluded from the idea of common good. The well-being of one contributed to the well-being of all. In Bolshevik ethics, any claim of an individual was regarded as almost treasonous and unpardonable egoism. Anyone with the right degree of proletarian consciousness was supposed and expected to put the interest of collectivity, that is, the working class, but in reality of the proletarian state, ahead of any personal interests. This disdain for an individual as a cultural phenomenon by the Bolsheviks is a blend of the two value systems distorting each of the original ingredients.

In the Bolshevik ethics, abstract morality was a fiction, it did not exist. There could only be class morality. "Who benefits from it?" was one of Lenin's favorite questions. In the given conditions the bourgeoisie and the landlords did. Therefore, all the laws and all the morality were at the service of the ruling classes. Existing laws did not matter because these were the laws of the oppressor. From here it followed that such laws were not binding on the revolutionaries. They would be guided by the revolutionary morality, that is, by that which is good for the cause. It was perfectly acceptable to forge documents, smuggle subversive literature, rob banks, change identity and organize assassinations. Everything was permissible. If the success of the socialist revolution required disbanding a parliament with a "counter-revolutionary majority," would it be moral and proper? Most Bolsheviks had no moral impediment to doing just that in 1918.

The well-being of Russia as a country was not of any particular importance for Lenin; the cause of worldwide proletarian revolution, meaning the success of his self-proclaimed vanguard party, was. Lenin considered the notion of patriotism to be an utterly bourgeois idea. It was held to have been invented by the ruling classes in order to cloud the minds of the proletariat. Patriotism in practical terms meant utilization of workers for the defense of the imperialist aspirations of the bourgeoisie. Workers did not have a motherland, they only had class solidarity. This well-known and often admired Leninist proletarian internationalism should also be seen in the context of Lenin's utilitarianism. Proletarian internationalism was useful as a weapon against class enemies, in practical terms Russia's establishment. In fact, as Lenin's subsequent record showed, he was as much an imperialist as those he had accused of being imperialists. Conquest of other peoples by force was perfectly permissible for the army of the victorious proletariat, because such a conquest objectively brought about liberation from capitalist exploitation. Use of force by a dedicated minority against all those who stood in the way of what he called proletarian revolution (in fact, Bolshevik seizure of power) was, for Lenin, moral, legitimate, and Marxist.

UTOPIAN VISION, 1917

Bolshevism up to 1917 was not identical with Leninism. What later became known as Leninism, that is, a voluntaristic adaptation of Marxism to the Russian revolution, was not yet an official doctrine of the Bolshevik Party. Officially the Bolsheviks still maintained that the coming Russian revolution was going to be a bourgeois–democratic one, that after the overthrow of autocracy political power would pass on to the institutions of parliamentary bourgeois order. Russia would have to go through the historical stage of capitalist development and then move on to the next stage of the socialist revolution. Just as Marxism was attractive to those who sought scientific proof of the inevitability of the revolution, Leninism was attractive to those who felt the urge to speed up the laws of history. They used Marxism to confirm in their minds that what they were doing made sense, yet they strove to rush ahead and get the capitalist stage over with as quickly as possible and arrive at the stage of the socialist revolution so that they, the vanguard, as they thought, could play the leading role.

The Bolshevik Party was an organization of professional revolutionaries, dogmatic, messianic, and ready to use force to recast society as they entered the fateful year of 1917. In February, they numbered 20,000 members, a small and rather insignificant political force. Yet in the course of 1917 they were swamped with tens of thousands of new recruits, just as all other political parties were. Their constituency comprised workers: mostly unskilled, unhappy, and rebellious new arrivals to the big cities.[20] The Bolshevik preaching appealed to them since it promised a better future. Yet what made the Bolshevik Party a force in national politics was increasing radicalization of soldiers, tired of the trenches of the First World War. The Bolsheviks' uncompromising rejection of the war, even at the cost of Russia's defeat, appealed to the soldiers. Bolshevik hostility towards propertied classes and privileged society won them many recruits as the revolution swept state authority away. In six short months after February, the small Bolshevik organization grew into a major political force set on seizing power if the opportunity presented itself.

One of the most confusing statements produced by Lenin was his small brochure *The State and the Revolution*, written in the summer of 1917. It comes across as an uncompromising defense of the people's power, and as a vision of the most thoroughly democratic order. In a famous phrase Lenin dreamed of every kitchenmaid participating in the affairs of government. The new democracy that the socialist revolution would bring about, wrote Lenin, would be very different from the bourgeois democracy as practiced in Western Europe, the United States or Russia after the February revolution. Bourgeois democracy, according to Lenin, was no democracy at all. It was in fact a dictatorship of the bourgeoisie. One clique of bourgeoisie replaced the other in power, manipulating the elections by restricted franchise and control of the press. The state for Lenin was not an instrument in the hands of society for the common good, but an instrument of coercion. From this reasoning it logically followed that it was essential "to smash to smithereens" the bourgeois state, the army, the police, and all other institutions of oppression. This message endeared Lenin to generations of critics of bourgeois democracy the world over. Lenin comes across here as a rebel, a true revolutionary in pursuit of a dream to empower the people.

What is misunderstood about Lenin's conception of the proletarian revolution is that he had no intention of leaving it up to kitchenmaids to determine the business of government, because as he repeated time and again, they were only capable of developing trade union consciousness. In other words, workers were concerned with wages and benefits rather than with the business of government. The vanguard of the proletariat (i.e. Lenin's party) would take over the state and the government. To endow Lenin with intention to respect the will of the people is to think of him as a Menshevik. He had no such intentions: Lenin had not spent two decades of his life building an obedient political organization simply to give it up and allow self-governing communes of workers and peasants to take over. For Lenin it was axiomatic that the will of the working class was expressed by its vanguard, the Bolshevik Party and its Central Committee, that is, himself and his cohort.

Lenin's praise of the soviets as institutions of people's power, as councils of direct democracy, is nothing but a political maneuver designed to use them for his own ends. As a brilliant improviser, he was ready to change tactics at a moment's notice if that would help him gain his objectives. In the political context of 1917, the supreme objective was to destabilize the Provisional government and make the country ungovernable – the more chaos, the more upheaval, the better it was for the Bolsheviks. If the soviets were useful for the task of delegitimizing the Provisional government, the Bolshevik slogan would be: power to the soviets. If the situation changed and the soviets ceased to serve that purpose, the policy could be changed, as indeed it was. The democratic rhetoric of Lenin in 1917 should not be taken at face value. It was merely a weapon like any other to discredit the Provisional government and seize power.

The fundamental drive in Lenin's personality was not pursuit of a positive vision of the future, but rather a destruction of the existing order. Lenin must be seen not so much as a creator of something new, but as a destroyer of the old. He profoundly hated the society in which he lived. He despised the liberals and intellectuals. He was disdainful of the peasants and patronizing towards the workers. He hated the Russia of his time – its institutions, social order, and culture. His lifelong ambition was to use his words to smash it to atoms, and he did. The system that emerged after the process of destruction was in many ways a product of his doctrinaire mind on the one hand and improvisation on the other.

SMASHING THE BOURGEOIS STATE

In the summer of 1917 it appeared that the seizure of state power by the Bolsheviks could take place if a very fortuitous combination of circumstances arose. The Provisional government could have pursued other policies, the mood of the revolutionary masses could have changed, the war could have taken another direction, the Allied powers could have acted differently, and the army might not have disintegrated as quickly as it did.[21] In many ways Lenin and the Bolsheviks were simply lucky that their opponents were so inept despite growing pressure to change the course of events. In retrospect it may seem incongruous. Yet it has often happened in modern Russian history that a ruler found himself abandoned by virtually all political forces, even by those who might have been expected to support him. Nicholas II, Alexander Kerensky and Mikhail Gorbachev were unacceptable both to the conservative forces of the old order and to the forces of change. Yet all three of them, despite the warnings of impending catastrophe, stayed the course and refused to change their policies.

By the fall of 1917, under the impact of chaos in the countryside, urban unrest, and disintegration of the army, the Provisional government was abandoned by all, even by the Mensheviks and SRs, whose party members served in the government. State authority ceased to exist, the empire's disintegration accelerated, the front eroded, and the economy collapsed. Russia was ungovernable. This combination of circumstances was exactly what Lenin had hoped for throughout 1917. The rest was easy. Several hundred sailors and soldiers were ordered to occupy strategic places in the capital in the name of the Petrograd Soviet in order to safeguard the convocation of the All-Russian Constituent Assembly and to prevent, as they were told, the surrender of the capital to the Germans, as Kerensky was rumored to be planning to do. A *coup d'état* was presented by its makers as a defensive action for the sake of democracy, peace, and land.

There are two ways of interpreting the demolition of Russian society that followed the Bolshevik seizure of power. One is that it was a Marxist experiment in action. Lenin began to fulfill what he had promised in *State and Revolution*. Within months, state institutions and societal structures were unrecognizable: the Constituent Assembly was disbanded; local self-government, the dumas and zemstvos, were disbanded as well; the independent courts and judiciary were abolished; the independent press was decimated, hundreds of newspapers were shut down, their editors arrested and their premises confiscated; independent trade unions were phased out; in almost all cases the opposition parties of the Mensheviks and SRs won local elections in spring 1918 and, as a result, the newly elected soviets were disbanded and replaced by unelected committees; by June 1918, opposition parties were expelled from the so-called parliament, the Central Executive Committee, even though only the Congress of Soviets had the authority to sanction this; the government presented the "parliament" with a *fait accompli*. By August 1918, virtually nothing survived of Russian civil society. All its institutions, organizations, political parties, associations, unions, and cooperatives had been disbanded, banned, abolished, or phased out. Was this an implementation of a Marxist program? Can a policy of disbanding workers' trade unions and soviets be called Marxist?

The second way of interpreting this catastrophic transformation of Russian society, this brutal simplification of social and political life, is to search for answers not in Marxism but in the culture of the people who called themselves Marxists. What was crucial in that culture was a boundless use of state power and coercion. It was a realization of Lenin's un-Marxist premise that a revolutionary minority would first seize power and then transform society by force. It was a manifestation of a utilitarian and patronizing attitude towards the Russian people by the revolutionary intelligentsia in general and by the Bolsheviks in particular.

This usurpation of the prerogative to decide for the people does not in itself explain why they went about transforming society in such a particularly brutal fashion. It seems there are four additional factors to be noted here. The first is that the Bolsheviks in power continued to operate exactly in the same conspiratorial fashion as they did in the underground. They were trying to hit the established order as hard as they could, only now they had the instruments of state power at their disposal. They could set up their own political police, mobilize their own army, set up their own newspapers, and so on. They realized that they were a small minority in Russia, and they feared that they might not hold power for long. Therefore, the imperative was to destroy the attributes of the old society and make their control over the instruments of state as irreversible as possible.

The second factor is that projection of state power downwards was based from the very beginning on a network of reliable comrades with unlimited authority. Lenin's interaction with his top lieutenants suggests that, as in the underground, everything was based on personal relationships.[22] When something needed to be done, Lenin's typical response was to entrust it to a trustworthy comrade who would be personally responsible and report immediately what concrete actions he had undertaken. In 1918–20 Lenin came across as an improviser of crisis management. One challenge after another was countered by Lenin sending a reliable comrade to deal with the situation: Stalin was sent to Tsaritsyn to make sure that grain stores there would be transported to central Russia. He charged Trotsky with creating the Red Army and sent Antonov-Ovseenko to conquer Ukraine. The political police was set up, the notorious Cheka, and Dzerzhinsky placed at its head. These plenipotentiaries were not to be held accountable to any state institution, but to Lenin personally.

All the members of the Central Committee were almost always on the road. It was a government of viceroys, who would appear in a province and impose Bolshevik requirements, by terror if necessary. This mode of operation made Lenin's government a personal dictatorship in the sense that no institutions were important or permanent. They could be abolished at a moment's notice. It was an emergency regime set up permanently. Its main function was to coerce, mobilize, cajole, enforce, collect, and terrorize the population into submission.

The third factor: once in power the revolutionaries became different people. Charming, brilliant journalists, democrats, and socialists, who had been guided by the noble ideas of creating a better society, became unrecognizable to Western observers who had known them in Paris and Vienna before the war. Toughness was now their main virtue. Not just Lenin and Trotsky, who had never displayed humanity and kindness as their more prominent characteristics, but Lunacharsky, Pyatakov, and Bukharin had no moral qualms about shootings, executions, and the suppression of peasant rebellions and workers' strikes. In 1919 and again in 1920 these people elaborated and partly executed a monstrous plan of de-Cossackization in the Don host area.[23] It involved mass relocation of population, the extermination of a rich stratum of Cossacks, the creation of concentration camps for the families of rebellious Cossacks, and systematic terror. Did anything change in Bolshevik morality to account for this?

Some would argue that nothing had changed. Lenin had always called for merciless suppression of exploiting classes. Consider the record of Trotsky, the brilliant orator who had demanded a government responsible to the parliament in October 1917. Insecure in the Bolshevik ranks as a late convert to the cause, he felt the urge to demonstrate that he could do whatever was required to safeguard the success of the Bolshevik venture.[24] In May 1918 he issued an order to disarm the Czechoslovak Legion in Russia. The Czechoslovaks disarmed the Bolsheviks instead and together with the SRs overthrew Bolshevik power in the entire territory from the Volga River to the Pacific. A more cautious approach was essential. Yet Trotsky repeated the same blunder with the same catastrophic consequences a year later. He issued an order to disarm the troops of Nestor Makhno, a leader of peasant bands and an unreliable ally in Ukraine. As a result, the White army of General Denikin broke through the Red lines and occupied the entire Ukraine and a large part of southern Russia. A military victory of the Whites and the capture of Moscow were quite possible. Trotsky's toughness brought the Bolsheviks to the brink of disaster twice in the civil war.

In 1920, upon the defeat of the Whites, Trotsky launched one of his most idiosyncratic fantasies: the militarization of labor campaign. Workers were turned into soldiers and soldiers into workers, as labor armies were created out of "muzhik raw material." Discipline and military order were the virtues Trotsky enforced after the victory over the Whites. Toughness, coercion, and terror were not temporary zigzags in Bolshevik policy imposed on them by the exigencies of the civil war. They were facets that expressed their very nature, policies they pursued when they had no constraints. The people were an object of state action, merely raw material for realizing Bolshevik utopian visions. The key here is a profoundly utilitarian attitude towards people, a lack of humanism and kindness in Bolshevism.

The fourth factor for the exceptional brutality of the Bolshevik rule was its insecurity. The Bolsheviks were never quite certain that they were going to last. Several times during the civil war they stood on the brink of defeat. Red Terror in September 1918 was a projection of their fear that they might lose at the front line. De-Cossackization of 1919 was to prevent Cossack participation in the anti-Bolshevik struggle. Ruthless suppression of hundreds of peasant rebellions was a direct consequence of a Bolshevik fear of peasant resistance. To hold on to power the Bolsheviks had to rely on violence. There was no alternative in this sense. As a result the "Geist" of Bolshevism changed by 1921. Leading the masses was replaced with deciding for the masses and then shaping the masses out of muzhik raw material. Society as a whole was perceived as an object of a military campaign: opposition parties had to be smashed, property owners dispossessed, workers taught to obey, and peasants forced to comply. Construction of socialism was understood as a military operation – fighting on the industrial front, the grain procurement front, the ideological front, and the transport front. Movement forward, progress itself, was understood as an unfolding of a military campaign. Mental categories were created which defined human aspirations in terms of warfare. From here it logically followed that traitors, deserters and saboteurs had to be unmasked and banished. An organization of conscious revolutionaries, a professional party, was going to build socialism from above:

eliminating hostile classes of population, mobilizing the masses for heroic feats on the industrial front, enforcing obedience by strict control over their ideas by the vigilant Cheka, educating them as to their purpose and destiny by means of propaganda, and spreading proletarian revolution westward if an opportunity presented itself. This was the reality and the program of the Bolsheviks in 1921.

As is well known, the Communist regime found itself in a deep crisis in February 1921. Bread lines in the cities, strikes of hungry workers, collapse of industry, and most importantly dozens of peasant rebellions were a manifest demonstration that the system was not working. Mobilization of resources by means of coercion and terror was sufficient in fighting a war against the Whites, but ineffective in organizing the normal economic life of the country. Bans on trade, forced grain requisitioning and labor conscription generated ever growing peasant resistance. Peasant rebellions in Tambov, Voronezh and Samara, Ukraine, and Siberia, strikes in Moscow and Petrograd, and on top of it all, a mutiny at the naval base of Kronstadt near Petrograd threatened the survival of the Bolshevik regime. In early 1921 Lenin made a truly historic decision to reverse this course and adopt the New Economic Policy – NEP.

NEP SOCIETY

NEP Russia should be seen as a conglomeration of social groups and cultures that had very little if anything in common. The Bolsheviks felt isolated and trapped in the cities surrounded by a suspicious peasant sea. They were in control but were not sure for how long and where exactly they were going. The abandonment of Communism (later renamed War Communism) had led to a moral and ideological crisis in the party. Restoration of private trade and property, the emergence of entrepreneurs, and talk of foreign concessions raised uncomfortable questions as to what the party of the victorious proletariat was going to do in NEP Russia. Lenin left some hope with his famous claim that, out of NEP Russia, a socialist Russia would emerge. This implied that NEP was not something desirable in and of itself, and that socialism remained the final goal. Yet Lenin also confused the issue by stating that private enterprise was going to remain in place for a long period of time. The terms in which Lenin defined the relationship between old economic policy, that is, Communism, and the New Economic Policy, NEP, were of offensive and retreat, construction and pause, leaving no room for a positive acceptance of NEP in Bolshevik minds. NEP was never conceived of as a path to socialism, but as a detour, as a temporary obstacle to overcome. The Bolshevik Party desperately needed a role to play; it needed a reaffirmation that it was leading Russia and not simply waiting for the conditions to arise when the socialist offensive could resume.

The intelligentsia

One social group that truly enjoyed the freewheeling spirit of NEP was the Bolshevik intelligentsia, whose culture and artistic output reproduced official Communist projections in its own way.[25] These were writers, poets, and filmmakers who within the parameters of pro-Soviet culture were relatively free to engage in their brand of experimental art. The paradox of their existence was that the best of what they created in its spirit prepared the ground for their own demise.[26] Take, for example, the masterpiece of the Soviet film industry, Dziga Vertov's famous silent classic *A Man with a Movie-Camera*.[27] The film is a spectacular kaleidoscopic montage of images. Its artistic value is in its dynamism, feeling of optimism, and impressionistic quality. The viewer is shown a series of images of a modern city. Everything is in motion: wheels and cogs and streams of people, and street cars. Life is vibrant and dynamic. There are no individual characters, instead streams of masses, streams of products, streams of a modern industrial city. New life was being constructed. It showed fascination with machines, progress, movement, and construction.

The key word here is construction.[28] The Communist avant-garde believed that the role of an artist was to plunge into the new era and participate in the construction of the new society. Yet already at this stage there were perils in these ethics. The next logical step was that an artist should not limit his creativity to reproducing in the form of art the images of construction taking place, but rather participate in construction. Following the principles already in place at the time of the civil war that art and culture should be useful for the masses, works of art were to be an intrinsic part of construction of the new society. Artists should participate in the production process. This logical progression in fact made individual artists superfluous in Soviet Russia. Cogs and wheels replaced individual artists with their own unique perception of reality. The concept that art had to be useful to the masses logically led to the conclusion that the only way it could be useful was if art production was performed by the Communist Party-led artistic brigades in accordance with an overall plan of building the new society.[29]

Cultural life during the NEP era went through a complete circle in terms of a relationship between the three participants: an artist, the party, and the so-called "revolutionary masses." The rise of the avant-garde was associated with an affirmation of the artist as an experimental innovator addressing the masses directly, bypassing the party or using the party for his own ends. Throughout the first half of the 1920s the party remained in the background, preoccupied with its own internal strife and search for its own identity and course of action. The revolutionary masses did not comprehend avant-garde art, and its appeal remained limited to a small and dwindling circle of the intelligentsia. By the end of the 1920s, the opposite relationship was in place: the party asserted its determination to guide the artist in the artistic construction of the new society.[30] The role of an individual artist was reduced to serving as a cog in socialist construction. The ideology of the avant-garde was bankrupt, having prepared its own demise. Now the party would use the artist to appeal to the revolutionary masses and inspire them to heroic deeds on the socialist construction front.

The non-Bolshevik intelligentsia was similarly misguided.[31] Some tried to adjust to the new reality since Russian statehood was in the Bolsheviks' hands, dealing with the Bolsheviks for the sake of Russia. During the war with Poland in 1920 when Tsarist generals responded to the call to serve in the Red Army without embracing the Bolshevik doctrine, when patriotism was partially rehabilitated, and especially after NEP was launched, many of the non-Bolshevik intelligentsia believed that the party was abandoning its utopian visions and becoming more pragmatic. One did not have to agree with the Bolsheviks but one could certainly try to coexist. The Bolshevik Party accepted the services of the technical intelligentsia but not their commercial, political, or any other organized activity.

The strain in the relations between the old intelligentsia and the Bolshevik upstarts is one of the key features of NEP Russia. This strain could be felt in every government office, bank, and educational institution. The old intelligentsia was contemptuously referred to as the *byvshye*, the former people. Bolshevik upstarts, propelled to positions of authority, felt insecure about their background and level of preparation, and resented their dependence on the skills and know-how of the old specialists. The non-Communist intelligentsia did not hide their indifference, if not hostility, to Communism and interpreted Communist claims, as well as the social, political, and cultural reality, in their own way. Students, professors, and engineers increasingly realized that instead of a return to normality, the NEP years were bringing the strengthening of the Communist dictatorship.

The masses

A stroll through the streets of Russian cities in the 1920s revealed to many foreign observers the diversity, even incompatibility, of Soviet society's many elements. Hundreds of petty traders with their little stalls, peasant markets with *babushkas* selling potatoes, private shops selling fake French perfume and other items of luxury, while at the same time Communist functionaries, leather-jacketed Cheka agents, and businessmen enjoyed luxurious meals in restaurants to the accompaniment of jazz. In contrast, hundreds of homeless children, orphaned during the civil war, swarmed on to the streets, or lived in abandoned housing. Dilapidated and neglected city centers and their palaces and squares, avenues and monuments were decorated with avant-garde posters and revolutionary symbols. And as a contrast one could see in some journals advertisements for Ford cars or other foreign objects, inaccessible to all but the very few. It was a strange mixture of capitalism and symbolism of socialism, with a government embarrassed by its own economic policy.

Divisions between the ruling party and the old intelligentsia were over status, culture, and authority. But at least both groups shared the same concern: the future of industrialization in Russia. The division between the Bolsheviks and the common folk, the workers and peasants, was even greater. The masses in whose name the revolution was made were the bearers of traditional cultural practices, mentalities and ways of rationalizing what was happening around them. They did not care about either the avant-garde or the party, much less a future-centered ideology. Their culture and their tastes had nothing to do with constructivism, productivism, or socialist construction. The only truly popular books, films, and songs during that time were entertainment, adventure, slapstick, and romance. As for the peasants, tradition, custom, and religion remained the foundation of their culture.[32]

Heroes in theory if not in practice, workers were off the center stage in the 1920s. Their daily lives were miserable and their disappointment in the "proletarian" revolution profound. Resignation and alienation were the main tones in workers' attitudes. They were completely at the mercy of the Red directors, the Cheka, and police. Any attempt to voice their opinions, let alone demands, was crushed as counterrevolutionary agitation, offenders being sent to camps filled already by 1923 by tens of thousands of political prisoners (Mensheviks, SRs, and Left SRs).

Each large social group had several subgroups with their own peculiarities. One can distinguish between workers in big cities and small towns, or between peasants in central Russian provinces and in Siberia, in terms of their attitudes to property and authority. In addition to these large social groups, there were many marginal groups with their own subcultures: Orthodox, Jewish, and Catholic religious communities who had to define ways and means of preserving their identity; merchants and traders, the so-called NEPmen; students and teachers; and homeless youths, prostitutes, beggars, and criminals, with their own sets of beliefs, cultural practices, and folklore. All these social and cultural communities had to interact with the Communist authorities. They were all targets of official social policies and Communist propaganda. The main purpose was to eliminate altogether most of these groups and to create instead a new Soviet Man, and a homogeneous society with one identity and one culture obediently following the vanguard of the proletariat.[33]

In almost every social group there were those who were identified for promotion and those who were deprived of opportunities. Thousands of peasants were deprived of voting rights, while others were recruited to the Communist Party and promoted to positions of authority. Tens of thousands of workers were singled out to be sent to schools and promoted to promising careers while others, "trouble-makers" and strikers, were "unmasked" and exiled to Siberia. Thousands of teachers were screened, some for promotion, and others to be purged. The same process affected university professors, students, engineers, army officers and factory managers. In each of these social groups the two polarities of promotees [*vydvizhentsy*] and the hold-overs [*byvshie*] defined the cultural tension most stark in the 1920s.

Political discourse

Political discourse in NEP Russia must be seen on three levels. The first and only one considered in the historiography thus far is the Bolshevik message to the masses. Its key elements are representations of reality in terms of idealized visions. The Bolsheviks' myths, rituals, symbols and ideological constructs reveal their vision of the world to be characterized by antagonism of the oppressors and the oppressed, the vanguard and the masses, the darkness of capitalism and the bright future of socialism.[34] Its vocabulary includes words like *smychka*, the unity of the working class and the toiling peasantry in Soviet Russia. According to such an idealized representation of social reality, the party and the working class were engaged in a construction of socialism. Since the Russian peasantry was influenced by age-old customs and property instincts, the party adopted the New Economic Policy in 1921, satisfying the peasants' desire to produce and sell their crops on the free market. Coercive methods of grain procurement dating to the civil war era were abandoned in favor of market relations and taxation of peasantry. Kulaks were the enemies of socialism, but their presence in the countryside had to be tolerated for the time being, though their actions were to be watched carefully. The long-term goal was introduction of collective forms of agriculture. All Communists' debates on policy had to be phrased in this framework.

The second level of political discourse is contained in confidential communication among top Communist institutions. To what extent did the Bolsheviks themselves believe their own official representations? One could not openly declare, for example, that there was no *smychka*, no unity of workers and peasants, nor that the Communist Party did not represent workers' dictatorship, nor that peasants had no representation in the so-called alliance and that they detested collective farms and destroyed them at every opportunity. To say this would invoke accusations of counterrevolutionary disloyalty and one would wind up in the cellars of the GPU. Most Bolshevik reports accepted the official ideological framework. Even if they understood the reality, they had to be careful in defining it in public. This gave rise to a coded language.

Failure to comply was defined as treason, a strike as desertion, peasant bargaining over prices as sabotage, and criticism as ideological subversion. There were offensives and retreats, deserters and conscious proletarians. Construction of socialism was associated with a mighty state, heavy industry, strong army, and obedient masses following their vanguard into the bright future. Communist revolutionary imagery projects violence, and a merciless struggle with the caricatural "enemies of the revolution" – the fat capitalist, the drunken priest, the vicious army officer, and the treacherous intellectual. Coded words, labels, and caricatures replaced reality in official Bolshevik communication.

And finally the third level of political discourse is revealed in popular attitudes, the most frank and honest of the three. The study of workers' culture, popular attitudes, and lifestyles shows a particular psychological tension caused by the gap between the official projections and the miserable reality. Workers tried to explain why in theory they were the ruling class and in reality they never got their wages on time. There was tension between promotees and ordinary workers, skilled and unskilled workers, and hostility to NEPmen and the Red directors.

Peasants lived in their own cultural world quite apart from the Communist visionary projections. This book will examine their voting records in the village soviets elections, *nakazy*, speeches, letters, petitions, rumors, religious practices, rituals, and holidays. The clash between official promises of emancipation and the reality of Soviet existence for women will be examined, trying to identify the main trends in the development of their cultural and political preferences. Similarly, the growth of the Young Communist League, Komsomol, will be considered in the context of the Bolshevik message and its reception by the Soviet youth in the 1920s. The purpose here is to determine the extent to which Communist official propaganda sank in. What elements of it were appropriated and internalized? In short, the Bolshevik message from above and its perception, appropriation, and popular reaction below are the center of attention on the pages that follow. Hopefully, a picture of interaction between the Bolsheviks and Russian society will emerge explaining the dramatic upheaval and the crisis of Bolshevism by the end of the decade.

Chapter 1

Extracting socially alien elements

Lenin defined NEP as a retreat. The country had to recover from the havoc of the civil war. The battle against capitalism would be a protracted one. For the time being, however, capitalism was back. The Bolsheviks held the reins of power, but Russia was still out there to be conquered. Thousands of traders filled the markets, homeless children roamed in the streets, and the newly rich enjoyed themselves in the restaurants and theaters. Factories were idle and famine devastated the Volga region. The Bolsheviks were keenly aware of their tenuous grip on the country and that their survival depended on creating a missing social foundation for their regime. But they were not certain how to proceed.

Lenin was apparently going through a major crisis in his own thinking. His notes, speeches, and recommendations were full of anxiety about the future. Russia's social reality convinced him that the restoration of market economy "chemically generated," as he put it, a petty bourgeois mentality in the population and hence a social basis for the Mensheviks, SRs and Kadets. Lenin resolved to proceed with the restoration of the market economy while physically extracting the by-product.[1] He was also worried by the signs of disunity in his own party. The remedies he proposed were remarkably simple and very much in accord with his style. Dissidents and heretics had to be weeded out, and the ban on factionalism strictly enforced. The party had to be expanded and proletarianized. It had to be linked to the masses and constantly reinforced by a steady flow of new recruits.

The main guidelines of Bolshevik policy in regard to other political parties, professional associations, and the Church were worked out in the early months of 1922 before Lenin's stroke in May. This was a policy of low-intensity warfare. Arrests, executions on the spot, and deportation were to be replaced by a new set of more subtle measures. In regard to the Church, it was to be the seizure of its assets, destruction of its organizational capacity, and the triggering of a split in its ranks. For the time being professionals and specialists, as long as they remained loyal, were to be utilized until they could be replaced by reliable cadres. The most dangerous, incorrigible, and famous were to be exiled from the country. Harmful ideological influences were to be restricted to a minimum. All enemies and opponents were to be arrested. The Bolshevik agenda was to expand Communist control over economy, education, and culture. The direct assault of the civil war era would give way to a steady and more methodical recasting of the entire society.

POLITICAL PARTIES AND INTELLIGENTSIA

The GPU, a successor to the Cheka, Lenin's political police, was to monitor and remove those hostile to socialist construction and silence those who were capable of generating alien ideas. The first on the list here were other political parties or dissident groups within the Communist Party; the second were priests and church functionaries; and the third was the intelligentsia in general: teachers, engineers, and specialists. That meant in practice purging all who had ever participated in any other political parties, exiling the most well-known and hence dangerous intellectuals, and destroying as much of the organized Russian Orthodox Church as possible. Teachers, professors, agronomists, engineers, and community leaders were to be replaced with loyal proletarian personnel. The Bolsheviks believed that once they had their people everywhere, their grip on the country would be secure.

Due to the secret nature of the GPU work, much of its activity is still unknown. In our possession are only those documents which were sent to the Information Department of the Central Committee by the GPU on the exile, deportation, infiltration and subversion of political opponents on a mass scale. They are professionally executed, matter-of-fact accounts on a number of accomplished operations. Even though many details remain unclear and bring to light more questions than answers, they do provide a glimpse of the GPU's contribution to the restructuring of society in the 1920s.

In 1923 at least five GPU departments were charged with domestic political surveillance: the Information Department, the Special Department, the Secret Department, the Counterintelligence Department, and the Eastern Department.[2] The Information Department was primarily preoccupied with information gathering. It received monthly, biweekly and weekly reports from the provincial GPU on the political situation in various provinces. These reports were matter-of-fact lists of incidents numbered and registered by place and date. All reports followed a clear pattern, presenting information by categories, such as "workers' attitudes," "peasants," "intelligentsia," "institutes and universities," "banditry," "terrorism," "anti-soviet groupings," and the like. The provincial reports were based in turn on the uezd GPU reports and on the information received from secret informers [*sekretnye osvedomiteli*].

In September 1923, the GPU chairman, Genrikh Yagoda, reported to the CC that: "The budget of the the GPU information department has been approved in the amount of 1,200,000 rubles in gold per annum." The GPU had been authorized to hire 18,000 secret informers in addition to 33,152 regular agents.[3] Tula gubkom's report to CC noted that in just one city district there were thirty-three secret GPU informers.[4] Little if anything escaped the attention of the Information Department. Every subversive speech at workers' meetings, every leaflet posted at the market square, and every anti-Soviet joke was duly recorded and included in the monthly compilation [svodka]. The Information Department systematized this data and sent its monthly report to the CC Information Department and to thirty-two other hierarchs who had clearance to read this kind of information.

The Special Department monitored the political disposition in the Red Army. The GPU agents collected information on former Tsarist officers as well as Communist commissars and were very attentive to the political views of the Red Army soldiers. The compilations of this department are full of quotations from the soldiers' letters, comments on political events, such as the SR trial, the death of Lenin, the political demise of Trotsky, and so on.

The Counterintelligence Department monitored what was called "banditry," meaning armed peasant guerrilla formations, and any other organized armed resistance to Soviet power. The Eastern Department monitored what was referred to as "nationalist movements." Its reports describe hostility between the Russians and the Kazakhs, anti-Russian and anti-Semitic attitudes in Ukraine, the strength of the Zionist sentiment among the Jews, and Social Democratic and pro-independence sentiment in Georgia. The Secret Department's sphere of competence included anti-Soviet political parties and the clergy. They infiltrated professional associations and intelligentsia circles, and decimated those groups that engaged in political activity at an appropriate moment.

In a letter to Dzerzhinsky dated May 19, 1922 (just a few days before his stroke), Lenin proposed to "exile abroad writers and professors aiding the counterrevolution."[5] He urged Dzerzhinsky to establish systematic monitoring of the press, and to follow closely the political views of writers, journalists, and professors. On June 22, the Politburo discussed a special Cheka report by Unshlikht on the proposed deportation of the Mensheviks. The Politburo instructed the Revolutionary Tribunal "to proceed with greater severity in conducting the SR trial" and to set up a special commission on the deportation of the "inimically inclined intelligentsia."

On August 9, a list of seventy-seven Ukrainian intellectuals subject to deportation was ready. It included professors from the Medical and Technological institutes in Odessa and Kiev, as well as agronomists and engineers. On August 18, Unshlikht reported to Lenin: "In accordance with your instructions, I am sending to you the lists of intellectuals in Moscow, Petrograd, and Ukraine confirmed by the Politburo." Lenin followed the matter with great attention despite his illness and communicated with the Cheka and the Politburo members on this subject almost every week. His instructions were anything but conciliatory. In a letter to Stalin, Lenin wrote on July 17, 1922:

Comrade Stalin:

On the matter of deporting Mensheviks, National Socialists, Kadets, etc. from Russia, I would like to ask a few questions, since this operation, which was started before my leave, still has not been completed.

Has the decision been made to "eradicate" all the NS's [Narodnye Sotsialisty] People's Socialists? Peshekhonov, Myakotin, Gornfeld, Petrishchev, *et al.*?

As far as I'm concerned, deport them all. [They are] more harmful than any SR – because [they are] more clever.

Also A.N. Potresov, Izgoev and all the *Ekonomist* contributors (Ozerov and many many others). The Mensheviks – Rozanov (a physician, cunning), Vigdorchik (Migulov or something like that), Liubov Nikolayevna Radchenko and her young daughter. Rumor has it they're the vilest enemies of Bolshevism. N.A. Rozhkov (he has to be deported; incorrigible); S.A. Frank (author of *Metodologiya*). The commission supervised by Mantsev, Messing, *et al.* should present lists and several hundred of such ladies and gentlemen must be deported without mercy. Let's purge Russia for a long while.

This must be done at once. Before the end of the SRs' trial, no later. Arrest a few hundred and without a declaration of motives – out you go, ladies and gentlemen!

With communist greetings.

Lenin[6]

By the end of 1922, the most prominent leaders of the Menshevik and Kadet parties, as well as philosophers, economists, and scientists – the flower of the Russian intelligentsia – were banished from Russia.

The trial of the SRs and the exile of intellectuals betrayed the Bolsheviks' profound insecurity in the early years of NEP. On September 2, 1922 after a meeting with Lenin, Dzerzhinsky noted down for himself "Directives from Vladimir Ilyich:"

To continue steadily the exile of the anti-Soviet intelligentsia (and of the Mensheviks most of all) abroad. To draft lists and thoroughly check them. Seek out literature specialists and have them furnish reviews. Divide between them the entire literature [periodicals for review]. To draft lists of cooperatives' leaders inimical to us.[7]

Dzerzhinsky tirelessly worked on systematizing political surveillance of the intelligentsia. He proposed to draft lists of all intellectuals by category: *belle lettres*; politicians and public affairs commentators; economists; financiers; energy and transport specialists; trade and cooperatives; technicians, engineers; agronomists; doctors; officers, professors; and teachers. "Data must be gathered on all of them by all our [GPU] Departments."[8] A file on every individual was to be created, and each person's record scrutinized. It was to draft lists of the SRs who had ever been elected to any public office beginning from 1905 and then check those names against the records of those detained so that the remaining SRs could be identified.

Arrests intensified in the fall of 1922 as the elections to the local soviets approached. In a letter to the local organizations, the Menshevik CC stated:

> A situation has been created where we in point of fact cannot participate in the Soviet elections. Posting lists of our candidates means supplying the Cheka with the names of party members still unknown to them. It means outright arrest and exile. Participation of our speakers in campaign rallies ends in the same way.[9]

The CC recommended that the local organizations boycott the elections but continue "the struggle for the legal existence of the party." In addition to expulsion from the soviets, raids on the local Menshevik clubs and party committee quarters, disbandment of Menshevik-led trade unions, and general arrests, some new methods were introduced. The GPU initiated telephone tapping, mail interception, the planting of informers, and dissemination of counterfeit proclamations to discredit the Mensheviks.[10]

The increasing viciousness in the GPU's treatment of the Mensheviks culminated in the final onslaught in May–June 1923. As usual, a defamation campaign in the press preceded the arrests. The Mensheviks were accused of scheming against Soviet power. An underground Menshevik journal, *Iz Partii*, reported 1,000 arrests in Moscow alone, 300 in Odessa, 100 in Petrograd, 70 in Rostov, and 30 each in Kiev, Kharkov, and Nizhnii Novgorod. The number of arrests in Tula, Bryansk, Tambov, Kostroma, and Ufa could not be verified.[11] The new element in this campaign was that the Mensheviks were being arrested en masse, without any pretext at all. An underground Menshevik journal published an emotional appeal of the Menshevik CC to the party members:

> Comrades!
> Our party has entered a period of hitherto unprecedented repressions. All over Russia, for two months now, a massive operation of the GPU has been unfolding. The repressions have attained a particularly wide scope in Moscow. Many hundreds of people have been arrested: on the streets, in offices, in ambushes. They arrest right and left: relatives, wives, and acquaintances [of party members]. They have decided to exterminate the Social Democratic Party to the last man. They have decided to wipe out the entire social milieu surrounding the party.[12]

On July 3, 1923 the last legal session of the Menshevik Central Committee took place in Moscow. When the GPU agents shut the meeting down, the Mensheviks were debating ways and means of continuing their legal existence.[13] Measures including surveillance, persecution, exile, and deportation continued unabated in 1923. In instructions sent out to all provincial party chairmen in May 1923 Viacheslav Molotov ordered: "To provide all available information on the activity of the Mensheviks to the GPU and to render all possible assistance to the GPU in its operations against the Mensheviks."[14] Virtually every month the GPU described victories in the covert war against the Mensheviks and SRs. In August 1923 thirty Mensheviks were arrested in Moscow after several leaflets at some Moscow factories were discovered.[15] The GPU report to Stalin boasted that: "A number of recent GPU operations weakened the work of Menshevik organizations. In Kiev the first All-Russian Conference of Social Democratic Youth was liquidated."[16]

Several Menshevik and SR *samizdat* journals persisted into the mid-1920s.[17] It is evident from their letters abroad that they thought they had organized their operations so well that the GPU would not be able to stop the circulation of the underground press. In fact, detailed information on the date, place, title, contents, number of copies, and authors in these journals was regularly included in the monthly GPU reports on popular attitudes.[18] In February 1924 the GPU described "several operations against the SRs, involving arrest of a group of students at the Petrovskaya Agricultural Academy who published an underground journal *Stremlenie*. The entire Vyatka SR committee, which had been functioning underground, was arrested, as well."[19]

By 1924 the GPU had inaugurated a new plan of ridding the country of the Mensheviks. In all provinces and especially in Ukraine, turncoat Mensheviks in the service of the GPU started campaigning in the press for conferences of former Mensheviks to condemn those in emigration.[20] Thousands of former Mensheviks understood this campaign as a chance to prove their loyalty to Soviet power. These conferences were well-orchestrated spectacles of public self-abasement, a ritual replayed on numerous occasions later in the 1930s. One speaker after another condemned traitors to the cause of the working class – the Menshevik delegation abroad – and praised to the sky the Marxist path of the Bolsheviks, swearing loyalty to the Soviet government. Alas, this public self-flagellation did not help many of them. As proof of loyalty, the GPU demanded that repentant Mensheviks become informers. As one Tula Menshevik complained to the CC:

> They suggested that I take up the role of an informer in relation to my former political comrades. Investigator Trofanov demanded that I enter the RSDRP again and engage actively in political life to be in the position to report regularly to the GPU.[21]

Those who refused were arrested and the lucky ones were exiled. The unlucky ones wound up in the camps. In the end the GPU proudly reported that: "The operation to liquidate the Menshevik Party by means of congresses of former Mensheviks was successfully carried out ."[22] Administrative exile without trial was widely practiced. Beatings, torture, intimidation and rape were often used to obtain repudiation of the Menshevik past, which would then be published for propaganda purposes.[23] By the mid-1920s, the Menshevik, SR, and Left SR delegations abroad had compiled lists of their comrades in Bolshevik prisons and camps. These lists contained thousands of names.[24]

In 1924 over a hundred Socialists who had been held in the Solovki camp in the north were transferred to various camps in Siberia. En route, they managed to compose a description of conditions they faced in Solovki and in their new places of confinement. The original document contained 121 signatures. They simply threw it out of the rail-car with a request to those who found the letter to forward it to the Mensheviks or SRs in Moscow. Miraculously, someone did find the letter, took it to Moscow and gave it to some Mensheviks and SRs. Sympathetic contacts in the Latvian and Estonian Embassy then passed the document on to the Menshevik and SR delegations abroad. The document described the humiliation, abuse, beatings, and mistreatment of political prisoners by GPU personnel.

> In the morning on June 17 [1924], armed detachments of Red Army soldiers and the Cheka [GPU] men unexpectedly surrounded Savvatiev *skit*, the largest in the Solovki camp. Infantry, cavalry, and even a machine-gun were deployed against the prisoners' barracks, in which everyone was sleeping at the time ... The chief of the directorate of northern camps himself – one Kostev – and the director of the prison department conducted this operation ...
>
> The staff of prison warders and Red Army soldiers had been selected especially for us. They had been taught to hate us and could not wait to put this hatred into action ... Swearing obscenely, yelling "Menshevik scum," and "traitors of Christ," the wild, drunken warders rushed up and down the corridors from cell to cell, threatening to shoot people and, aiming rifles and revolvers at us, shouting "Don't spare bullets."

The letter also provides a general profile of 115 prisoners in the group: 112 of them were members of socialist parties (Menshevik, SR, and anarchist); 66 of them had entered those parties before February 1917, and 28 before 1905.[25] Few could have known that after 1926 their ranks would be augmented with dissidents from the Bolshevik Party as well. The arrest of thousands of Trotsky's supporters after their defiant protest action on the tenth anniversary of the October revolution should be seen in the context of the earlier arrests of the Mensheviks and SRs. It was simply one more operation in the climate of escalating repression of political opponents of any persuasion.

The story of the GPU operations in the 1920s has still not been told. It is an enormous and fascinating subject. Some of the more spectacular operations are well known, but others have not yet reached the public domain. In

July 1923, for example, the GPU claimed to have smashed underground organizations linked to Petliura and Titiunik in Ukraine and to have infiltrated an underground group "The Center for Democratic Action," which was, according to the GPU, preparing to overthrow the Soviet state by means of a *coup d'état*.

The operation "Trust" involved the GPU's infiltration of Boris Savinkov's underground "Union in Defense of Fatherland and Freedom" in Russia. An SR terrorist before the revolution and an associate of Kerensky in 1917, Savinkov was an uncompromising enemy of the Communist regime. He lived in Warsaw and believed that he had a following in Russia. As it turned out, his following was mostly made of the GPU infiltrators who managed to convince Savinkov to return to Russia and lead his underground organization. Eventually, he took the bait and crossed the border. He was immediately arrested and forced to write letters to his friends abroad saying that he had changed his mind on the Soviet question.[26]

Another example of a spectacular success was the GPU infiltration of the monarchist officer circles in Paris.[27] Similarly, the GPU infiltrated what was left of the People [*Narod*], a legal political party, which in 1921 united SRs who had repudiated their formerly uncompromising opposition to the Bolshevik regime. By 1925, most members in this group were GPU agents. The sole purpose of its existence was to attract those who held anti-Soviet views and thought that they were joining the company of likeminded people. In fact, they would all be arrested by the GPU in due course and wound up in the Solovki prison camp.

Detailed study of even the most important operations of the GPU would take volumes to describe.[28] The NEP years witnessed a steadily diminishing spectrum of permissible political expression and a steadily widening category of opponents to be identified, isolated, and annihilated.

OPERATION "THE LIVING CHURCH"

Much of the first- and second-generation scholarship has assumed that the split of the Russian Orthodox Church into traditionalist and renovationist wings was a normal consequence of the revolutionary upheaval. Social change brought about by the October revolution found its counterpart in revolutionary theology. Elements in the Russian Orthodox Church felt a need to adapt to the revolutionary society and the renovationist movement emerged in response to this pressure from below.[29] The revolution was held to have liberated the Church from Tsarist-era state tutelage, state and Church to be genuinely separated, and freedom of conscience to be guaranteed by the Soviet government. This was the official line.

Some historians of the Orthodox Church have described persecution of the clergy, destruction of the churches, confiscation of property, and the split as stages in a progressive escalation of the Bolshevik campaign against the

Church.[30] The Bolsheviks considered different ways and means with which to undermine the authority of the Orthodox Church, to deprive it of financial resources, and to disorganize its potential to preach the creed. Gregory Freeze cites Trotsky's report to the Politburo filed on May 24, 1922, outlining three main tasks in disorganizing the Church – the Patriarchate had to be controlled by a loyal Patriarch, the church administration had to be placed in the hands of loyal renovationists, and the church administration had to be decentralized.[31] The assumption underlying these goals was that the Church was to be treated as a political organization. Deprived of its centralized structure, leadership, press, and finances, and subject to the control of trusted people, it would be rendered harmless.

Until now there have been no documents available to prove unequivocally that the split in the Church was engineered by the GPU.[32] Fortunately, a document, "A Report of the Chief of the Sixth Secret Department of the GPU On Accomplished Work in the Church and the Sects during 1923," sheds some light on this matter. The report is addressed to GPU Deputy Chair Viacheslav Menzhinsky.[33] It is written in a matter-of-fact tone, listing major facts, actions, and specific events without much comment. In form, the report is an internal GPU paper not intended to be read by the CC or anyone outside the GPU. It is therefore unlikely that facts mentioned were distorted significantly, though one can detect some arrogance and boasting in the account. The author was certainly very proud of his department's accomplishments.

The report begins its narrative in 1922. Up to that moment, Patriarch Tikhon had controlled the church hierarchy. During the Bolsheviks' direct assault on church property through the confiscation of valuables campaign, a plan was devised to break the resistance of the Church by undermining Tikhon's authority.[34] In this sense, Operation "The Living Church" was a direct outgrowth of the confiscation of valuables campaign. The GPU's first task was to identify those in the church hierarchy who were unhappy with Tikhon and willing to cooperate with the GPU:

> To achieve our objective, which was to make sure that anti-Tikhon elements gained control over the church apparatus, we first had to create a network of informers so powerful and widespread that we could direct [*rukovodit*] the entire Church through that network. In this we have succeeded.[35]

The network of informers, no matter how widespread, proved to be powerless in undercutting Tikhon's control of the hierarchy. So the next step was the launching of the operation "The Living Church." Moscow was the first place where a group of clergy was organized who claimed publicly to espouse what was known as the "renovationist theology." Calling for reform of the Church, they began identifying themselves as the Living Church. In the initial period there were six clergymen involved: two archbishops, Antonin and

Leonid, and four priests, Krasnitskii, Vedenskii, Stadnik, and Klinovskii. The GPU report continued:

> It is self-evident that to achieve this was going to be impossible without expenditures of money. Having already established a network of informers, we had been trying to set the Church on a path which we wanted. And so in Moscow the first renovationist group was formed which later became known as "The Living Church." Shortly thereafter, a congress of the renovationist movement was convened, which the GPU welcomed since it widened the split and undermined Tikhon's authority.[36]

Up to this point (the first months of 1923), everything was going according to plan, at least as portrayed by the GPU. But then the renovationists started to squabble among themselves. Antonin broke with the others and formed his own "Church Revival" group while Vedenskii called his group the Apostolic [*Drevneapostol'skaya*] Church. The GPU was unhappy with this schism, since Tikhon could overcome small challengers easier than a unified one. There was, however, a benefit to be derived from the renovationist groups' intrigues, as the report explained:

> This situation of the renovationist groups made them willingly or unwillingly resort to denouncing each other. And in the process they became regular informers to the GPU, which we used in full measure.[37]

This was the situation on the eve of the All-Russian Church Council which convened in May 1923. The renovationists won de facto control of the Church and defrocked Tikhon. This well-known outline of events acquires a new meaning in light of the information in the GPU report:

> The reason for our influence at the Church Council was that more than 50 per cent of the congress participants were our informers and we could have turned the council either way.[38]

What the GPU bosses did not quite control was the energy with which their various hirelings fought for power among themselves. Four groupings emerged at the assembly: the Living Church, the Apostolic Church, Church Revival and the supporters of Tikhon. Out of the 560 delegates, three-quarters were associated with the first two groups. The Tikhonites were hopelessly outnumbered. Their attempt to place Agafangen at the helm of the Church was defeated with GPU intervention. The renovationists, controlled by the GPU, took control of the Russian Orthodox Church. For the moment it appeared as if the victory was total and complete. This was felt in the uncompromising – almost Bolshevik – language with which the Church now spoke.

What the GPU and the Bolsheviks did not take into account, however, was that controlling the apparatus was not like controlling the religious community. They quickly discovered that congregations did not like the radical changes introduced by the renovationists, and many openly identified with

Tikhon regardless of whether he was officially Patriarch or not. At this stage the GPU had been welcoming anything that widened the split and therefore did not root out all the Tikhon supporters among the local clergy right away. The GPU instead decided to dismantle Tikhon's image as a martyr and pressure was applied on him. Unfortunately, the report does not specify what kind of methods were used on Tikhon:

> At this point we had to work over [*obrabotat'*] Tikhon in such a way that he would not only apologize before Soviet power, but repent for the sins he had committed . . . We succeeded in convincing Tikhon and he signed a document of repentance.[39]

Tikhon was released and the Synod was restored as the governing body of the Church. Yet factional infighting between Tikhonites and renovationist groups continued on its own.

> Being in the state of war, these two currents are trying to blacken each other in the eyes of the authorities and prove their loyalty. Their favorite method is denunciation, to which they resort often.[40]

The report cites Tikhon as complaining that he and his supporters were "stepchildren" of the GPU, while the renovationists were the "sons." By that he meant that the authorities favored the renovationists and merely tolerated the Tikhonites. The GPU report concluded on an optimistic note:

> The system of information gathering which we have created during the past year corresponds fairly well to the requirements which will enable us to keep control [*rukovodstvo*] over the Church, if, of course, we have appropriate financial resources.[41]

The GPU saw money as the sure way to control the Church, or at least the church hierarchy. In operation "The Living Church," the GPU revealed its style once again.[42] Similar to operation "Trust" against Savinkov and operations against former Mensheviks and SRs, the GPU infiltrated the organizations it perceived to consist of political opponents, destroying them from within.

THE "FORMER" PEOPLE

The exile of intellectuals, the arrest and incarceration of the Mensheviks and SRs, and the split of the Church affected tens of thousands. Yet these were not the full extent of the Bolshevik efforts to reduce the potential of society to resist state policy. Entire population groups were subjected to systematic discrimination, enforcing conformity and silencing voices that might challenge Soviet power. The majority of those repressed were either "former people" [*byvshie liudy*], persecuted on the basis of social origin, or groups prospering under the New Economic Policy. The "former people," or "has-beens," typically included members of the pre-revolutionary elite, former officers or high-ranking bureaucrats in tsarist state service, religious functionaries, those who profited from hired labor ("exploiters"), and those who lived on the return of investments ("unearned income"). These people were officially disenfranchised by Soviet electoral laws until 1936. Hence the title *lishentsy*, the "disenfranchised" (from the verb *lishat'*, to deprive). Anyone who had been "someone" under the old regime ran the risk of being identified as a "former person." The term was generally synonymous with "socially alien," "politically unreliable," "exploiter," and "parasite." While the term *lishenets* differed from the rest in that it had a legal definition, statutes were vague and contradictory enough that in practice it was just as arbitrary as other slurs related to the Bolshevik class-based lexicon.

Being included on *lishentsy* lists was a serious social disability, even in the relatively tolerant atmosphere of the 1920s. One was officially deprived of voting rights and the right to hold public office. Voting rights were a sign of inclusion. People deprived of the right to vote on the basis of social origin or occupation shared the category with convicted criminals and the certifiably insane. *Lishentsy* typically became outcasts or pariahs, their presence tolerated but undesirable. They experienced restricted access to employment, housing, higher education, and medicine. Such limitations would affect entire families, even if only one member had been disenfranchised. For many, the label was permanent.

During campaigns to redistribute living quarters in 1923–4, owners of large townhouses and apartments were forced to accommodate working-class tenants, often losing all but one room for themselves. Simultaneously, *lishentsy* were barred from housing in cooperatives.[43] Priests and religious functionaries were evicted as church buildings were nationalized and converted. The seizure of property from the former people aimed to impoverish this social grouping. In larger-scale industry, *lishentsy* were banned from trade unions, and refused access to government employment, pensions, medical services, paid vacations, certain kinds of housing, and unemployment services at the labor exchange.[44]

The state taxed *lishentsy* by rates that based levies on social origin as well as income. Throughout NEP, these rates penalized those in the private sector, becoming prohibitive after 1928. Higher rates among the so-called "independent professions" (handicraftsmen) and "non-laboring classes" (people who rented rooms or received money from abroad) suppressed their standard of living to subsistence levels.[45] Rents and fees for municipal services such as water, gas, and electricity also penalized the *lishentsy* as they paid two to five times higher rates than workers in the state sector.[46] Fees for primary and secondary education were also scaled according to social origin. Higher education was more rigidly policed. After 1923, all but roughly 10 per cent of enrolling students had to be nominated by the Komsomol, trade unions, or party. Background checks into social origin were unavoidable, and after 1927 an outright ban on *lishentsy* in higher-education institutions was adopted.[47]

Conditions were gradually worsening for the *lishentsy* in the mid-1920s. Stunning defeats in the 1925 rural elections brought about the reintroduction of intensive disenfranchisement policies. Electoral laws expanded the categories of people to be disenfranchised. Tax rates in the cities were raised and new levies introduced. In 1928, Deputy Commissar of Finance Moshe Frumkin was able to boast that "in some places we have almost completely abolished private trade by our tax policy."[48] On the local level, tax collection brigades often dispensed with complex formulas and invented sums that would require traders to surrender all their belongings. An American correspondent wrote of an assessment made of five NEPmen who had thought they had abandoned their trading professions in time in the late 1920s:

> That was a sad day for those poor NEPmen and for thousands of their ilk in Moscow, Leningrad and other cities . . . the next morning, they were informed that a new retroactive tax had been imposed upon all NEPmen of 2 or perhaps 5 or 7 per cent upon the total turnover of their last business year. Whatever the tax was, it coincided neatly with the values of their apartments and furniture! Vainly they protested that they had retired from business after paying all their taxes. This, they were told, was a new tax, and retroactive. Within three days, they were all out on the streets with little more than the clothes they wore and some bedding.[49]

Several campaigns in the 1920s were specifically directed at the "former" people. One was the eviction of the former landlords campaign in 1924 and the eviction of the "former people" from the big cities in 1928–30. In both cases the Bolshevik state resorted to collective punishment of an entire social group whose only fault was its identity. These people had been property owners years earlier, and they were not charged with anything. Their mere presence in the cities or the countryside was found objectionable. Dispossessed landlords were suspect automatically. They were likely to have kept a negative view of the Soviet system. Their education, social background, and potential influence were their main faults. The Tula gubkom was complaining to the CC that the former landlords were giving advice to the village soviets and that peasants were listening to their advice eagerly. Most landlords in the Tula province were employed as accountants, statisticians, jurists, or economists. They lived in houses rented from peasants and some of them resided in apartments at their old estates rented to them by the current owners of these buildings, mostly Soviet agencies, schools, and clubs. The eviction campaign in Tula province started in the fall of 1923. By the end of 1924 all former landlords had been evicted.[50] In the spring of 1925 the government made the decision to evict former landlords from the Russian countryside everywhere.

In 1929 NEPmen and "speculators" were expelled from urban apartments with any former landlords who had managed to evade earlier campaigns. As Eugene Lyons described:

> To be among the *lishentsy* was to be an outcast. They could not work in government enterprises, except in the lowest categories of "black" or unskilled labor. Their children were the last ones to be admitted into elementary or higher schools, which under conditions of overcrowded schooling meant that they were not admitted at all. When food rationing was introduced, from the end of March [1929] forward, they were denied rations. When revision of the rights to occupy "living space" was undertaken, the *lishentsy* were the first to be ejected from their homes. In their totality the number of these pariahs (even babies were not spared) came to millions.[51]

The demands of industrialization triggered massive rural–urban migrations which strained the beleaguered Soviet housing and distribution system. The *New York Times'* correspondent quoted a Soviet paper's commentary on the process: "in the cities, the overcrowding is so great that news that hundreds or thousands of apartments will be vacated by the expulsion of the NEPman tenants is good news to all." Apartment building committees prompted expulsions of *lishentsy* in an effort to relieve the terrible housing shortage; neighbors denounced each other in a contest over coveted space. An urban rationing system was introduced in 1929 and periodically reorganized to exclude *lishentsy* from state supply networks.[52] At the end of the 1920s, a NEPman told an American tourist in Moscow that:

> Six years ago they took away my right to vote; because I had a store and a few employees I was branded an exploiter of labor. Do you know what it means to be "deprived"? No trade union card, therefore no bread card – yet everything is sold by rations. My room costs me five times what a factory hand would pay, and there is no guarantee that one day we will not be swept out like old rubbish when some loyal worker needs the room. Thank God I have no small children for they would be barred from school.[53]

Disenfranchisement provisions gave the Bolshevik authorities a powerful mechanism of social control. The social origin of any individual could be investigated, scrutinized, and used as a leverage. Some intellectuals, former Mensheviks and SRs, and former Tsarist officers and bureaucrats managed to escape becoming *lishentsy* by serving in the new Soviet state as specialists, providing skills that employees of proletarian origin did not possess. These jobs were respectable and highly paid, yet many were not fortunate enough to receive such exemptions. These unfortunates, the majority of the "former people," were forced to live stigmatized as "has-beens." The Bolsheviks used them for propaganda purposes, as constant reminders that a new elite had taken the place of the old. An American correspondent described the pathetic appearance of the "former people" on the streets of Moscow:

Most pitiable is the lot of those aristocrats, male or female, who are devoid of any qualifications of practical value. One sees them stand patiently for hours in the open-air markets, holding coats, furs, small pieces of jewelry, by the sale of which they can eke out existence for a few weeks longer.[54]

Because association with the *lishentsy* virtually guaranteed marginalization, many naturally tried to conceal their social origin: using false identities they shifted from job to job and locale to locale, taking advantage of the bureaucratic inefficiency to escape detection. Most common were attempts by children to disown their parents, thereby escaping the family's stigma. Provincial papers in the 1920s carried announcements that such-and-such a son of a priest or a landlord had renounced his ties to his parents, severing all links to his shameful origins. Divorce was an option for spouses of *lishentsy*, as it would be for those married to those accused of being "enemies of the people" during the 1930s Great Terror. While many renounced family bonds only *pro forma* in order to refranchise family members, some broke completely with family members, fearing seemingly inevitable compliance checks by the authorities.[55]

Appeals to the state became increasingly common in the late 1920s during the intensification of discrimination. As one observer described, those standing in line outside the Central Electoral Commission were remarkably diverse:

The waiting crowd was a cross-section of Russia geographically, racially, linguistically. Peasants in bark sandals from far-away Siberian provinces, who had not taken the government's land programme seriously and were shorn of their property and civil rights, rubbed shoulders with "declassed" landowners and ex-army commanders of the Ukraine. Former military contractors, provincial officials of the old regime, lawyers, teachers, intellectuals who in the early stages of the Bolshevist regime had their doubts about the stability of the government, and had remained non-committal too long, now waited to plead their case.[56]

Instead of addressing electoral commissions as objective, impersonal, governmental organs, petitioners threw themselves at the mercy of the authorities, claiming one of two possible identities. Either they styled themselves as harmless, insignificant, pathetic creatures deserving pity and mercy, or, more rarely, they claimed to be loyal proletarians involved in cases of mistaken identity.[57] The petitions in many ways recreated the traditional landowner–peasant relationship, only this time the tables were turned, with the working class considering the pleas of the former elites. In any case, it does not seem that many petitions were even looked at, much less granted.

Suicide, too, was an option in resolving the dilemma between family loyalty and state requirements for inclusion. A Russian professor told an

American tourist during a train journey about a student he had known who had been forced to admit to falsifying his social profile:

> He was summarily dismissed from the university. The fellowship for future study was at once withdrawn. And while the education which he already possessed could not be taken away from him, the right to employ it usefully was withheld. He was not permitted to teach; he had no right to use his training otherwise.
>
> The youth had now no home or occupation. He slept one night in one place and the next night somewhere else. His teachers, believing that the young man had the making of a great scientist, searched the educational world of Moscow for a place where he might fit in . . .
>
> After eight months, they finally found a laboratory which would risk employing this youth. They looked for him in his usual haunts, but he was nowhere to be found. He was finally traced – to a cemetery. He had committed suicide.[58]

Throughout the 1920s, the public humiliation of the "former people" was a deliberately pursued policy. The Bolsheviks needed them to reassure the proletarian masses that the regime was pursuing goals favorable to them. And, indeed, the most unfortunate in society did seem to be "former people," demonized in cartoons, satire, and propaganda art. The social equation did seem to have been turned on its head. Even though the common workers were worse off than before the war, the presence of the *lishentsy* in society suggested that the working class enjoyed some degree of privilege at the expense of the officially designated class enemies. Denunciation can be seen as a safety-valve, allowing ambitious working-class elements to improve their standard of living without expense to the state. An American observer illustrated the situation in the late 1920s:

> When a prominent proletarian wants a room occupied by a member of the former intelligentsia or middle class, a Soviet official will frequently sign an order for the evacuation of the premises. Similarly, if a job held by a former intellectual is wanted by some unscrupulous or envious proletarian, he will obtain it through the simple expedient of casting a slur on the man's "social status." An investigation will be ordered and the former intellectual will be "cleansed," or removed from his job for the good of the proletarian.

Many tried and some succeeded in melting into the working class, and hiding their compromising backgrounds. Though there were exceptions, most survived by living inconspicuous lives, avoiding opportunities for advancement that might have attracted unwanted attention.

Seen in isolation, any one of the campaigns against the intellectuals, Mensheviks and SRs, the Church, and the "former people" does not seem particularly ominous. The party was weeding out the dissidents and the members of the former opposition. It controlled admission to universities and removed undesirable elements. It promoted splits among its ideological rivals, including secular parties and religious congregations. The "former people" were harassed, stigmatized, and impoverished. The NEPmen were phased out. In contrast to the hundreds of thousands of kulaks deported in 1930–1 and hundreds of thousands of party officials arrested or shot in 1937, these measures during NEP do not appear particularly harsh. Yet they are revealing in regard to Bolshevik objectives. They highlight the boundaries of the permissible. They show that there was no "retreat" in Bolshevik attempts to reshape Russian society under NEP.

Chapter 2

The Culture of the New Elite 1921–5
Ascetic knights and drinking pals

The history of the Communist Party during the years of NEP has been largely seen as the interaction of prominent personalities.[1] The extent to which the political history of the CP intermingled with cultural history has been limited to what is called political culture.[2] Here the emphasis has been on the culture of debate as a Bolshevik virtue. It is reiterated over and over that in the 1920s Bolshevik political discourse was mainly deliberative. Bolsheviks debated issues at public forums. The decline of the culture of debate within the Bolshevik Party is usually attributed to the rise of Stalin and his entourage.[3]

The rise of dictatorial culture within the Bolshevik milieu by 1929 cannot simply be explained by the political record of factional struggle. Culture does not change by order from above. Behavioral norms, attitudes, and cultural practices do not materialize overnight. They are usually reflections of deeply rooted values, of norms that are understood as natural and self-evident. Change in political culture was a result of the profound social, political, and cultural transformation of the Bolshevik Party in the 1920s.[4]

OLD HABITS AND NEW TASTES

As the civil war was winding down, the Bolshevik official culture was still that of asceticism, self-sacrifice, and service to the people. The Bolshevik self-image was that of a selfless, humble, and ascetic knight of the revolution, a seasoned fighter who had gone through the upheavals of the civil war, risked his life, and fought against the Whites. A Communist was a hero who had won despite all odds, a natural leader, a union organizer, whose main preoccupation was the cause, the revolution, and victory. Many Bolsheviks adopted this identity in public. In real life, however, the Bolsheviks did not live up to the official image. During the civil war, many local Bolsheviks used grain requisitioning and redivision of property to enrich themselves. People who abused power were labeled hangers-on [*primazyvshiesia*], scoundrels, and opportunists to be exposed and purged from the party ranks.

With the transition to NEP, when the survival of the Bolshevik Party in power was no longer in doubt, the strict enforcement of the ascetic principles of the Old Guard was relaxed. It was time to reap the benefits of victory. Top-ranking Bolshevik leaders, provincial party chairmen and Soviet executives stopped hiding their privileged positions. In their private lives they stopped pretending that they were ascetic knights of the revolution. They began to perceive privilege as an entitlement for their contribution to victory.[5] As early as 1920–1, when Russia was in the midst of famine and hundreds of thousands of peasants were starving, Yulii Martov, a Menshevik leader living in Moscow in poverty shortly before emigrating, wrote in a private letter never intended for publication:

> As far as the "Commissars' Estate" is concerned, its superior standard of living is almost out in the open or should I say less concealed than last year. People like Riazanov, Radek, and Rykov, who had earlier fought against "Inequality," now display on their tables white bread, rice, butter, meat, and at Radek's and Rykov's a bottle of good wine or cognac. Karakhan, Kamenev, Bonch- [Bruevich], Demian Bednyi, Steklov, *et al.* obviously enjoy life. Only Angelica [Balabanoff], Bukharin, and Chicherin, among the stars of the first calibre are still noted for their simplicity of disposition.[6]

Asceticism was giving way to indulgence in the pleasures of life: a comfortable home, a glass of cognac accompanying a conversation about the world revolution. The cultural level of the Old Bolshevik leaders, despite all their claims, remained what they themselves called bourgeois. They were journalists and propagandists who claimed proletarian identity only in the public sphere. In their habits and way of life, the intellectual Bolsheviks returned to what they were before the storms of the revolution, when they were spending time in Zurich, Geneva, and Paris in endless conversations about politics, revolution, and the labor movement, writing articles and making speeches, organizing party meetings, schools, and congresses. Now they did the same from the luxurious National Hotel in Moscow where most of the top Bolsheviks resided. Luxury, *per se*, was not the priority for most of these people. Nor did they accumulate material possessions. They simply required a level of comfort they were accustomed to. They surrounded themselves with luxury and began to display it in public. In a top-secret letter addressed to all gubkoms in October 1923 entitled "On the Struggle with Excessive Luxury and Criminal Abuse of Office Prerogatives," the CC wrote:

> There are at the disposal of the Central Control Commission a series of facts available which indicate that both the central and the provincial party organizations . . . maintain fleets of automobiles and horse-drawn carriages without any work-related need . . . It has come to our attention that very often special rail cars have been dispatched to the southern resorts for the sole purpose of delivering one passenger to the resorts. At state expense, entire freight rail-cars were dispatched to the southern resorts transporting automobiles.[7]

1919

1922

1927

Figure 1 The Three Epochs
Source: *Bich* No.9 (1927), p. 10

The Central Control Commission referred to this as a widespread practice. High-ranking party officials did not distinguish between personal and state expenses, systematically using state funds and facilities for personal gain or enjoyment. They did not think that they were violating any ethical norms, as privilege came with the job. They believed they were entitled to any resources under their control because that is what confirmed their rank in their own eyes as well as in the eyes of the masses.[8] The Central Control Commission continued:

> Some high-ranking officials [*otvetstvennye rabotniki*] have at their disposal or as personal property their own automobiles, their own stables filled with race and riding [*vyezdnye*] horses, as well as a variety of horse-drawn carriages.[9]

These high-ranking officials imitated the lifestyle of the overthrown gentry. The CC did not ban those practices outright. It was concerned, though, that the ostentatious lifestyle might incense the masses, and recommended that display of luxury be curtailed.

What was the role of the Bolsheviks to be? – that was the question. The party was groping in the dark for an answer, as is clear from the debates at the Xth Party Congress in spring 1921. The problem, according to Bukharin, was that the party had "detached itself from the masses."[10] The Communist upstarts found themselves under NEP in leadership roles as supervisors, administrators, and executives. They had to define for themselves what attributes of power and authority were appropriate. The first thing most upstarts tried to do was to put some distance between themselves and the milieu they had just abandoned. They wanted to be perceived as higher in social status. They surrounded themselves with the material attributes of a superior social class such as large apartments, cars, maids, good clothing, as well as an authoritative or even condescending mode of address to the proletarian masses. In its report for 1923, the GPU described the lifestyles of the Communist administration in Donbas:

> They are engaged in drunkenness. They set themselves up comfortably. They are rude to workers. In Yuzovka high-ranking party officials are riding about in automobiles under the influence of alcohol.[11]

The Workers' and Peasants' Inspectorate received hundreds of complaints about unlawful distribution of apartments among the bosses.[12] According to the CC investigation at the Vladimir textile factory, "usually at workers' meetings, members of the RCP and workers met as two inimical camps," because the Communists had appropriated available apartments. They stuck to themselves and engaged in drunkenness.[13] At a factory in Bryansk, a CP secretary, one Sidorenko,

> was the subject of undesirable gossip. Workers regarded him with distaste because he indulged in an abundance of luxury. His wife was seen

promenading with a little dog. He demanded a large apartment for himself, threatening the plenipotentiary in question with expulsion from the party if his demand was not met.[14]

A lady with a little dog is a familiar image in Russian literature, automatically associated with the character in Chekhov's story of the same name. It is an image of a noble and refined lady. In this incident, the workers perceived Sidorenko's wife as acting as if she were a lady of high society. In the workers' minds, she was parading her superiority. Sidorenko defined his party membership as an entitlement to a better apartment.

Communist Party membership was the only thing which separated people of the same cultural milieu. Those who were members knew it guaranteed access to privileges that were denied to others. In countless cases, authority was understood as superiority over others, as a source of material well-being, and as an ability to demonstrate to others who was subordinate to whom. In the popular perception, the Communist bosses had only replaced the Tsarist ones. According to the Agitprop analysis of the questions posed by workers at the Moscow factories and plants, there was much gossip about those who lived in luxury and rode in automobiles. "They referred to them as Soviet bureaucrats and complained about the high salaries of party officials."[15]

Among workers, party membership was almost never associated with a set of political views or programs. It was first and foremost a matter of moving into a different social world. For some, party membership was an insurance policy. In Samara province, for example, 244 party members were listed as unemployed. These were workers without any skills or education. When the party secretary suggested that they acquire a skill and go to school, their response was that they did not need to study and did not want to work. They expected the party to take care of them.[16] Party membership was a way to free oneself from physical labor. Once one became a party member one did not need to work as hard as before. The association of party membership with career and privilege was so commonplace that the satirical journals of the time openly published verses poking fun at it.

partbiletik partbiletik
ostavaisya s nami
ty dobudesh nam konfet,
chaya s sukharyami,
slovno raki na meli
bez tebia my budem
bez bileta my nuli
a s biletom lyudi.[17]

party card, party card
stick by us please
you're the one who'll earn for us

pretsils, sweets and tea
like crawfish in shallow water
without you we will become
without party cards, we're zeros
but with you we are "someone."

A party card was seen as a ticket freeing one from work, and party
assignments as an unwelcome chore to be avoided. Once one achieved party
membership, and its consequent superior social status, why should one bother
with fulfilling tasks and obligations? This was the reasoning of the local
Communists in Novosilskii uezd, Tula province. "Nobody fulfilled party
assignments," stated the report. "The cells were engaged in systematic and
pervasive drunkenness."[18]

Party members were expected to perform certain rituals which would
prepare them for leadership roles, at least according to the expectation of the
CC. These included reading Communist propaganda materials, attending
party meetings, paying membership dues, and participating in provincial
propaganda campaigns. Doing all this with enthusiasm qualified one to be an
activist. The description of the trends in Votkinsk party organization, located
in a large industrial city, reads:

> There is weakness of party discipline. Many party members systematically
> skip party meetings, do not pay party dues, do not want to study, and do
> not read newspapers.[19]

The activist identity was understood by many in the rank and file to be a
springboard to a higher status. If one was successful enough to reach a high
rank in the party, one could afford to skip meetings, readings, and even paying
dues. "Party activism" for most was merely a role to play to gain promotion.
"Activism" was perceived as a necessary initiation rite to be dispensed with
once one made it to the top.

The rural Communist Party was small in number and terribly insecure.
These people had bitter memories of the Green detachments. Their old habits
and experiences were still with them. They perceived NEP exactly as Lenin
phrased it, a retreat. Their relative weight and power in the countryside had
diminished considerably and they had to respond to Moscow's unpredictable
demands and to those of the autonomous village community. The situation
in Tambov province is instructive. There were only 3,500 Communists, a
hopelessly small number for a province of 2.5 million.[20] Most were upstarts
of the civil war years and had very primitive notions not only of what
socialism was, but of who led their own party. A test of political literacy
showed that: "even the secretaries of party cells believed that the party leader
was called the secretary and he was appointed by the Cheka, and that
Comintern was running the party and Comrade Zinoviev the Comintern."[21]
When asked the question, "What kind of person should a Communist be?",
many answered, "A person who fulfilled decrees of Soviet power."

With minor variation the socio-cultural profile of rural Communists was fairly similar. Most were from poor rural families but not those of practicing farmers. Most had received only rudimentary education and had only recently converted to Communism. In Tula province for example, of the several thousand Communists in the province, only 0.4 per cent had joined before 1917, 15 per cent during the civil war, 22 per cent during 1922–3, and 62 per cent in 1924; 84 per cent had primary education, meaning that they could barely read.[22] The party secretaries from many provinces complained that the cultural level of rural Communists was very low. No one understood "the tasks of socialist construction." The CC wrote to the province committees that "there were cases in Donetsk province when Communists were beating their wives for attending party meetings."[23]

On every possible occasion village Communists paraded their power. In Tambov province a chairman of the district EC felt he was entitled to ride in a luxurious carriage and engage in debauchery.[24] The Tambov GPU admitted that "pervasive drunkenness of local officials was a common occurrence throughout the entire province."[25] The situation was no different in Saratov province. The city committee letter described intrigues, embezzlement, and drunkenness among party members as "showing a tendency to grow."[26] The CC criticized civil war habits, localism, acquisitiveness, abuse of power for personal gain, lack of discipline, and lack of secrecy in business transactions [konspirativnost'] among party members in the Don province party organization.[27] Much of what these people internalized from Communist propaganda was to obey orders. The Communists' job was to enforce grain collection, first and foremost. The Tambov party secretary admitted that as late as 1924 old methods persisted: "To enforce agricultural tax collection, repressive measures are being applied everywhere. They practice mass arrests and confiscation and sale of personal belongings at auctions."[28] Particularly notorious in this regard was "the work of assessors in Morshansk uezd. For failure to pay taxes, they were destroying stone granaries, ignoring complaints and petitions."[29] This senseless destruction had no economic imperative and was discouraged by the provincial authorities. The GPU was worried by the excessive zeal of local officials.

In order to intensify extraction of tax, they usually rely on repressions: such as inventory and sale of property and arrest of non-payers. In some provinces the numbers of those arrested reached several hundred per uezd, and in Stavropol' province they arrested more than 10,000 tax evaders.[30]

The civil war upstarts had become used to seeing their tasks in military terms. It was about storming and destroying the enemy; it was about enforcing procurements; and delivering on time, no matter what the cost. These methods were now officially discouraged, but the civil war veterans did not know any other. They found themselves disoriented, and disconnected to the new reality. Reluctance of many to part with the old habits, a spate of suicides in the party, and a general sense of disorientation were signs of a cultural shock. It was a sense that the military victory in the civil war was hollow and Russia was remaining to be conquered. But nobody seemed to know how exactly. Nostalgia for War Communism in the early years of NEP was a natural reaction of the party to the new and unfamiliar role. It was a nostalgia for simple and easy solutions and for clear goals. But first and foremost it was a sign of difficulty with settling into NEP.

To project power for most local Communist upstarts involved instilling fear. If peasants did not fear them they felt their status was threatened. The Tambov GPU described in its report an incident it called typical:

A member of the Communist Party cell in Kuzminskii district, Lipetskii uezd was systematically drunk; he often beats peasants. On several occasions they tied him up and wanted to bring him to the city but did not, fearing him as a CP member. They were afraid that when he returned he would send them all to prison or shoot them, as he had threatened.[31]

Incidents like this abound in the GPU and party reports from the provinces:

The chairman of the district EC in Morshanskii uezd was habitually drunk, and shot his revolver to threaten peasants. An uezd party secretary got drunk with the chief of district police and shouted that they'd shoot them all with revolvers.
The drunken chairman of Zamyatchinskii district EC attempted to rape a schoolteacher.
The chief of the Kromovskii district police went to a peasant's house and demanded some vodka. After he got drunk he ordered the peasant's wife to go to bed with him.[32]

The frankness of the GPU and party reports on the lifestyles and tastes of rural Communists is astonishing. If this kind of information had appeared in a non-party journal, it would have been shut down immediately and its editors arrested as counterrevolutionaries. The CC referred to incidents like these in a letter to the provincial committees as a "malaise of the party." The rank and file were seeking compensation for their diminished status under NEP in debauchery and abuse of power. Rural party members resented NEP because it put limits to their arbitrariness and required abandoning extraordinary procedures for normal governance.

Reminiscing about the good old days of the civil war with a bottle of vodka in a company of drinking pals was now a favorite pastime. Drunkenness was so widespread that party reports did not even consider it to be a serious offense. Members were expected to demonstrate to each other that they had special bonds, which in the Russian context generally took the form of drinking vodka together. Communists socialized only with those of their status: other party members. Pervasive drunkenness of the Communist bosses must be seen as their cultural reaction to the onset of NEP. Even though they were hopeless enterprises, periodic campaigns against drunkenness were waged. The provincial reports showed local Communists' propensity to use their job as a source of personal gain. Once the funds were flowing, they had to drink together. Slobodskii uezd committee in Vyatka province wrote in its report:

> Although seasoned, among our party members the tradition of a drinking party [*pianka*] is strong. Our Communists bless their daughters for marriage, marry them in churches, marry their sons to priests' daughters, associate with kulaks, and do absolutely nothing, besides hanging around with other party cell members.[33]

These Vyatka Communists clearly defined their status as equal to the economic and spiritual elite of the countryside. Hence they spent time with the most prosperous peasants and wedded their sons to priests' daughters. They brought their own traditional understanding of hierarchy, order, and power into the workings of the Communist Party. The image of a rural Communist was that of a kulak's drinking pal.

At a Leningrad workers' conference in 1925, workers related their experiences and impressions after spending summer months in the countryside. One woman worker from Tver' province described rural Communists:

> In our locality, a Communist, shameful as it is, got into the habit of going to church; he baptizes his children, produces self-made vodka, and drinks together with the kulak – that's what our typical Communist is like.[34]

The portrait she painted was all too familiar to many. Local Communists were not models of conscious proletarians but a part of the local cultural milieu. Just like everybody else, they used the party to rise a notch above the rest.

A CC investigation of the Vologda province party revealed the usual compilation of violations: drunkenness, hobnobbing with kulaks, embezzlement, bribery, and church attendance. The report stated that the chairman of the uezd party committee had turned official premises into "a place for their amorous affairs with women and drunken parties."[35] A survey of conditions in the Leningrad rural organizations likewise spoke of pervasive drunkenness, embezzlement, falsification of documents, and links to alien social elements.[36] A brief glance at the categories of party reprimand by period and province suggests that drunkenness, abuse of authority, detachment from the masses, and other social ills were widespread. In Vyatka province, for example, of the 2,027 Communists in 1924, 115 were censured for various violations, 53 of those reprimanded for drunkenness and hooliganism.[37] In the city of Samara, there were 272 Communists charged with crimes in 1924: 163 (50 per cent) were accused of abuse of authority, 33 (12 per cent) with economic crimes, 39 (16 per cent) with embezzlement, 28 (10 per cent) with bribery, 20 (7.7 per cent) with theft, and 23 (8.5 per cent) with document falsification.[38]

Official campaigns were launched to bring the masses and bosses closer together. Party rank and file were encouraged to "alert" the center if they felt violations of party discipline were taking place. This became a long-lasting feature of Soviet political culture, as denunciations flowed to Moscow. The CC and GPU studied them and usually dispatched a commission to investigate the validity of the allegations. The results varied, but the general pattern was that the affairs were white-washed, a few minor scapegoats being sacrificed to assure the silence of the rest. As one local party member said to the CC commission during its visit to study the situation in the Vologda province party organization: "You will go but I will have to stay behind."[39] Rank and file Communists' only recourse – denunciation to the center – was a highly dangerous weapon.

All these countless incidents and pieces of evidence add up to the impression that the officially propagated image of the CP members as ascetic knights of the revolution, burning with ardor to construct socialism in Soviet Russia, was no more than a utopian, idealized vision, and a myth which had nothing to do with reality. The CC was well aware what kind of people constituted the so-called vanguard of the proletariat. In secret party instructions and letters to the provincial organizations, it used a number of terms to define what was called the "malaise of the party," "bureaucratization," "detachment from the masses," and "pervasive drunkenness." Thousands of instances could be cited here to illustrate these practices. Primarily, Communist Party membership was about access to privilege and power over others. The people who joined the party wanted to break out of the working-class or poor-peasant identity and act as if they were of a higher social status. Their ideas about what that implied had nothing to do with officially propagated images but with deeply ingrained cultural traits. The Communist upstarts imitated the role models familiar to them. They tried to act exactly in the same fashion as the overthrown elites. Their notions of what it meant to be in charge, to administer, and to supervise were inevitably associated with large apartments, servants, and giving orders to be carried out without question. Dreams of proletarian culture were the utopian visions of people like Bogdanov and other theoreticians of proletarian culture. But the authority relationships of the old regime were simply restored and reproduced. "Comrade" replaced "sir," but the yell, "Do you understand who you are talking to?" remained the same. Lenin's Communists imitated as best they could the old pre-revolutionary elite. They acted the way they thought bosses should: enjoying life, holding drinking parties, taking bribes, demanding better apartments and houses, and expecting reverence and obedience from the masses. Most of them were barely literate. Intellectual debates between high-ranking Bolsheviks on the meaning of socialism were of no interest to the new ruling elite, as long as they held the reins of power and privilege.

"You, my dear, as I see, do not forget the revolution. Even the furniture in your office is of red wood."

Figure 2 Revolutionary Comrade
Source: *Bich* No. 17 (1928), p. 9

EDUCATING THE NEW PARTY CADRES

By the time Lenin died, it was apparent to many that the Bolshevik Party was not what it claimed to be. It was not the party of the proletariat in the country building socialism. It was a party bereft of revolutionary spirit, a party of social-climbers and bureaucrats, a party whose elite was far from confident in the success of the enterprise it had embarked upon. It was a party of the voiceless rank and file and a few who knew what was going on around them but were not allowed to communicate. The Bolshevik organization had little to do with a political party. It was a mobilization and recruitment agency producing cadres for state administration. It was a propaganda and tax-collection agency, and a police agency. It was a self-sustaining and perpetuating ruling elite claiming to be proletarian and Marxist.

The top party leaders and the Central Committee were just as aware of this as were the dissidents and the critics. They knew that the party could not remain in power if it remained a party of directors, commissars, and executives. In the minds of the party leaders, the solution was in opening up the party to the tens of thousands of worker recruits. New cadres were to proletarianize the party and replace the doubters, critics, spineless bourgeois intellectuals, and inefficient drunkards. The solution was in educating a new generation of Communists from the factory floor. New proletarian cadres would save the party from degeneration into corrupt and drunken networks of cliques. New proletarian cadres would make the party immune to ideological heresies and cement its unity. They would ensure the party's connection to the working class in the uncertain times of NEP. These were the goals of the "Lenin levy" recruitment drive.

The entire party-building procedure was orchestrated from Moscow. The CC decided how many new members were going to be admitted and sent the targets to the provinces. Since the percentage of workers from the factory floor remained consistently low, the CC instructed local gubkoms to increase workers' membership.

> In accord with the decision of the XIIIth party conference and the CC plenum on January 31, 1924, the Bryansk gubkom is to recruit to the party 2,000 workers from the factory floor within three months.[40]

Party recruitment was the most important task of any provincial party committee. So the professional agitators and propagandists went out to the factories and offered all kinds of enticement for workers to enroll. Terms of admission were relaxed for workers. Applicants did not have to have recommendations from party members. Virtually any worker who wanted to could join. The campaign was well covered in the press across the country as a symbol of unity of the Communist Party and the working class. It was portrayed as an example of a true worker democracy in the country of the victorious proletariat, because in no other country were there so many opportunities for a simple worker from the factory floor. At the end of the campaign the Bryansk gubkom reported: "In the end the task of the CC on Lenin's recruitment drive was fulfilled by 88 per cent."[41] In Kursk province the target of 1,000 new recruits was over-fulfilled by 141 new Communists.[42] The Lenin enrollment drive was, however, just another bureaucratic campaign and the province committees simply fulfilled targets by processing people.

Despite all the perks associated with party membership, the party committees had a hard time fulfilling those targets: there were not enough volunteers to join the party. The Kostroma province had a majority female population, and poor land. Men had traditionally left their villages in search of employment in cities. So the Kostroma party committee had to be inventive in increasing party membership figures. It distributed guidelines to local cells on individual approach to party enrollment. Every local party cell was required to identify "politically advanced persons" whose job was working over [obrabotka] specific individuals with the aim of recruiting them into the party. A chosen comrade was to name two or three persons who were the targets of his "agitation activity." Their names were to be kept secret. The party task of the chosen comrade was to establish regular meetings with them in an informal atmosphere, to invite them for tea, visit them in their homes, and establish friendship.

> The entire work on individuals must be conducted secretly. The peasant in question should not know that the party comrade is attached to him for the purpose of working him over [obrabotka] as a party task. The party comrade must prepare him for entering the party ranks without him being aware of the process.[43]

These recruiters represented the act of joining the party to the potential members as an act of joining a superior caste, a pantheon of wisdom, a vanguard, and as a source of power over other people. In the Don host area the individual approach targeted primarily workers and miners.[44] The Bolsheviks were clearly unable to let go of their pre-revolutionary conspiratorial techniques.

One of the main tasks of the provincial Agitprops was educating the new cadres. For this purpose the Agitprops ran a network of schools and courses of long and short term and different levels and purposes. Among these were: the province sov-party schools, workers' faculties, circles for the study of Marxism–Leninism, and centers for the liquidation of illiteracy. The sov-party schools trained reliable administrative cadres and propagandists. Their short-term crash courses lasted only one month. "Students faced a difficult task of mastering elementary political literacy and learning the methods of conveying this knowledge in their future propaganda work," and graduates of the crash courses were required to lead circles for the study of Marxism–Leninism or to supervise village reading houses [izba-chital'nya].[45] In

Vladimir province, 113 students selected from among rural schoolteachers (almost all of them women) were to be trained to lead reeducation courses for schoolteachers after graduation.

The Vladimir sov-party school encountered difficulties recruiting students for training as propagandists. It tried to follow Moscow Agitprop admission guidelines but finally had to relax standards because there simply were not enough "young conscious proletarians" to fulfill the admission targets. As a result, they had to admit illiterate people. The problem was, according to the report, that "elementary literacy of those admitted was very low." Before they could be trained as propagandists they had "to be passed through" the crash courses at the centers for the liquidation of illiteracy and through political literacy courses. Only after that would they be ready for a crash course at the sov-party school. The Gomel province committee reported that most of the 1,800 party recruits of the Lenin levy were functionally illiterate: "Some of them had to be 'passed through' the liquidation of illiteracy centers, others through the schools for semi-literate and some through the sov-party schools."[46] The total number of students at the Vladimir province sov-party school was 148 – 133 men and 15 women; 69 were CP members or candidates; 74 were Komsomol members; and 5 had no party affiliation.[47] To suggest that the future Bolshevik professional propagandists lacked refinement would be to state the obvious. The most these people could do upon graduation was reiterate the party line on a given subject. Fortunately, that is exactly what was required of them.

Political literacy schools were a step below the sov-party schools. In Vladimir province there were thirty-eight of them with the total enrollment of 1,109.[48] Their main purpose was to provide basic political literacy for young Communist Party recruits. Many of them had no idea what the relationship between the Communist International and the Central Committee was, let alone some more complex issues of Communist theory. The crash courses taught the future propagandists the history of the Communist Party, the foundations of Leninism, and the practice of Communist construction, all in a much simplified version.

The centers for the liquidation of illiteracy were at the bottom of the educational pyramid. They taught students to read and write. For the most part they were not regular workers or peasants but new recruits to the Communist Party who happened to be illiterate. In Vladimir province, for example, 366 centers graduated 7,600 students during 1924–5 school year and in Orel province 18,000 people attended, and 11,000 graduated.[49]

Workers' faculties ran courses for mostly Communist workers who were earmarked for promotion and further education. These were essentially preparatory courses for entering institutions of higher learning in big cities. The Vladimir province workers' faculty had 150 students: 67 of them were CP members, 58 Komsomol members, and 25 without party affiliation; 130 were men, 20 women, and almost all were under 25 years of age.[50] Successful graduates of workers' faculties could be selected to be sent to college or university. The central Agitprop or Central Committee's Department of Cadres Distribution [Uchraspred] usually sent target allotment numbers [razverstka] to the provinces. Naturally, future students had to have proper credentials, such as proletarian origin, party or Komsomol membership, and distinction in party political education. Provincial authorities sometimes had a hard time meeting those targets in view of the poor level of education of their recruits. The Vladimir gubkom, for example, reported:

> Despite the fact that the target figures were sent well in advance, we could not fulfill them for the lack of qualified candidates. We could fill only 30 of the available 42 slots with difficulty and some of those returned since they were not adequately prepared.[51]

A special term was coined for those to be promoted in NEP Russia: vydvizhentsy, or promotees. These were mostly young people, poorly educated graduates of various crash courses and schools. In addition to Agitprop, the CC apportioned target figures for admission to military schools, while the Komsomol hierarchy had its own resources and target allotment figures for educational placement. Through all these channels, the Vladimir province, for example, dispatched 223 promotees (193 men and 30 women) to study at various institutes and universities in 1924. Of these, 70 were CP members, 122 Komsomol members, and 111 without party affiliation, but politically reliable, educated comrades.[52]

Admission to Leningrad institutions of higher learning was possible at that point only through the admission targets set by the party. Each educational institution received a target allotment list [raznaryadka] of how many students from which province and which institution they were to admit, who was going to be admitted through the allotments of the workers' faculties system or Komsomol or promotees' commissions. Of the total of 3,462 students admitted to all Leningrad institutes and the university, 55 per cent were dispatched by workers' faculties from various provinces.[53] This means that by 1925 at the latest, the majority of students in big cities had "proletarian" social origin credentials and had passed through political screening.

The networks of courses and schools the Bolsheviks set up had no precedent in Russia. This impressive recruitment drive was conditional upon political loyalty. The crash courses and political-education schools hardly provided an education if that is defined as knowledge and the capacity to think. They disseminated a pre-packaged myth, a staple diet of simple propaganda lines to be used as a guide to proper behavior. The propaganda machine turned out people to staff the growing Bolshevik state agencies who thought that they were being educated, though in fact they were denied an education. Educational opportunities were taken out of the domain of individual free choice. Students were trained to obey the party and fulfill orders in exchange for career opportunities. A new class of people was being created: those who believed they owed everything to the party. The higher on the nomenklatura scale these people moved, the less freedom of expression they had. Can this kind of mobility be called upward?

DISSIDENT VOICES

Lack of culture, drunkenness, bureaucratization, and detachment from the masses – these were the officially recognized and widespread social ills of the Communist Party. Yet no group could discuss on its own the ills that the CC discussed in its secret letters to gubkoms. Such a discussion would be considered subversive and suppressed immediately. Rank and file could appeal to the CC but never initiate any independent action from below. But how large was the audience of critics in the Communist Party in the early years of NEP? The exact answer is probably buried in the archives of the GPU. Judging by the CC instructions to the provinces and by the GPU reports to the CC, it was a minority. These people belonged primarily to three very different constituencies: old guard party members, the so-called Old Bolsheviks, associated with the labor movement; the civil war veterans who had failed to adjust to NEP; and worker activists on the factory floor.

The Workers' Opposition and the Democratic Opposition of 1920–2 belonged to the first group. These were Bolsheviks from the intelligentsia, like Aleksandra Kolontai, who had been linked to the labor movement throughout their lives. They defined their identity as pro-worker and they had the internal need to express their views. They called themselves the Workers' Opposition, but in fact had little to do with workers, although they were convinced that the revolution had not brought about the liberation of the working class. They were mostly alarmed by the loss of revolutionary elan and by the privileges and bureaucratization of the party.

Myasnikov's dissident group was a genuine workers' opposition from the factory floor. A worker himself, he assumed that the proletarian revolution in Russia promised liberation for workers. For him and his supporters it was obvious that this had not happened. He referred to NEP as a new exploitation of the proletariat. Myasnikov was particularly active in 1921 and early 1922. Zinoviev, the Petrograd party boss, was so uneasy about his revolutionary, anti-establishment rhetoric that he exiled Myasnikov to Perm province, home of a huge Motovilikha plant. Myasnikov quickly became a workers' hero there, attacking the bosses' privileges and betrayal of the working class. Myasnikov and his supporters campaigned for restoring the soviets as genuine organs of workers' self-government. They supported peasant unions and welcomed their participation in the regulation of prices. They favored workers' self-management and complete freedom of the press. In short, Myasnikov's politics had a flavor of revolutionary egalitarianism, populist democracy, and class partnership. It echoed some of the themes of the Left

SRs or of the Bolsheviks themselves in October 1917. In 1922, however, this was counterrevolutionary heresy for the Bolsheviks.

In March 1922, with Lenin's consent, Myasnikov was expelled from the Communist Party and arrested. Despite the censure, he published leaflets articulating workers' grievances, attacking the bureaucracy and the new bosses, and wound up in a GPU cellar.[54] In 1923 the GPU intercepted an appeal of his Workers' Group to party members. In it, dissidents wrote that the soviet and party apparatus had detached itself from the masses, that bureaucratization of the party was proceeding at an alarming rate, and that internal party stratification was separating the elite from the rank and file. All these accusations were almost identical to the ones identified by the Central Control Commission. Nevertheless, it was politically incorrect to address embarrassing facts that were common knowledge. In another underground dissident appeal, critics wrote:

> Comrades: Despite the fact that the statute of the party allows one to dare express opinion and campaign in defense of one's views and against the line taken by the CC, the leading circles of the party resort to repressions against any attempt to utter a critical word.[55]

The CC knew that the charges were true, yet the GPU was instructed to arrest the oppositionists, not for what they were saying but for daring to organize themselves into a group and for criticizing the party publicly. This typified what was to be a long-standing trait of Communist political culture: no public criticism of the party, and no organizing would be tolerated. In a secret letter to provincial organizations on May 8, 1923, Molotov called on all gubkoms to launch a merciless struggle against all those who "put forward leftist slogans" and appeals against the NEP. The party committees were advised to pass information on such heretics to the GPU.[56] This suggests that the Bolshevik intra-party debates in the 1920s went on not thanks to Bolshevik tolerance but despite Bolshevik intolerance. They continued for years because it took a long time to extinguish the natural human desire to have an opinion and try to articulate it.

Dissident views among the Bolshevik intelligentsia were widespread in the early years of NEP, but they were seldom part of a coherent world-view. Those who signed petitions could be counted in dozens. Those who sympathized with the criticism numbered perhaps in the hundreds. Many more, however, shared the feeling of alarm in 1923–4. Questions discussed at numerous private meetings included: How would the party manage without Lenin? How would the rivalry between Trotsky and Stalin be resolved? Was NEP viable in the long run and if not what would replace it? Doubt crept into the Bolsheviks' minds.

A new spate of suicides hit the party. As Victor Serge, an observer and journalist noted: "Expelled from the party for opposing the 'New Line,' some young men have gotten hold of revolvers – to turn against themselves . . .

What good is life if the party refuses us the right to serve?"[57] Of the more famous people, the suicide of Yevgeniya Bosh shocked the Communist elite. She was the epitome of the tough Bolshevik commissar of the civil war era. She had fought peasant rebels and the Whites during the civil war, and she had worked in the Cheka and the Ukrainian government. Life had had a meaning and a purpose. The NEP years brought with it nothing but dis-illusionment. The party lost its sense of direction. Party functionaries were sucked into the world of shady deals and financial schemes. Corruption was rampant. As an old Chekist explained his frustration to Victor Serge:

> Figures on unemployment, wage-scales, seizure of the home market by private businessmen resulting from plunder of the state; privation in the villages and the creation of a peasant bourgeoisie; weakness of the Comintern and the Rapallo policies; wretchedness in the cities and the arrogance of the newly rich – do these results seem natural to you? And have we done all that we have done, just for this? . . . We did not fight the revolution for this.[58]

These doubts were seldom recorded and rarely found their way into the opposition petitions or programs. This, however, does not make them any less a part of the history of the cultural climate of the mid-1920s.

Several years after the end of the civil war, as NEP was in full swing, thinking Bolsheviks were asking themselves whether the revolution had succeeded. Who had benefitted from the revolutionary transformation of Russia? Was it really possible to build socialism, especially in one country? These and many other questions were debated endlessly in private apart-ments, around dinner tables with friends, among students of the universities, workers' faculties, and, of course, at the Institute of Red Professors, the center of the Communist intelligentsia. Critical views were seldom com-mitted to paper, not so much because it was dangerous at that time, but because they were so much a part of the mainstream thinking. It was something that was on "everyone's mind." Some diaries survive of the mid-ranking Bolsheviks, from the circles of Red Professors, and CC functionaries. The diary of I.I. Litvinov, a graduate of the Institute of Red Professors in 1924, reflected the topics of these conversations, the mood in the party, and the views expressed by many at that time:

> People who had set themselves a goal of changing the world and fighting against prejudice must be brave, fearless, and revolutionary themselves in their deeds and thoughts as the Bolsheviks used to be. And now? What is the party today? Nothing but a herd of sheep, not daring to have opinions but only trying to please, fearing any independent act.[59]

Litvinov describes conformity, time-serving, and subservience. The culture of the party did not encourage independent thinking or judgment. NEP as a system was generating a search for comfort and career opportunities.

Nevertheless, the outcome was not predetermined. We learn from the diary that two points of view were most prevalent. Either the NEP climate of freedom would infect the party and propel it forward or the process of degeneration would continue. If it turned out to be the latter, in the end the CP would "turn into a caste," and it "would be abandoned by everything that is live and cultured" and only "careerists, thieves, opportunists, and conservatives would remain."[60]

This sort of criticism against the party was commonplace in the mid-1920s among the Bolsheviks. Culturally, it was an assertion of one's individuality, and the right to have an opinion. In a sense, it was a public manifestation of a claim to belong to the Russian intelligentsia. Criticism of corruption was not, strictly speaking, as subversive as heretical thoughts about Marxist–Leninist ideology. Criticism of corruption implied interest in improving things rather than totally rejecting them. However, even in the relatively mild atmosphere of the mid-1920s, one could share critical thoughts about the ideology only with trusted friends. Committing some of those heretical views to paper, the future Red Professor Litvinov wrote in his diary in 1922:

> One cannot reject personal initiative; one cannot turn the world into barracks with impunity. One cannot defend the idea of class dictatorship when mankind has come to resolving gigantic problems of the entire humanity . . . Marxism has been turned into a religion. It is petrified. It is a mummy. And its end is near.[61]

The GPU would have found these thoughts counterrevolutionary. They cast doubt on the validity of the entire Bolshevik undertaking. They undermined the confidence in the belief that the party was, in fact, building socialism.

As the Communist Party approached the height of NEP, it was in the process of fundamental cultural change. The far-reaching consequences of that change were not immediately apparent. The Bolshevik Party consisted of three cultural entities: the ever shrinking old intelligentsia core, the civil war veterans, and the new recruits. The old Bolshevik intelligentsia was splintered into various factions, preoccupied with what they had been doing all their lives – arguing about the fate of the revolution. These people were concentrated at the top of the state administrative apparatus, which made them visible, and outwardly powerful, as if they were the ruling class, but also vulnerable to changes in political climate. In the provinces there were practically no intellectual Bolsheviks. These were fiefdoms of civil war upstarts, who tried the best they could to break with the milieu they had come from and imitate the overthrown elite. Some succeeded in adapting to NEP, others did not. Those who did, as we shall see, thrived with the new opportunities; those that did not remained bitter and angry with the establishment.

Their counterparts in the cities were the proletarian upstarts of the "Lenin levy" recruitment drive. The promotees were the lucky worker and peasant upstarts who benefitted from new career opportunities. They were singled out, trained and given careers, jobs, and power. The CP was creating a new privileged class recruited from the masses. These people were the basis of the new order, but their world-view was cast by the sov-party schools. Most of them had been functionally illiterate when they entered the party. They were rewarded and promoted not for their skills, knowledge, or talent, but for their loyalty and obedience. In sov-party schools or workers' faculties they received training not education. This was the generation of people who were given myth instead of history, a crude ABC of Communism instead of Marxism, a vastly distorted picture of life in the West, and no knowledge of philosophy, history, economy, or psychology at all as it was understood in the rest of Europe. This was the first generation of the Russian elite since Peter the Great to be cut off from access to Western civilization. These were the people trained to learn how machines work and how to administer an enterprise but not how to think independently and how to make decisions. They were the future of the party.

The combination of these qualities in the short run insulated the Communist regime from perilous political heresies. It made party leadership more independent from the rank and file. It provided more opportunities for manipulation of rules and procedures. It made it easier to keep the intellectual Bolsheviks in check. In the long run, however, the sov-party school's output made old intellectual Bolsheviks an endangered species.

Chapter 3

Bolshevik actions and peasants' reactions, 1921–5

Face the village, face defeat

Social and political trends in the Russian countryside in the 1920s are usually seen in the context of what happened before and after NEP. It was a period between the two greatest upheavals in twentieth-century Russian history: the civil war and Stalin's revolution from above. As I have argued elsewhere the real civil war was not between the Reds and the Whites but between the state and peasants, a period of requisition detachments, Green bands, and the burning of villages, taking of hostages, and deportations; a period of famine and devastation, a disaster of monumental proportions.[1] In 1928 a new campaign of violence against the peasants commenced. Misnamed "collectivization," it was a new war on peasantry, a new cycle of deportations and famine. Seen in the context of these upheavals, the NEP years were relatively good times. Peasants are assumed to have been content, if not happy with their situation.

For the Bolsheviks the peasant question was primarily one of the perceived backwardness of Russian agriculture.[2] By "backwardness" the Bolsheviks meant not only economic performance but traditional way of life, habits, attitudes, and religious and cultural practices. They were convinced that a movement towards progress and socialism was only possible if peasants' deeply ingrained instincts were overcome at some point in the future. The disagreement among the Bolsheviks was over the tempo and the method of changing the traditional rural economy. Trotsky and Preobrazhensky's phrase "primitive socialist accumulation" summed up their reasoning that just as capitalists in Western Europe during the first industrial revolution accumulated capital by appropriating wealth and its accumulation, the socialist state, building socialism, should accumulate wealth by taxing peasants in order to invest in industry.[3] In principle, other Bolshevik Party leaders did not object to this plan in the mid-1920s. The disagreement developed later in 1927–8 not over whether to overtax peasants but to what extent and how quickly to abandon individual farming and the market.

How did peasants understand Bolshevik policy objectives during NEP? And how did they act in response to their perceptions? To understand the drama of the late 1920s and the demise of NEP, it is essential to follow the interaction of the Bolshevik administration and the peasants during the six short years of NEP, 1922–8. The key is to understand that top Bolshevik leaders adopted decisions in response to what they knew was happening in the countryside. What they knew was not what was written in the newspapers and not what they themselves were saying at the party meetings. To interpret their decisions we must decipher the coded language being used. We must know who knew what, what they knew and how they defined their facts.

WHO KNEW WHAT

How many people in Bolshevik Russia knew the real situation in the country? What exactly did they know? And how did they perceive the facts? The stream of information to the party leaders flowed essentially through two channels: the party apparatus and the GPU. Every provincial party secretary wrote once or twice a month a report on the political situation. It described the disposition of the population and party work, the economic situation, strikes, protests, and other relevant developments. These reports mostly present the facts in a favorable light as the party secretaries worried about their own standing. The provincial reports were processed by the Central Committee's Information Department, which composed its own report to the Politburo on the political situation in the country province by province. These reports condensed but did not alter the substance of the provincial chairmen's reports. In addition the Information Department drafted reports and memoranda on specific topics, such as the Peasant Union movement, or the situation in the Don and Kuban' hosts.

In addition to the party channel, every provincial GPU wrote its own weekly, biweekly, or monthly report to the All-Russian GPU. The Information Department of the GPU processed these materials and drafted monthly reports on the "Political Situation in the USSR." These were essentially factual compilations with little or no analysis. Incidents were listed by number, province, and topic, such as "workers," "peasants," "the Church," "intelligentsia," and subtopics, such as "Peasant Unions," "strikes," or "terrorism." All the relevant facts for the period in question and where they took place were listed. Comparison of the GPU and party reports makes it possible to verify specific facts. The GPU had no stake in presenting the situation in a particular province in a positive light. Its task was to be vigilant, to see and hear everything, and to report it systematically. Thanks to the hard work of the GPU we now know what questions peasants and workers asked at numerous conferences and meetings, what leaflets appeared where and when, what rumors circulated, how many strikes took place, and how many local Communists were guilty of corruption. The GPU took note of it all in its surveys.

The front page of each report bore an inscription, "top secret." The document was supposed to be kept in a safe with the same level of security with a code key to decipher top-secret instructions. Most GPU compilations of data bore an inscription on the front page which read as follows: "To make copies and take notes is inadmissible under any circumstances." Not only was it forbidden to make any references in public to the GPU data, but even to acknowledge their existence. Then followed the list of persons who had access to this information. Every copy was numbered and each number corresponded to a certain name on the list. Some copies were meant to be read by more than one person.

At the beginning of NEP, in January 1922 when Lenin was still in control, the daily Cheka compilation [*svodka*] went to the following persons: Copy no. 1 Lenin; 2 Stalin; 3 Trotsky and Skliansky; 4 Molotov, and Mikhailov; 5 Dzerzhinsky; 6 Unshlikht; 7 Medved' and Avanesov; 8 Samsonov and Blagonravov; 9 Redeneu; 10 Artuzov; 11 Menzhinsky and Yagoda; 12 Chicherin and Litvinov; 13 Andreev and Shmidt; 14 Steklov; 15 Meshcheriakov and Sol'ts; 16 Velensky; 17 Radek; 18 Khalatov; 19 Kantsev for the CC of Communist Party of Ukraine and Siberian Bureau; 20 Pavlunsky; 21 Grushin; 22 Pankratov for province leaders; 23 Peters; 24 Moroz; 25 Voroshilov; 26 Ivanov; 27 Messing; 28 Gusev; 29 Yel'tsyn; 30 Katsnel'son; 31 Kratt; and copies 32 and 33 stayed with the Information Department of the Vecheka.[4] Of the 31 copies then, 9 went to the Cheka departments' chiefs, and the rest to top party leaders and a few people's commissars. Not all Politburo members were informed, nor all the members of the Central Committee. Some province secretaries presumably had access through the CC of the Ukrainian Communist Party and the Siberian Bureau.

In July 1925, the access list to the monthly GPU survey of political conditions in the country contained, in order, the following names: Yagoda, Menzhinsky, Kamenev, Kalinin, Kiselev, Zinoviev, Stalin, Molotov, Andreev, Bubnov, Khataevich, Bisiarin, Syrtsov, Tsuriupa, Unshlikht, Chicherin, Tomsky, Doletsky, Kotov, Kuibyshev, Artuzov, Blagonravov, Piliar, Zalin, Deribas, Katan'ian, Ol'sky, Trilisser, and Bokiia.[5] Stalin's copy was only number seven at that date. However, by the end of the year Stalin's copy was number one in all GPU compilations. If we compare the 1922 and the 1925 lists, it is clear that a serious personnel change took place. Only nine names appear on both lists. The total number is slightly diminished. It included only the top party secretaries, some Politburo members, and GPU department chiefs, and a token number of government officials, like Chicherin, the People's Commissar for Foreign Affairs. Every copy had a number and the name of the person for whom it was made; then followed a list of people who had been allowed to read it, when they read it, and how long they kept it. Some country-wide GPU surveys, based on the provincial GPUs' reports, were accessible to the provincial GPU chiefs, as is clear from the instructions on some front pages: "The chiefs of the provincial GPUs may furnish this compilation to provincial and city party committees, as well as the Bureaus for reading only." The provincial political police department chiefs decided whether the party bosses would be allowed access to intelligence assessments of popular attitudes in their provinces.

Very few people in Soviet Russia had access to complete information on political and social trends. Those who did (the twenty-nine), read week after week, month after month, a steady flow of information, drastically different from the official Communist representations. They knew that the peasants insisted on ending their economic exploitation and political discrimination; that the rural party was unfit to govern, that the vast majority of the party was composed of unskilled and politically illiterate men who guarded their privileges and cheated Moscow in the process. They also read, as we shall see, that strikes were endemic to socialist industry, that the Red Directors were incompetent, and that most state enterprises were producing losses. What they read qualified in the public sphere as malicious counter-revolutionary vilification of socialism.

This flow of information had a peculiar effect on Bolshevik political discourse. On the one hand, those who knew the facts had to discuss the real situation without admitting to those facts in public. The Bolsheviks had to devise such formulations that would explain their policies in a Marxist framework without revealing their underlying rationale. Class struggle was intensifying in the countryside, vigilance had to be brought to a higher level, discipline had to be strictly enforced, and enemies had to be unmasked – this was the politically correct representation of the problem and of what could be done about it.

PEASANT CONCERNS

The transition to the New Economic Policy was a painful and drawn-out process. Famine still gripped the Volga provinces. Trains functioned irregularly, and almost every day the Cheka reported the discovery and removal of corpses from frozen trains in numerous locations. The Cheka characterized the disposition of the population in Samara "as agitated, and the attitude towards the Communist Party as unfriendly due to the fact that the population did not receive any famine relief."[6] Peasant bands were still roaming in Ukraine and the lower Volga region. Communist Party officials were still ambushed and slaughtered on the roads. In Donetsk, a Green band had dismantled part of the rail track, causing a train wreck.[7] As late as 1923, the GPU reported the activity of forty-three armed peasant bands:

> The period under consideration is distinguished by the growth of banditry of a purely political coloring. It is especially strong in Ukraine, and . . . the Volga basin where a number of previously defeated bands have been resurrected . . . The bands particularly stand out in the following provinces: Penza, Astrakhan', Saratov, Tsaritsyn, and Bashkir Republic . . . In

the Don host area the population provides a favorable climate for the development of banditry.[8]

The horrors of the civil war and famine retreated only slowly and the situation did not normalize until the financial stabilization reform of 1923. Punitive detachments, Green partisans hiding in the forests, the burning of villages labeled "nests of counterrevolutionaries," summary executions, the taking of hostages, and deportations came to an end. Fear of expropriations and confiscations diminished, and production increased dramatically. Markets reopened. The target collection of grain by force was slowly phased out and replaced by taxation. Peasants were free to sell their surplus at market price. This was the keystone of NEP.

The Communist Party still monopolized political power. Economic concessions were, for the Bolsheviks, a way to avoid granting political concessions. The essence of NEP, as Richard Pipes puts it, was "to purchase political survival with economic handouts that could be taken back once the population had been pacified."[9] The center's objective was to generate revenue by taxation while preventing possible political domination of the countryside by the prosperous peasants. Party leaders realized that the rural Communists were dispirited, disoriented and did not understand their role. The peasants' economic interests focused on easing the burden of taxation and diminishing the political domination of the party. The framework of NEP was therefore inherently contradictory: it combined relative economic liberalization with political dictatorship. Political process in the Russian countryside was to develop as a competition between two sides over taxes and power.

In a country of over 100 million peasants it is extremely difficult to generalize about political attitudes. Economic conditions, customs, local government, and even party policies varied a great deal in central Russia, Ukraine, the Volga Basin, and Siberia. Peasant attitudes changed over time depending on the region. The issue is complicated by the fact that virtually everything that was printed distorts the true picture. It was simply impossible even in the relaxed atmosphere of the 1920s to print information on peasant opposition to Communist policies. The third difficulty is that the Russian peasantry did not speak with one voice, especially during NEP, a period of social and political stratification. Proceedings of local assemblies and district executive committees, peasant letters, resolutions [nakaz], petitions and protests, leaflets, and actions carefully monitored by the party and the GPU can all be assessed as sources for understanding peasant attitudes.

The system of taxation was based on taxable property, which took into account the size of herds, fields, and estimated harvest. The richer peasants were taxed more, the poorer less. Lists of taxable property [oplatnye listy] for each household were drawn up. Special commissions measured the sown acreage and the size of the herds. This system generated a natural desire on the part of peasants, especially the prosperous ones, to hide their taxable property, as the GPU report for 1926 attested: "In the districts of North Caucasus, the Urals, and Siberia, the work of commissions to measure the acreage and to verify the size of herds encountered well-organized sabotage of the kulaks."[10]

Peasants almost everywhere objected to the very structure of taxation. Their reasoning was that it was natural to try to gain more. Yet as soon as one increased one's herd or acreage, one was considered a kulak and taxed mercilessly, undercutting any desire to try harder. A secretary of a district EC in Omsk argued that the current system of taxation was preposterous and senseless because taxes hurt most those who worked the hardest: "Just wait a couple of years and peasants would clamor for political power." The CC memorandum to the Politburo cited as typical a concern expressed by one peasant in a letter from Smolensk province:

> The newspapers are full of claims that the Bolsheviks gave land to peasants for free. But where is it, your free land? Even though it was divided for free, one had to pay later in order to confirm it for oneself. And then, the food tax, is it not a form of payment as well? And so it turns out that you did not give it for free but leased it to us and at a high price at that.[11]

The tax burden is the most prominent feature of peasant complaints throughout this period heard from all provinces. The GPU in its assessment of the tax burden wrote in 1924 that: "In order to pay the monetary part of tax, peasants had to sell grain and even cattle and agricultural implements for nothing [*beztsenok*]."[12] Peasants compared the level of taxation with what they had experienced earlier. Admittedly, what they called "the robbery of War Communism" was gone, but the situation was still worse than under the Tsar. Peasant complaints over taxation alarmed Communist Party leaders enough that the CC sent a memorandum to all Politburo members:

> Discontent over taxes is reflected in pronouncements like these: "When the Communists took power they promised that there would be no taxes and now they rip you off more than the Tsar. And the tax money is spent covering expenses of bosses [*zapravily*] who are getting fat at the expense of peasantry."[13]

From the peasants' point of view the level of taxation in the first years of NEP hardly changed in comparison with 1920. In Tambov province the tax target for 1924 was based on the previous year's target. Peasants were required to pay a tax under the threat of confiscation of property or other reprisals:

> Our agitation in favor of paying agricultural tax had to be replaced by more direct measures, such as itinerant [*vyezdnye*] court sessions and actions of the shock troykas. Peasants feared their appearance so much that at their arrival the entire villages would flee to the forests.[14]

Even with such expenditure of effort, the authorities had managed to collect only 82 per cent of the apportioned target. The arbitrary collection by extraordinary troykas emptied reserves and led to serious food shortages in Tambov province later in the year.

To pay the agricultural tax in cash, peasants had to sell their crop first. Most of them had to sell right after the harvest to procurement agencies. The state agencies invariably fixed a low price for grain. This amounted to double or triple taxation. For example, in Tambov province in the fall of 1924, the fixed procurement price was 50 kopecks for a pud of rye. By spring the free market price on rye went up to 3 rubles 60 kopecks.[15] As a result peasants felt cheated by the state's procurement agency. Naturally, they insisted on flexible time frameworks to pay the tax and, most importantly, freedom to sell to anyone at a fair price.

Controlling the prices on manufactured goods, the government extracted from peasants more than what the latter considered fair. As one peasant put it at the Dmitrovskii uezd meeting in Moscow province: "The Soviet power takes a ruble's worth but gives back a kopeck's worth."[16] At the Rossoshanskii uezd peasant meeting in Voronezh province, one peasant summarized his understanding of the prices: "In the old days, one could buy a shirt for a pud of rye, and now you've got to sell four or five pud; and in order to buy leather boots you've got to sell no less than 15–20 pud of grain. We would rather go barefoot but will not deliver grain for nothing." Another peasant added: "What kind of free trade is it when they control the prices?"[17] Peasants were also angered because, in addition to levying heavy taxes and controlling prices on manufactured goods, the local authorities tried to control the prices the peasants charged at the free market. The peasants in Dubrovino village near Novosibirsk rejected unanimously these (state) prices ... and announced: "we will not accept them until city products become cheaper. But at present please let us charge the prices we wish and do not dictate to us in this matter."[18]

A great number of peasant letters, petitions and resolutions concerned various forms of anti-peasant discrimination in Soviet Russia in virtually every sphere of life: taxation, education, insurance, medical care, job opportunities, and voting rights. The leitmotif in peasants' discourse is their legal inferiority. At a village meeting in Ryazan' uezd, one peasant said: "In the old times there were two classes in Russia, the bourgeoisie and the second class, workers and peasants. And now we also have two classes, the Communists and the peasants. Access to everything is open to the first, but nothing is open to us."[19] The Tver' party committee in its report for December 1924 admitted that peasants in the province were demanding equal voting rights in elections.[20] Countless other peasant resolutions at the village or district levels protested Communist attempts to dominate, supervise, or direct elected local bodies. A peasant resolution in Voronezh province opposed the party's "striving to unite the peasants in organizations where peasants would have no power at all since they would be compelled to work under the dictates of the party."[21] Peasants clearly resented their inferior position. In the frame of reference available to them, Communists in positions of authority could only be compared to the officials of the old regime. Kaganovich sent to Molotov a copy of a peasant letter from Kostroma province:

> Why is it that the party is preaching to the dark peasants about collective labor, about the future of communism and socialism, but the party itself, both the central and the local one, does not practice this and does not even strive to? Party officials live by themselves separately in private apartments ... They receive all kinds of salaries and they have servants ... They enjoy all the benefits of life just as the old civil servants.

The letter went on to say that the Communist Party had turned into a class of exploiters and ended with the words: "Comrade Communists, you have hurried to set yourselves up comfortably, loading all the burden of economic dislocation on peasant shoulders."[22]

The GPU made lists of questions peasants asked most often at district and uezd congresses of soviets. The clustering of questions on certain themes indicates which problems mattered more to peasants than others. The greatest number of questions asked at the district and uezd congresses of soviets of Orekhovo-Zuevo, for example, focused on peasant discrimination:

- Why is it that only the intelligentsia is getting through to the institutions of higher learning, and it is hard for peasants to be accepted?
- Why is it that only Jews are sent to the sanatoriums but for peasants it is virtually impossible?
- Why are workers and peasants represented disproportionately at the uezd congress of soviets?
- What exactly and how much did peasants receive in terms of social services [sotsial'naya zashchita] during the last seven years?
- Why are the majority of officials Communist Party members?
- How much is paid to the people's commissars?
- Why are Communists armed?

The second set of questions concerned peasants' perceptions of unfair taxation and prices:

- Workers owe an unpaid debt to peasants. And still why is it that under War Communism we paid 20 pud of grain and now under the tax system 200 pud?
- Why was the tax last year 550 rubles and this year 800?

In addition to taxes and civil rights the questions dealt with other aspects of social, political, and cultural life of the country.

- What is the strength of the Red Army?
- What is the amount of grain exported abroad?
- Where is Trotsky? Is he a member of the CP?
- Why is it not allowed to hang icons in schools?[23]

What is most remarkable about these questions is their simplicity and openness. City dwellers would know better than ask questions on Red Army strength, grain exports, and Trotsky's status. These questions could be construed as counterrevolutionary agitation in disguise. Peasants were not trained yet to observe the taboos of Soviet political discourse and they were not punished yet for their naivety and curiosity.

A sample of questions in other provinces shows similar concerns. In the Kolomenskii uezd, Moscow province, peasants asked:

- Where do the means to support the Communist International come from?
- Where did the valuables removed from the Church go?
- Why are peasants not covered by social insurance?
- Why is it that in other countries there are peasant unions and here we can't [unionize]?[24]

The Communist speakers simply did not know and could not discover the answers to these questions. In Novozybkovskii uezd, Gomel province, the peasants' questions at pre-election meetings were characterized as more hostile than average by the top secret Central Committee report.

- Why is there no freedom of speech?
- What did the revolution give to peasants?
- Is it possible to equalize human talents and bring everyone to the same level?
- Why is tax now three times as high as under the Tsar?
- What was the goal of NEP and what has been achieved?
- On whose orders are the priests persecuted?
- What is the opinion of the Communist Party about organizing a Peasant Union?

Some of these questions were simply hidden expressions of criticism. Others conveyed skepticism about Communist representations, such as:

- Why is a peasant who owns two cows considered a kulak?
- What kind of peasant exactly should be considered a kulak?
- How soon is your ruble going to be equal to the pre-war ruble?
- When we arrive in socialism, will there be one cow, two cows, several cows, or no cows at all?[25]

In addition to questions revealing peasant apprehensions there were resolutions and petitions of various district and uezd soviets which expressed outright hostility to Communist objectives. The above-mentioned

Kolomenskii uezd peasants resolved plainly: "We do not want any hegemony of the working class." In the Moscow province compilation, peasants were reported as asking: "What do we need the world revolution for? And why should we care about it?"[26] In some provinces such as Gomel, questions defined as explicitly political were particularly bitter:

- How long are you going to torture the peasantry?
- What happened to your promises?
- When are you going to stop inciting one part of the village against the other?
- How long are you going to hang around our necks as parasites?
- When will the Soviet power cease ruining peasant agriculture?
- When will we have a Peasant Union?

In terms of practical policies, peasant preferences boiled down to expanding the free market and eliminating Communist economic and political controls. For example, a village soviet chairman at a plenum of the district EC in Orenburg province reasoned that since, in the past, supplies in the countryside were cheaper and of better quality, it was necessary to transfer all industry into private hands.[27] The GPU reported with alarm that "agitation for unlimited access to grain procurement by the private sector" was gaining in intensity and that in many provinces peasants demanded "expansion of free trade."[28] Peasant resolutions in the North Caucasus proposed that a commodity exchange between town and country should be set up directly, bypassing state intermediaries.[29] In numerous other provinces peasants insisted that "agricultural cooperatives become independent of the state."[30] And finally, perhaps most disturbing from the Bolsheviks' point of view, demands of outright peasant ownership of land sounded more and more insistent.[31] The Tula gubkom chairman wrote that, among peasants of some districts, "there was a striving to receive land as private property with the right of buying and selling up to 15 desiatin."[32] The CC was quite aware of the peasants' relative dissatisfaction by early 1925, generally considered to be the height of NEP:

> Manifestations of discontent and even hostility on the part of peasants towards the workers and the party are emphasized more and more often and more emphatically in the materials arriving at the CC Information Department from the province committees and non-party organizations.[33]

Peasants saw through Communist propaganda. They measured official Communist claims against their real situation and based their concerns on sound common sense. They were not afraid to express these concerns publicly. Unfair taxes, exorbitant prices, privileges for the Communists, peasant discrimination, and constant interference in local affairs were the most frequent complaints.

STRATEGIES OF COPING

Representations

The Bolsheviks represented themselves as the urban allies of the toiling peasantry. They knew, of course, that in reality the alliance [*smychka*] was merely a propaganda device to produce a favorable impression among the peasants. Both the authorities and peasants knew their real roles. The state set the taxes and the prices. It tolerated private farming but clearly preferred collective farms. It relied on poor peasants and endowed them with tax privileges. Peasants had to operate within the confines of these realities and they developed a number of strategies of coping.

One such strategy involved their own representation of themselves to the authorities compatible with ideology. As a rule prosperous peasants resented artificial class division of the rich, middle, and poor peasants. At election meetings in Tula province, for example, villagers favored their own norms, insisting on classifying peasants as lazy or hardworking.[34] Everyone tried to avoid being cast as a kulak at all cost, as that entailed excessive taxation and deprivation of civil rights. Since the definition of who was a kulak varied a great deal, peasants could avoid acquiring those characteristics which would cast them as kulaks. If cultivated acreage was a factor, they would split up the land into acceptable parcels, making arrangements with other peasants to cultivate their land in exchange for labor, forgiven debts, fixed prices, or loans. For public record it looked like they were all hardworking middle-income peasants. If a kulak was defined as one who used heavy machinery and hired labor, one strove to avoid this public identity by a number of arrangements. For example, in Voronezh province, prosperous peasants were aware that the few tractors sent to the province were to be sold to the collectives rather than to individual farmers. Three prosperous peasants organized a partnership collective and applied to buy a tractor with seemingly impeccable credentials. They were a collective, they had 50 per cent membership of poor peasants and 30 per cent CP members.[35]

Middle-income peasants had a direct incentive to come across as poor peasants because then their tax burden would be lighter. Poor peasants had no incentive to become better off as that would lead to a reduction of tax privileges and political clout. There is extensive evidence that those parading about the public identity of "poor peasants" were in fact more prosperous than the less astute middle-income peasants. Poor peasants simply did not want to improve their performance, reasoning that: "It was much more convenient to be a poor peasant, much easier that way: you did not have to work too hard, you paid lower taxes, and the bosses looked favorably upon you."[36] Peasants' public identity should not be seen as necessarily reflecting real identities, but that which the peasants wanted to project.

The Peasant Union movement

The second strategy of coping was an attempt to deal with the authorities in an organized fashion. The idea of a Peasant Union was first put forward by the SR Central Committee in May 1920 as an organization which could resist the Communist onslaught in the countryside. In 1920–1, Peasant Unions sprang up in the black earth provinces, on the Volga, and in Siberia. During the height of the peasant war in Tambov and Voronezh, Peasant Unions played a prominent role. Truly autonomous of any political party, they were the de facto supply mechanism for the rebel army. They also played a crucial role in the peasant insurgency in Siberia.[37] Liquidated in 1921, Peasant Unions seemed to disappear, but the memory that they had been extremely effective in defending peasant interests remained.

In 1923 calls for creating a Peasant Union were increasingly appearing in various provinces. In 1924, "the idea of a Peasant Union spread throughout a majority of regions of the USSR." By 1925, campaigning for Peasant Unions was reported from twenty-five provinces.[38] In the village of Deniskovichi, Gomel province, at the district EC session, a revealing episode took place. One peasant put it this way: We've got to act as the *Internationale* song says:

> No one will give us liberation
> Neither God, nor the Tsar or hero!
> We will achieve liberation
> With our own efforts!

The party secretary asked the peasant how one should understand this citation. Someone from the audience shouted: "We've got to create our own Peasant Union, that's how!"[39] The peasants reasoned like this: If it was true that there was an alliance of the working class and the toiling peasantry for the cause of socialist construction, then there could not be anything wrong with the toiling peasants forming their own unions, parallel to the workers' unions. These unions would give credence to the claim that peasants were partners of the working class in Soviet Russia. The unions would defend peasant economic interests since Russia under NEP was still a class-based society where every class had its own economic interests. This reasoning amounted to peasants' skillful use of Bolshevik official representations to their advantage.

Campaigning for Peasant Unions was most intense during tax collection, and local elections to the soviets. "Why do the Soviet authorities not allow us to organize Peasant Unions?" This question, stated a GPU report, "is being asked more and more insistently at numerous regional conferences." In Roslavl' uezd, Smolensk province, it was raised by middle-income peasants during the election campaign, and by poor peasants at the district congress of soviets. Virtually identical demands were reported from Saratov,

Samara, and Altai provinces. The report stated unequivocally that the Peasant Union movement embraced all income groups of peasants and all areas of the country: "Therefore, against the background of the general rise of anti-Soviet attitudes among all strata of peasants, the question of the Peasant Union stands out prominently."[40]

In 1924–5, Peasant Unions' objectives were to defend economic interests. In most provinces this involved lightening the tax burden and ensuring fair prices. The Don Cossacks wanted their union to restore their right to sell grain abroad. In the North Caucasus peasants defined the tasks of their proposed union as "defending peasants from the unlawful actions of authorities and creating direct commodity exchange, bypassing state intermediaries."[41] In Smolensk province, one peasant proposed at a meeting "to create a union of grain growers and not to surrender grain at 40 kopecks, but to say instead, one ruble and that's it."[42] Peasant voices in favor of a union sometimes had clear political overtones. At a soviet election meeting in Orel province one peasant proposed to convene a congress of non-party peasants: "If not today then tomorrow we will create our union." And at a local election meeting in Gomel province, a candidate argued that: "The RCP had become weaker and peasants should organize their own political party." This proposal was greeted with applause. On the basis of an enormous number of similar speeches and resolutions, the GPU concluded that "presently the Peasant Union was thought of not only as an organization pursuing exclusively economic objectives, but political ones."

The line dividing economic and political demands was very thin, especially for the Bolsheviks. It was certainly a matter of political action if Peasant Unions were to organize what amounted to a strike, as a resolution in the Moscow province suggested: "The Peasant Union will play its role. We will not give grain to the proletariat for three weeks. Then they will come and bow low to us." No less disturbing was the proposal of a peasant meeting in Irkutsk province: "We must unite on the all-Russian scale and then diminish the sown acreage immediately. Then the Soviet power will feel the punch."[43]

During the opening months of 1925, campaigning for Peasant Unions gave way to setting them up. The Samara province GPU informed the CC that: "Peasant Unions appeared . . . and embarked upon pursuing political objectives . . . The provincial GPU ordered immediate dissolution of those unions."[44] As the year progressed, attempts to set up Peasant Unions multiplied to such an extent that this was no longer a series of attempts, but a Peasant Union movement across Russia. In August the GPU admitted that: "The trend to organize Peasant Unions was gaining momentum literally everywhere, intensifying with each passing week."[45] A special top-secret GPU report covering just two weeks in May 1925 described in great detail attempts to set up Peasant Unions in Samara, Saratov, the Urals provinces, and in the Moscow province.[46] Other reports added Vologda, Tula, Voronezh, Ukraine, and Omsk. A top secret CC memorandum sent only to Politburo members stated: "In a number of provinces, the present disposition of the peasantry takes the form of demanding organization of Peasant Unions to defend peasants' economic interests."[47] The GPU systematically arrested agitators for the Peasant Union, confiscated leaflets and broke up organizations that claimed to be Peasant Unions. As a result, peasant spokesmen began to argue that the peasants' position in Soviet Russia was meant to be inferior. The claim that there was an alliance [smychka] with the peasantry was said to be a lie.

Virtually any assembly of peasant representatives, from regional congresses of cooperatives, to mutual aid societies, from district to uezd congresses of soviets, turned to the question of setting up the infrastructure of Peasant Unions. In Tsaritsyn, a provincial non-party rural conference raised this issue, while in Ryazan' the uezd soviet did, and in Penza province, Saranskii uezd EC declared that the majority of the population favored creating a Peasant Union.[48] The tone of most peasant resolutions suggests that organizers did not see anything illegal about their actions. They usually argued that workers had trade unions, so why should peasants not have their own as well? A secretary of a district EC in Omsk argued that in other countries where the bourgeoisie was in power, like in Germany, there were peasant parties and peasants were represented in government, but in Soviet Russia, where peasants were supposedly allied with the working class, they were not allowed to have their own unions.

In some areas, kulaks and village teachers were identified as leaders of the Peasant Union movement. Many rural Communists and Komsomol members shared the pro-union views. They did not resist and some even joined in the attempts to set up the unions. At the Tula province Komsomol conference, one speaker addressing professional propagandists said:

> You come to our villages and try to comfort our dark masses just as the priests used to. But what have you delivered to peasants with your revolution? You have enslaved the peasants . . . they will soon rise in another revolution.[49]

A CC memorandum stated that in Siberia there were cases of Communists publicly raising the question of organizing a peasant party.[50] This was labelled a pro-peasant deviation. When rural Communists sided with the peasants they must have had divided loyalties. On the one hand, they were agents of the center; on the other, they had countless ties to the village community through family, friends, relatives, and economic interest. According to the GPU, "The officials of the local Soviet apparatus actively participated in hiding taxable property."[51] With meager salaries they had to fend for themselves and they did. They were not averse to cheating their superiors, accepting bribes from peasants, paying bribes to uezd authorities, and entering into all kinds of economic arrangement with the kulaks. In other words, peasants resorted to many traditional strategies of coping, such as adopting politically correct identities, bribing local officials, and organizing their own representation. The GPU registered 150 attempts to create unions across the country in 1926 and 229 in 1927.[52] The GPU report hastened to add that Peasant Unions were liquidated as soon as they were created.

ELECTIONS, 1925

The year 1925 was not supposed to be one of rising tension in the countryside. The official Bolshevik policy – "Face the Village" – was a policy of compromise, a partial decrease in levels of taxation, partial reversal of disenfranchising quotas, and other measures perceived as concessions. At the same time the "Face the Village" campaign was designed to energize the party through positive involvement. Communist Party cells were to transform the rural political community by becoming involved in elections, taxation, land use, and other matters of local government.

Peasants perceived the new policy as a window of opportunity. If it was possible to compete and maybe even oust the Bolsheviks from the soviets, why not try? Clearly peasants had no chance of influencing Bolshevik policies even if they won overwhelming majorities (policies were made not by the rural soviets but by the party committees) yet at the uezd, district, and especially village level, the soviets were linked to the tax collection apparatus and it was vitally important for the peasants to influence the process of who was taxed and by what criteria. The CC described the political situation in Ukraine in 1925:

> This year a serious electoral struggle manifested itself for the first time since the establishment of Soviet power in Ukraine. Striving for political power is noticeable on the part of both the kulaks and the middle peasants.[53]

The Communists took elections seriously, of course. A propaganda campaign was launched under the "Face the Village" slogan. Party propagandists tried to expose "malicious scheming" of the kulaks, to split the peasant community by income, and to find reliable partners among poorer peasants. This policy had worked in 1918, but in the conditions of NEP poor peasants and especially middle peasants had identical economic interests with the prosperous ones – to sell their produce at a higher price and buy manufactured goods at a lower price. According to the Voronezh gubkom:

> The kulaks were the most active elements politically in the countryside. Our slogan "Face the Village" they understood as our retreat, as our weakness. He [the kulak] reads the newspapers, knows Soviet laws, and decrees ... he is trying to make politics in the countryside, maneuvering between the middle and poor peasants.[54]

The Bolsheviks were handicapped in rural election campaigns because the peasant leaders were more politically sophisticated than during the civil war. Local rural party activists were no match for peasant leaders in terms of education and leadership. The Tula gubkom wrote:

> More and more noticeable is the stratum of peasants who know their way [*razbirayutsya*] in politics better than the members of the party cell. In the countryside these people are known as law defenders [*zakonniki*] . . . Non-party peasants are clearly ahead of the party cells in their political development.[55]

The Tula gubkom could not possibly know that at about the same time the Vyatka gubkom dispatched an almost identical assessment:

> An active non-party peasant is head and shoulders above your average party member and sometimes he is more literate than the majority of party members working in a district. Peasants read newspapers, follow political life, which we cannot say about our Communists. Often peasants pose questions to our Communist speakers which they cannot answer.[56]

One reason for this was that only the poorest of the poor were attracted to joining the Communist Party. Yet their background did not prepare them for competing in elections with the prosperous and literate section of the rural community.

Everywhere, the most striking feature was the extraordinarily low level of education. The Voronezh gubkom survey showed that 72.2 per cent of Communists in five uezds were either totally illiterate or semi-literate. In the village cells, the illiteracy rate reached 80 per cent. "Those Communists who could read did not read books because they did not understand them. Some read newspapers reluctantly."[57] In the neighboring Orel, the numbers and ratios were quite similar: 1,595 party members, of whom 1,069 were illiterate.[58] In another black earth province, Kursk, there were only 3,320 party members, most of them "politically illiterate."[59] In Vladimir province in central Russia, there were only 2,569 party members, likewise mostly politically illiterate. The rural party showed signs of malaise: NEPization, that is involvement in private enterprise, acquisitiveness [*khozobrastanie*], excesses in consumption [*izlishestvo*], drunkenness, and other vices.[60] The rural party comes across in these reports as very small and poorly educated. Most reports showed that they had ceased practicing agriculture and consequently lost touch with peasants. As a result peasants could not regard party members as capable of understanding their concerns. The Samara gubkom described its party cells as:

> far removed from the peasants. They pulled away from agriculture. And there was nothing strange in the fact that the peasants sometimes did not know about the existence of the party cells.[61]

Rural party cells were indeed isolated. They did not want to become involved in political campaigning, and opposed the emphasis placed on soviet elections and other populist themes. In Samara province, rural Communists "had become used to relating to peasants as strict bosses. It reached a point of serious abuses of authority; then they tried to escape accountability and peasants were convinced that Communists generally could not be held responsible for their actions." Their role was to give orders and instructions and that of peasants' to obey. They publicly opposed elections, arguing that the "Face the Village" campaign was in fact going to lead to capitulation to the kulaks. Usually, radical posturing is interpreted as an indication of ideologically inspired revolutionary zeal. The Samara gubkom report, however, explained it by more prosaic causes. Many Communists were "simply afraid" to be left without a job.[62]

Some rural Communists perceived the new policy in the countryside as a crusade against them by the party's central institutions. Some understood it as punishment for their heavy-handed methods of the past, as is clear from their speeches in self-defense: "We are not to blame that we were issuing orders. We were forced to from above. And now our superiors want to score points [otygratsya] at the expense of the rural Communists."[63] Provincial party leaders warned the center that the Communists' reputation was so low that they were unlikely to win elections. Again from the Samara gubkom report:

The drawbacks of the Communist Party cells, from drunkenness and intrigues, to abuse of power and acquisitiveness, are so glaring that it is understandable that the peasants tried to get rid of such Communists at elections, as soon as they had the opportunity.[64]

At most district conferences, peasants elected non-Communist presidiums, passed resolutions in favor of creating Peasant Unions, and refused to sell grain at "unfair" prices.[65] Prosperous and middle-income peasants were the most active politically, many speakers demanding guarantees that they were not going to be arrested for their speeches. As always, taxes were at the top of the agenda.

You keep on talking about raising the level of agriculture. But at the same time you have raised taxes several times higher than under the Tsar and then you say it is a unified single tax. Wait a second here. And who fixes the prices on manufactured goods? You fix them. And we are paying much more for them than in the past, right, so that is a tax too, is it not?

You should know that we have one pair of boots per family. You keep on saying we should bring our wives to meetings. But it is hard to walk in straw shoes in mud. So I came but my wife is sitting at home barefoot. If you keep on this tax, there won't be any boots at all.

Another speaker proposed that agricultural tax be calculated against a consumption minimum so that peasant incomes were comparable to the wages of workers. Demands for lower taxes, fair prices, and Peasant Unions were so overwhelming, the reporter noted, that they had to be included in the official resolutions of many district conferences.[66]

Another subgroup of peasant speeches can be seen as responding to Communist ideology, specifically that kulaks were exploiters, that the soviets were organs of popular will, and the Communists were the vanguard of the proletariat and the toiling peasantry.

> Human talents cannot be brought to a common denominator. And a person who is more developed and has more talents would strive for a better life and therefore you will not be able to abolish exploitation of man by man.

> In the cities the Communists have everything, kindergartens and orphanages and servants, and for their children they stage Christmas parties, and here the orphans of the Red Army soldiers are lucky if they get a piece of bread for Christmas.

> If we calculate who is going to give us credit on better terms, the kulak or the bank, it is clear, the kulak is not going to lead away your last cow. No, comrades, deal with your banks yourselves.

> Why are you shouting about elections to the soviet? The authorities bypass the soviets and this is not likely to change.

> You keep saying that the elected institutions should govern, but in reality the bureaucrats do. For example, a land surveyor comes and says: "You'd better do this and that or else I'll submit a report and they'll arrest you." This kills any desire to deal with the soviet, in any case it is a pawn of the bureaucrats.

> You keep on saying that you want peasants elected in the soviets. In district soviets they perhaps can accomplish something, but at the uezd level and higher you will carry on with your policy as you have done up to now. What we must have is a true proportional representation between workers and peasants all the way.

Peasants seem to have been guided by their common sense. Some speeches were a response to unfulfilled promises, perceived injustices and extravagant propaganda claims:

> We are fed up with your tales. The only thing you've learned to do in seven years is blab. You are not improving agriculture but ruining it. You, Red executioners, you'd better know that the steam engine of peasant patience is going to explode some day. You'd better know that the peasants curse you usurpers in their morning prayer. You are stealing the last cow, the last belongings. What do you pay to a peasant invalid who had lost a leg

defending your revolution? You can't pay a ruble to him, but to a Tsarist general you pay 300. Where is truth? Where is justice? Why did you fool us with words such as freedom, land, peace, equality! Now we understand that the government of Kerensky was better to us.

The disappointment over unfulfilled promises was exacerbated in peasants' minds by the reality that the Communists themselves enjoyed comfortable lives:

> You promised to give equality, freedom and land, but what you have given us instead is a yoke around the neck . . . You promised to provide universal education but in fact the schools are falling apart. You promised to provide pensions at age sixty and instead are stealing from the young and from the old . . . You are sucking our blood . . . We are suffering without grain, and you are getting fatter, enjoying smoking cigarettes, living off the province's salary. You are the new nobility!

At one of the meetings an old man came up to the podium and, addressing the Communists, asked: "How long are you going to rob us?" Officials did not bother to respond, but voices from the floor could be heard: "Hold on, man. Soon there'll come a better day."[67]

Some peasant speakers went further than expressing doubt in the Communist claims. They wanted to organize politically in defense of their rights:

> We need a Peasant Union. You [authorities] had decided in the fall to take grain at 60 kopecks, you started to pressure us with taxes. But if we had had a Peasant Union, we would have refused in an organized fashion to surrender grain at 60 kopecks, and we would have forced you to reverse your decision. Next point: Your prices on manufactured goods are unacceptable to us. But without the Peasant Union we can't do anything about it. But if we had had a Peasant Union, we would have resolved to stop buying all manufactured goods. We would have held out for a year without your manufactured goods but you would not have had bread and would have agreed to sell at the right price as in the old times.[68]

The sample of peasant speeches shows that they reiterated the same themes: unfair taxes, privileges for the Communists, and unfulfilled promises. They show that peasants had opinions on all kinds of issues from banking to social welfare and the role of the soviets. They understood what the official representations were, did not trust them and ridiculed Communist practices and objectives.

Usually the district or uezd ECs proposed a Communist list of candidates at election meetings. The task of its opponents was to block it either by invalidating the elections or attempting to nominate their own candidates. At the election of the Staroatlashenskii district EC in Saratov province in August 1925, for example, Communist opponents launched a successful campaign under the slogan: "Soviets without the Communists." The social profile of those elected was: 60 per cent kulak, 30 per cent middle-income peasants, and 2 per cent poor peasants.[69] In Tula province, wrote the gubkom chairman, the electoral lists drafted by the party were rejected as a rule. It was a crushing defeat for the Communists. The Komsomol members fared even worse: "Almost everywhere they were defeated."[70] In Samara province, peasants did not allow Communists to draft election lists, saying: "Your time has passed."[71] In Moscow province, the popular slogan during village soviet elections was again: "Soviets without the Communists."[72] In Voronezh province, a total of 16,700 persons were elected to the village soviets, only 9.2 per cent Communists.[73] This proportion seems to have been average. In Vladimir province, 9,984 were elected, only 307 being Communists.[74] In Tambov province, poor and middle-income peasants sided with the prosperous ones in elections against the Communists. In a report to the CC for the first quarter of 1925, Provincial Party Secretary Birn wrote:

> The disposition of the poor and low-income middle peasants shows signs of . . . discontent in regard to the authorities and the party. On the one hand, it is a consequence of drunkenness, rudeness, hooliganism, and abuse of power by local officials, and on the other, it is caused by the extraction of agricultural tax.[75]

Birn cited peasants as saying at election meetings: "We should not elect Communists to the soviets. They were sitting in the soviets doing nothing. You've got to elect the kind of people who would give us bread, would let us go to the church, and hang icons in the soviets." In the provinces of Tambov and Voronezh, the considerable majority of those elected were "formerly active participants in the bandit movement," stated the GPU.

In Gomel, just as everywhere else, the prestige of party cells was low. Party policies were unpopular because the authorities had set the procurement price for grain at 65 kopecks a pud. Most peasants refused to sell at that price and as a result were unable to pay their taxes. The Bolsheviks applied "decisive measures," as the "apparatus of the GPU was deployed in the uezds to remove those conducting malicious anti-tax agitation."[76] The outcome of local elections was unfavorable for the party. Kulaks and "anti-Soviet elements" were said to have gained tremendous influence.

Don and Kuban' Cossack lands were areas of large-scale grain production. During the civil war they were centers of resistance to Bolshevik rule. Rich Cossacks were dispossessed and exiled at the end of the civil war and peasants received equal rights with the Cossacks. A CC memorandum to Stalin pointed out that the Cossacks perceived the Communist slogan "Face the Village" as a weakness. They were saying at election meetings:

> The Communists' power is at an end. Now the time has come to defend our rights. The Communists feel shaky and that is why they have started

negotiations with the countryside. And they are even sending important people to the villages . . . But they will not be able to impose their lists upon us. We know whom to elect. And we will elect ourselves.[77]

The "Face the Village" campaign caused a panic among the rank and file. They feared for their jobs and privileges. As in other regions of the country, there were very few Communists on the Don: 4,987 on January 1, 1925. They had no idea how to campaign in elections. Party membership was "for many nothing but a company of buddies and a source for procuring income without any control." The party report characterized political attitudes on the eve of elections as "negative among peasants and inimical among the Cossacks." The "Face the Village" campaign increased interest in elections and well-organized peasant and Cossack groups led a boisterous election campaign. They sent observers to neighboring settlements and publicized election procedures and violations. In some Cossack settlements, election meetings demanded the restoration of voting rights to all, without any exception, including the priests. "Kulak activists," as they were called, drafted lists of candidates. The party report attributed to them a determination to have as many "opponents of Soviet power" elected to the soviets as possible:

> The poor peasants were under their influence. In a private conversation, one poor peasant pointed out: "You Communists have not done anything good for us, only words, whereas Ivan Ivanovich helps me . . ."
>
> The election meetings nominated candidates on the spot and candidate lists drafted by the CP were systematically rejected by the electorate if one or two Communists' names were on the list.

Fortunately, there is a fairly detailed data on the outcome of rural elections in the Don region. Out of 675,782 residents, 321,364 or 47.8 per cent were eligible voters. The share of Cossack population in relation to peasants fluctuated from 45 per cent to 55 per cent depending on the district. Of the electorate, 1.7 per cent were deprived of voting rights in 1925 (fewer than in 1924 by 1.5 per cent). In accordance with the electoral law, living on unearned income, hiring labor, working as a religious functionary, or opposing Soviet power merited disenfranchisement. In a conciliatory spirit some categories of deprivees were reenfranchised.

Of all the eligible voters, only 130,579 cast their ballots (41.2 per cent). Only 35 per cent of eligible Cossacks took part in voting, while 64.5 per cent of the peasants did. Voter turnout was higher in comparison with 1924 by 10 per cent. A total of 5,419 persons were elected to the rural soviets which was almost double the number of those elected in 1924. Of those elected: 41.6 per cent were Cossacks, 58 per cent peasants, and 8.9 per cent women. Only 7.8 per cent of the newly elected soviet delegates were Communist Party members. This represented a decrease of 36 per cent from 1924.[78]

In some districts the Communist Party was simply wiped out. In Mechetin-skii district, 111 candidates competed for the 22 seats. The party list was rejected and voting for individual candidates went on for hours. Not a single Communist was elected. Generally, in Cossack majority districts all official candidates were defeated. Those elected were either individual farmers or, as the party report put it, "one or two Communists elected as a cover, to avoid attracting attention [*kak shirma, dlya otvoda glaz*]." Most of the newly elected soviet members were described as middle-income Cossacks and peasants. Some had counterrevolutionary credentials from the Bolshevik point of view. In Sinyavka a former aide to the Ataman was elected, as was a deputy chairman of the church council. In Krivlyana two women were elected, but one was a daughter of a priest, and the other the wife of a former Cossack colonel. Election returns were a political disaster for the Communists on the Don. The Don party committee explained defeat to Moscow as having much to do with the activity of kulaks. Yet their own data on voting results showed that Communists failed to win popular support in a fair contest.

The Kuban' party leaders did not and could not have known the content of the top-secret report on elections by the party committee in the neighboring Don. Yet the overall picture in Kuban' was very similar. The prosperous peasants and Cossacks were well versed in Soviet law and in their campaigning successfully used this knowledge by pointing to all kinds of violation of the law by the local authorities. "In terms of the level of their culture," stressed the report, "this stratum surpassed the party and Komsomol by far."[79]

What distinguished Kuban' was that local leaders were members of the rural intelligentsia: teachers, agronomists, former elected officials, and civil servants. In their election campaigns they spoke about proportional representation, rule of law, freedom, and democracy; speeches were inevitably followed by thunderous applause. They criticized the Communists and offered plans to create a Union of Grain Growers. Almost everywhere the lists of candidates put forward by the Communist Party were rejected and time-consuming name by name voting took place.

Kuban' is the only province that provided data on the social composition of the CP members not by class (which is meaningless) but by estate [*soslovie*]: of the 4,074 members, 6.2 per cent were Cossacks; 10.8 per cent townspeople [*meshchane*]; 78 per cent outsiders [*inogorodnie*], the majority of whom were recent arrivals to Kuban'. There were no workers in the Kuban' party at all: "The majority in the village party cells were people from administrative personnel, civil servants, unconnected to agriculture, in rare cases, craftsmen, but almost never grain growers."

The social and cultural profile of Communists was similar to the Don and the black earth areas: most did not practice agriculture; 80 per cent, and in some locations 90 per cent, of party members were described as "politically illiterate," only 3 per cent having an educational level sufficient to give a lecture on political affairs; most were detached from the rural community and had no interest in farming; they had no links to the local population, and stuck to themselves in an almost conspiratorial fashion; most of them desperately tried to incite hostility between the poor peasants and the kulaks but without much success.[80] The Kuban' party committee saw one of the reasons for the Communists' defeat in the fact that, "The initiative to criticize the old system of elections based on fraud and manipulation belonged to the political right [i.e. Cossack leaders], whereas the CP cells persistently defended the old methods. This was one of the reasons why the majority of the middle peasants supported the right."[81]

Local Communists had a habit of issuing orders, relying on "coercion," as the report put it, "they feared for their material well-being, they feared losing their jobs." Just as on the Don, the local Communists regarded the "Face the Village" campaign with apprehension. It was contrary to their habits and attitudes. In private conversations comments could be heard that "mass participation in elections is nothing but perversion [razvrat]." One of the local cells denounced the official report on party policy in the countryside as counterrevolutionary. The very admission of elections was "a political NEP," a capitulation to the class enemy.

The population, as the report put it, "vigilantly" controlled the work of the counting commissions. The counters were watched and tallies verified, not allowing anyone to approach the ballot tables. The election returns were disappointing for the Communists. In the old soviets the CP held 21.3 per cent of seats, but in the new ones its share sank to 12.2 per cent. The Cossacks' share increased from 32.3 per cent to 52.2 per cent, and the peasants' share fell from 60 per cent to 42.7 per cent. The election returns were similar in Ukraine.[82] In Siberia, kulaks were reported to have won control over village soviets.[83]

From the Communists' point of view, the election returns were a disaster. The Communist Party cells found themselves completely isolated. They wanted to have nothing to do with "counterrevolutionary soviets." "Rich" Cossacks had become members of soviets, speaking in the name of Soviet power. They refused to accept directives from the party cells, which were increasingly perceived as good-for-nothing groups of poor peasants tied to Bolshevik paymasters. The newly elected soviets started behaving in ways the Bolsheviks perceived as counterrevolutionary. Their first priority was to establish control over the land-use departments. Taxes, class identities, and civil rights depended on the rulings of these departments. New soviets also started repair work on desecrated churches to the jubilation of the rural community. Some soviet members served in the church councils. They also began assistance programs for dispossessed priests. Some soviets began discussing restoring confiscated houses to their former owners. They set up mutual-aid funds, providing cheap loans to poor peasants at rates more favorable than those of the state. Worse was that the new soviets "dared to reject the decisions and rulings of higher-standing presidiums," because, they argued, the latter were legally subordinate to the elected assemblies. The CC memorandum to Stalin concluded that: "The political disposition of the Cossacks remained inimical to Soviet power and the activity of the newly elected soviets, composed primarily of prosperous Cossacks, was contrary to the directives of Soviet power from the very first days."[84] The non-Communist soviets were popular, strengthening their hold on the countryside, and reducing party cells to insignificance.

Clearly a picture of a content peasantry under NEP is misleading. Peasants knew what their economic interests were. They were suspicious of state authorities and did not want city agitators to tell them whom to elect to their soviets. What is most striking is their relative political sophistication. They were no longer confused by the difference between the soviets and the Bolsheviks or the Bolsheviks and the Communists, as they were during the civil war. They had very clear notions on who the Communists were and what they wanted. They were remarkably unaffected by Communist propaganda. They knew the system, saw through Bolshevik rhetoric, and utilized a number of strategies to achieve their objectives. Their elected leaders formulated a coherent set of political proposals all by themselves, without political parties, an independent press, or radio. In conditions of peaceful competition the "Face the Village" campaign turned out to be a "Face a Defeat" result for the Communists. Peasants wanted free elections, their own union, free trade, and private ownership of land. And they were prepared to take them.

Chapter 4

Propaganda and popular belief

AGITPROP: ERADICATING ALIEN INFLUENCE

Two features distinguished Communist propaganda during NEP. The first was the persistence of elements of civil society. Even though there were no longer opposition party newspapers, multiparty elections, or free unions, private printing houses, clubs, and theater groups remained. Independent cultural and literary journals espoused views and values that were distinctly non-Bolshevik. Private enterprise had been legalized for the time being as capitalism and bourgeois culture had deep roots. The Bolsheviks found themselves on the defensive on the ideological front. Therefore, the task was to redouble efforts in preaching Communist ideals among the masses.

The second feature was that the Bolsheviks had more resources available now to be thrown at the ideological front of mass education. They began to build a huge bureaucratic machine to treat agitation and propaganda as state business. It was no longer a matter of tokenism – an occasional propaganda train passing through the countryside or a spectacular show for foreign Communists – as during the civil war. Now it was an everyday business of ever-multiplying agencies which launched propaganda campaigns in rapid succession. The key institution here was the Agitation and Propaganda Department of the Central Committee. During the NEP years, it grew into an elaborate bureaucratic structure of more than thirty subdepartments on the press, publishing houses, science, schools, cadres training, cinema, the arts, theater, radio, and literature, to name only a few.[1] As early as the mid-1920s, all these departments systematically monitored activities in their field. They wrote regular surveys, recommendations, and guidelines. They received instructions from the Central Committee, and their top officials were given access to OGPU (NKVD) reports on popular attitudes. The paper trail stretched from the CC Information Department to Agitprop and then to studios, theaters, and editorial offices, which enforced "politically correct" presentation of ideas and information. The main task was to monitor the views disseminated by non-Bolshevik sources on the one hand, and to build up the infrastructure of dissemination of Communist views on the other. Launched in 1922, various commissions drafted guidelines on supervision of theater, the censorship of film, the work of clubs and associations, and control over anti-religious propaganda.

The Commission for Newspaper Supervision drafted guidelines on what was admissible for publication.[2] Coverage of capitalist countries was to focus on capitalist exploitation. Strikes, protests, and disturbances were to be featured prominently. Domestic coverage had to focus on achievements in socialist construction. These basic principles would stay constant until the end of Communist rule. A rivalry developed over the prerogatives of censorship between the GPU and the Commissariat of Education. Its Main Committee on the Press was in charge of preventing "agitation against Soviet Power" in the press. On March 22, 1922 the Central Committee considered:

> it necessary to unite all kinds of censorship in one center under the People's Commissariat of Education, though the supervision and monitoring of the activities of the printing presses shall remain in the competence of the GPU.[3]

In this connection, Rykov wrote to Stalin in April 1922: "The discussion of this question revealed the fact that at the present time the censorship apparatus numbers 2,500 persons." That, Rykov believed, was a waste of resources. Why should a censor be sitting in every printing shop? It was much more efficient to make directors of the printing presses responsible for what they published.[4]

The chief of the Agitprop himself, A.S. Bubnov, chaired the Commission to Monitor the Private Book Market. He set up a system whereby every article and every book published by non-Bolshevik printing houses and associations was carefully read, numbered, and registered, and its content summarized. In November 1922, the commission reported that the Russian Technical Society's journal *Ekonomist* expressed "critical views of the New Economic Policy and the Soviet government." The House of Literati, in its journal *Letopis'*, persistently defended the independence of the press, which amounted to subversive agitation. Another journal, *Utrennik*, "showed a clear tendency to discredit Soviet Power." The Commission listed eighty-five private publishing houses or associations in Petrograd alone as "Menshevik" or "Kadet" in their political orientation.[5]

The Bolsheviks made every effort to keep abreast of what was on the intellectuals' minds. Guidelines were drafted for cleansing the library collections of books that could undermine Soviet power. The first priority was to remove all newspapers and pamphlets published during the revolutionary years by the socialist opposition parties (the Mensheviks, SRs and Left SRs) as well as whatever publications libraries may have received from the Kadets, Monarchists, or other parties. After that the pool of undesirable literature was broadened to include most of the pre-revolutionary political and cultural journals, publications by religious philosophers, and the work of numerous non-Marxist scholars. Possession of these materials was limited to a few scholarly libraries and required advance clearance. This was a serious attempt to sever the link to the past, to the outside world, and to "bourgeois" cultural heritage.

By 1923 Agitprop extended its coverage to film, theater and music.[6] The Main Repertoire Committee [*Glavrepertkom*] defined its task:

From the very first days . . . our entire attention has been focused on making our cinematography healthier. As a matter of first priority, our task was to remove all that garbage which had flooded our cinemas until the formation of the Main Repertoire Committee.[7]

The problem with the existing system of acquisitions and release was that both the state and private cinemas were guided by revenue. They showed films which did not appear explicitly political in content, dealing with everyday situations, adventure, love, and feelings, explained the MRC. At first glance, there was nothing subversive in those films. Since the audience loved them and money could be made, why not show them? was the reasoning of the release authorities. According to the MRC, "The cinema establishment's release policy was essentially pre-revolutionary. The release process was not Soviet. It was in fact counterrevolutionary."[8] Those films' subversion was worse than explicitly anti-Soviet appeals because they conveyed bourgeois values to the masses and distracted them from acquiring proletarian consciousness:

The films imported from abroad are, almost all of them, contaminated with petty bourgeois ideology, some of them have a touch of mysticism, others defend the old "unshakable" foundations of life: marriage, family, etc. Many are chauvinist pictures, as, for example, *America* or *Madness and Horror*. All this is pseudo-culture [*salonovshchina*], tragedies about nothing, vapidness, [*pustiak*], and sufferings and joys of noble Grand Dukes, Princes, bankers, and landlords. And all this is shown in luxurious surroundings, with balls, parties, receptions, decadence [*kutezh*], and happy, care-free life. And almost everywhere you hear fox-trot.[9]

If left to their own inclinations, the masses would continue to favor romantic adventures, entertainment and fox-trot on screen. The MRC resolved that every film slated for release had to have a permit. Those films that failed the test were to be marked "not for worker/peasant audiences." During the first six months of 1923, the MRC surveyed 941 imported films and banned 118 of them.[10]

By 1924 the MRC had spread its surveillance over theater and music as well. Out of 269 theater plays, 23 were banned. In a classified memorandum, the MRC sent out lists of plays allowed and/or banned to the provincial literature sections [Gublit]. Lists of plays were followed by lists of gramophone records which were allowed for circulation. The MRC listened to the tunes and song lyrics of 1,510 records and banned 106 of them.[11] The deputy chair of GlavLit (the Main Literature Department) explained:

> Enclosing with this memorandum the catalogue of the gramophone records, the Main Repertoire Committee informs you that all gramophone records listed in this catalogue, excluding those crossed out by the MRC, have been checked by the MRC and are therefore cleared for listening without any audience restrictions.[12]

The former leader of the Proletarian Culture movement, Lebedev-Poliansky, now a censor, explained that all known records containing monarchist tunes or amoral material were to be confiscated immediately. The MRC admitted that an outright ban on all imported bourgeois films and songs was impossible because there was nothing as yet to replace them. For the time being, only the most objectionable material was to be removed, but the long-term plan was to create films about Soviet explorers, Soviet heroes, and Soviet life. Idealized representations of a visionary world as if it were reality was the long-term goal of the Agitprop many years before Comrade Stalin codified this approach as socialist realism.

POTEMKIN VILLAGES ON THE IDEOLOGICAL FRONT

Provincial Communist bosses were aware of the ideal that one had to strive for and represented the social and political situations in their provinces to the Central Committee as closely to the required ideal as possible, knowing that their success or failure was dependent on it. Material addressed to Moscow claimed that the disposition of the population towards Soviet power was favorable. It was the norm to report that peasants' attitudes were stable and workers' enthusiastic. The CC consistently encouraged the Agitprops to do more and to try harder: "deepen the contents, widen the audience, and strengthen the efforts." That is why provincial Agitprops always reported how many events were staged and how many people they were able to involve. The gubkoms projected an image of themselves as tireless campaigners involving the masses in socialist construction. The party was getting stronger and better all the time, or so they said. Its membership grew steadily and surely. The campaign to attract workers from the factory floor to the party was a tremendous success. It demonstrated the wisdom of the Central Committee and made the party younger and closer to the masses. It brought new, talented proletarian cadres into the party ranks.

The gubkoms claimed to have made enormous strides involving women workers in social and political life. Thousands of women workers took part in delegate meetings. Thousands were elected to village soviets. Thousands more were helped to overcome illiteracy and religious superstition. Work among youth was usually represented as one of the most successful enterprises. Youth was simply flocking to the Communist cause in tens of thousands. It was filled with enthusiasm, optimism, and belief in communism. The Komsomol ranks were growing in spectacular fashion. A reliable junior partner of the party, the Komsomol was the vehicle of many successful propaganda campaigns against religious superstition, gender-based inequality, illiteracy, and backwardness, all advocating the new socialist lifestyle and morality.

In addition to the tremendous growth in the ranks of the party, Komsomol, and women's organizations, spectacular progress was reported in communicating the Communist message to the rest of the population. Hundreds of thousands of people had joined trade unions, and voluntary associations, such as the League of the Godless, the Liquidation of Illiteracy, Help to Children, and so on. Illiteracy was being overcome. Subscription to newspapers and journals grew steadily and surely. The Bryansk gubkom reported that "as required by the directive of the CC," they increased subscription rates on all newspapers.[13]

Reading rooms dotted the countryside.[14] Dozens of clubs were designed to attract working people to cultural activities – the study of Marxism, singing, dancing, and crafts. A large network of elementary schools, and soviet and party schools was being developed that would produce ever more well-educated and politically conscious propagandists. New career opportunities had been opened to thousands of workers and peasants sent to study at workers' faculties, institutes, and universities. Education had never been so easily available to the masses as it was under Soviet power. The country was in the midst of nothing less than a cultural revolution. This was the message from the provincial party committees to the Central Committee.

Propaganda, judging by the monthly reports to the Central Committee, was one of the main preoccupations of the provincial CP committees, besides industrial production, rural tax collection, and grain output. In a typical provincial party committee, in addition to the Agitprop, various sections or departments dealing with the cadres, the soviets, trade unions, women, youth, and the Church worked full time on the business of propaganda. In some provinces, Agitprop was a section, in others a full-fledged department of the gubkom. In some, women's departments were a section of Agitprop; in others, they were not. In Bryansk province, for example, Agitprop itself had four sections: the culture board, political education board, the bureau of workers' correspondents, and a women's department. The task of all these departments and sections was to involve the masses in what was called socialist construction. Provincial Agitprops were to increase subscription rates to the Communist press and reach every corner of the country and every village by creating reading huts [*izby chital'ni*], Marxist study circles, and the so-called centers for the liquidation of illiteracy. Learning to read and write was to be combined with reading Communist literature specifically designed for the masses. The ultimate objective was to introduce a new lifestyle, new holidays, and new rituals – a new identity for the people.[15]

The daily work of the Agitprop was structured around propaganda campaigns, which occurred one after another. All campaigns originated in the Central Committee. Directives went out to the provinces to stage such and such a campaign and report back on how many rallies were held and how many people participated. In the first years of NEP, Agitprop's activity was somewhat erratic. One campaign was launched with great fanfare, then attention would shift to another, the first to fall into obscurity. Some campaigns crowded out all others at certain moments. In 1921 it was a vindictive campaign against the Mensheviks and SRs as hirelings of the bourgeoisie. In 1922 it was a campaign to force the Allied powers to drop their sanctions against the "first workers' and peasants' republic." Then followed a campaign to confiscate valuables from the Church and another against the SRs in the lead-up to one of the first show trials. The next year the anti-SR and anti-religious campaigns were slowed and attention shifted to economy's "scissors crisis". One campaign followed another as through the lens of a kaleidoscope: "the new morality in daily life" campaign, the "liquidation of illiteracy" campaign, the "Lenin enrollment" campaign, the "Trotsky heresy" campaign.

Depending on which holiday was approaching, this or that campaign gained prominence and became the focus of intense organizing. For example, the Bryansk gubkom reported in 1924 that it had conducted a series of campaigns. In February the fifth anniversary of the Communist International triggered a stream of articles in newspapers, lectures, courses, processions and marches to promote world-wide working-class solidarity. The anniversary of the February revolution was celebrated as the day of the overthrow of the monarchy. This was the occasion to lecture on the advantages of Soviet power over Tsarism and the glorious achievements of socialist construction in Russia. March featured the celebration of International Women's Day. Other themes were put on hold and working women's issues received top priority for the duration of the campaign. In April and May the main holidays were the anniversary of the Paris Commune and the Komsomol Easter, followed by the celebration of May Day, which included parades and rallies of the revolutionary masses expressing solidarity with oppressed proletarians in capitalist countries. In August the focus was on the tenth anniversary of the beginning of the imperialist war. This day was to be used for lecturing on the imperialist scheming of capitalist powers and the revolutionary movement of the working class abroad. In September the main campaign was tax collection. Agitators and propagandists criss-crossed the countryside trying to convince peasants to pay their taxes. In October and November the main focus was on the celebration of the Great October socialist revolution, the centerpiece campaign of the year. The Kursk Agitprop, for example, reported that it had convened 232 village assemblies, 59 rallies, 4 demonstrations, 50 conferences, 40 discussions, and 7 honorary sessions [*zasedan-iya*] in the province associated with this gala occasion.[16] The schedule of holidays and celebrations was fairly tight. The point was to keep attention focused on the new revolutionary festivities and crowd out old religious holidays.

The Communist representation of 1917 reconstructed major turning points: the overthrow of the autocracy in February, the arrival of Lenin in Petrograd in April, the Kornilov putsch in August and the glorious popular revolution in October. The chain of events still focused on the masses as the main vehicle of history. Lenin and his role were featured prominently in 1924. The revolutionary calendar reinvented history of the recent past as a pre-history of October, inevitably leading to the victory of the proletariat under the leadership of the Communist Party led by Comrade Lenin. It was a quest for legitimacy through historical myth-making.

In addition to these regular propaganda festivities, the Agitprops staged thematic campaigns which usually targeted a specific class enemy, such as the bourgeoisie, NEPmen, or priests. In campaigns like "Boycott private traders," a stream of newspaper articles, rallies, and conferences explained to the laboring masses that even though private trade was legal it was still dishonest and exploitative by its very nature, and private traders were speculators and parasites. Class-conscious proletarians were encouraged to buy consumer goods in cooperatives and state stores instead.

The demonstrations, processions, and rallies were, in effect, variations on the same basic script: the masses rise in revolution and overthrow the power of the landlords, capitalists, and priests. The latter were always represented as caricatured reincarnations of vice, avarice, and evil. Effigies of fat capitalists, drunken priests, and haughty officers were paraded through the streets as a part of the new ritual on public holidays. This caricatured representation of enemies with counterparts in heroically idealized images of the proletariat was to be the standard staple of Soviet propaganda for decades to come.[17]

A matter of first priority was to establish control over schools. All children had to be exposed to Communist ideology as early as possible.[18] At the provincial level there were still very few Communist-trained schoolteachers. Most of them were trained before the revolution and were feared to espouse SR or "old regime" ideology. The Bolsheviks launched periodic campaigns to involve schoolteachers in what was called "Communist construction," in practice enforcing ideological correctness. In this vein periodic congresses of teachers were held at the district and uezd level. Those teachers whose speeches were found objectionable were labeled "unreliable" and sub-sequently disqualified from teaching. To facilitate the process, schoolteachers had to go through attestation, involving verification of their credentials. Those of alien social background, such as the children of priests or landlords, were sometimes fired even if there was no immediate replacement. Those with any kind of association with any opposition parties would be purged as well.[19] The Bryansk Agitprop set up reeducation courses which passed 120 teachers in 1924.[20] Regular Agitprop staff would pay unexpected visits to village schools and monitor the work of individual teachers. They organized supplementary courses on Communist education and coached teachers on the correct interpretation of party decisions and policies.

In the fall of 1924 a country-wide campaign was launched in preparation for the All-Russian Congress of Teachers. The purpose, as before, was to purge undesirable elements from the ranks of rural schoolteachers. The Vladimir gubkom reported:

> Before the convocation of the All-Russian Congress of Teachers, we conducted a mass purge of schoolteachers. We exposed ninety teachers for dismissal because they were from the families of the intelligentsia and clergy . . . Many of them had worked in village schools for two or three decades.[21]

This seemingly innocuous report suggests that the Bolsheviks had introduced what can be called new cultural practices – people were judged not by their personal records but by an ideological identity imposed by the state. Needless to say, these categories were highly artificial and rarely flexible enough to provide for rational implementation, even by Soviet standards of the day. At uezd- and district-level conferences, many teachers had to undergo a specific-ally Soviet ritual of cleansing [promyvanie].[22] The personal record of individual teachers was scrutinized at general meetings to reveal political loyalty. The outcome of most of these meetings was that senior, experienced, and independently minded teachers were fired, and younger Communist teachers promoted (if they could be found).

The public ritual of cleansing transformed the relationship between the state and the individual. From the point of view of "bourgeois" ethical norms, it was a blatant invasion of the private sphere by the state. The sum total of views, convictions, and utterances, no matter in what context – private or public – was brought out. The purpose of this new Soviet ritual was to condition subjects that anything said or done could be used against them. The message was that if one wanted to keep one's job, status, and security, it was necessary to parade loyalty to Soviet power. This invasion of the mind, a new Bolshevik ritual, had a long-lasting effect on generations of Soviet public servants.

At the All-Russian Congress of Teachers Bolshevik leaders gave re-assuring speeches that the Soviet state and teachers could overcome mutual distrust and past misunderstandings, as long as teachers would become true "conduits" of Communist ideology to the young generation.[23] Despite this rhetoric, schoolteachers remained a suspect social category throughout the NEP years. Screening and verification of political reliability continued as a matter of routine.[24]

In 1922, 1923, and 1924 three successive waves of screenings and purges affected students in higher education as well. In 1922 those identified as students with Kadet political sympathies were arrested and exiled to the Solovki camp. In 1923 the purge targeted leftist students, especially those displaying affinity to Trotsky's ideas. In 1924 a general purge of the entire student body was launched which was analogous to the schoolteachers' purge, the centerpiece of that campaign being *promyvanie*, entailing individual screening of 135,000 students for social origin and political reliability.[25]

In Voronezh every student was called upon to appear in front of a commission composed of the leading figures [*aktiv*] of the party and Komsomol in 1924. If one wanted to remain in school, one had to go through with this humiliating ritual, admit to past sins, and swear loyalty to the party and the Communist cause. Many students refused to participate and published an underground protest leaflet against the purge, posting it all over town. Ultimately, 30 per cent of students at the university and 25 per cent at the agricultural institute were expelled.[26]

The Nizhnii Novgorod gubkom reported that a special commission had examined the social background of all students and had cleansed institutions of higher learning of "socially alien elements" – the children of priests, nobles, entrepreneurs, and traders.[27] Periodic screenings and cleansing of educational institutions became a matter of routine business. Social origin and political correctness were criteria by which anyone could be expelled. The Agitprop explained:

> In order to cleanse the universities of politically unreliable and generally undesirable elements, the university council shall appoint a screening commission composed of the [party] secretary, Komsomol secretary, and the dean. The screening commissions will conduct a political verification of students at the time of admission and periodic purges of students throughout the entire university, as well as in separate classes.[28]

The CC instructed provincial party committees that admission to institutes and universities was to be conducted on a class basis. The selection committees were to scrutinize the credentials of all those who had been nominated by local party, trade union, and Komsomol, or other organizations.[29] Access to education, just as with access to films, books, or music, was the business of the party; it decided who could see what kinds of film and read what kinds of book and who could be a teacher and a student.

Most official documents described spectacular achievements of Soviet power on the cultural front, upward mobility for the workers and peasants, women's delegate meetings, and the progress of mass education.[30] However, in addition to the reports from the gubkoms, the Central Committee had two more channels to verify these claims. One was the GPU and the other the CC's own investigative officers [*instruktory*]. They traveled to the provinces to verify reported facts and assess the situation themselves. Their communication with the Central Committee provides a very different picture of the social and cultural reality in the provinces.

According to the CC plenipotentiary in Bryansk province, the gubkom's claims of spectacular achievements in the field of Communist education of the masses were much exaggerated. The province, with a population of 1,250, 000, still had a 58 per cent illiteracy rate.[31] Provincial authorities increased subscriptions to newspapers, but most subscribers could not read them, and even if they could, they were not interested. The total circulation of all periodicals in the province was 19,000, "for 9,000 semi-literate subscribers."[32] This meant that the number of readers had not increased but the number of subscriptions in state agencies had.[33]

The numbers may have been correct on paper but they do not necessarily mean much. Thousands of members of voluntary associations, observed the CC envoy in Bryansk province, were members on paper only, "dead souls" as he put it. The factory administration enlisted entire worker collectives as members, and workers did not mind as long as it did not cost them anything.[34] The Don host party committee insisted in its report that the voluntary associations' large membership was not fictitious. Members paid their dues, but these funds were usurped by the boards for their personal needs without any accounting.[35] In the so-called centers for the liquidation of illiteracy, students were rarely regular workers and peasants; more commonly they were illiterate party recruits. The number of schools decreased because church schools were shut down and priests (and teachers who were sons of priests) were being slowly but steadily barred from teaching.[36] In Gomel province, for example, there were 815 schools, and 1,326 teachers. Of these, 205 in the course of 1924 were forced out through the screening and attestation ritual.[37]

The Kursk gubkom could not afford to pay teachers even the minimum wage. There was no money in the local budget and no subsidies from Moscow. As a result, teachers were paid one of the lowest wages of all, 16 rubles a month.[38] In Samara province only 40 per cent of children of school age actually went to school since there was no available space for the others.[39] School budgets were the last priority for uezd and district officials. In the Bogorodskii uezd of Tula province, the Karachevskii EC paid 500 rubles to its members, covering the deficit by laying off seven teachers.[40] In Vyatka province the budget for rural schools was 36 rubles a year, whereas a member of the CEC from the province was paid 400 rubles.[41] Teachers were overburdened with large classes, averaging forty-five pupils. Of those who went to school only 40 per cent had textbooks. There was no money for teachers' salaries, school supplies, or construction of new schools. Teachers in Tula province complained that there was no chalk and they had to write on the blackboard by dipping their index finger in water. Illiteracy rates in the countryside were actually increasing, despite the campaign to liquidate illiteracy, concluded the report. According to the Vladimir gubkom, "schoolteachers were unhappy." They did not like the propaganda campaigns that they were required to take part in: "Outwardly, they pretend to participate in social work but in reality one cannot see the results."[42] To be sure, the threat of purge and dismissal made rural teachers fear for their jobs. Some of them tried to enter the party.[43]

Peasants generally wanted more regular schools for children and fewer propaganda campaigns. As one peasant at a village soviet election meeting in Gomel province asked: "What concrete measures for the improvement of rural schools has the Communist Party undertaken?" Another added: "Why are there not enough local teachers in the countryside?"[44] And another peasant reproached the Bolsheviks: "You promised to give us universal primary education, but in reality the schools are falling apart."[45]

The work of rural reading huts [izba chitalnya] likewise did not correspond to the gleeful official representations. In Voronezh province, for example, on paper there were 360 rural libraries, but in reality only 125.[46] The librarians [izbachi] had the miserable pay of 5 or 10 rubles a month, a salary impossible to live on. There were no books, journals, or funds for maintenance. Only propaganda pamphlets from the civil war years on Denikin and Kolchak were on the shelf. By contrast, in Tula province in Plavskii uezd, the only books available were reminiscences of the German Crown Prince, the corres-pondence of Nicholas and Aleksandra, and memoirs of Bismarck. An inspection in Saratov province also showed that rural libraries had no political literature of any kind, not even posters. The Communist cells neglected the libraries and, as a result, "they often became places for dating [mesto svidanii] or turned into dirty and filthy shacks."[47] When workers and peasants did use the local libraries, they were interested in anything but politics or Marxism. The most popular books were detective stories.[48] According to one survey, official Marxist–Leninist books remained uncut, proving that nobody bothered even to glance through them.

In some cases, Communist representations were clear fabrications, as is reported by a district education board member after his unexpected tour of rural libraries in Gomel province:

Our cultural institutions work badly. There is more noise and pomp than real business. In one village I entered the reading hut and asked: "How is your work, attendance?" The librarian started to treat me to statistics that startled me. There are three study circles, the masses are involved, and attendance is excellent.

As it turned out, this was all a pack of lies. There were no study circles, no masses involved, nothing. These were only plans for the future, represented as if they were reality.[49] As a regular pattern, rural reading huts were run by Komsomol activists: in Kursk province, out of the total of 86 rural librarians, 66 were Komsomol members.[50] This in itself scared off potential peasant visitors, as one peasant put it at a soviet election meeting: "What use is there for the library if one cannot do anything there because of Komsomol members."[51] Peasants detested the libraries as centers of anti-religious campaigns. In Vvedenskii uezd, Kostroma province's former noble estate was turned into a club. On paper it looked like a major cultural center for the surrounding districts. Lectures, films, and meetings were reported to take place there. An independent inquiry however, showed that:

> It is true that the club is housed in one of the best buildings in the province. An auditorium and the library are there. If there were active work one could have created a cultural center there. Alas, it is not so in reality. There is disorder and dirt everywhere. The furniture is broken and some has been stolen. There are no locks and no guard. There are no funds. The building is dying.[52]

In Leningrad province, the gubkom survey of rural clubs found that membership figures were fictitious. They contained "dead souls" because rural people had exceptionally low interest in attending Communist-run clubs.[53]

In a typical Russian province there was perhaps one theater in the provincial capital, if that. Gramophones were more readily available but certainly not in every household. There were no literary journals nor a thriving book market. In most towns they only heard about cinema or saw films on rare occasions. Orel gubkom admitted that printed matter seldom reached peasant audiences. The traveling cinema had twenty showings in the countryside in spring 1925 with tremendous success. The only problem was that the ticket price of 10 kopecks was excessive for many peasants and in frustration those who could not afford the price broke the windows of the clubs where films were shown.[54] Peasant audiences did not seem to care what the films were about, as long as they were shown something, anything. They were willing to watch the same film more than once if there was no other. All reports indicate that worker and peasant audiences craved shows, theater plays, concerts, and cinema.[55]

In a small town in Moscow province the factory administration convened a general workers' meeting, and six times it could not take place "in view of a general no-show of workers." Then the factory administration posted an announcement that before the business part of the meeting a play would be shown and a concert given. Twice as many people showed up as the auditorium could hold. The chairman of the factory committee announced: "You know comrades we have deceived you a little bit. Before the show you will have to listen to the report of the town soviet and then conduct elections." When the chairman started his report, shouts broke out: "Down! Down! We have come to see the show and not to listen to your reports."[56] Workers and peasants were not interested in lectures on socialist construction but they would wait for hours to see a concert or a film. A journal in Moscow noted that even workers who lived in the city outskirts were not deterred by the relatively high prices of tickets to see *Tarzan*.[57] Before the age of radio and television, plays, concerts, and occasional films were the only forms of exotic entertainment available. In small towns and especially in the country-side such events took place rarely enough to make them all the more desirable.

Gubkom propaganda reports to Moscow echoed in the official media misrepresented cultural life in provincial Russia. Propaganda campaigns were often on paper only and membership drives enrolled "dead souls." Official claims of a cultural renaissance or even a cultural revolution were nothing but Potemkin villages on the ideological front. Popular tastes remained "bourgeois," from the Bolshevik point of view, or, to put it another way, normal. Common people wanted entertainment, shows, films, concerts, and detective stories; they wanted *Tarzan* and the fox-trot. Despite a gigantic effort to excite the masses with the prospect of socialist construction, popular tastes, values, and aspirations still remained beyond the grasp of the Bolsheviks.

ANTI-RELIGIOUS CAMPAIGNS[58]

In 1926 an All-Russian Conference on Anti-religious Struggle convened to work out new approaches in promoting atheism.[59] The central Agitprop explained that anti-religious propaganda had to be based on Marxist–Leninist teaching. Religion was an ideology of class enemies like any other. Struggle with religious belief had to go hand in hand with class struggle. Religious belief was defined as a tool of class enemies – the priests, landlords, and kulaks – for spiritual control over the minds of the peasant masses. Commun-ist propagandists had to:

> say clearly not only that religion was a weapon in the hands of capitalists, but expose the counterrevolutionary character of all idealistic clerical teachings of priests in our message to workers and peasants. We must say to them: "If you are a believer and if you think that without God you will not be able to live, you ought to know that these ideas were imposed on you by the bourgeoisie, and that all this talk of good and evil is a reflection of that which is good and evil from the point of view of capitalist exploiters."[60]

Workers and peasants were to espouse a different class morality, since that which was good for the capitalists was not good for the oppressed masses.

The message to provincial propagandists was that religion was a mental construction of the bourgeoisie designed to dupe the masses. All they had to do was convince the masses to shake off religious belief and that would lead to spiritual liberation. The masses would then see the light of true freedom under socialism. Materialist explanations of the world and scientific ex-planation of spiritual phenomena were to be the cornerstones of anti-religious propaganda.

We have never asserted: "Do not believe in God because it is not the truth." We have been saying that science disproves talk of the existence of God. And if someone is spreading lies about the existence of God, these people are doing it with an explicit purpose to darken one's consciousness, to close one's eyes to the laws of societal development and to direct one's attention to the heavens in order to knock the class weapon out of one's hands.[61]

Class struggle, underlying social relations and science, was to prove the falsehood of religious teaching. It was the main message to the provincial propagandists, who had to be guided by those two notions in their work. The tone of the conference was upbeat. It was an easy task, they thought. All one had to do was expose, unmask, and explain. The priests and the Church had to be exposed as liars, manipulators, and extortionists. More pamphlets on the Marxist explanation of the falsehood of religion had to be published, more propagandists trained, more grass-roots atheist organizations founded, and more secular rituals introduced to replace tenacious customs.

The journal *Antireligioznik* argued in 1924 that anti-religious propaganda was most effective when focused on specific priests or on specific rituals or sets of beliefs. A peasant was more likely to agree that a specific priest was no good rather than that all clergymen were. He was more likely to believe that a miracle-making icon was a fake if miracles did not happen. Propaganda had to appeal to peasant experiences relying on science.[62] There were numerous instances when local party and Komsomol cells tried to expose "lies" of the Church. One participant at the All-Russian Conference gave this example: "A Communist took an icon into the street and shot it with a rifle. The message he was trying to convey was: 'You see, nothing is going to happen to me. God has not punished me.'"[63]

Administrative measures were often applied and encouraged by Moscow. In November 1924 the Bryansk gubkom conducted the operation of removing the sacred relics from Ploshchanskii monastery in Sevskii uezd. After the monastery was shut down, the monks refused to depart, settled in the neighboring villages, and conducted anti-Soviet agitation, using the sacred relics for their purposes. "A necessity arose to expose the lies of the monks and to knock the weapon of counterrevolutionary propaganda out of their hands."[64] Apparently the monks were saying that the relics were miraculous and that the Bolsheviks would pay for their abuse of the Church. The Communist propagandists were sent to remove the relics and convince the peasants that the monks were bluffing and no miracles would occur. The main purpose of this operation was to discredit the monks and to force the peasants to deny refuge to them.

Article after article in anti-religious journals praised the power of science as the weapon of propaganda. "It is essential to demonstrate to the peasants that man possesses the true power in his struggle against the forces of nature.

Man can do everything that he expects from God."[65] A village newspaper in Tver' province argued that the biblical story of the Annunciation and pregnancy allegedly caused by the "Holy Ghost" were no more than legends rooted in the pagan communities "in which the mother did not know the father of her child."[66]

The main strike force on the front of the anti-religious struggle was the young – Komsomol members. Much of what they did was on the instruction of the party committee or provincial Agitprop. In June 1924 in Bryansk province the Komsomol members were mobilized to discredit the holiday of Ilia the Prophet. Several instructors taught Komsomol members how to argue with believers. They were supposed to say that Ilia was not a prophet at all and that belief in prophets was nothing but a fairy tale invented by the clergy to cloud the minds of the toiling peasantry.[67] The Komsomol members were encouraged to disrupt Easter celebrations and stage a counter-ritual, the so-called Komsomol Easter. Usually this boiled down to marches and processions of young Communists singing revolutionary songs in the vicinity of churches, making speeches on the dawn of the new era of liberated labor and the falsehood of religious belief. It was supposed to be a colorful, solemn, and attractive alternative to offset the magnetism of the Easter service. In practice the Komsomol Easter often degenerated into acts of hooliganism, insulting the believers. In the village of Trubchina, in the Bezhetsk uezd of Bryansk province, for example,

> The Komsomol members decided to disrupt [sorvat'] a religious service and attract peasants to the celebration of Komsomol Easter. To accomplish their plan, they surrounded the priest's house with barbed wire, trapping him inside. In the meantime, they stole holy books and vestments [oblacheniya] from the church through the window. At the beginning of the service, peasants gathered in front of the church but there was no priest. Instead, they saw Komsomol members who pushed their way into the church and started dancing and playing the harmonica. When the indignant peasants threw them out, they started to bombard the church with stones and broke the church's windows.[68]

Komsomol Central Committee files contain hundreds of reports on excesses of Komsomol activists in the anti-religious struggle. In one province local activists decided to burn the church, and one activist was assigned the job of setting the priest's house on fire. In Tula province, a local cell in one of the uezds threw a barrel of tar from the church tower down on to the procession of Easter prayers.[69] Komsomol cells often resorted to vandalism in their campaigns. In Kostroma province local Komsomol cells destroyed crosses at the local cemetery.[70] Actions like these earned Komsomol the reputation of a hooligan organization, a meeting place of village riffraff. One speaker at the Agitprop Anti-religious Struggle Conference recalled:

I had an opportunity to glance through the materials of rural Communist Party cells. There I found the following facts. Some Komsomol members light cigarettes during the service from the Icon-lamp [lampada] or release sparrows into the church during the service.[71]

It was not so much a manifestation of mischief as a self-righteous affirmation that God would not punish them. Their acts aimed to humiliate and inflict pain on believers. As a cultural expression, this was certainly an act of defiance of traditional authority, a claim to other, superior, and more advanced cultural community. To believers, flag waving, fiery speeches, and stones cast upon church windows only underscored Bolshevik impotence.

The Komsomol Easter was a counter-ritual affirming Bolshevik values over religion.[72] It was supposed to attract village youth away from religious Easter celebrations and communicate the message of working-class solidarity of the oppressed. Agitprop Komsomol activists chose the same forms to communicate their message as practiced by the religious congregations. They staged loud processions, singing revolutionary songs, and displaying the revolutionary iconography in a vain attempt to compete with the Easter service. In fact, Komsomol Easter was a false counter-ritual. In its form and presentation it mimicked the religious Easter but was devoid of any depth or meaning. It failed to offer anything that could compete with the solemn, mysterious, and miracle-like feeling believers experience in the procession celebrating the resurrection of Christ. Bolshevik counter-rituals remained rather superficial, hollow imitations which found a niche for themselves in popular celebrations in addition to rather than instead of religious festivals.

The split in the Russian Orthodox Church between the Tikhonite traditionalists and the "Living Church" renovationists was explained as an ideological struggle between the reformers and the conservatives. Provincial authorities were required to keep an eye on religious congregations and report how many were loyal to Patriarch Tikhon and how many were renovationists. While no grouping was to be supported publicly, the provincial Agitprops were instructed to stimulate, if they could, the rivalry and hostility between the two. This was done by discrediting campaigns focusing on particular priests or vicinities. In 1924, for example, the Vladimir gubkom reported:

So far, the Tikhon followers are particularly strong in the province. As before, the campaign to discredit the clergy in the eyes of the masses has continued. We have been defrocking the priests.[73]

In their reports, the Provincial party committees consistently represented the clergy as the hidden enemy. There is nothing surprising in this, of course, since they perceived the clergy as being the direct competitor for the hearts and minds of the people. In spring 1924, for example, the Kursk gubkom reported that supporters of Patriarch Tikhon in the Russian Orthodox Church were gaining the upper hand in their struggle with the renovationist Church in their province and that

> The church pulpit is consistently used by the clergy for agitation against Soviet power. Most of the time it is concealed in preaching that the drought and famine were God's punishment for our sins, strongly implying that the soviets are responsible.[74]

The struggle with religion was supposed to unfold at the initiative of the masses. The gubkoms were required to mobilize anti-religious elements of the community and promote their cause. If there were no such elements, they were to create them. In Orel the Agitprop set up anti-religious courses and opened a local chapter of the League of the Godless.[75] The Voronezh gubkom reported that: "In connection with the projected creation of the League of the Godless in the USSR, we have given the directive to localities to set up anti-religious associations."[76] Local branches were not voluntary in any meaningful sense. They were creatures of Agitprop. In 1926 the League of the Godless claimed 86,000 members, in 1927 138,000, and in 1929 465,000.[77] From this miraculous growth one would have the impression that the movement caught on. In fact most members were "dead souls" listed for statistical purposes.

Initially, the Bolsheviks were so confident that their message would prevail that in several cities from 1923 to 1925 public debates between Bolshevik propagandists and priests took place. On some occasions renovationists debated with Tikhon supporters. These were events that attracted enormous crowds. When in March 1923 Archbishop Vedenskii, the leader of the renovationists, took part in the "Science and Religion" debate in Moscow, it was virtually impossible to get tickets for one of the most interesting cultural events of the season. People's Commissar of Education Lunacharsky himself spoke for the Bolsheviks. He repeated the main Bolshevik message, that science proved that God did not exist, because science explained natural phenomena and exposed church teaching as nothing other than superstition. Lunacharsky's comments were rather simplistic, clearly closer to the Agitprop level than his own refined tastes would have preferred.[78] Vedenskii's rebuttal drew boisterous applause from the audience. He argued that it was only possible to sense and feel the existence of God – it could not be proven or disproven. Science would not replace religion as it could not satisfy the inner spirituality of mankind. Science could explain natural phenomena but not the meaning of life.[79] The Bolsheviks concluded that the debate did more harm than good because it familiarized the masses with the issues of religiosity.[80]

The Orel gubkom decided to encourage anyone who would denounce the established Church and allowed a public debate on the topic: "Was there a Jesus Christ?" Warring branches of the Orthodox Church were invited, as well as atheists and representatives of Evangelist, Baptist, and Adventist congregations. It was the most popular gathering organized by the Agitprop.

The Bolshevik calculation was that all these diverse factions would fight each other in public and that the anti-religious propaganda would profit. The result was the opposite of the one expected. The debate stimulated tremendous interest in religion. Warring religious congregations gained ground from one another but there were few gains for the atheists.

Every time the Bolsheviks tried to debate matters of Christian faith or ritual with the clergy they lost. Debates were clearly counterproductive, doing more harm than good. As Christmas of 1925 approached, the Central Committee sent out a secret directive to all provincial party and Komsomol committees:

> In the conditions when there are no cadres well prepared for anti-religious propaganda in the overwhelming majority of places in the countryside, it is imperative to abandon attempts to conduct widely attended lectures, reports, and most of all, debates on religious topics.[81]

Reporting on anti-religious struggle to Moscow, provincial Agitprops conveyed a contradictory message. On the one hand, they claimed new victories on the anti-religious front and new recruits for the League of the Godless since new relations in society and science were on their side; on the other hand, they admitted that religious belief was tenacious, due to the scheming and plotting of class enemies and priests. The implication was that a clear victory on this front would be achieved when all the exploiting capitalist classes were smashed and when the authority of the Church was undermined. The journal *Antireligioznik* prophesied: "Religion will not last [*izzhivet sebya*] because it is an ideological construct which will find less and less correlation to current economic and political relations."[82] These were excessively optimistic forecasts, as it turned out.

It is astonishing that Bolshevik "theoretical journals" did not consider or discuss the spiritual quality of religion, reducing it to materialistic profit-seeking. They never addressed issues of Christian ritual, tradition, or custom. Religion was trivialized to a level of superstition or merely enemy propaganda. For the Bolsheviks, peasant religiosity was a problem of information. If only peasants would listen to simple and rational explanations of natural phenomena, they surely would understand the veracity of the materialist and atheist world-view. The Bolshevik rational, atheist, and materialist mind-set inclined them to believe that scientific facts, propaganda, unmasking, and exposing would fit the bill, decreasing peasant religiosity, and wiping out peasant superstition. For the Bolsheviks it did not make sense that peasants believed what appeared to them patently false propaganda of the priests. Their natural reaction was to counter propaganda with propaganda. Hence the counter-rituals, renovationism, lectures, and debates. The Bolsheviks failed to grasp that any change in the ritual endowed with religious meaning was going to encounter fierce resistance. Peasants held on tenaciously to their own explanations and rationalizations. Science was a strange concept to them. They believed in miraculous wells and sacred icons.[83] The Bolsheviks were naive to believe that rational explanations were going to convince peasants. Here we have a clear-cut case of a collision of cultures.

POPULAR RELIGIOSITY

Russia was still a country of traditional culture. Religion was inseparable from the general cycle of peasant life. It gave it order and meaning. As Nicholas Berdiaev put it, the majority of the Russian people lived by faith.[84] To live by faith for a Russian muzhik meant to observe the religious calendar and ritual. Events in the year were connected to Christmas, Easter, Trinity, and so on. As one scholar put it: "Another point on which the Russians have reflected is the universal presence of God and his Providence. In all the events of life, they discern the workings of his Providence."[85]

The power of the Orthodoxy over the minds of the Russian people was precisely in the ritual. It was the singing and the candles, the icons and processions, and the congregation that gave meaning to the believers. Ritual, in the mind of a Russian peasant, was a part of something sacred and deeply connected to the mystery, miracle, or punishment sent from Heaven. Holidays could not be simply erased from the minds of people by order of the new authorities. Even though religious holidays fell on regular work days, many workers, especially women workers, observed them despite fines. The Voronezh gubkom admitted in 1924 that on the Day of Transfiguration on August 19, more than 50 per cent of workers across the province did not show up for work even though they knew they would be fined. Despite an all-out propaganda campaign, a religious procession took place in Voronezh with thousands of believers participating.[86]

In the countryside sacred wells were discovered which peasants believed did not go dry because of divine intervention. In Arkhangelskii uezd of Orel province, the rumor spread that if one looked into a miraculous well, one could see the image of Jesus and the Virgin Mary. Peasants in their thousands made pilgrimages to the holy well, swearing that they had seen the image of Jesus. Rumors spread that "even the Communists who were there and looked into it believed in God and donned the crosses."[87] In popular consciousness it was certainly an affirmation of the righteousness of the Christian faith which would prevail over the Communist blasphemy.

When in 1924 drought hit the black earth provinces of Tambov, Voronezh, and Orel local peasants understood it as God's punishment for offenses against the Church. Salvation could only come through prayer and pleading for a miracle. The Voronezh gubkom informed the CC:

The absence of rain caused the strengthening of religious belief. The result was that the masses of peasants led by their priests were walking into the fields singing and praying that rain be sent from the Heavens. There also appeared miracle-making icons. In these cases we could not avoid interference of the GPU. Some of the offenders were arrested.[88]

In Tambov province a rumor quickly spread that in Rannenburg uezd a miraculous well had been discovered. A pilgrimage to this well sprang up quickly. Religious services were held and processions with priests and crosses in many villages took place praying for the end of the drought.[89]

To the Bolsheviks' minds, miracle-making icons and holy wells were nothing but manifestations of superstition at best and malicious scheming of the priests to confuse peasants at worst. Their natural response was to intensify anti-religious propaganda or to unleash the GPU against the priests. For example, in Gomel province, a rumor spread in Regitskii uezd that a miracle had happened when sacred scrolls were discovered in a baked loaf of bread. The scrolls commanded the peasants not to sell grain to the Bolsheviks at 65 kopecks a pud. The local authorities were furious. They were convinced that counterrevolutionary priests were using peasant religiosity to set them against Soviet power.[90]

Rumors were manifestations of popular culture uncontrolled by the authorities. They reflected in most cases wishful thinking or spontaneous expressions of fears, hopes, frustrations, or hidden aspirations.[91] They provided a simple explanation of reality that appeared to make sense: "A drought was God's punishment," or "War will come and the soviets will perish." A piece of information was picked up and passed on to others, thus becoming a rumor. The fact that others passed it on means that they believed in the plausibility of the rumor's content. Rumors therefore brought private inner understandings and rationalizations into the public sphere. They uncovered the pre-existing explanatory parameters of the popular mind.

Rumors always had an element of the fantastic, unbelievable, and supernatural in them. Something extraordinary was rumored to have happened which would lead to a resolution. Either everything would be better or everything would become much worse. This duality of the rumor content is perhaps one of its most salient features. A great many rumors contained references to a coming war.

Pskov: Rumors circulated here that the Allies demanded that the USSR disband the Comintern and elect a president. Kuban': July 1925, Maikop okrug: Rumors among the Cossacks spread that soon separate Cossack land holding would be restored, Cossack uniforms would be permitted to be worn, that outsiders [non-Cossack settlers] would be thrown out of the Kuban' lands, and that this had already been done on the Don because war with France had just begun.[92]

A special CC report to Stalin on the Cossacks' political attitudes cited rumors about the war with Poland and England, the impending fall of Soviet power and the restoration of Cossack traditional liberties. A considerable oral folklore developed about legendary Cossack heroes who were conducting secret negotiations with the Communists on Cossack autonomy. On the Don there were rumors about Cossack uprisings in Kuban', and in Kuban' about uprisings on the Don. Another rumor predicted the coming election to the throne of "father Tsar." The CC report concluded that the Cossacks "continued to live by their old illusions and hopes for a speedy fall of Soviet power."[93] These rumors clearly reveal Cossack nostalgia for the good old days and their hopes for some miraculous intervention that would put things right.

The GPU political survey for March 1925 noted an increase in monarchist rumors across the country, predicting the return of the Romanovs – in some versions this was made possible by war with the Western powers. In Volyn' and Vyatka provinces rumor had it that the war had already started, that Ukraine and Siberia had seceded from the Soviet Union, and that Moscow and Leningrad were being evacuated.[94] Quite a number of rumors predicted various kinds of cataclysm, upheaval, uprising, and a possible end for Soviet power. In Moscow province, rumor predicted: "a coming split in the Communist Party, changes in the New Economic Policy and war by spring."[95] In the Volga Basin provinces, the GPU reported a rumor spread by the kulaks that "the RCP would split into pieces and Soviet power would fall."[96] And in Dmitrovskii uezd, Moscow province, peasants were saying that the time had come to convene a Constituent Assembly. The Tambov GPU reported in May 1925: "the kulaks and traders are spreading provocative rumors about war with Bulgaria and Germany, the fall of Soviet power and election to the throne of Tsar Mikhail Fedorovich."[97]

The theme of miraculous salvation had its counterpart in rumors predicting a turn for the worse. These were apocalyptic visions. Rumors of this kind were particularly widespread in times of political uncertainty. In a special memorandum on popular attitudes after Lenin's death, the GPU identified two themes in all reports: one was that things would get worse; and the other that enemies were responsible for Lenin's death. In Vladimir province, for example, rumor had it that Lenin had been poisoned by Jewish doctors and that Trotsky had fled.[98] The theme of a Jewish conspiracy was widespread in rumors circulating in numerous provinces: in Novgorod, the rumor expressed fear that "a Jew would replace Lenin."[99] And in Belorussia:

> In military units, rumor has it that Lenin died three months ago, and that a wax figure was made to look like his body, and that it was this wax figure which was displayed in the Hall of Columns. Some poor peasants are completely indifferent to Lenin's death and kulaks are secretly happy. Who will replace him? Some Red Army soldiers say that peasants should not pay taxes since they would fall into the Jews' hands without Lenin. Trotsky has fled abroad and Soviet power will fall by spring.[100]

Here the explanatory scheme fit into the pre-existing prejudices. Lenin was endowed with positive qualities and villains had to be those traditionally assigned that role, the Jews. All the themes combined to say that things were bound to get worse, Jews were to blame, and perhaps deliverance from Soviet power would come soon. An almost identical rumor was reported in Smolensk province:

> Rumors are that Trotsky will replace Lenin and then the Jews will take power into their hands. War is inevitable. And Lenin did not just die. He was killed. And Trotsky was arrested because he had sent the murderer.[101]

This rumor is a forecast of doom and identifies a villain to blame. Nevertheless, Trotsky was sometimes endowed with positive qualities in some provinces and peasant aspirations were pinned on him. In Tula province, the gubkom chief wrote that: "The population defines Trotskyism as the abolition of taxes."[102] Among the peasants of Gul'skii uezd, rumor had it that

> Trotsky has departed to meet Kerensky and that they together are going to organize against the Bolsheviks and then the end would come to Bolshevik rule, because Trotsky is for us peasants. He is against taxes and the Bolsheviks are for taxes.[103]

Apparently it was because Trotsky was abused in the official press that some peasants interpreted this as a sign that he stood for peasant interests.

Several rumors endowed Lenin with all kinds of positive qualities. In Terskaya province, for example:

> In connection with Lenin's death, the population is spreading rumors that Lenin did not just die, but was poisoned. The kikes [zhidy] are striving to seize power, because Lenin supposedly believed that it was necessary to abolish agricultural tax for peasants and other taxes for traders and that Trotsky and others did not want this.[104]

Another rumor likewise praised Lenin "as the only defender of peasants and that it would have been better if Trotsky had died instead."[105] This rumor parallels the rumors during the civil war when peasants identified Lenin and the Bolsheviks as those who had given peasants the land and Trotsky and the Communists as those who were trying to take it away. Rumors ascribed what they would like to see happen to the positive heroes and all that could go wrong to the negative villains. They reflected flights of fantasy, nostalgia, and wishful thinking. Rumors depict peasants facing spontaneous elemental forces beyond their control. Peasants do not come across as active participants in the cataclysms they predict. They pin their hopes on miraculous icons, war, valiant Cossack heroes, or divine intervention to put things right. Rumors necessarily presented the past, the present, and the future starkly black and white. There are recognizable characters and forces in them from Russian folklore: the good father Tsar, the bad villain, miraculous and divine intervention, apocalypse and salvation. In this sense, rumors reflect traditional popular religiosity.

The spiritual world of the Russian peasant was beyond the reach of Communist propaganda. The intensity of Communist anti-religious campaigns, posters, outright repressions against priests, and closure of churches generated a backlash. Religious life became more intense. Debates, arguments, and campaigns between the authorities and various Orthodox factions stimulated interest in the issues at stake. In Bryansk province peasants beat up renovationist priests. The Tikhonites clearly held the upper hand in the province. Out of the total of 442 churches, 300 supported Tikhon, 62 supported the renovationists and 80 congregations denounced both.[106] In Kuban' and Don the general pattern was similar: the Tikhonites were clearly much stronger than the renovationists, but Old Believer, Evangelist, and Baptist congregations thrived as well.[107] The Tula gubkom wrote frankly that propaganda campaigns had very little effect. In the entire province only three civil marriage ceremonies had been performed: "The clergy enjoys the support of the population."[108] From various provinces, reports were coming in that: "renovation of the icons caused an outburst of fanaticism on the part of peasantry and a part of youth, including Komsomol members."[109]

According to the Orel gubkom assessment, the sectarian movement was growing in the province at the expense of the renovationists.[110] New congregations of Baptists, Evangelists, and Adventists arose in addition to the old sects of Skoptsy and Old Believers; 99 per cent of the adherents of these congregations were new converts. In 1917 none of them had any meaningful presence in the province, stated the report. The preachers of these congregations capitalized on the anti-religious campaigns of the Bolsheviks against the Orthodox Church and even more so on the recriminations between Tikhon supporters and renovationists. The sectarian preachers denounced Orthodox priests of both branches and won over new adherents to their congregations. The gubkom admitted that the League of the Godless had few adherents whereas the sectarian congregations were growing fast. In Samara province, the life of various religious congregations was not altered in any significant way by the Communist propaganda efforts. In the Russian Orthodox communities attempts to promote the renovationist Church failed because, of the 26 congregations in the city of Samara, 24 remained Tikhonite. As elsewhere, some gains were made by the Baptists, Evangelists, and Molokans at the expense of the Orthodox. Congregations of Lutherans, Catholics, and Jews remained stable, not experiencing growth or contraction.[111]

An unexpected consequence of the Bolshevik-promoted struggle between the renovationists and the Tikhonites was that the relative influence of local parishes increased. The Bolsheviks realized their objective of depriving the church hierarchy of its central role in dictating procedure to the parishes. In the conditions of rivalry between the two Orthodox branches, each parish suddenly was free to choose for itself. The Bolsheviks' calculation had been that by weakening the organizational structure of the Church they would actually weaken religious belief. Yet, as their reports suggest, they were mistaken. The genuine democratization of the church structure, the opportunity to choose and debate issues of ritual and reform actually enhanced the cohesion of the local parishes. The result was the opposite of the one expected.

In his study of popular religiosity in the 1920s, Gregory Freeze has demonstrated that resistance to renovationism came from the local parishes which in turn reflected the preferences of the parishioners. It was not so much that political issues such as loyalty or opposition to Soviet power preoccupied parishioners, but rather that purely liturgical reforms generated tenacious resistance. Moreover, the common division of Orthodox factions into reformers and conservatives is inappropriate because Tikhon likewise consented to and tried to implement reforms, the most important of which being the acceptance of the new calendar. Both renovationists and Tikhonites were reformers of varying degrees, and both, as we know, cooperated with the GPU. Both encountered fierce resistance of the parishioners to any liturgical reforms, including the introduction of the new calendar. Freeze has called this phenomenon a counter-reformation in Russian Orthodoxy. It was a genuine popular religious movement against church reform of any kind. The congregations tenaciously held on to their customs, traditions and holidays, dating them by the old, familiar calendar.

It is not difficult to explain why popular response was so defiantly conservative. It was a natural reaction to the onslaught of the new. The countryside experienced the new, secular, dynamic Bolsheviks preaching the new ideology. The Church, custom, and tradition provided a defense against this onslaught. The parish was a familiar, safe group that sheltered members from hostile change. Parishioners' bonds were strengthened by the virulent attacks of the Godless and Komsomol hooligans. The Church, even without its hierarchy, was the only anchor of stability available. And when even the clergy began to talk of reform, it caused total consternation and overwhelming repudiation. In spite of official discouragement, most congregations flocked to Tikhon as a symbol of the old non-reformed Orthodox Church. When Tikhon agreed to introduce the new calendar, he was astonished by the vehemence of popular rejection as epitomized in a report to him from the Bishop of Tambov:

> The transition to the new calendar woke up the people and caused them to discern here a precedent for the encroachment on their "holy of holies." ... The clergy is caught between two fires: an order from renovationist diocesan authorities that they – under penalty of losing their positions – unfailingly perform liturgies according to the new calendar. But the people threatened retribution and expulsion from the parish if the priest should dare to violate the centuries-old way of life and order in the Church by conducting services according to the new calendar.[112]

In the end Tikhon was forced to acquiesce and abandon calendar reform for the foreseeable future.

Communist propaganda did not undermine the religious congregations. On the contrary, it invigorated religious life. One of the main reasons for this was that the Bolsheviks, as believers in organization, hit the church organization, hoping to weaken religion. What they did not comprehend was that a Russian peasant did not necessarily need an organized Church to sustain his religion. As one scholar put it:

> We can only conclude that Russian popular religion is about as unclericalist as it could be, not in any way tied to the clergy. It would not cross the peasant's mind to abandon the Church and the sacraments because he thought his priest unworthy. The inadequacy of clergy will never put his faith at risk.[113]

Faced with the Communist challenge the local clergy responded to the needs of their community in new ways. They tried to make religious life more meaningful and respond to their flocks' economic as well as spiritual needs. The Don party committee wrote to the CC that the Orthodox clergy, in their attack on the renovationists, imitated Communist methods. The clergy started organizing discussion groups and Bible readings, explaining the meaning of religious holidays and practices, something that they had never done before. Moreover, church councils on the Don started giving out small loans to peasants at interest rates much lower than those offered by banks, money-lenders, or cooperatives. This brought grateful peasants closer to the Church.[114]

Faced with the challenge of state-sponsored anti-religious propaganda, the Church responded in new ways, trying to adapt to the new conditions. The Vladimir gubkom reported with alarm that new religious societies were appearing, such as "The Struggle against Disbelief." There were many collective petitions submitted asking for the reopening of closed churches and for permits to build new ones.[115] In the Don and Kuban' Cossack lands, the local population's defense of the Church went further than mere petitions. Numerous newly elected soviets in 1925 tried to reverse the anti-religious campaigns of the Communists. Village soviet members took seats on the village church councils. They allocated funds for the maintenance and repair of local churches and in some cases tried to return confiscated church property.[116] In Saratov province, as well, church councils had amicable relations with the village soviets and with local teachers. The Church had its own fields and, consequently, income. Two church choirs were thriving.[117]

One senses in the reports of provincial authorities that by 1926 they began to regard the anti-religious struggle as a hopeless undertaking. In Ukraine some provincial Agitprops decided to cease anti-religious propaganda entirely because it fueled peasant hostility to the party. The propagandists complained that there were no published texts on the Marxist history of

Christianity. In most provinces there were no people who could debate these issues. As a party cell chairman in Kostroma province summed up: "With the kind of people we have, we do not risk to engage in it."[118] The All-Russian Anti-religious Propaganda Conference likewise acknowledged that:

> The League of the Godless carries on its miserable existence, because we do not have appropriate literature, nor do we have the authors who could produce the necessary literature ... We must admit that we face the strengthening of religious organizations and religious belief. In some places there exists what we could call a religious revival.[119]

The second half of the 1920s, until the so-called cultural revolution of 1929, were years of a rich religious life in Russian towns and villages. Religious congregations were thriving. Especially inventive were some evangelical groups. In their missionary work, they competed directly with the Bolsheviks for the youth constituency. As an American observer noted:

> The law allows these religious associations to conduct worship but does not permit them to carry on social work of any kind. Several evangelical groups managed to circumvent the strict interpretation of the law and had gathered under their guidance many young workmen and peasants, it was announced. An organization of the youth competing with Komsomol was being started, in some cases calling itself "Baptomol" or "Christomol."[120]

Unable to compete, the Bolsheviks withdrew from the struggle. Like so many of the Bolshevik campaigns, the initial assault had quickly fizzled out. Yet the shock of the 1922 robbery of the Church and the 1923 state-induced split galvanized the Russian Church, at least in this period. Religious life had changed and new forms had appeared that had not been present before. It was not reform *per se* that was impossible, but a reform which aimed to contradict tradition and custom. Reform which appeared to strengthen the religious congregation, and new practices that enhanced the parishes' power were accepted. From this perspective, the counter-reformation was a popular response from below to reform from above, a genuine religious revival in defense of traditional forms and practices.

The violent attack on the Church during the so-called cultural revolution in 1929 was an admission of failure by the Bolsheviks, if seen against this backdrop. Ten years of anti-religious propaganda had brought no voluntary decline of religiosity in the countryside. The Bolsheviks responded by draconian legislation and anti-religious activity. The teaching of religious creeds was banned. All religious schools were closed. Hundreds of churches were destroyed, hundreds more shut down.[121] It was an admission that in the conditions of NEP, the religious congregations had been winning. Their number was increasing, their message was being heard, and their appeal was growing.

One may conclude that ambitious Bolshevik campaigns of the 1920s on the ideological front, to overturn customs, traditions, way of life, and religiosity failed dismally. Was this a setback for the forces of progress and enlightenment in their struggle with peasants' backwardness and superstition? This, of course, is how the Bolsheviks wanted to represent the issue. In reality, resistance to change was not resistance to progress but resistance to lawlessness and indecency. It was an affirmation of collective solidarity in the face of brutal state intervention into the private sphere in ways hitherto unprecedented. The rural community was showing once more its resilience and internal strength.

Chapter 5

The Komsomol and youth
A transmission belt that snapped

REPRESENTATIONS

Agitprop operated under the assumption that the youth were an easy target of Communist propaganda, as the young are always likely to be attracted to revolutionary ideals. The job assigned to Komsomol [Young Communists' League] was to tap into this creative energy, to provide recruits to the party, and to spread the Communist message among the youth. Agitprop's message to youth was that a new society was to be built, a just society of workers and peasants, with great opportunities for the downcast, free from exploitation and from the landlords and capitalists led by the vanguard of the proletariat, the Communist Party. The task, then, was to overcome the legacies of the preceding capitalist order such as avarice and greed, religious superstition, and bourgeois tastes and manners. A model Komsomol member was supposed to excel in loyalty to the Communist Party, and be driven by Communist ideals as an honest, dedicated, and conscientious proletarian. Communist propaganda has largely succeeded in representing the Komsomol as a mass organization of young Communists, eager defenders of Soviet power, a reserve battalion, a pool of recruits, a transmission belt, and a striking force in the socialist offensive, involving hundreds of thousands of young men and women in socialist construction.

Komsomol's ranks grew dramatically during the 1920s, suggesting that there were hundreds of thousands of young people who voluntarily chose to become ardent Communist supporters. The record of anti-religious struggle as well as many other Communist campaigns also seems to show that the main striking force was the Komsomol. Almost all cultural campaigns of the 1920s, be they anti-religious, or oriented towards overcoming illiteracy or introducing socialist morality, deeply involved the Komsomol. Hence it is described as an ardent supporter of the new regime.

Gubkoms were expected to demonstrate to the center that the business of Communist propaganda among the youth was at a high priority and went out of their way to report how many Red weddings took place, how many meetings and rallies were held (and on what occasion), and how many young

Communist enthusiasts participated. Gubkoms had to approve the agendas of this "voluntary organization," which usually followed the same protocol: work among peasant youth; among young workers; among young female workers and among children; anti-religious campaigns; support for the new Soviet lifestyle [*byt*], the Red Army draft, and so on. Statistical charts, campaign descriptions, and impressive numbers were all designed to demonstrate that youth was actively involved in socialist construction under the leadership of the party.

Provincial Komsomol committees were expected to show rising membership. Thus they did. In the early 1920s admission in the provinces was essentially open to all who wished to join. The Bryansk gubkom reported 5,752 Komsomol members in 1924, Vladimir over 7,000, and Voronezh 6,118.[1] Party committees set the targets for Komsomol organizations' membership growth. The Voronezh gubkom, for example, decided to set a target of 12,000 Komsomol members by the end of 1924.[2] In synch with the Lenin levy, the CP recruitment drive in 1924–5, the Komsomol expanded rapidly. In most provinces Komsomol membership outstripped that of the party. In 1925 alone 525,224 new members were admitted to the Komsomol.[3] The same rapid pace continued in 1926 and 1927, enrolling more than 200,000 members. Campaigns were launched to strengthen party leadership over the Komsomol. In September 1925 the CC issued a directive to all gubkoms to identify 30,000 active and politically reliable Komsomol members across the country and grant them simultaneous party membership. The gubkoms had target figures to fulfill proportionate to their provinces. Since there were local Komsomol cells without a single party member, the Vyatka gubkom, for example, instructed the uezds to reach the level of 10 per cent party membership in local Komsomol organizations.[4] The party controlled Komsomol composition, defined its agenda, and monitored its activity. By the end of the decade the grand total of Komsomol membership stood at one and a half million.[5] The image conveyed to Moscow was of a vibrant, dynamic, and constantly growing organization of young Communists.

RURAL CELLS: HOOLIGANISM AND DRUNKENNESS

The Komsomol's rapid expansion in the mid-1920s was largely due to peasant recruits, as they joined much more willingly than workers.[6] The CC constantly reminded province committees that Komsomol growth should be strictly controlled by the party. Gubkoms were required to maintain worker preponderance in the Komsomol's social composition so that peasant youth did not dominate local cells, even in agricultural provinces. This was easier said than done because party organizations remained comparatively small, especially in agricultural provinces. As it worked out, these rural cells failed to meet the worker quotas and had to achieve the prescribed percentages in other ways. In 1925, 141,240 members – 27 per cent of the newly admitted –

were expelled, the majority being rural residents.[7] Admission and expulsion figures demonstrate that the party pursued two objectives which proved to be incompatible: on the one hand it tried to expand membership and involve as many of society's youth as possible, while on the other it tried to retain urban control. This was nearly impossible in an agrarian society.

The problem inherent to the rural Komsomol was that it was not integrated into the fabric of rural community. In rural areas Komsomol never became a transmission belt for the party, linking it with the peasant masses. Rather it became an escape-valve mechanism for young and ambitious, mostly male, recruits, to take them away from the rural community. The problem was, as a report from Siberia explained, that "as soon as a rural fellow becomes a Komsomol member, his first priority becomes leaving for the city to study or work."[8] Membership was viewed as a ticket out, and as a result Komsomol members paid little attention to agriculture and acquired the reputation of a lazy bunch, interested only in mischief and girls. For those who stayed, there were few other opportunities in rural areas. Komsomol membership implied access to clubs, funds, entertainment, and association with other young people. The Komsomol CC investigation of the cells in Ivanovo-Voznesensk province showed that

> virtually no cultural or political educational work was carried out. Pervasive drunkenness and hooliganism was prevalent. Quarrels, rivalry, and discord plagued the cells. Rural youth unaffiliated with Komsomol had a negative view of it in all districts.[9]

The Omsk province committee wrote that "many cells were engaged in drinking to the last man [*pogolovno*]."[10] The Samara gubkom admitted that: "Komsomol members do not enjoy respect. People do not want to elect them to the soviets."[11] In Gomel province, for example, 200 Komsomol candidates in elections to village soviets were defeated, despite pressure of party officials to get them elected. A secretary for local affairs of the CC Information Department described an incident he called typical at the soviet elections in the village of Tulgovichi, in the Yurovichesky district of Gomel province in 1924:

> The secretary and members of the CP cell were trying to get a Komsomol member elected to the village soviet against the wishes of citizens who pointed out that he was dishonest. Three times the voters rejected his candidacy and abandoned the meeting, and three times they had to gather again. In the end the party secretary pulled out his revolver and threatened to arrest some of the voters. This had a desired effect and the Komsomol member was elected to the village soviet.[12]

Defeat of Komsomol members in elections was commonplace. Secret data assembled by the Komsomol Central Committee showed that as time went on the small percentage of Komsomol members in rural soviets dwindled even further. In 1924 the percentage of Komsomol members in uezd towns' soviets was 5.1 per cent and in 1926 it amounted to only 4.3 per cent; in the provincial capitals, the share decreased from 5.9 per cent to 3.8 per cent.[13]

In general the attitude of rural people towards Komsomol members was even worse than to party members. They were perceived as rowdy hooligans who had little respect for custom, tradition, law and order, or religious feelings. Citing the Tambov provincial GPU, the all-Russian GPU reported to the CC that:

> The peasants' attitude to Komsomol is negative. The most wretched elements in the countryside enroll: hooligans, drunkards, and outright thieves. Komsomol cells organize real drunken orgies. When drunk, they swear. Komsomol members of the village of Kuratovo robbed a mill.[14]

In 1922–3 rural Komsomol acquired notoriety because of its provocative actions in the anti-religious campaign. As mentioned above, rural Komsomol members disrupted Easter processions, took priests hostage, threw stones at churches, and took part in other mischief, parading their struggle with "religious superstition."[15] A monthly survey of the Komsomol's activities in Siberia in 1925 listed dozens of examples of Komsomol's anti-religious struggle. In one town a Komsomol cell made a list of believers, imposed a 10-ruble "indemnity" upon them, and appropriated the funds. In another during the Komsomol Easter they publicly abused God with the dirtiest of oaths.[16] The North Caucasus committee reported that one cell wrote a letter to a priest threatening to shoot him if he did not stop preaching. Another cell member extinguished a cigarette butt on the forehead of a priest during Easter service.[17] And the Voronezh province Komsomol committee reported that a local cell bombarded a sacred icon with rotten eggs during the service.[18]

The party officials were appalled by how the Komsomol attracted "activists," who were in reality trouble-makers, gang leaders, and drunken brawlers. A Komsomol district committee in Ivanovo province described cultural practices in the countryside:

> Carousing is always followed by fist fights among the young. They come from far away villages deliberately to get revenge against someone, some old enemy, who had done something in the past. This usually serves as a pretext for a fight which usually ends with beatings and killings.[19]

A village female schoolteacher in Nerekhta uezd complained to the district EC that Komsomol activists were regularly having boisterous parties with drinking and dancing in the library. The inquiry confirmed the complaint. The Komsomol activists refused to discontinue their parties.[20]

The Komsomol was not a vanguard of worker and peasant youth, but a marginal organization in rural Russia, confused about its purpose and identity. By 1928 Komsomol cells in the countryside were mostly ostracized and an insignificant minority, while, by contrast, religious youth associations were experiencing a genuine upsurge, as were religious congregations in general. Relatively little is known about the numerous religious associations in the countryside. All indications are that they involved hundreds of thousands of young men and women. These were genuine and truly voluntary youth movements that by far eclipsed the Komsomol as a social and cultural presence in the countryside. In a secret memorandum to Molotov on the activity of anti-Soviet organizations, the Central Committee's Information Department wrote:

> All over Siberia, cases are being registered of spontaneous organizing of associations of youth, such as Union of Non-party Youth, or the Socialist Union. Recently all the Baptists' congregations have received instructions to organize sections for youth in the uezds.[21]

Under the term "anti-Soviet organizations," the CC listed associations with very different memberships and constituencies. The Socialist Union was basically an association in the tradition of the SRs. Without explicitly identifying this connection, it resembled the Peasant Union movement in its emphasis on peasant self-rule, free elections, and fair taxation. Another memorandum, "Anti-Communist Organizations of Youth in Siberia," explained:

> In order to avoid "Communist contamination" – and this is how they refer to the Komsomol in villages – village elders organize youth into a union, which they call the Union of Peasant Youth. And they are trying to attract all the youth in the village into it.[22]

Orthodox, Baptist, and Evangelist associations were somewhat different. They did not pursue political objectives, at least in public. Their aim was to attract youth to a religious community, where spiritual themes were dominant. In Leningrad province alone the official report listed twenty-five religious associations of various denominations with a membership of over a hundred thousand.[23] In addition to Bible reading and discussion, regular activities included tea parties, harmonica playing, choir singing, religious theatrical performances, and, of course, celebration of all the rituals and holidays in the Christian calendar. In Moscow at several factories groups of a Christian Union of Youth were formed, inviting young workers to their evenings, discussions, and Bible readings in their leaflets.[24] In the countryside and small industrial towns sectarian and even Orthodox religious ideas were making a strong comeback. The special report explained:

> The religious and sectarian movement is noticeably livening up both in cities and in the countryside . . . Sectarians organize evenings, concerts, choirs, musical shows, discussions of various topics, and so on. There were instances when Komsomol members came to these evenings just to look and then went over to them, quitting the Komsomol. Anti-religious struggle

almost everywhere has died down, and systematic work is not carried on anywhere.[25]

In the conditions of free competition, the Communist offensive on the rural youth front collapsed in disgrace. Komsomol cells in rural areas had little to do with Marxism, Leninism, or socialism. They were simply groups, mostly of young men, who used their Komsomol membership for social activities and drinking parties.[26] What comes across as revolutionary zeal in the anti-religious struggle to some and as common hooliganism to others was in fact a rebellion against authority in the countryside. The Komsomol attracted youth who did not want to submit to established cultural practices. In "hooligan" or "revolutionary" acts these young men showed their independence from the village elders. Before too long, the party, in addition to the village elders, discovered that rebellion against authority was a major problem among Komsomol members.

WORKERS: VODKA, SEX, AND DEFIANCE

Vodka

As in the countryside, most Komsomol cells in workers' neighborhoods and townships were least of all concerned with grand political issues of the day. Many of those who joined saw Komsomol membership as a means to improve their situation in life. A study of the Moscow city Komsomol organization noted that the unemployed were particularly anxious to join:

> Among the unemployed, the majority of Komsomol members are inveterate trouble-makers. Many of them flaunt their Komsomol membership, demand jobs without waiting for their turn, saying: "Since we are Komsomol members, send us in."[27]

When Komsomol membership did not interfere with young people's other activities and aspirations, they willingly joined. When, however, they felt that there was nothing particularly interesting to be gained from that membership, they quit without hesitation. At the Diad'kovskaia factory in Bryansk province, 50 out of 170 members submitted petitions to quit: "We ask you not to consider us members any longer because there is nothing to do in the Komsomol." A report to the Central Committee cited what it claimed were typical pronouncements about the Komsomol by young workers:

> You don't have anything good in the Komsomol. There isn't order . . . What difference does it make whether I am a member or not? I can be a hooligan regardless, so what's the point? What good would it do for me?

And one young man explained his refusal to join like this: "If I want to get a drink, I'll get a drink, if I want to go to a party, I can go to a party, but a Komsomol member can't. So why should I join?"[28] The membership turnover in the Komsomol was greater than in the party. In 1926, for example, for every seven new recruits there were two who quit or were expelled.[29] As a result local party officials reported vastly inflated membership figures. In Bryansk province, for example, there were 1,040 "dead souls," as they were called, whose names were kept on the books for the purpose of inflating the statistics. At the locomotive plant alone, there were more than a hundred "dead souls."[30] In numerous local organizations, no records were kept and no dues were paid. No one knew how many Komsomol members there were.

Komsomol membership for many was no more than a chance to socialize with other young people. Dancing, partying, and drinking were their main preoccupations. The Leningrad Komsomol Committee admitted that Komsomol members "attended meetings reluctantly, and were not interested in political education, but in organizing dancing parties instead."[31] What the young people detested most, it seems, was attending propaganda meetings and being lectured to. Most meetings were held for the sole purpose of listing them in the monthly or quarterly reports on conducted campaigns and activities to the CC, as one of the special reports from Bryansk describes:

> Usually no explanatory work of any kind was conducted. What kind of meeting was going to take place? What kind of questions would be discussed? What would they vote for? The working youth is not aware of any of this . . . One has the impression that the Komsomol cell gathers a meeting for the rubber-stamping of its activity. Having come to the meeting, the young people can't wait to take to their heels [*smotat' s nego*].[32]

According to the GPU in 1925 pervasive drunkenness of Communist and Komsomol cells in Leningrad province "became an everyday occurrence." And workers of the Liberated Labor factory in Yaroslavl' province were complaining about "drunkenness of Communists and Komsomol members, calling them profligate drunkards and self-seekers."[33] A report from the Krasnaya Presnya district in Moscow admitted that: "drunkenness and hooliganism are widespread primarily because our Komsomol cells are ill-adapted to address the needs of youth."[34] As a result, Komsomol cells regularly degenerated into companies of drinking pals. An investigation of the *Rabochaya Gazeta* cell revealed:

> abnormal relations between the guys and girls. The leadership of the cell has degenerated morally. It organized systematically wild parties with the consumption of alcoholic beverages. (Sixty bottles of various kinds were found.)[35]

Likewise, Komsomol weddings conformed to the revolutionary standard on paper only. In actuality they were rowdy parties with lots of food and drink which hardly differed from traditional weddings except for the absence of a priest. Hundreds of reports like these from virtually everywhere suggest that

Komsomol workers were no different from other youth. They wanted entertainment, excitement, and a good time. Party officials and the rest of society defined it as mischief, hooliganism, and alcoholism.

Party reports frankly described the miserable living quarters of young workers in dorms, their pay being barely half that of adult workers. Having no place of his own, a teenage worker spent most of his time hanging around with his gang after work. Fist fights, drinking, swearing, and mischief were their main preoccupations. The Ul'yanovsk province committee identified the

> causes of pervasive drunkenness in the unsatisfactory work of clubs. It is boring and the guys run away to the movies to watch films like *The House of Hatred* or *The Hero of Alaska* . . . The activists busy themselves with playing cards and drinking and the rank and file follow the example of the activists.[36]

Working-class youth seem to have been interested in Komsomol only insofar as it could add spice and excitement to their lives. Their own subculture was far removed from the concerns of proletarian revolution or construction of socialism. After a work day at the factory, they wanted to get as far away as possible and have fun: go to a party, date girls, or drink with friends. A CC report from Bryansk described young workers' habits:

> After the siren, a young worker breaks loose and runs home. At eight or nine in the evening, he goes out until one or two in the morning. What they usually do is walk up and down the main street, polishing it, as the saying goes here. If they have a girlfriend, they see her off home at about three or four in the morning. Then they go to bed, to get up in a few hours and go to work and then it starts all over again. The folks here call this schedule the "devil's wheel."[37]

On pay day the custom was to get drunk with one's buddies. In winter there were typically several parties on every block. At such drinking parties, young workers played cards and boasted about how many girls they had slept with. The other kind of party was with girlfriends:

> And so they go to the party. They dance and drink and sing abominably obscene couplets [*chastushki*]. Pervasive drunkenness is on the rise. The parties usually end with fist fights and acts of hooliganism.[38]

In the official press, it looked as if workers' clubs were the bustling centers for the ideological education of the masses. In fact these were clubs like any other, attracting large crowds – only not to lectures on Marxism–Leninism, but to occasional films and more regular dances. In Bryansk these were usually followed by fist fights:

> In winter the club is a favorite meeting place for the hooligans. The extent of hooliganism in the clubs is such that it is suppressed with difficulty by

the most decisive administrative measures. Quite often, the police prefers not to interfere, fearing the hooligans.[39]

A survey of workers' clubs in Leningrad showed that most of them were half-empty or dominated by adults. Only one, "attached to the Rabotnitsa factory, had a youth evening, but that consisted of only a loud band and young people dancing the fox-trot."[40] As Preobrazhensky put it in 1926: "Our clubs are empty but the pubs are full."[41]

The Komsomol leadership was so worried by the stream of reports from the provinces on drunkenness and hooliganism that it issued a special resolution in 1926 on "Strengthening Mass Cultural Work in Connection with the Growth of Drunkenness and Hooliganism among the Youth."[42] The resolution instructed local cells to make Komsomol clubs centers of the struggle against drunkenness, mischief, swearing, and promiscuity. The task of the Komsomol was strengthening "healthy forms of entertainment." Instead of drinking parties, vodka, fox-trot, sex, and lechery, the Komsomol was to organize folk-dancing groups, sports activities, storytelling, evenings of readings, games, and harmonica playing.

An important role in combating "hold-overs of the bourgeois culture" was assigned to workers' amateur theater groups.[43] These groups seem to have been genuinely popular during the height of NEP precisely because they dramatized everyday situations. The main themes were hooliganism, anti-Semitism, alienation, and gender relations. Workers recognized themselves and identified with the views, attitudes, and problems depicted in the plays.[44] Young workers were crazy about the fox-trot, fashionable dress, and merry-making. Factory boys' and girls' heroes were not conscientious proletarians building socialism, but characters from Western films. As one study put it:

> One of the most visible and to many Bolsheviks problematic expressions of cultural resistance were those Soviet youth who adopted flapper fashions of Paris and New York and danced to the seductive rhythms of American jazz. These young people resisted the serious and sometimes puritanical images of Bolshevik ideology and culture in favor of playful forms of entertainment and personal expression that studiously avoided politics.[45]

The paradox was that the 1920s saw Western popular culture affect Russian working-class youth to an extent unheard of before. Thus, at the time when Soviet youth was bombarded with Agitprop's exhortations to build a new socialist culture, they were actually drawn to Western popular culture – fashion, dancing, and jazz.[46]

Sex

The Bolsheviks expected to replace "bourgeois" morality with a new socialist morality; instead young workers responded with a rebellion against

The announcements read: "Today. A Debate on Sex," "A Lecture by Professor ... The Problem of Sex in the Middle Ages and Today," "Auditorium of the Polytechnic Museum: A Debate on the Problems of Sex," "A Report: The Question of Sex in Contemporary Literature."

Figure 3 The Spring Freshet
Source: *Bich* No. 16 (1928), p. 7

propriety, conformity, and decency.[47] A special report to Stalin spoke of the "widespread growth of drunkenness, hooliganism, and sexual promiscuity."[48] Young people had appropriated the Bolshevik "Down with Bourgeois Morality" campaign in their own way. Marriage was associated with hardship, responsibility, and constraint, especially since obtaining living quarters for young couples was virtually impossible. Sex without marriage was in vogue, as was vodka and partying. Young women who wanted to get married were sneered at as bourgeois maidens. As one report explained: "Young men regard sexual relations lightheartedly. They try to make young women sleep with them and then dump them. A girl who does not agree is called petty bourgeois."[49]

A prevalent view among those who considered themselves advanced was that marriage was a bourgeois hold-over. According to a survey of attitudes among young women, "the majority of male Komsomol members continued to regard female Komsomol members primarily as a means to sexual pleasure rather than as comrades."[50] The Kursk province report admitted that among male Komsomol members the usual practice was "to go feel-up [*polapat'*] the girls."[51] Many male Komsomol members retained disdain for young women who took initiative in public or did not guard themselves in their relations with men. Any openness was misinterpreted as sexual availability; as a consequence many women endured sexual harassment. According to the Voronezh Women's Department:

> As a result of our work in all the uezds of the province among young unmarried women, 1,872 entered Komsomol ranks. Despite this achievement, the process of their integration goes slowly because there is an unfavorable climate for young unmarried women in the Komsomol. Hooliganism, swearing, sneering, and sexual advances – these are the negative phenomena slowing down the female membership drive.[52]

In theory the Komsomol ranks were open to both young men and women. In practice, however, young women shied away from Komsomol membership. On average there was no more than 15 per cent female membership in the Komsomol throughout the 1920s. In some urban centers the level reached 20 per cent, but in rural areas it hovered at 5 per cent to 10 per cent.[53] In some instances the very attempt to attract more young women to the Komsomol degenerated into sexual harassment. A Ukrainian rural Komsomol cell decided to enroll more women, their slogan being "Let every Komsomol member draw one woman in!" It was supposed to be a Komsomol link-up [*smychka*] with young women. The campaign ended with a stream of complaints from pregnant village girls claiming that Komsomol activists had promised to marry them, but had instead abandoned them.[54]

Komsomol women were often expected readily to enter into sexual relations. Somewhat misrepresenting the practice, provincial Komsomol reports referred to it as "prostitution," whereas what they really meant was unrestrained, promiscuous sex. For example, a Black Sea Coast province report referred to "pervasive drunkenness among Komsomol guys and prostitution among Komsomol girls." One young woman was asked why she refused to enter Komsomol, and her answer was that if she became a Komsomol member she would be expected to have sex with whoever asked her to.[55] Sexual advances against female Komsomol members were cited as typical in the Komsomol. In Zvenigorod, Moscow province, one activist asserted that Komsomol was "making hooligans out of nice fellows and whores out of good girls. Once members they all begin to engage in promiscuous behavior: 50 per cent of female Komsomol members are screwing around and making abortions."[56]

Identical reports came to Moscow from virtually all provinces. In Tula 40 per cent of female Komsomol cell members had had abortions. The Komsomol CC wrote with apprehension about "entire cells engaged in debauchery to the last person. They organize drunken bacchanalia followed by sexual orgies."[57] In Simbirsk "guys regard girls only as sexual objects, evaluating them from the sexual point of view exclusively, and all their conversations revolve around the topic of the sexual act, and variety thereof."[58] In some provinces groups, circles, and associations began to spring up celebrating free sex without marriage or obligation. In Zlatoust' in the Urals, for example, a "Down with Virginity" society was formed.[59]

The infamous glass of water theory was indeed quite popular among the youth. According to an attentive observer, "Books, like those of Aleksandra Kolontai were promoting an absurdly simple theory of 'free love'; childish materialism was reducing the 'sexual need' to a fundamental of carnal desire: 'We have intercourse for the same reason that we drink a glass of water, to slake our thirst.'"[60] Whether Kolontai meant her theories to be understood in the way that they were, the outcome was liberation from restraint. According to the special report, "Young Women in the Komsomol":

> Such phenomena as hooliganism and sexual promiscuity generate un-healthy consequences. At the Nogin factory in Moscow, for example, the youth, including Komsomol members, both male and female, swap "wives" and "husbands" as gloves. Sometimes girls turn into hooligans no more virtuous than the guys.[61]

Another report noted that factory girls and especially female students including Komsomol members "simultaneously had several rich 'husbands' who supported them financially."[62]

Consensual sex among Komsomol members often degenerated into little more than rape. The Ul'yanovsk province Komsomol committee reported an "abnormal situation, with group consumption of alcohol, followed by hooligan-ism and gang rape of girls."[63] At the end of 1926 the entire country followed the infamous Chubarov alley rape case. A young woman was raped by twenty-seven assailants in Leningrad. Dozens and dozens of articles discussed the problem of hooliganism, sexual promiscuity, and abuse of women.

The Chubarov case acquired notoriety as a particularly gruesome incident which triggered a new round of anti-hooliganism campaigns. Dozens of rape cases were reported in monthly provincial reports. Some of them stemmed from drinking parties, while others were cases of abuse of authority. As the Komsomol CC report explained: "Such cases [of rape] are not isolated incidents. In some places, sexual promiscuity assumes particularly disgusting forms. All kinds of circles and groups are created with the active participation of Komsomol members."[64] Several reports listed cases of rape involving Komsomol members province by province. The overall pattern reflects an increase in the incidence of rape between the mid- and late 1920s both in urban and rural areas.[65]

Clearly, hooliganism, sexual promiscuity, and rape were not merely hold-overs from the "bourgeois" past. The problem the Bolsheviks did not want to face was that the debunking of religion and attacks on courtship, the family,

A Thousand and One Nights

Figure 4 Unfortunately, not a fairy tale
Source: *Buzutyor* No. 21 (1926)

and the private sphere necessarily encouraged a "utilitarian" attitude to women. On the other hand, the reappearance of "bourgeois" mind-sets in NEP Russia generated another explosive cultural conflict, as one researcher explained:

> In contrast to these youths, who, depending on their behavior, were classified as "uncultured" or "pessimistic," were those who threw themselves wholeheartedly into NEP, drinking and gambling, ready to exploit and be exploited. Often the line between the rejection and acceptance of NEP was blurred, as portraits of youthful depravity combined elements of War Communism's crudeness with self-destructive despair and with acquisitive egotism.[66]

Comrade Semashko: "Citizen Hooligans! Don't kill. This is not hygienic!"

Figure 5 Special Edition on Hooliganism
Source: *Buzutyor* No. 21 (1926)

Restaurants, cafés, cabarets, exquisite food, foreign cars, fox-trot, and elegant women – all these attributes of "bourgeois" civilization were present in the capital cities in quantities enough to be tempting. Working-class youth and Komsomol idealists were instructed to condemn all of it, and yet the allure was overwhelming. Unable to be a part of the world of the rich and famous but drawn by the seductive images of fox-trot and Western films of the "good life," all the while encouraged to reject it in public, youth reacted unpredictably. Hooliganism and rape were therefore youth's violent responses to social and cultural realities of NEP Russia.

Defiance

Tens of thousands – in fact more than a hundred thousand – Komsomol members had to be expelled for drunkenness and hooliganism in 1926 alone. Statistics indicated that the number of people voluntarily quitting the Komsomol each year was on the rise. In working-class neighborhoods the Komsomol was unpopular "as an organization dominated by the intelligentsia and a meeting place for hooligans."[67] Many comments ridiculed "the endless political study, and boring lectures on political literacy."[68] The survey of Komsomol members' attitudes in Moscow was titled "Malaise." According to the Komsomol CC in 1927:

> Apathy, disillusionment, and decadent attitudes are not only among the main body of youth, but among the leaders. And as a direct result of these attitudes, we find a growth in manifestations of malaise such as drunkenness, hooliganism, and suicide.

This report was published only for key Komsomol and party leaders in eighty-five copies, frankly admitting that the Communist message and the organization called upon to spread it among the youth were in crisis.[69]

Manifest avoidance of "politics" was itself a political act. By ignoring political involvement, most young workers were sending a message that they did not care about official campaigns. When explicitly political issues affected their lives and interests, they got involved with as much vigor and passion as they could muster.[70] In the last years of NEP, the biggest issue of all was the so-called rationalization campaign, which sought to increase production rates without pay raises. Unskilled teenage workers, who received no more than 30 per cent or 40 per cent of adult workers' wages for similar work, were ardent opponents of rationalization.[71] They lived mostly in dormitories and ate in cafeterias. A lot of them had the reputation of being hooligans and trouble-makers. Those who joined Komsomol ridiculed the bosses, the party leaders, and Komsomol itself.

In the Khamovnicheskii district, a party official wrote down some of the sentiments expressed: "They were complaining that NEPmen were riding in automobiles and homeless children were everywhere."[72] Hostility to the newly rich was widespread among the workers. Someone deciphered the acronym NEP as new exploitation policy. Party officials did not discourage hostility to specialists and NEPmen, interpreting it as revolutionary zeal. Yet, at those same meetings, most speakers equated the NEPmen and specialists with party officials: "Why are party officials riding in automobiles, taking vacations at resorts, and entertaining their wives in restaurants, while workers can't afford any of this?"[73] At the Hammer and Sickle plant Komsomol members voiced the views of many workers, saying: "They keep talking about raising the productivity of labor but they themselves get high salaries. The director is riding in an automobile and we workers, supposedly the owners, walk on foot."[74] The GPU intercepted a letter from a Komsomol worker from the Urals working in Moscow:

> The majority of those who hold the levers of the dictatorship of the proletariat here in Moscow, as well as what remains of the rotten intelligentsia, live in luxurious apartments and regularly commute to their country-houses [*dacha*]. On one hand, a part of the proletariat – entire families – sleep on bare floors and plead for a piece of bread, hungry, cold, and barefoot. The other "part of the proletariat" glut themselves in restaurants.[75]

Komsomol speakers showed little respect for top party leaders and their teachings. At meetings comments could be heard like: "Zinoviev and Stalin are fighting with each other. Why should we study them?" And one female Komsomol student said: "Yes, comrades, we know what kind of disagreement he had with Zinoviev. They fought over portfolios."[76]

A special study, based on an analysis of comments and questions at various meetings, and commissioned in 1927 for the top party and Komsomol leadership, highlighted inter-ethnic friction in the Komsomol:

> Data is coming in from many local organizations about growing nationalist sentiment. All organizations state the fact that chauvinism is increasing. Anti-Semitic attitudes are on the rise not only among the peasants and workers, but among Komsomol members.[77]

No discussion of any problem in this regard was permitted in official media. Any manifestation of ethnic prejudice was brushed aside as a hold-over of the bourgeois era. In a country of workers and peasants there was no (and *could* be no) ethnic prejudice. In fact, popular anti-Semitism among workers and Komsomol members was often linked to NEP. Jews were envied as they were perceived to be those who enjoyed upward mobility. Views like these were typical: "Jews live well. All Jews are traders and NEPmen, and those who are in the party are there only for their own benefit."[78] As to what should be done about it, the views varied, but some were quite extreme: "A pogrom is needed" or as a Communist worker in the township of Serpukhov put it: "If someone said: 'Go beat the Jews,' I'd be the first to go."[79] To underscore the point that these were not isolated incidents, the report concluded: "Such reasoning is noted almost without exception by all organizations – in Ukraine, Moscow, Leningrad, Tula, Tatariya, Vologda, Ryazan', and others."[80] In Kuban' young peasants and Cossacks were saying: "If it were not for the Jews, there would be no Soviet power and it would be easier to live; the Jews hold everything in their hands in the USSR." Among the working-class youth anti-Semitic attitudes were also growing more pervasive.[81]

In some cities, underground anti-Semitic groups formed. Their main objective was "struggle with the Jews with all means available, up to and including terror." In Moscow an anti-Semitic group, the Russian National-Communist Union of Youth, was plotting to blow up the synagogue. It consisted of eighteen adherents (all Komsomol members) and had branches in other cities. The key ingredients in its ideology were virulent anti-Semitism, Russian nationalism, and Communist egalitarianism.[82] Another anti-Semitic group calling itself Russian Komsomolets made its existence known through a demand to "shake off the yoke of the kikes" in its leaflets.[83]

Jewish youth was very sensitive to the problem of anti-Semitism. The Komsomol CC reported that in Ukraine, particularly in small towns with large Jewish minorities, well-funded Zionists were making tremendous gains among the Jewish youth. They accused the Soviet government of continuing the same policy as the Tsarist government had. Anti-Semites were still in power, discrimination was still a menace, and the authorities encouraged anti-Semitism. Zionist leaflets demanded Jewish self-rule, free religious practice, and unobstructed emigration to Palestine.[84]

That anti-Semitism persisted in the Russia of the 1920s, especially in conditions of economic hardship, is not surprising. Ethnic prejudice, however, was widespread in Tatariya, where Russian residents complained that "the Russians are being squeezed out," while Tatars countered that "Russians control everything, and we are not free."[85] The Caucasus and Central Asia were rife with ethnic enmities, and anti-Semitic attitudes in Ukraine were matched by anti-Russian sentiment.

In 1927 radical rejection of NEP and privilege gave way to political protest. Worse, Komsomol members were often "taking active part in work slowdowns and strikes at the factories and plants."[86] Political and religious teachings critical of Communism found eager audiences not only among working-class and peasant youth, but among Komsomol members, including activists:

> In search of the new ideas and while trying to satisfy their cultural needs, a part of the Komsomol – the least conscious and politically illiterate – is falling under the influence of parties and groups which are ideologically inimical to Soviet power. The development of anti-Soviet, Menshevik, Socialist Revolutionary, and anarcho-syndicalist attitudes

takes root quickly among this politically unstable part of the working-class and peasant youth.[87]

If we decode the meaning of these politically loaded terms, it appears that "anarcho-syndicalism" meant a protest against higher production rates without a corresponding pay increase; "SR deviation" meant sympathy with the plight of peasants; while "anti-Soviet" meant hostility to the party hierarchy. In July 1927 the Komsomol CC informed the party CC that anarchist, Trotskyite, and Menshevik groups had been formed in Voronezh, Ul'yanovsk, Kharkov, and Leningrad and their leaders were former Komsomol and party members.[88] In Moscow, Leningrad, and Kharkov, a platform for the Komsomol convention was drafted which focused on production rates, wages for teenage workers, and privileges for the party bosses and Red directors. The opposition printed leaflets, appeals, and proposals. They established informal channels of communication between various cities and distributed dissident literature across the country.[89]

Things came to a head in October 1927. Well before the well-known protest action by Trotsky and his supporters on the tenth anniversary of the October Revolution, dozens of Komsomol functionaries were arrested by the GPU and charged with "counterrevolutionary activity."[90] After the October démarche arrests were widened to include hundreds of oppositionists and critics. The Komsomol CC and the Bolshevik leaders refuted their critics with violence and repression, not well-crafted argument – a pattern to be repeated in the following months and years. After the wave of purges and arrests, a mass flight of youth from the Komsomol began. According to a secret Komsomol CC report to the Central Control Commission:

> During 1927 and the first half of 1928, 442,396 people left the Komsomol. In comparison with the previous years, there is a definite increase in the number of those voluntarily quitting the Komsomol. Today, for every fifteen newly admitted members, ten quit the Komsomol.[91]

STUDENTS: POVERTY, "DECADENCE," AND DISSENT

Poverty

The traditional culture of Russian students was socialist oriented towards "serving the people." This spirit remained after the civil war, although the student body was changing. The social and cultural tensions in the institutes and universities set old intelligentsia against newly promoted cadres on the one hand, while pitting a shrinking body of regular students admitted on the basis of merit against proletarian promotees on the other. These ill-prepared students were insecure and disoriented, resenting the intelligentsia professors who judged their knowledge and skills rather than social origin. Close encounters between the two generated incomprehension, distrust, and hostility. Non-proletarian students were appalled by the new students' lack of culture and low level of education. They were barely literate and unprepared for the level the universities required. They also resented the new students calling them "bourgeois parasites," "capitalist exploiters," and "privileged scum." The old-time students not only considered themselves sons and daughters of the people too, but knew that they had the years of learning behind them to qualify them for university study. They felt that the upstarts called them abusive names because they envied their culture and knowledge. As one student put it: "They call us bourgeois but it is they who are getting privileged rations, whereas we are starving."[92]

Workers' faculty graduates believed that old-time students looked down upon them, and, basking in their superiority, tried to convey that they did not deserve to be at a university. The proletarian promotees responded in a variety of ways. Some could not handle the pressure and returned home; others tried to work hard and reach the required level; still others developed a strong resentment of the cultured and spectacled "bourgeois parasites" and clung to the milieu of the Communist or Komsomol cells where they felt at home.

According to the Don host party committee, the proletarian students' level of preparation was poor. A senior workers' faculty student in her fourth year of study made twenty-five spelling mistakes in her application for a stipend.[93] The situation was not easy to remedy, since there were no textbooks and no funds. Facilities were in terrible shape. The pay scales for the teaching faculty were miserable. Many professors had no living accommodation: in Rostov-on-Don, forty-two professors slept in their offices, lacking their own housing. To improve their situation was not the party's priority, since they were "bourgeois specialists." They stayed in their jobs out of a sense of duty, or simply because they had nowhere else to go.

Students' material situation was just as miserable. Most of them arrived in the big city full of enthusiasm. Typically they had nothing but a piece of paper that such and such a party committee had sent them to study. When they went through all the bureaucratic procedures of enrollment, they were often disappointed to find that a bare minimum of food and shelter were lacking. As late as 1926, only 36 per cent of all students received a stipend.[94] All others had to find means to support themselves on their own. A CC report admitted that: "A student with a stipend and a dormitory is indeed lucky."[95] Those lucky ones could barely make ends meet on their 23 rubles a month.

The quality of dormitories varied a great deal. Some had basic facilities for a minority of students; most did not. Students had to endure truly unbearable conditions. An official of the Commissariat of Education sent a troubling letter to Molotov on the conditions in dormitories. There were only 25 beds for 176 resident students and those without beds slept on dirty mattresses on the floor. Some windows were broken.

- It goes without saying that some residents of such dormitories get colds very quickly. The lighting is poor. There are few textbooks. Students' food rations are very meager and delivered irregularly. Some students support themselves by selling their belongings. Some would like to return home but lack means to do it. There have been cases of suicide caused by terrible poverty.
- Some cases are worse: Female students, who have literally no means of support, resort to prostitution. There have been cases when a young female student has had to endure two other female students engaging in prostitution in the same dormitory room.
- In a short article I cannot use all the materials at hand. But the overall picture is depressing. Hundreds, indeed thousands of youths fruitlessly waste their time and efforts, ruining their health. Some degenerate morally.[96]

A resolution of the CC Secret Department written on the front page of this memorandum banned it from publication.

"Decadence"[97]

Student life in the 1920s was almost automatically equated with poverty. The majority of students had to work on the side to make ends meet. If a student was married, the best he could hope for was a room somewhere, but more often a rented "corner" of a room with privacy provided by a curtain. Shortage of living space was one of the central concerns. In such conditions, the boundary between married and non-married sexual unions became blurred. Living together was considered a civil marriage. Only some marriages were registered. Some lasted, others did not. Students' material and emotional lives were unsettled and unstable. Promiscuous sexual bonding was in vogue, unbound by commitment to family building.

The poet Yesenin became a cult figure. His popularity was so strong that the Communist authorities coined a new term – Yeseninshchina – to describe decadence, apathy, and escapism. It was a cult of melancholic reflection, detachment from reality, and withdrawal into sensuality and mysticism.[98] Lunacharsky, People's Commissar of Education, cited what he called typical attitudes: "Yesenin – that is interesting, that is for your soul, and the revolution is stale and dry and we are tired of it."[99] Reflecting on these trends among students, *Komsomol'skaya Pravda* summarized views expressed in what it termed as typical letters:

The youth is right to be crazy about Yesenin. Yesenin is a part of every young person's soul. There is no freedom of thought. The only way out is to withdraw into one's self. The youth is beginning to be genuinely interested in religion. Religion is becoming necessary for youth.[100]

Interest in religion and Yesenin was, in a sense, a protest against Soviet collectivism. It was an affirmation of the self. The official emphasis on the public left no room for the private; official exuberant optimism left no ways of dealing with doubt. The official cheapening of religion as mere superstition intensified interest in the eternal questions of the meaning of life, faith, love, and belief. One person and his inner world fascinated young men and women. Various circles of students appeared studying religious philosophy, reading Dostoevsky and Berdiaev. To quote from another letter of a Komsomol member reflecting on the mood of the young people:

> I have been in the Komsomol for six years already. I feel that the foundation is collapsing below us. All my old convictions which saturated me during the revolutionary years are slowly being undermined, are being displaced from my mind by the flow of our day-to-day life. Our "apostles" are leading us in darkness, sweetening us with the illusion of a bright future, which hardly promises anything good . . . Our life is beautiful and joyful only in the press . . . What reigns in the institutions of higher learning is either indifference or discontent.[101]

Dozens of cases of suicide were reported among students, usually accompanied by a protest letter. Typical in this regard was a letter from an art school student:

> It has always seemed to me that scandalous injustice reigns in Soviet land. On the one hand, enormous riches, on the other, depressing poverty. On one hand, fat NEPmen in bustling cafés, on the other, homeless children and starving students.[102]

Another student from Moscow University who committed suicide left a note full of bitterness about the Komsomol, saying it was

> rife with glaring careerism and bureaucratism. The Komsomol has split into two parts: activists and non-activists. All one has to do to those who are "activists" is pin stars in their lapels and you will have perfect state assessors with the right to occupy some important posts; as for the non-activists, some of them work hard to pass a test and then go to a tavern to get drunk or look for a prostitute. Out of the present generation of students will come either disgusting bureaucrats or lusty bribe-takers.[103]

Some students submitted their protest declarations in writing to the Komsomol or university administration. Guided by idealism, they refused to contemplate injustice quietly. They knew that a defiant act would lead to their expulsion at best, if not to a charge of anti-Soviet activity. And yet, hundreds of protest letters were submitted in the late 1920s. One of them was from a student from the Institute of People's Economy:

> Don't we have enough of the shameful facts when some enter Komsomol in order to have a chance to enter a university? Don't we have enough

examples when they enter Komsomol to receive a stipend? In fact, the majority of students just want to make a career by using the Komsomol to that end.[104]

Most suicide letters focused on social injustice, poverty, and bureaucratization, conveying a feeling of there being no way out.

Dissent

Those interested in politics, especially among the leadership, were naturally drawn to the forbidden, to the controversial, to the exciting and new ideas circulating in self-produced pamphlets and journals.[105] One student summarized objections of many to the doctrinaire and intellectually suffocating ideological requirements of the party line in an open letter:

> The Komsomol organization provides its members with only the monotonous teaching of Communism, without any reference to or arguments and views of other socialist parties and their leaders. And even if it refers to these views, they come prepackaged by the Main Political Enlightenment [Committee] or by the Central Committee or some other committee in such a distorted fashion that, as a result, there is no way whatsoever for critical thought to develop.[106]

Officially required polit-study was boring, socialist teaching of a non-Communist genre was banned, and Trotsky's ideas were taboo. This was hardly an inspiring intellectual atmosphere. As a result new, genuinely voluntary, and unsanctioned informal political associations sprang up, led by current or former Komsomol members.

One of the most interesting in this regard was the Union of Young Marxists. These were young people genuinely interested in Marxism in a country that professed Marxism as its official state ideology. And yet the unofficial study of Marxism, of Menshevik or European Marxism, was not allowed. Komsomol leaders found no better tactic to deal with the Young Marxists than to inform the GPU. In Crimea an underground student organization "Freethinking Youth," professing SR political philosophy, spoke in its underground leaflets of the Constituent Assembly and democracy.[107] In 1927 this definitely qualified as "counterrevolution."

In Moscow, a Left SR informal student association was likewise "exposed" by vigilant GPU agents in 1926. In the "Open Letter to Students and Workers' Faculties," they attacked bureaucrats and careerists who had sold out to the GPU. They praised the revolution, the development of critical thought, individual liberty, and open debate among all socialists, both in Russia and beyond. Without it, the revolution and the cause of socialism were turning into an atrophied dogma.[108] In Saratov University a Baptist student organization was suppressed in 1928.[109] Marxist, neo-populist, and liberal ideas in the tradition of the Menshevik, SR, and Kadet parties were wide-spread among urban youth, especially students.

The GPU surveys for 1927 and 1928 show an increase rather than decline in the critical attitudes of professors and students, especially in big cities:

> During the elections of the Leningrad soviet, anti-Soviet activities took place among teachers, students, and professors. They campaigned against electing Communist Party members. They were going from school to school, trying to persuade [people] not to vote for Communist Party candidates. At open election meetings, they spoke out against the Communists. They were saying that the teachers of the USSR have been deprived of political rights.[110]

These teachers were not doing anything illegal by campaigning in elections and yet the GPU described their actions as "anti-Soviet activity." The GPU report continued: "At the election meeting of fourteen teachers' committees, the mood was anti-Soviet. The decision adopted was to fail the Communists at elections."[111] In virtually every city in Russia and Ukraine the teaching faculties of schools and universities argued that Communist Party candidates should not be forced on the electorate; that the freedom to campaign should be guaranteed; that political rights be granted to all citizens of Soviet Russia; and that schools and universities should retain their traditional academic freedoms.

Consider basic data on all institutions of higher learning in Leningrad in 1926. There were 33,475 students in all fourteen institutions of higher learning plus workers' faculties in 1926, without Rabfak, 29,058. Of those, only 13 per cent were CP members and only 13.9 per cent Komsomol members. Among professors and teaching faculty the percentage of CP members was in single figures.[112] More unsettling was that the non-Communist professors' and students' influence was expanding among the majority of the student body. The party bosses expressed their concern over several cases when rectors who openly opposed Communist policies were elected at institutes and universities. In Leningrad Polytechnic, for example, by the overwhelming majority of professors' and teaching faculty votes, Professor Boykov was elected rector. Students campaigning in his favor posted leaflets and appeals, and even made the rounds of the voting faculty's homes. At a conference in Moscow Boykov sharply criticized Soviet policy in higher education: "It is inadmissible to lower the standards of science to the level of the proletariat. One has to raise the level of the proletariat to the level of science."[113] This was an undisguised attack on the class approach in admissions. Boykov argued that merit and performance, not social origin and Communist credentials, should be the basis for admission.

A similarly scandalous incident occurred at Leningrad University. As a confidential report explained:

> The university faculty is connected with the Academy [of Sciences] which generally defines the consciousness of the faculty and of intelligentsia.

> Right-wing professors have proposed the candidacy of Professor Deriugin [for rectorship]. The campaign for his candidacy has been exceptionally strong. Several private meetings of various groups of right-wing professors preceded the official nomination and election meetings.[114]

Among the professors 54 votes were cast in favor of Deriugin and 33 against, while among the teaching faculty 155 voted in favor with only 42 against. In his acceptance speech, Deriugin made his priorities clear: the university's academic autonomy had to be restored. Interference of political organizations in academic affairs of the university was impermissible. The so-called "political minimum" examination at admission was to be discontinued as a useless ideological test. Some campaigned for the return of exiled professors and reinstatement of full academic freedom. Leningrad party committee annulled Deriugin's election on the grounds that he espoused anti-Soviet views.

The situation in Moscow University was remarkably similar. There, as well, a campaign was in full swing to limit, if not phase out altogether, the interference of party committees and the Komsomol in academic affairs. Campaigners protested the purge of old specialists: "to believe that Communist professors can replace famous scientific specialists simply because they are Communists is an exercise in empty and harmful arrogance."[115] The promotion of upstarts into faculty positions without adequate knowledge was bound, they argued, to lower the standards of research and teaching, and produce graduates incapable of performing their duties. "Bourgeois" and "counterrevolutionary" from the Bolshevik point of view, rectors and administrators were elected to numerous academic institutions across Russia in 1925–7. These elections took place in Voronezh University, Saratov, and other institutions.[116] In 1927 get-togethers [skhodki] and spontaneous meetings became a matter of daily occurrence at numerous institutes and universities. Leaflets were posted and campaigning conducted under the slogans: "For the free development of youth! For democracy! For free elections."

That university professors demanded academic freedom and ideologically free admissions is not surprising, especially in the conditions of NEP. What stunned the party officials was that Soviet students with proletarian credentials were falling under the influence of "bourgeois" professors and accepted their, rather than the Communists', agenda. The GPU, it seems, could not comprehend why teachers and students who had moved up into those positions thanks to the Communist Party would not be grateful but succumbed to Kadet, SR, or Menshevik views. The answer probably lay in the simple fact that the culture of academic life, the culture of individual self-worth, was stronger than the gratitude for upward mobility. Many of those students who campaigned for free elections would not have considered their actions anti-Soviet. They regarded their actions as perfectly consistent with the high ideals of socialism. They campaigned not against Soviet power as such, but against party domination of elections, which rendered them meaningless. Propaganda trumpeting about equality for the toiling masses collided with the reality of a bureaucratic, hierarchical, one-party dictatorship.

There is nothing unusual that youth was drawn to new ideas and found the Komsomol less and less appealing. It was an organization tightly controlled by the party, ideologically rigid, and highly bureaucratized. In a society where unconventional ways of thinking were not yet automatically associated with the Gulag, it was only natural for diversity to assert itself as a matter of course. The best word to describe students' political and cultural preferences in the last years of NEP is diversity. It was a remarkably rich spectrum. Starting with a few Komsomol enthusiasts on the left (mostly Trotsky's supporters), who criticized social injustice, bureaucratization and detachment of the bosses from the masses, there followed a variety of groups and associations of neo-Menshevik, SR, or liberal views, which advocated free elections, academic freedom, and a removal of indoctrination from education. On the right, there were nationalist groupings of all kinds.

What the Bolsheviks called mysticism, apathy, and decadence, in fact was fascination with poetry, sentimentalism, contemplation, sensualism, and religiosity. Having studied Tolstoy and Dostoevsky, Soloviev and Berdiaev, and Merezhkovsky and Lavrov, young people were drawn to the Russian philosophical heritage of the preceding century. As ever, they debated the eternal question of the destiny of the Russian people, the reason for the failure of the revolution, the relationship between the hero and the crowd, and the meaning of escaping into the private. The mystical and the poetic clashed with Agitprop's bombastic and simplistic.

The gap between the official representations of Soviet youth and reality was enormous. Instead of conscious proletarians building socialism under party leadership, Soviet youth showed hostility to NEP, denounced miserable living conditions, and openly attacked inequality, party privilege, and low wages. The Komsomol as a transmission belt of Communist ideology into urban working-class youth failed dismally in the 1920s.[117] Those who propagated the official ideology were mostly paid state bureaucrats. Very few were inspired to become class-conscious fighters for the party of Lenin. The trend was, in fact, in the opposite direction. In the realm of political ideas the Komsomol was a breeding ground for many "anti-Soviet" political and religious associations. The 1920s saw the revival of interest in populism, liberalism, Menshevism, and religiosity. Dissident groups proliferated and religious associations eclipsed the official "transmission belt" in their popularity. Many espoused prejudice against Jews and other ethnic minorities.

The vast majority remained apolitical and could not have cared less about socialism. They craved entertainment, not politics; for vodka, sex, and fox-trot rather than for Lenin or the ABCs of communism. Attitudes to women were anything but socialist. Bolshevik "new morality" campaigns seem to have made things worse. Sexual contact became freer and the family structure weaker. Most youths were attracted to Western popular culture and music, ignoring Agitprop's message and propaganda. In their lifestyles, tastes, dress, and aspirations, Soviet youth espoused "bourgeois" values rather than some ephemeral proletarian consciousness.

Despite hundreds of thousands of rural members, the Komsomol remained a marginal force in the countryside. It attracted only those who wanted to leave and make a career in administration elsewhere. Moral standards alienated women, and anti-religious campaigns the rest of the rural community. The sheer numbers of young people affiliated with religious congregations and the Peasant Union dwarf the Komsomol's presence in the countryside. Ten years of ceaseless Communist propaganda among the youth in the conditions of a press monopoly, expenditure of enormous financial resources, and the absence of a legally tolerated opposition failed to generate enthusiasm or excitement.

Chapter 6

Women: false promises, dashed hopes, and the pretense of emancipation

The party initially showed almost complete indifference to women's issues. Leading party figures resisted creating anything separate for women, or for anyone else, for that matter. Only after much soul-searching and delay did the Bolshevik CC agree to set up women's departments.[1] They were not created to promote women's rights or a feminist agenda in Russia but "as a transmission belt downward only, a way of conveying the party's objectives and instructions to a hitherto inaccessible constituency."[2] The Bolshevik leaders of women's departments hoped that, in the end, women would benefit, and accepted the underlying principle of women's subordination to the party, even though Aleksandra Kolontai, the first chair of the All-Russian Women's Department, made some feeble attempts to turn it into an institution representing women's interests.[3] Nevertheless, women's departments were conceived to be, and actually performed as, organizations of the party and for the party, auxiliary mobilization agencies recruiting women for the hospitals, factories, and other institutions. Women's departments worked under the assumption that the female masses would be grateful to the party.

In 1923 women's departments existed in most provinces; 35,539 women attended delegate assemblies in cities and towns, and 55,688 more in rural areas. Their principal achievement was that 3 per cent of that number (455) had entered the Communist Party.[4] This was a modest beginning. The party had its sights set on hundreds of thousands of organized women and tens of thousands of female party members. The official message to women was that following the victory of the socialist revolution, women were equal. The Bolsheviks implemented concrete policies designed to equalize the status of women with men, improve their educational level, and involve them in society.[5] It is therefore essential to examine political and cultural responses of rural women, factory women, and party women to the Bolshevik message and the new reality they faced.

RURAL WOMEN: STAYING OUT OR
GETTING INVOLVED?[6]

The Bolsheviks perceived peasant women as a backward, superstitious, and religious constituency that needed to be shown the way forward.[7] They were the hardest to reach and found the Bolshevik message most incomprehensible. Studies on rural women undertaken by the women's departments painted a grim picture:

> Peasant women face extremely difficult conditions. Beatings at the hands of the husband are frequent occurrences. There is sneering at those women who attend the village assembly and participate in [party] social work. They are in the grip of superstition, prejudice, and darkness. Abortions in domestic conditions ruin their health.[8]

The main thrust of the rural women's departments was to encourage women to participate in village soviet elections, attend women's assemblies, and promote Komsomol membership. The Bolshevik mission was to enlighten the "backward female masses," overcome their "religious superstition," undermine male domination, and draw them closer to the party. To accomplish all these formidable tasks it was necessary first of all to get women to attend delegate assemblies and empower them in soviet elections. The women's departments were effectively subordinate to their respective gubkom bureaus. Thus, in 1924 the Voronezh gubkom coordinated 177 delegate assemblies across the province, with total attendance figures reaching 7,607 women.[9] In Vladimir province the 1924 organizing drive reported spectacular success: 3,182 peasant women delegates were elected in the province, amounting to more than a 200 per cent increase over 1923's figures. The women's department proudly reported on its accomplishments:

> Almost in all uezds all kinds of women's bureaus, women's commissions, and women's societies are being created at the initiative of the politically active peasant women and village schoolteachers.[10]

In 1923 Kursk gubkom estimated that its women's department had reached 30 per cent of the local women, and, by 1924, 46.5 per cent.[11] In Bryansk the provincial women's delegate assembly of 875 deputies, representing 28 local delegate assemblies, successfully fulfilled the gubkom-drafted campaign plan. They organized an honorary seeing-off of Red Army draftees, recruited for political-education circles, and celebrated twenty "October baptisms" – a secular ceremony substituted for Christian baptism. Women's departments were also active in promoting Red weddings, another new ritual designed to replace its religious equivalent. The Voronezh women's department accomplished much along similar lines:

> The practice of Soviet rituals in the countryside is becoming more and more frequent. In accordance with the decisions of the VIIth Province Party

Conference, the women's departments are taking part in staging Red weddings and October baptisms in the countryside.[12]

In just two months in the fall of 1924 Voronezh claimed to have held six Red weddings and six October baptisms. The Vladimir province women's department consisted of three women: one chairperson and two lecturers. As was the case everywhere else, they engaged mostly in propaganda campaigns on subjects like the army draft and its correct understanding, hygiene and first aid, and literacy.

Rural women and especially younger women responded favorably to new opportunities which were opened up to them through involvement in social work.[13] They regarded women's departments in terms of what they could do for them. The Voronezh women's department wrote to Moscow that "failing to obtain justice, peasant women were writing letters full of despair" and complained that they could not get help or even an explanation from anyone.[14] On numerous occasions various women's departments took up the legal defense of women in court. In just one uezd of Voronezh province, the local department represented women claimants in the court in 56 cases dealing with the division of land, 83 regarding divorce settlements, 14 about non-payment of wages, 9 for unfair dismissals, and an unspecified number involving sexual harassment and rape.[15]

The provincial women's departments studiously tried to increase the percentage of women in the soviets. In this they were largely successful. The number of women in local soviets grew steadily. In Voronezh province, for example, 845 women (5.7 per cent) were elected as soviet members in 1923, and 1,879 (8.9 per cent) in 1925.[16] In Vladimir province 1,052 women were elected to village soviets out of 9,984 delegates in 1924.[17] In some places women activists' names were included on the election slates of the Communist Party. This, however, had a negative effect in areas where the Communist Party's reputation was tarnished. In the Don and Kuban' Cossack lands, these attempts backfired. Male Cossacks opposed electing women if they had any connection to women's delegate assemblies, women's departments, or any other Communist-dominated organization. Those women who were elected in the Cossack lands had credentials which granted them respect in the eyes of the local community. They were members of the village church councils, daughters of priests, or wives of former Cossack officers.[18] From the Communists' point of view, it was better to have no women in the rural soviets at all than face women like this. Women in the rural soviets not only failed to follow the Communists' lead, grateful for their liberation, but turned into the most articulate, fearless, and vociferous opposition.

Propaganda work among women encountered tremendous resistance from all sides almost everywhere. Local party organizations regarded this line of work as their last priority. The gubkom in Kursk put the blame on the lack of women organizers and funds.[19] A party survey of work among peasant women of Vvedenskaya district in Kostroma province showed that:

The district women's department is weak. Hardly any meeting of delegates took place. You have to drag delegates to meetings. They persistently refuse to attend. The same situation remained after new delegates were elected. They say that all the same, they are not going to attend any meetings.[20]

Peasant women were for the most part reluctant to break with their traditional roles and attend women's delegate assemblies. Male peasants were against female participation in any separate meetings. They were quoted as saying: "You are not going to fool us this time even though you are the smart Bolsheviks. You are trying to drag our wives to your meetings and fool them. This is not going to happen."[21] Peasants perceived the enticement of their wives or daughters to separate meetings as interference in their family lives. Girls' fathers forbade them from attending meetings where Komsomol members were present because, the saying went, "they only spoil [impregnate] the girls there."[22] A report from Volyn' province in Ukraine noted that it was typical for fathers to ban Komsomol meeting attendance to prevent fraternization with the "Godless Bolsheviks."[23]

Some women objected to the meetings because of the Bolsheviks' anti-religious message. As one peasant woman at a women's delegate meeting in Gomel province explained in 1925:

Here you hang a poster showing a muzhik harnessing himself to pull a capitalist and a priest in a cart and the Godmother is shown to put on a yoke. Shameless people you are! Obscene people you are! You have lost all shame. It is not the Godmother who puts on a yoke, but you, the Communists, who have put a yoke on us peasants and are strangling us. Why do we need freedom and equality if there is no bread and there is nothing to eat? Yes, indeed, you have already equalized everybody – men and women are all hungry and barefoot. Yes, indeed, you can say there will be good life. But now there are no jobs. Your plants are idle. There are no jobs for our men. They are sitting at home and what results from that is only a bunch of kids. There is nothing to eat. This is what you've led us to.[24]

In most provinces young women stayed away from mixed social gatherings on their own when these became associated with indecency and impropriety. The Komsomol committee from Vyatka province reported that sewing and discussion groups had to be led by hired female teachers because the girls would all run away if Komsomol members appeared.[25] Popular wisdom held that sexual advances were commonplace in the Komsomol or party. The conclusion for many rural unmarried women was obvious – stay away from secular, non-segregated, Bolshevik-run organizations since they offered nothing but trouble.

However, rural women attended willingly female village gatherings [posidelki] and traditional courses on sewing, cooking and child-care, and church-run women's choirs. Such meetings offered social contact with other women. Voronezh province gatherings were popular, as was captured in this verse:

Khot' rugaite ne rugaite
no po vashemu ne byt'
na yacheiku na sobranie
ne zakazhite khodit'.

Scold me or not
it won't be as you say
I'm off to a meeting
you can't bar my way.[26]

These were activities where young women felt safe, and their honor was not compromised. The rate of young women's involvement in non-segregated religious associations was much higher than in women's assemblies or the Komsomol. At the former, a young woman could enjoy respect, stability, safety, and social contact with young people (including young men) without the fear of unwanted sexual advances. Moreover, if her social contacts did lead to marriage, her role in the congregation would not change appreciably. The party or Komsomol alternate was not as appealing.

The main preoccupation of young rural women remained finding a perfect match. The overwhelming majority of *chastushki*, popular poems in the countryside, were about a woman's beloved one.[27] Very few addressed any other topic. Provincial Komsomol committees considered it a big achievement on the cultural front when rural women sang *chastushki* casting Komsomol members in a favorable light, since this was a rarity. Severo-Dvinsk gubkom cited a poem:

Ne rugai menia mamasha
menia ne za chto rugat'
zapishus' ia v komsomolki
budu knizhechki chitat'
mne teper' ne nado kolets
i braslety ni po chem
priglianulsia komsomolets
nam s podruzhechkoi
vdvoem

Save your yelling mama
No need to give me dark looks
I'm going to sign up for Komsomol
and I'm going to read some books
I don't have use for rings now
and bracelets not at all
because together with my girlfriend
I've got my eyes set on a guy
from the Komsomol.[28]

At first glance this poem reflects new socialist reality in the village. A young unmarried woman does not want traditional trinkets but, instead, books and a social life. The punchline, though, is that she likes a young fellow who happens to be in the Komsomol. Affection and traditional love are still the main theme here rather than socialist construction or political correctness.

A report to Moscow noted that a woman who married a Komsomol or party member had to be written off.[29] She would have so many obligations with cleaning and raising children that there would be no time for the Komsomol or anything else. Essentially, many men thought that once a woman got married she was no longer supposed to take an active part in public life. Once married, a woman belonged to the man; she had to obey her husband, her master. A husband expected her to cook, wash, and raise children, and, on occasion, he would beat her.

At one of the conferences on the new lifestyles in Moscow, Comrade Toporova lamented that Komsomol and Communist married women mostly quit public life because:

> As soon as she gets married, starts having a family and all those kitchen implements, she is sucked in. They marry mostly party members. And what do we see? After a couple of months they are already divorcing. There were cases when a husband simply announced: "If you do not come home at five o' clock and clean the room and cook dinner, we shall divorce."[30]

This role was, of course, difficult to accept for young energetic women who sought comradeship and equality. What a disappointment it was for them to discover that in real life a Communist husband was seldom different from any other. Even if a Komsomol or party member himself, he would not let her remain a member after marriage because it was widely perceived to be a euphemism for promiscuousness. Komsomol membership was seen as inappropriate and indecent for a married woman. Many women complained that the liberal divorce law gave advantages to men. They could leave women at a moment's notice and all the resulting hardships – especially if there were children – fell on the woman's shoulders.

There were hundreds of cases in rural women's department files of young women complaining that so and so had promised to marry them, made them pregnant, and abandoned them, and now they did not know what to do. The variation on this truly classic plot in the specific conditions of NEP was that a party official married a young woman, lived with her for three months, and then announced that they were no longer married once she became pregnant. The young woman was left with nowhere to go and no one to complain to.[31] Alas, nothing could be done. No court would accept cases of this kind. Sometimes womanizing by party officials became known to the public and scandals broke out. In Shchekinsky district of Tula province, for example, Red Army draftees discovered that Political Commissar Kagushkin had ten "informal" wives. They published an article about Comrade Kagushkin's

You should be ashamed of yourself, neighbor, to beat your wife.
You are, after all, a member of New Lifestyle society.
So what, I am also a member of the Old Moscow society.

Figure 6 The Old in the New
Source: *Bich* No. 9 (1928), p. 9

"Work among Women" in a wall newspaper, which embarrassed the Commissar and caused some jokes, but the case was not considered a serious offense.[32]

It was commonplace in the mid-1920s to refer to two types of wife: "legal" and "actual." Cohabitation constituted actual marriage, which complicated divorce and child-support cases.[33] In Vologda province Komsomol activists decided to conduct a poll among soviet, party, and Komsomol male officials about their habits and lifestyles – all of which went under the rubric of the "New Lifestyle [Byt]". They received remarkably frank answers to their detailed questionnaires about the most intimate spheres of private life. One of the questions was: "How often do you have sex?" Most typical answers were: "whenever," "sometimes," and "two or three times a week." "With whom do you have sex?" Answers: "with whomever," "with various women," "with more than one." "Do you have a legal wife or an actual one?" The fact that this was asked implied that there was either one or the other. Interestingly, most respondents answered: "both."[34] This adds credibility to women's complaints that the liberal family code made it easier for men to be promiscuous.

Some women enthusiasts, perhaps feminists, debated vigorously at their meetings what could be done to empower women in gender relations, to increase their independence as a check against the whims of their male partners. The women's department in Shadrinsky uezd of Ekaterinburg province, for example, organized a public debate "New Morality and the Free Woman." Some feminists argued that women were to be protected in case of pregnancy, regardless of their marital status. Since women gave birth to children, and since no man could be legally held responsible in the conditions when sexual partners were equal before the law, regardless of marriage bonds, a new mechanism had to be devised to protect single unmarried mothers. All men were to pay a special tax to cover the expenses of unwed mothers.[35] The reaction of the party committee was quite revealing. These proposals were perceived as extreme leftist heresy. The issue was not considered and subsequently made taboo.

Rural women's interaction with Bolshevik authorities is a record of rational choices in accord with their values. They were not the backward, superstitious, and dark masses the Bolsheviks painted them to be. They did not stay away from involvement in public affairs. They were interested in women's gatherings of all kinds, exactly as they had been before the Bolsheviks ever appeared in the countryside. They availed themselves of new opportunities and willingly ran in elections to rural soviets. They participated in public organizations of their choosing. They stayed away from party and Komsomol membership and their interest in women's assemblies declined, whereas their dominance in religious associations was overwhelming. Bolsheviks failed to coopt traditional female networks in the countryside. Rural women got involved not in socialist construction, but in the defense of traditional values, Church, and family.[36]

FACTORY WOMEN: FROM COMPLAINTS TO PROTEST

The work of women's departments varied a great deal from province to province. They were most active in the textile industry provinces east and north-east of Moscow, Ivanovo, Vladimir, and Kostroma, and weakest in the agricultural provinces of the black earth region south of Moscow, along the Volga, and in Siberia. At the Bryansk Profintern locomotive plant, ninety-nine women delegates held regular meetings once a week to discuss several on-going projects, including subscription to the *Bryansk Worker* newspaper, the work of the cultural commission, and activities among the Pioneers (a Communist children's organization). Once a week the delegates washed children in a bathhouse. Women delegates were also involved in the "liquidation of illiteracy campaign," since illiteracy was highest among women. Reporting on its accomplishments, the Bryansk women's department proudly stated that: it had opened 3 illiteracy liquidation centers in the city and 5 in the countryside, held 15 public lectures, staged 11 rallies, and convened 5 conferences with the total number of 7,100 women participants.[37]

The main task of every women's department was to increase the percentage of Communist Party membership among women. The bulk of women's departments' activity went into preaching and organizing, trying to convince women to elect representatives to attend their delegate assemblies. The most receptive female audiences to the Communist message were initially women workers, especially those who held low-paying jobs. Delegate assemblies gave them an opportunity to vent their grievances, break their routine, meet other women, and share experiences. Many women delegates simply could not comprehend, however, what the Communist propagandists were talking about. As one woman worker recalled:

I'll tell you comrades about a women's conference. So they were going to call a women's conference and elected three delegates but they refused to go. So I had to go by myself. So I went. You know, we are sitting at the conference, I'm sitting there too. They are presenting a report to us. Some kind of an outsider is delivering the report. So she is reading this report and you know she uses some kind of bookish words, unfamiliar words, you know. And more than half of us present just can't get it. The young delegates are listening attentively, not understanding either, but they listen anyway. But we, the older ones, are sitting there and just sitting and then we dozed off. And so many of these conferences were like that: completely useless. They'd just sit there and sit and then doze off a little and then talk a little and leave.[38]

They did not comprehend the message, nor did they care about surplus value, the workings of capitalism, or the prospects for world revolution. Working women often perceived intelligentsia organizers as society ladies, despite their efforts to come across as proletarian sisters. The cultural divide between them generated misunderstandings, disorientation, and hostility. Professional propagandists, for their part, often paraded their superior education and culture, widening the gulf between the two. Cultural difference and tension between working women and "society ladies," and even the women's own elected delegates, made agitation and propaganda among female masses much more difficult than the Bolshevik hierarchs anticipated.

Delegate assemblies were to identify and promote those who might be useful in spreading Communist propaganda. In some cases delegates developed the identity of a privileged elite. They imitated the behavior of party committee members and began to act as if they were bosses as well. They sent out demands, instructions, requests, and even tried to set quotas on how many women delegates should be elected to the village soviets. The Kuban' gubkom claimed that "the women delegates were not the vanguard of the masses, but a caste who regarded the delegate assemblies only in terms of how these could be used to improve their material situation."[39]

Some delegate assemblies regarded themselves as the voice of their constituencies and provided an opportunity for women to air their views. Most speakers tried to juxtapose the sweet words they heard about equality against the reality they faced. Many asked why women workers were paid less than men. Why were their jobs the lowest-paying jobs?[40] Why were there so few kindergartens and day-care centers? In Vladimir and Ivanovo delegates asked repeatedly why production rates increased with their transfer to three spinning machines instead of two, but pay did not. As the Ivanovo women's department summarized, "the women are interested in schools, kindergartens, pay-scales, bathhouses, laundry facilities, and they are upset about the rude behavior of the administration."[41] As the workday was lengthened to twelve hours at the sugar-beet factory in Voronezh women workers pleaded with the provincial women's department to intervene on their behalf. The small staff of the women's department was swamped with petitions and complaints it could not handle; and this was the case even though 90 per cent of women workers were illiterate and had nowhere to go and no one to ask for help. Reports noted that many women's petitions viewed all Soviet institutions "with suspicion and hostility."

Three sets of women's concerns were beyond the jurisdiction of the women's departments. These were wage rates, labor disputes, and, most importantly, gender relations in the work-place. The Bolsheviks' priority was to increase productivity of labor. This is why they introduced new production rates across the board in various industries. At the Bryansk locomotive plant 1,097 women were employed in the hardest and lowest-paying jobs.[42] When the pay-scale was cut and production targets increased, women workers were the ones most affected because it was easier to impose unfavorable rates on them than on the highly skilled male workers. At the textile mills in Vladimir province, where most workers were women, new standards were introduced whereby spinners were to work three machines instead of two. The women delegates were required to set an example to others. This generated intense hatred for the women's vanguard among the rest of the women workers:

> The disposition of the women workers has been rather bad lately. The cause for this was the transfer from two machines to three. There was a lot of noise and shouting at the Gus' Khrustalnyi. Women workers simply refused to accept the new rates. We had to transfer first the Komsomol members. There were cases when rank-and- file women workers spit in the eyes of those who had begun work at three machines and cases when they banged their heads.[43]

In 1925 the pay-scale of the lowest paying job at the textile mills of Nizhnii Novgorod province was cut from 15 rubles a month to 12.50. This, predictably, affected women. They went on strike and won their old wages back, but the women's departments had no authority to interfere in these matters. As a result women workers complained that when they needed the women's departments most, they were as helpless as the trade unions: "What good is there that they assembled delegate assemblies and lectured to us about women's equality?"[44] In Smolensk province most women workers were set against their delegate assemblies, saying: "We do not need your meetings and we will not attend them."[45] Almost identical was the reaction of women workers in Tver':

> Give us bread, eliminate lines, and do not introduce the so-called rationalization, because you create merciless unemployment with that. We don't need your delegates. They don't defend us anyway.[46]

As the campaign for production-rate increase gained momentum in 1926 and 1927, it generated more and more unemployment. Women's departments were helpless and factory women's interest in them plummeted. In many provinces women's departments had to resort to a purge of the delegate assemblies.[47] Unemployment was the greatest fear of women textile workers, since fewer than a third received unemployment compensation. Others had to fend for themselves. Out of 171,000 unemployed in Moscow, only 56,000 received some form of assistance.[48] For many women, even the lowest-paying job as a textile worker for 15 rubles a month was inaccessible. Faced with unemployment and starvation, some women turned to prostitution. It was a serious problem in urban Russia, but seldom discussed in official propaganda. Women from all social groups could be seen in the centers of big cities, at railway stations, and on the main streets, in restaurants, and bars. In Orel the number of full-time prostitutes varied from 57 to 126. By social origin, they were 7 per cent former noble ladies, 12 per cent former townswomen [*meshchanki*], and 80 per cent women of proletarian and peasant origin. Over 40 per cent of them had practiced their trade for over two years.[49]

Entire categories of offences affecting women were never acknowledged to exist in Soviet Russia. Most working women had no access to the courts. Even if they did, no court accepted cases involving sexual harassment. Neither courts nor the women's departments wanted to get involved precisely in the area where common women needed help most.[50] The Ivanovo-Voznesensk women's department handled dozens of complaints from female textile workers about the rude treatment they suffered at the hands of factory foremen.[51] In a special report to the CC on women workers' political attitudes, Artiukhina, the chairperson of the All-Russian Women's Department wrote that foremen in industry "compelled women workers to have sexual intercourse against their will."[52] She clearly referred not to isolated incidents, but to widespread practice. The gubkom of Votkinsk province, home of a large armaments plant, mentioned in passing in one of its monthly reports, "unfortunate cases of gang rapes of young unmarried women, and that it was a lifestyle [*bytovaia*] tradition." The province authorities did not know what measures to take against this "tradition," which was blamed for the high rate of syphilis in the province and "was leading to degeneration among local cadres."[53]

On numerous occasions, women workers initiated protests and strikes which caused serious concern for the Communist authorities. Women were more direct, brave, and emotional than men. They demanded exactly what they wanted and did not stop before fist fights. In Leningrad a work slow-down in 1928 caused by the reduction of wages escalated into a full-fledged strike. Women workers were accused of being trouble-makers, as they had led the crowds of angry workers in breaking down the plant gates and beating up party officials.[54] In 1927–8, hostile rejection of delegate assemblies seems to have become a standard response almost everywhere. From Ul'yanovsk, the city committee wrote that: "It is only possible to force women to attend delegate assemblies by mounted police."[55] As women workers realized that the purpose of women's departments was solely party-oriented, they responded with disappointment and indignation, resulting in purges, absenteeism, and the refusal to attend meetings.

A NEW SOVIET WOMAN: DATING, FASHIONS, AND FOX-TROT

The official representations of a new Soviet woman focused on her social standing, not her gender. A foreign observer described a column of Soviet women, wearing red kerchiefs and carrying guns, marching across Red Square, following the Red Army and the GPU detachments, indistinguishable from men.[56] A new Soviet woman was supposed to walk briskly and energetically as a fighter and a worker. She was to stop styling herself after bourgeois maidens of the pre-revolutionary epoch and shake hands rather than allow her hand to be kissed. The feminine part of her appearance was dismissed as a bourgeois hold-over. To look attractive, use cosmetics, or act in a coquettish manner were values of the past. A new role model was of a tough leather-jacketed commissar with short hair and a cigarette in the mouth. Many travelers were struck by the stern appearance of Soviet women:

> I can only make out the head of a teacher. She must be about sixteen, dressed like a worker with a red kerchief over her hair – a face without femininity or charm but concentrating persistently on the Idea. Millions of women here have faces that are fierce; their femininity has been transformed, shifted from its sexual center to new and sterner areas.[57]

All attributes of femininity were to be rejected as hold-overs of bourgeois culture. Women were supposed to be seen as comrades, not objects of sexual appeal. Quite revealing in this regard were propaganda poems sung by the so-called "blue blouse" propaganda theater troupes of the 1920s:

> Tomu zadam muzhchine vzbuzhchku
> kto mne vop'yotsya gubami v ruchku
> s takim dub'yom kashi ne svarish
> kto ne zovyot zhenu tovarishch.

> I'm gonna give a scolding to the man
> who would latch his lips on to my hand
> from such dummies
> nothing can be made
> who don't call their wives comrade.

They wanted to shake off the image of young timid maidens, waiting to be courted and married. Another poem in that genre made fun of the bourgeois norm of using makeup:

> My postupaem vo vsyom premudro
> gub'yov ne mazhem, ne syplemsya pudroi
> kolets ne nosim i ne seryozhek
> i kirpichom ne mazhem rozhi.

> We act wise in everything
> don't use powder or paint our lips
> don't wear rings or hang earrings
> and don't stain our mug
> with red-brick rouge at all.

The Bolshevik-propagated image of an assertive and independent woman related only to the public sphere, but contained virtually nothing appealing in regard to private life. A good Komsomol or Communist member was raising productivity of labor and striving for socialism. Unanswered remained the question of falling in love. Could a conscious proletarian woman fall in love? And if she did, how was she supposed to behave? At some Komsomol meetings in debates over new morality, young women asked whether it was permissible for a young man to declare his love for a girl. Komsomol officials argued that romantic love was to be rejected as an escape into the private sphere. Those in love typically were preoccupied with their own feelings and would neglect social and political tasks of the day. They often detached themselves from the masses and thus succumbed to bourgeois individualism. For a true Komsomol or party member, the collective was superior to the private, and common good was superior to personal happiness. Building a family was not a cultural value for the Komsomol. Quite the contrary. Loyalty to one's husband was secondary to loyalty to the cause. The closest bonds were to be fostered with the collective rather than with the chosen loved one, or family.

Factory girls were also not interested in production rates, or in the cause. The Bolshevik puritanical asceticism was unappealing and the political message simply boring. Young women were the largest category of those quitting the Komsomol. When some of them were asked why they quit, they answered that they had thought that "they would have fun at meetings." Bored, they quit.[58] According to a female Komsomol activist, unmarried women workers talked mostly about their boyfriends: "I love so and so, or I date so and so, or I lured so and so away from so and so." They were not interested in their factory. As one might expect, their attention was focused on free time after work. "They just love dancing. Don't give them honey, just give them a chance to go dancing."[59]

They wanted to forget their meager existence as soon as the work day was over. This led to precisely the quasi-bourgeois tendencies the party feared.

> Komsomol activists in the Krasnyi Treugolnik factory reported that there were many cases of female workers who literally starved because they spent all of their wages on silk stockings, makeup, and manicures, while *Komsomol'kaya Pravda* described young women working in the Vysitskii factory who wore "fashionable" low-cut dresses and scanty shoes that pinched their toes.[60]

Many urban unmarried working women wanted to escape the routine and socialize with young men, go to parties, and be independent. The fox-trot mania of the 1920s is an important cultural phenomenon. It satisfied many crucial aspirations of young men and women. Dancing was about equality. On a dance floor, in her one and only fashionable dress, a young woman factory worker could abandon her proletarian identity and mingle with all kinds of people. She danced with one partner, not a collective as in traditional Russian folk dance. Dancing gave freedom of choice *vis-à-vis* partners and an illusion of glamor. Komsomol leaders took the problem seriously and organized conferences of female Komsomol activists to improve propaganda work among young unmarried women factory workers. At one of those conferences in Moscow in 1927, Comrade Smirnova from the Nogin factory explained that:

What class, Vasia, do you consider to be your own?
To tell the truth, the dance class.

Figure 7 "Social Position"
Source: *Bich* No. 5 (1927), p. 7

We know that streets exert great influence on our factory girls. The evenings we organize do not satisfy them and they come, if at all, only when the second part of the evening begins – dancing. They come in silk dresses, powdered and made-up, despite the fact that wages at our factory are not very high (2 rubles and 96 kopecks a day) they manage to carve out for cosmetics and silk dresses. Our agenda is of no interest to them and we are powerless to draw them away from dancing parties.[61]

Many young women factory workers, including Komsomol members, imitated what was officially called "bourgeois" styles in their behavior and clothing. Despite an all-out propaganda effort to change their habits, they tried to look attractive, flirted with young men at dance parties, and put on sexy clothes. A party secretary from the Gomza plant described the cultural preferences of young women factory workers:

The girls work at the factory all day long. Then they come home and put on powder and makeup. Evening parties at the factory have an outright non-Komsomol character. Young women, Komsomol members, come in dresses with low cuts, without sleeves.[62]

This certainly shocked the factory administration. Bourgeois culture was rearing its head again. One of the problems was that Bolshevik propaganda could not compete with the alluring dream world of Hollywood films. As a recent researcher put it:

the flurry of fashionable Western images from Hollywood movie productions encouraged some young people to forgo the advice of Bolshevik moralists and Komsomol enthusiasts and imitate the sophisticated dress and dance of the American movie star ... Women wore bright red lipstick and narrow-toed high-heel shoes, bobbed their hair, and shortened their skirts.[63]

Sex on demand without marriage was not appealing for most unmarried young women, who wanted to have a partner and a family at some point. The dream world of a Soviet female factory worker was not focused on building socialism and overfulfilling a plan. She was interested in dating, dancing, looking attractive, and building a family. Her role model was not a tough, leather-jacketed, masculine-looking Bolshevik commissar, but a bourgeois lady in silk stockings and low-cut dress from Holywood films. The subculture of female factory workers was as distant from the Bolshevik iconography as ever.

BOLSHEVIK WOMEN

Factory women and rural women, as we have seen, were largely immune to Communist propaganda. They elected delegates and attended women's gatherings to defend their economic interests and cultural values. As of January 1, 1928 only 63,835 out of nearly a million CP members were women. In Komsomol female membership never exceeded 20 per cent in urban centers and 5 per cent in rural areas. Bolshevik women were a very small social group indeed. At the center of that group were old-time Bolshevik intelligentsia women. Most of them had joined the revolutionary movement before 1917. Very few regarded themselves as women's representatives in the Communist Party. On the contrary, female Old Bolsheviks shunned the emancipation agenda, avoided assignments to women's departments, and preferred tasks in mainstream administrative, economic, and political agencies. In their behavior, culture, and posture they de-emphasized that they were women. They wanted to be seen as revolutionaries first and foremost, equal to men.

Those Bolshevik intelligentsia women who were assigned to women's departments in the provinces were dedicated, hard-working, idealistic revolutionaries, spreading the word among the "dark masses" with the same kind of zeal as their predecessors had in the 1870s and 1880s. These enthusiasts helped rural women in court cases in Voronezh and tried to defend abandoned unwed mothers in Ekaterinburg. The majority of provincial women's department organizers were recent graduates of the sov-party schools. Themselves of humble proletarian origin, they were trained to spread the word among the female masses.

The second category of Bolshevik women was the Communist's wife. Some of them were revolutionaries of long standing in their own right, usually married to Old Bolsheviks, like Kolontai, or Smidovich, the successive heads of the All-Russian Women's Department. Others were just wives of high-ranking officials. What mattered to them was not dedication to the cause, but belonging to the ruling elite. As NEP began their culture was increasingly that of conspicuous consumption. They held receptions, organized literary evenings, served tea, went to the theater and restaurants – in short, acted in accord with their notions of the lifestyle of the elite. Their ostentation was so glaring that in 1923 the CC issued a complete and unconditional ban on the public display of diamonds and other precious stones. Party officials and their wives were not required to surrender them, but simply not to wear them in public.[64] Communist wives perceived party membership as joining an elite club. The Moscow gubkom reported that wives of Communist Party functionaries accused new female party members of having "entered the party to seduce their husbands."[65] They interpreted prospective members' motives as stemming not from the burning desire to build socialism, but as seeking career opportunities and a broader social calendar, and consequently they perceived these recruits as a threat.

The third category of Bolshevik women were from the factory floor. Recruiting women into the CP was a well-regulated process, like any other. Provincial authorities had to fulfill recruitment targets, which was not easy. Most women perceived enrollment as entering into a foreign world of male command in which they felt uncomfortable. A three-month-long female recruitment drive in Bryansk fulfilled only 20 per cent of the target figure. Most of those recruited were wives of party members and all except two were illiterate.[66]

Once in the party ranks, women were seldom rewarded with career opportunities typically extended to men. In fact, women were the most insecure and vulnerable constituency in the CP. Their proletarian origin, supposedly a benefit, was often used against them, as it usually implied a low educational level. During periodic campaigns to cleanse the party of "passive elements" women were the first to be expelled. To fulfill orders from Moscow quickly, the gubkoms would typically identify women as dead wood, unproductive, or politically illiterate. During the 1925 verification of political literacy in Kuban', one woman purged in this way was a certain comrade V.I., a party member from 1920, and a peasant by social origin. She had worked as a nanny and a day laborer at a tobacco plantation before the revolution. In 1918 she followed the Red Army as it retreated from the Kuban' host. Subsequently she worked in the GPU and after the civil war took a job at a tobacco factory. The verification commission found that she had no knowledge of the party statute or program, and had no understanding of basic political issues. Another woman purged was a party member since 1924, and a worker by social origin. Having learned how to type while a salesperson in a cooperative, she worked as a typist in a Red Army unit in 1919–20. Subsequently she worked in the GPU and as a women's organizer. She was expelled as "politically illiterate" in 1925.[67] Women were convenient scapegoats. They were easy to intimidate as most of them had no powerful connections.

Rural female graduates of the sov-party schools in the provinces had perhaps the most difficult jobs. The party machinery was supposed to help them organize the female peasant masses. However, women's organizers found themselves practically alone. They were lucky if they were simply ignored. More often they were harassed by male party officials. According to a CC investigation of party work in Saratov province,

> The district women's organizer was unable to conduct business negotiations with the secretary of the party cell, because whenever she addressed him, she had to listen to his vile proposals.[68]

In another case a female candidate-member of the party asked a party secretary to write her a recommendation so that she could become a full party member. His answer was that "she had a choice: either he would write a recommendation and she would have sex with him, or, if she would not have sex with him, he would not write the recommendation."[69]

Rural women's organizers were poor and defenseless, and hence easy prey for officials on whom they were dependent. Women's departments in the provinces received dozens of letters describing the poverty, misery, humiliation, and sexual harassment of women's organizers, librarians, and other

Unlucky is the one who is not beautiful: the bosses won't give you a raise.
Well it's not easy to be beautiful either: they don't leave you alone.

Figure 8 Either Way You Lose
Source: *Bich* No. 5 (1927), p. 6

female personnel by their male superiors. A female librarian in the Taganrog area wrote to the Kuban' women's department:

> I have been in the party since 1919. Now I am exhausted, I have no strength any more; it is all gone after five years of hardship. I have no place to live. Is selling your body the only way to survive? At every corner you are confronted by your own colleague, a man, who asks you to come by in the evening. If you go, you are finished. Some of them say: "You are poor and hungry – why don't you find a man who would provide for you?" In response you would just start crying and go away, and he would say: "Who do you think would worry about you for nothing?" I don't know what to do? There is no food and there is no hot water for two months already. Should I beg? Should I go to the mines? Barefoot? And I am not the only one in such a situation. Please help women workers. Please save us from prostitution. Save us from selling our bodies for a piece of bread.
>   With Communist Greetings.[70]

Women's organizers' enthusiasm quickly evaporated when they found themselves in such conditions. They realized they were just being used by the party without providing the minimum for subsistence. In this dismal reality they gave courses on Marxism, the bright future, and equality under socialism. The clash between propaganda representations and Soviet reality led some women to protest. One N. Alekseeva wrote an angry letter to the central women's department that abject poverty of women workers and women's organizers was clearly a responsibility of the party. She wrote, "high-ranking party officials are not barefoot, have enough clothing and food. And they, like predators, are on the watch for a woman to blackmail her, and to coerce her to cohabitation. During the past year we know of dozens of cases in Donbas when comrades in power used their positions of authority to coerce women to sex."[71] Alekseeva expressed the frustration of many Bolshevik women in 1927–8. Many of them were aware that women in the party did not have equal standing with men. They were the last to be promoted to positions of authority and the first to be purged as politically illiterate. Equality and emancipation was as distant as ever.

With all the variety of experiences and patterns of interaction between the local party and women's departments, between delegates and the departments' leaders, and between delegates and their female constituency, overall trends over the NEP years suggest that agitation and propaganda among female masses in favor of socialist construction did not work. Most women remained resistant to the Communist message. Worse for the party, by mobilizing the female masses, they got more trouble than they bargained for. In 1928 the chairperson of the All-Russian Women's Department, Artiukhina, wrote a special memorandum to the CC outlining reasons for the extremely low number of women in the CP. In the textile industry 56 per cent of all workers were women, but only 3.7 per cent of them were party members. The party plan to use delegate assemblies as conduits of recruitment did not materialize either. Only 2.9 per cent of women's delegates enrolled in CP membership.[72] Artiukhina explained:

> The main theme in the speeches of women delegates at the textile industry congress was that behavior of men was the main cause breaking the process of women's enrollment in the party. It is drunkenness, and the beating of wives, not only by non-party workers but by Communists as well.[73]

The party leaders were clearly disturbed by the trends showing decreasing party influence among the female proletarian masses, decreasing female enrollment in the CP, and increasing numbers of women-led labor protests. According to the CC Information Department, in 1925–6 there were 12,350 delegate assemblies, involving 401,214 women. In 1926–7 the number increased to 15,147 assemblies, representing 477,738 women. But in 1924 6.9 per cent of women delegates entered the party, while this figure shrank in 1925–6 to only 1.7 per cent and in 1926–7 to 0.9 per cent.[74] From the point of view of top party leaders, the women's departments failed to act as conduits to draw female activists into the party and failed to guide delegate assemblies towards pro-Soviet work.

The party did train a tiny minority of women activists who joined other promotees, but it also faced increased political awareness among working women. Women took propaganda on equality and opportunity seriously and when they saw no tangible improvements, they flooded women's departments with an ever increasing flow of petitions. Instead of complacent women workers grateful to the party for expressing concern over their miserable conditions, the party faced women who bombarded state agencies with complaints, requests, and demands. Women workers were not ready to accept the reality that some of them would be promoted but that the rest would have miserable wages, and the patronizing disdain of their male superiors. Women's departments in industrial towns found themselves squeezed between the party and their constituency. They sensed the anger of women factory workers, but were helpless to change much, since wage rates, labor conditions, and gender relations were not under their jurisdiction.

Perhaps the most remarkable change occurred in the status of rural women. Despite traditional male resistance, thousands of them were elected to village soviets. The main reason for their election was that male peasants would rather agree to having women in the village soviets than Communists. Women were still members of their own communities. Under pressure to elect Communists, Komsomol members, or women, the last were the least objectionable. Very soon male peasants discovered that their female representatives were just as articulate and aggressive in defense of the traditional values as men, if not more so.

Liberal divorce and abortion legislation contributed to male promiscuity and unwed mothers' misery. Wage rates and the authority structure discriminated against women in employment. Sexual harassment was commonplace. Promotion and purge practices discriminated against women in the party. Can this record be called beneficial for women? Does this record explain their low enrollment in party, Komsomol, and state institutions? Can this record be qualified as having anything to do with women's emancipation? The demise of women's departments was an admission by the Bolsheviks that they had failed in their endeavor to mobilize the female masses for the cause of socialist construction.

Chapter 7

Towards showdown in the countryside, 1926–8

By 1926 there were clear signs that the countryside was in ferment. The Communists' defeat in rural elections to the soviets in 1925, the rise of the Peasant Union movement, the curtailment of production, the shrinkage of cultivation, and in some places the appearance of peasant bands all indicated that peasants wanted to expand their economic freedom and political rights. The rural party was in a state of confusion, weakened by electoral setbacks and uncertain about the purpose of NEP and its own future. The party leaders faced some difficult questions. Was economic recovery in the countryside possible without losing control? Was it really advisable to rely on the rural party cells who were mostly poorly educated, corrupt, and ill-equipped to direct economic recovery? To what extent was a soft policy in the countryside acceptable? These issues were hotly debated in 1925–6 at Communist Party meetings at all levels. Some major decisions were made in 1926 which set up a chain of events leading to the procurement crisis of 1928 and the demise of NEP.

RURAL PARTY: ADAPTATION, DEFIANT REJECTION, AND INTERVENTION

By mid-1925 Communists at all levels faced a difficult question. What to do next? Economic recovery brought tax revenue and investment capital as well as the Communists' defeats in rural elections. A variety of views and opinions were expressed. The response of the Communist Party as a whole developed along three lines: adaptation, defiant rejection, and intervention. Obviously, the rural officials did not like the trends because every peasant gain was their loss. If peasants gained everything they wanted, there would be no role for the Communists to play. If peasants had their own unions, could bypass state procurement agencies, and elect their own candidates, what would the Communist Party do? It had identified itself beyond the point of no return with state coercion. The Communists tried to adapt and survive.

Adaptation

Partly inspired by Bukharin's pronouncements, perhaps, some defended NEP as a market system that had to develop and grow. The logic of their reasoning was that the New Economic Policy was a success. Over a short period of time agricultural production in most provinces recovered to a pre-war level. Essentially, all economic indicators – area under cultivation, size of herds, and levels of income and consumption were on the way up. Constraints on NEP had to be loosened, prices liberalized, and competition encouraged. Some Communists went even further. At a November 1925 Moscow party committee conference, a Comrade Yakovlev proposed to codify peasants' possession of land as private property. Land was a commodity like any other and therefore it should be possible to buy, sell, and inherit it. Yakovlev argued that peasant ownership of land would increase output since peasants would till the land with full knowledge that it was theirs and they could pass it on to their children.[1] Sokolnikov's speech was a little more cautious. As an architect of the 1923 financial reform, he had well-known pro-NEP credentials. He tried to defend market relations but not capitalism, cultured farmers [kul'turnye khoziaeva] but not kulaks. Sokolnikov pointed to an obvious contradiction in the party's policy: "We are encouraging the middle peasant up to a certain limit and then we begin strangling him."[2] The implication of his speech was that the limitations on market activity were impeding economic growth.

Some rural Communists shared peasants' views. Many of peasant stock themselves, they defended local and regional interests. They may have felt that the well-being of their province would be safeguarded if peasants were not overtaxed excessively. They saw nothing anti-Soviet or counter-revolutionary in peasants' attempts to create peasant unions or in trying to sell at a higher price. A telling example is when a party member in Luga uezd of Leningrad province came with a delegation of peasants to the uezd soviet and submitted a petition demanding permission to set up a Peasant Union.[3] This was not an isolated incident. Low-ranking party officials at the uezd and district level increasingly acted as peasants' spokesmen. Some party reports suggest, however, that the local Communists' pro-peasant stance was motivated not by sympathy to the peasants' plight but by "a desire to butter up the peasants," after the election defeat, trying to find a niche for themselves in the countryside.[4] These Communists represented themselves to peasants as having connections to the higher-ups. To the party elite, this sounded very much like pure and simple opportunism.

The most typical response of local officials was to adapt to the growing financial power of the prosperous peasants. One of the most typical ways was loans. In the Belevskii uezd of Tula province the party debt to the co-operatives stood at 5,174 rubles on January 1, 1925.[5] Peasant cooperatives typically granted loans to party cells which were seldom collected. The extent of the rural party's indebtedness by 1928 is extraordinary. Rural officials regarded their positions as a source of revenue. They delivered what they thought a fair share to Moscow and kept some for themselves. The GPU wrote with alarm that: "Lower soviet officials actively cooperated with the kulaks in underreporting taxable property."[6] Since uezd officials assessed taxable property, they had an important source of revenue. As the Tula province party chairman reported to Moscow:

> Comrade Ivitskii, the EC chairman of the village of Troitskoe, came with a bunch of pals to Citizen Anikieva's home and demanded vodka, promising in return to lower her agricultural tax. After drinking vodka they went to Citizen Alenicheva, Evdokiia. She lives alone. They banged on her door and demanded to be let in, but she refused, to which they responded with threats: "You will learn how to treat authority."[7]

Those officials clearly wanted to project an image of power defined as their capacity to strain peasants' budgets. They expected awe and reverence from their peasants. Instead they often faced ridicule as peasants were saying: "What kind of authority is this? This is a gang."

According to a special report, embezzlement rates in the tax-collection apparatus were high in Siberia and "the embezzlers were the administrators, and the administrators were the party members."[8] In Kuban' the process was labeled "capitalist regeneration." The Communists there appropriated the best parcels of land. Since they had no time or skills to till it, they rented it out to the Cossacks. By Soviet official standards they received what was called "unearned income," qualifying them for the kulak tax bracket. Yet the practice went on for years. The most serious problem of the party cells, continued the Kuban' report, "is pervasive drunkenness. This was the cause of numerous cases of debauchery, scandals, fights, often accompanied by shooting ... Embezzlement, waste of public funds is often connected with drinking ... These manifestations of malaise have a tendency towards spreading."[9] The rural party was learning to live under NEP.

Defiant rejection

Rural party officials were not happy with the rise of a prosperous and independent peasantry. The CC compiled for Stalin typical questions asked at the rural party conferences in 1925. In one way or another they all boiled down to Lenin's question: Who will beat whom?

QUESTION: How can we approach a middle peasant so that he will ally with us if in fact every middle peasant under NEP is striving towards the kulaks and not to us?

This question touched upon the painful reality the Bolsheviks had to face. Middle-income peasants wanted to become rich peasants. For them it was just as natural as the fact that day followed night.

QUESTION: Why are the kulaks allowed to expand, whereas a poor peasant still lives badly?

Next to this question there are two red lines in pencil drawn presumably by Comrade Stalin since it was his copy of the compilation. Without reading too much into this, one wonders why. Was he concerned as early as December 1925 that NEP was contributing to the economic strength of the prosperous peasants? And if so what could be done about it?

QUESTION: Can it happen that the poor peasants would succumb to the influence of the kulaks?

QUESTION: Where would the kulaks' activity lead to if they possess financial means?

The party officials were worried that economic development of the country-side could lead to squeezing the party out. The Tula gubkom wrote that the kulaks were trying to establish political leadership over the peasantry.[10]

QUESTION: Why are the tractors sold to those who cultivate 100 desiatin and not to those who cultivate 20?[11]

This question brought home the fundamental contradiction in Communist policy in agriculture: to increase output in order to raise tax revenue and finance their industrial projects meant encouraging prosperous peasants. However, ideologically and politically this could not be done.

Some rural Communists could not hide their outright hostility to NEP and engaged in what was called Red banditry. Most cases were reported in Siberia where prosperous peasants had larger acreage under cultivation than did peasants in central Russia, while the Communist cadres were spread very thin. Rural Siberian Communists were mostly former Red partisans who had just a few years earlier fought against the Whites and felt that they were being robbed of what was rightfully theirs, political power won in battle. Expressions of hostility to NEP literally fill pages of the reports from Siberia. As the GPU survey for August 1925 put it, "in many districts of the Tomsk province a strengthening of Red banditry was noticeable," while in Altai province, "local Communists allowed themselves partisan escapades against the local population."[12] The Omsk party reported that a rural cell resolved to kill a priest after they had heard a lecture on anti-religious struggle.[13] The most common form of abuse of power was illegal confiscation of property in excess of official taxes.

Prosperous agriculturalists were complaining that they received anonymous threats and demands to surrender such and such an amount of grain or else a revolutionary people's court would wreak punishment on them by burning their crops.[14] In the judgment of the Siberian kraikom, NEP was widely perceived as "a concession to kulaks, and a Communist retreat." In Novosibirsk the Communists were bitter that the soviets "were now in the hands of the kulaks, and the Communists were being thrown out." Their reaction was "either apathy or tough dictatorial methods." Some started setting up "Committees for Struggle with the Kulaks," unauthorized from above. Many rural cells ignored or boycotted district executive committees of soviets or soviet assemblies and wanted to have nothing to do with them any more. Some CP cells were linked to arson. Some started "terrorizing the population," as the kraikom admitted.[15]

Recourse to intimidation, threats, arson, and violence was for many a way to vent their frustration. As a party cell secretary in the Barnaul uezd, Altai province, put it, "Soon there will be no Communists in the countryside, thanks to the New Course taken by the party."[16] In Biysk, also in Altai province, a party secretary complained that the party cell did nothing: "Party folks have been saying that you've got to quit party work in the countryside because nobody needs it any more." In the view of the dispirited official, it was a hopeless task to engage in propaganda and agitation in Siberian villages. The kulaks were already in control.[17] The party officials felt betrayed. This explains why many paraded their claim to power by criminal acts.

In the village of Tokarevo of Altai province, one Communist raped a woman and publicly boasted: "Don't worry, the court won't take the case."[18] The peasants there indeed complained that the authorities were not accepting claims against party members. Another Communist in Shchiglovskii district refused to surrender weapons, claiming that "there was no order from the Central Committee to disarm the party."[19] In much of what these people were saying there was a keenly felt nostalgia for the good old days of the civil war when they could use guns against "the enemies of Soviet power" without asking any permission. In the village of Salairki of Bochatskii district, a group of Communists threatened to liquidate the kulaks: "You just wait! Soon the year 1920 will come back upon you again."[20]

In many cases these Communists were buddies during the civil war. They had drinking parties reminiscing about the old times and then engaged in Red banditry. A certain Gavrilov in Shchiglovskii district set a barn of a poor peasant on fire hoping "that the fire would spread and burn all the kulaks." Another Communist was observed waving his gun and shouting: "I shall shoot you all!"[21] Local people were afraid of these types and constantly pleaded with the authorities to put an end to lawlessness. But the authorities preferred to ignore most of the complaints. Why should they defend kulaks against old-time party comrades?

Some cases of Red banditry sound almost like a deliberate replay of the civil war scenes. In a village of Slavgorodskii uezd in Omsk province a letter came to the village soviet. It ordered the kulaks to surrender surplus grain to the poor peasants. The letter threatened to burn households of those who failed to comply with the order. It was signed: "the Chief of the Food Supply detachment, Savinov, and the Chief for the Struggle with the Kulaks."[22]

There were no food supply detachments in 1925, nor were there any "chiefs for the struggle with the kulaks" in either 1920 or in 1925. Comrade Savinov just could not part with the past. What is most interesting in this incident is that the peasants complied. They began to surrender surplus grain to the village soviet with no compensation just as in 1920. For someone of the twenty-nine reading these reports such incidents could have reinforced the notion that the use of force, or just the threat of the use of force, still worked.

Defiant rejection of NEP was most prominent in Siberia, but certainly not limited to that area. It is best to think of this phenomenon not in terms of geography, but in terms of a state of mind. Defiant rejectionists were the people who did not or could not adjust to NEP. Market relations and political pluralism held no promise of a better life for them. They represented their views as an ideological commitment to the proletarian cause, but in fact they were bitter about their own failure. According to the editor of the journal *Novaya Derevnya* some people in the countryside were bound to remain poor not because they were lazy, but because others had better land or more start-up capital. Income differentiation was a natural by-product of market relations. Those who did fall through, or those whose hopes did not materialize, were particularly bitter since they envied those who succeeded. The editor claimed he had received many letters and:

> So much anger and frustration can be felt in these letters that one is truly overwhelmed. Never before have we had letters with so much resentment, hatred, and envy of the growing new agricultural households as now. A hungry and poor peasant is beginning to hate the prosperous toiling agriculturalists so much that he wants to bring ruin upon them. "If it is not for me, then for nobody," he says.[23]

Intervention

The top party leaders were worried by the trends in the countryside, perhaps obsessively so. The terms "cultured farmers" and "prosperous peasants" were increasingly replaced by the ominous "kulaks." The top twenty-nine knew that the party failed in elections, but in public Zinoviev repeated in one speech after another that in 1925 the Soviet state had paid 600 million rubles for 600,000 puds of grain; 60 per cent of all grain was produced by 14 per cent of the peasantry who had earned 500 million rubles.[24] The "kulaks" were getting more powerful and better organized all the time. They were going to challenge the party's leading role. Time was working against the Communists.

In 1926 important decisions were made. The prosperous peasants were to be taxed out of existence and deprived of electoral rights. From 1926 on, taxes on prosperous peasants were increased substantially, so that by the beginning of the new assault on the peasantry no prosperous peasants were left. The electoral law expanded the social category of those deprived of civil rights. In 1928 they were condemned to hard labor, their property was confiscated and their children not admitted to schools. They were being destroyed "as a class," in Bolshevik terminology. Two years later they would be deported from their native villages en masse.

The Bolshevik leaders tried to maintain their control over the countryside by targeting an entire social group they perceived as dangerous, the prosperous peasants, so-called kulaks. In fact dangerous elements were not necessarily prosperous. This was merely a convenient label. Dangerous were those who expressed political opinions, campaigned for Peasant Unions, opposed Communist domination, defended the churches, and defeated the Communists in elections. The absolute majority in that category were not the ephemeral kulaks but middle-income peasants or simply peasants. Recourse to administrative measures was in a sense an admission of the Communists' weakness. Despite the efforts of a huge propaganda machine, monopoly on communications, and enormous financial resources, the party was unable to compete with critically minded peasants who had no organization or national leadership. The experiment with unobstructed village soviets elections showed that with the kind of the rural party that was in place and with the kind of a reputation the Bolsheviks had in the countryside they had no chance of winning the peasants' trust.

RADICALIZATION, 1926

The political temperature in the countryside was rising. GPU reports noted increased kulak activity in the local soviets, insubordination to provincial authorities, circulation of anti-Soviet rumors, and even calls for armed insurrection. Some non-Communist soviets openly debated ways and means of raising prices on agricultural products by withholding supplies from the market. In some areas prosperous peasants bought up grain from poorer peasants hoping that grain prices would rise later. In other areas they began decreasing cultivated acreage since it was no longer profitable to produce more. This, in turn, affected poorer peasants who lost their jobs. In short, peasants were resorting to a form of bargaining at the market place. The Communists defined it as sabotage, hoarding, and malicious scheming by the class enemy. In its survey for July 1926 the GPU regretted that: "The soviets are contaminated by social elements alien and inimical to Soviet power; a widespread campaign to withhold taxes is on; appeals to refuse payment, to conceal taxable property, to agitate for tax-boycott organizations; and countless cases of protests against the level of taxation, as well as the organizing of Peasant Unions are widespread."[25]

Political trends unfavorable to the Communists were strongest in the areas which during the civil war had been the hotbeds of peasant resistance: Ukraine, the Cossack lands, the black earth southern Russian provinces, the

Volga Basin, and Siberia. Cases of anti-Communist campaigning, leafleting and rallies were reported in Tula, Vladimir, and Moscow provinces. Some leaflets talked about establishing peasant power [*krestyanskaya vlast'*].[26] At a peasant meeting in July 1926 in Dmitrovskii uezd of Moscow province, one peasant said: "Communists are very sly. If they had allowed a secret ballot, they all would have been thrown to the devil because peasants feel like this everywhere now."[27] The tone of peasant speeches and resolutions sharpened:

TAMBOV: We've got to organize ourselves and stop grain deliveries to the market. Let workers sit without bread.

SAMARA: Let the Communists sit for a while without food. It seems they have too much.[28]

KHERSON: Let the grain rot, but we will not surrender it for nothing.

TULA: The devil with them! Let them do whatever they please. Let them put us into prison, let them shoot us, but all the same we will not pay.[29]

GOMEL': The tax is sheer robbery. We've got to start an uprising and overthrow the Soviet power with arms, destroy the Communist Party, and establish the power of the democratic peasantry.[30]

The GPU survey for December 1926 noted "appeals to launch an armed insurrection against the soviets and the Communists."[31] Peasants in Tula province were agitating for a new revolution: "The peasants will rise against the soviets soon, led by well-known people, and then the end to Communists will come."[32] The number of angry peasant resolutions and letters was in the thousands from all regions of the country.

TSARITSYN (STALINGRAD): "Pass it on to Kalinin that we will not sow any extra grain, because peasants' produce is too cheap and the factory goods are too expensive."[33]

IRKUTSK, UDINSKII DISTRICT EC: "Soviet Power is not People's Power but is like another Nicholas II. There is no People's Power but a gang which is not interested in the peasants' situation. It is time to create true People's Power."[34]

In some situations peasants' actions were clearly a manifestation of a rising exasperation:

UL'YANOVSK (SIMBIRSK): A crowd of peasants, fifty people, after leaving the church destroyed the library, tore to pieces portraits of the CP leaders and beat up Komsomol members who were there.[35]

In March 1925 in the township of Yuriunin in Tsaritsyn province, a leaflet was posted at the city market square saying that the Communists were parasites filling up their own pockets and living at the expense of others. A Komsomol member started to tear down the leaflet and shouts were heard from the crowd: "It looks like you do not like hearing the truth."[36] One of the main themes in protest leaflets was that the Communists were robbing the peasantry. An appeal: "To You, the Quiet Don" spoke of "arrogant and unbridled boors who rip off the people to the end."[37] Another leaflet found in Donetsk drew a parallel between War Communism and NEP:

> During the so-called target grain collection, a robbery unheard-of in history, a wave of peasant resistance threatened to overthrow the Bolshevik dictatorship. But the sly swindler Lenin, who has kicked the bucket thank God, managed to deceive the people by a maneuver of trickery. The robbery of target collection he replaced with the robbery by tax. The hope that the Bolsheviks will change their economic policy is nothing but the ravings of a madman. They intend to create on the bones of millions something impossible to create – Communism.[38]

The GPU surmised that a group of the rural intelligentsia wrote that leaflet. In some cases protest leaflets contained open calls for violence. In May 1925 "An Appeal of the Starving Peasants to Soviet Power" was found in Borisoglebsk uezd, Tambov province: "If you do not provide relief to us, we shall rise against you. We will destroy, burn, beat, rob, and agitate against you!"[39] The Tula gubkom wrote that at peasant conferences one could often hear: "If the party is going to carry on with this tax policy, we will rebel."[40]

A special category in monthly GPU surveys was "Terror." Cases of arson, violent protests, activities of peasant bands, and political assassinations were counted and reported province by province, month after month by the watchful GPU. In the Volga Basin and Siberia in January 1925 there were 160 cases, and in February, 125.[41] In October alone there were more than a hundred incidents of violence against the local Soviet officials reported from Bryansk, Gomel, North Dvina province, and Altai in Siberia. As usual the word "terror" went together with the word "kulak" whether the prosperous peasants were involved or not. In Ukraine numerous peasant bands sprang up as during the civil war:

> UKRAINE: Pavlogradskii district: widespread arson of the households of Soviet officials and party members has begun. Among the peasants, rumors are circulating that some people have turned to revolution.

In Yekaterinoslav kulaks set party members' houses on fire. In the Don host country, Cossack bands reappeared and staged assaults on warehouses, soviets, and party cell premises.[42] And in Ishim district in Siberia peasants were quoted as saying: "Soon we peasants will turn to arms again. And then there really will be the last and decisive battle."[43] In 1926 the frequency of "acts of terror" increased: more than 100 every month, and in November 171.[44] In 1927 the GPU reported 61 cases of "kulak terror'" in February, 80 in January, growing to more than a 100 a month later in the year. The party leadership concluded that a soft policy in the countryside generated demands rather than gratitude for concessions.

ELECTIONS, 1927

In November 1926 a new electoral law deprived more kulaks and persons engaged in trade of voting rights.[45] As a result, the number of disenfranchised doubled.[46] In some areas the increase was severalfold. In Siberia, for example, in 1926 14,564 persons were disenfranchised, but in 1927, 76,958.[47] According to the official statistics, in 1927 a total of 1,338,158 persons in rural areas were deprived of electoral rights.[48] The local CP was instructed to rely on poor peasants, to take advantage of social tensions, isolate the kulaks politically, and create a solid social basis of support for Soviet power in the countryside.

Peasants cared a great deal about who would be elected to rural soviets because they determined who was a kulak and who was not. Taxes were assessed on the basis of class and income. Income was assessed on the basis of property listed in the property surveys. The surveys were conducted by local soviet functionaries. Who surveyed and what they surveyed determined higher or lower taxes, social identity, status, and later, survival. In Novosibirsk province, for example, 26,994 taxable households, or 22.5 per cent of the total number, were freed from paying any agricultural tax as poor peasants. Investigation later showed that the recipients were not poor peasants, but drinking pals and relatives of those in power.[49]

The electoral commissions drafted electoral lists to their own advantage. In many provinces middle-income peasants and even poor peasants were disenfranchised. Under the guise of struggle with the kulaks, the rural intelligentsia was disenfranchised almost everywhere. The qualification "persons engaged in trade" made it possible to disenfranchise any peasant for selling potatoes at the market. In Moscow province local authorities invented their own categories, such as "not yet unmasked elements" and, in Vyatka, "trouble-makers."[50] Local cliques and clans, insecure and isolated after the crushing defeat in elections in 1925, used the disenfranchisement campaign to preserve control over rural soviets. And that meant control over taxation and revenue.

The middle peasants almost everywhere opposed the new electoral law. They feared that some kind of excuse would be found to deprive them of voting rights as well. As one peasant in Ryazan province put it: "Now they want to cut off the peasants from power completely. You can't sell a single sheep without risking being disenfranchised."[51] Not just fears but common economic interests united middle-income and prosperous peasants. According to the GPU: "A bloc of middle peasants with the kulaks was noticeable even before the elections. Most of them followed the kulaks under the slogan: 'Elect businesslike and independent farmers.'"[52] In some areas the disenfranchised peasants refused simply to accept their exclusion from the electoral process. They tried to bribe local officials to restore their voting rights and sent appeals to Moscow. And in some cases they tried to organize themselves politically. In Troitsky district in the Urals, for example, the disenfranchised peasants resolved:

> Fine, let them deprive us of voting rights, but we shall declare our autonomy. Let us, all those who have been disenfranchised, gather a general meeting and nominate our own candidates.[53]

In general the prosperous peasants did not regard their situation as hopeless in 1927 despite heavy taxation and voting discrimination. Their confidence was based on an assumption that the authorities needed them as providers of revenue. In Novosibirsk the kulaks were reported as saying: "The state is afloat only thanks to us, the prosperous peasants. That's because we are the ones who pay taxes. And what can you take from a poor peasant? Whatever you give him, it's a waste, because he is lazy."[54]

Poor peasants were generally happy with disenfranchising the prosperous ones. However, there are indications that this was not always the case. The GPU cited poor peasants as saying: "The master is deprived of his voting rights and I lose my job."[55] Poor peasants expressed concern that the Communists only made promises. The words of one peasant were cited as typical:

> You comrades only know how to talk. But you have not done anything tangible for peasants. You just talk and the wind blows. What do we get out of your organizing? What good is there that we have assembled? We will not have enough to eat from that. But prosperous peasants will give us something real without much talking, and the authorities just promise but give nothing.[56]

The rural Communists campaigned vigorously in 1927. Province committees usually mapped out campaign strategy. Party meetings would be held, a core of propagandists traveled across the province and held pre-election meetings with the "activists" in the uezds. The party cells then held meetings with groups of "poor" peasants, that is, reliable supporters, drafted lists of candidates, and presented these at general election meetings. In their speeches they repeated old familiar themes, on the unity of the working class and the toiling peasantry, the wise policy of the Central Committee, the threats to Soviet Russia from the imperialist countries, and successes in socialist construction in the USSR. Communist campaigning was always too general and avoided specific issues that interested peasants most: taxes, prices, and civil rights. After brief speech-making the Communist cell usually moved that the Communist list be accepted by an open show of hands in favor. Quite often this system worked and desirable candidates were elected. In hundreds of cases in all regions of the country peasants resisted Communist control of election procedure:

KIEV: These are not free elections when they send us the chairman of the district EC from Kiev.

KANSK: They have sent the district EC chairman by mail to us. Are they going to send us a village soviet chairman in the envelope too? What kind of elections are those? This is simply appointeeism. A bunch of party people decide everything.

TAMBOV: The congress of soviets should be the true master and not a bunch of party folks.

TOMSK: They write all the time that elections are free, and then here some kind of a conference appoints candidates and imposes them on us.[57]

In what was a typical electoral situation in Bronnitskii uezd, Moscow province, the village soviet chairman read out the list of candidates, all members of the Communist cell. Shouts were heard: "Down with pressure! Enough orders!" The party cell list was rejected and candidates were nominated by the peasant meeting right there.[58]

A vigorous election campaign raged all over the Soviet Union. Speeches of peasant candidates at election rallies, the formation of opposition electoral blocs, and the appearance of concrete policy programs all testify to the peasants' remarkable political maturity which had no precedent in Russia. In Saratov province several groupings were holding election meetings in one village: the church council [tserkovnyi sovet], the CP cell, the committee of the poor, the Komsomol cell, and the disenfranchised caucus.[59] What distinguished the election campaign in 1927 was that peasants tried to put on the ballot alternative election slates and to compete in elections within the bounds of Soviet law. The number of political groups in opposition to Communists which were labeled "kulak" drastically increased, from 84 in December 1926 to 274 in January 1927. At the same time, the GPU registered 229 attempts to set up Peasant Unions.[60]

Electoral groupings are being formed primarily for the purpose of securing victories for the kulak candidates and the defeat of the candidates of the poor peasants and the Communist Party cells.[61]

In Ivanovo-Voznesensk province, for example, a pre-election meeting of the Communist Party cell and the "poor" peasants was canceled on the grounds that it was illegal. A schoolteacher led a group of protesters, arguing that peasants of all income groups had the right to attend election meetings.[62] In other places prosperous and middle-income peasants argued that if the Communists and the poor peasants had a right to organize their separate pre-election meetings and nominate candidates, the kulaks had the same rights. The GPU referred to such incidents as "heightened political engagement of the kulaks."[63] Moreover, at the district congresses of soviets in the Leningrad, Stalingrad, Orel, Tomsk, and Ivanovo-Voznesensk provinces, the Communists' opponents managed to create their own "non-party factions" whose main purpose was to defeat party candidates. In Tambov province, for example, non-party factions were organized at two uezd congresses of soviets. As one peasant delegate in Morshanskii uezd explained:

If we do not nominate our own candidates in an organized fashion, the Communist Party is going to squeeze us because the party nominates first of all party members and only then sometimes peasants. However, the Communists are small in number, but we, the peasants, there are 100 million of us.[64]

A truly universal peasant demand in 1927 was to reduce taxes. The entire taxation system based on class had to be abolished. It was counterproductive, since all middle-income peasants feared to produce more lest they be bracketed as kulaks. Prosperous peasants subdivided their assets to avoid being labeled kulak and risk dispossession and disenfranchisement. Poor peasants usually enjoyed a tax exemption but many resented the label "poor" which did not confer much respect. Peasant delegates worried about specifics: forests, water, insurance, and schools. The rights and obligations of communities and province authorities had to be defined. Peasant delegates did not want to hear about imperialist threats but about road construction in their provinces. A peasant *nakaz* at the Omsk electoral district demanded:

The entire peasantry must have insurance, must be provided with medical aid, educational facilities, and places of rest and recreation proportionate to its size in the country's population. All this can be paid for from the funds raised by the agricultural tax. This is our peasant understanding of the agricultural tax.[65]

In short, the peasants wanted to see concrete improvements in their lives. They were not interested in ideology or abstract theories. Their leaders complained that though peasants were the largest taxpaying group in the country they had no idea how their money was being spent. They did not understand why so little was returned to them.

Many proposals revolved around the problem of prices: high prices for industrial goods and low prices for agricultural products. A peasant speaker in the Volokalamskii uezd of Moscow province explained: "Our products are very cheap. The authorities are riding on the peasants' back. They deliberately raise prices in order to squeeze more out of the muzhiks. We've got to have our union to protest against high prices." The best way to oppose the state fixed price was to cut out the state intermediary altogether and do business independently. As a peasant in the Moscow province explained:

What we have to do is create peasant partnerships and a Peasant Union so that we could establish contact with the trusts and syndicates and then we will buy cloth, and so on, from them and we ourselves will sell them our agricultural products at a price we set.[66]

Several speeches and resolutions at election meetings implied that the Bolshevik state was an obstacle which had to be removed. In Belgorod uezd of Kursk province a Communist resolution was rejected and a peasant speaker said:

The power of soviets and the CP does not reflect the peasants' interests. How long are you going to fool us peasants? You have exhausted us with taxes ... You pay 70 kopecks for rye ... We are not going to support you and we do not trust you.[67]

Russian peasants were against taxation without representation, for lower taxes, fair prices, social services, insurance legislation, and educational opportunities – a wish-list that would be considered normal in any society. They proceeded in their politics from the empirical reality they saw. Every year their perception was reinforced that the authorities treated them only as a source of revenue. Taxes were high, elections unfair, and production discouraged. The weapon at peasants' disposal was to store grain in their possession until the price was right. In 1928 in many regions of the country the peasants did just that. And in some areas they refused to pay any agricultural tax at all. Party leaders either had to raise procurement prices or return to grain collection by force.

BOLSHEVIK DILEMMAS, 1928

From 1925 to 1928 Russian agriculture showed remarkable growth. In most provinces cultivated acreage reached the pre-war levels and cattle herds began to surpass those levels. Those who had one cow in 1925 qualified as poor peasants but if they added another cow, by 1928 they moved into the middle-income tax bracket. Those who had three cows in 1925 and six in 1928 became kulaks in terms of their social identity and tax status. This meant that the success of NEP in increasing agricultural output consistently generated more kulaks. In Vologda province, famous for its dairy products, the growth of the well-to-do peasantry was extraordinary. In just two years from 1926 to 1928 the acreage under cultivation increased by 30 per cent, cattle herds by 35 per cent, and the number of horses by 30 per cent. Peasant households in the tax bracket over 500 rubles a year (i.e. kulak) grew from 6,315 in 1927 to 8,462 in 1928, an increase of over 2,000 in just two years that threatened to overwhelm the 2,500 rural Communists in the province.[68] In the neighboring Votkinsk province, "there were only 900 rural Communists and a marked tendency of the rural party cells to shrink."[69] The rural party was losing out to the kulaks both in sheer numbers and wealth.

Communist propaganda portrayed collective farms as inherently superior to backward individual farming. In fact those familiar with the real situation knew state farms were mostly loss-making. They could not survive without state support nor compete with peasant partnerships. As early as 1924 the GPU gave the following assessment of the state farms:

The condition of the newly created state farms is almost everywhere unsatisfactory. Everywhere we can see sloppiness, negligence, and sometimes clear criminality of administration in regard to the property in its custody. In Yaroslavl province grain is rotting in the granaries, and agricultural machinery is being stolen by the administration.[70]

To Bolsheviks who wanted to believe that collective and state-run farms were superior it was difficult to face the fact that they were not. From the point of view of the party leaders, the continued existence of "kulak partnerships" begged unfavorable comparisons and generated heretical views in the party. Did capitalist production outperform the socialist version? Would reorganization of agriculture along socialist lines lead to the creation of an inherently inefficient agriculture? This was the line of reasoning in many discussion circles in the party in 1928.

The level of violence steadily rose in the countryside from 1927 onward. Provincial reports were full of accounts of arson, assaults, ambushes on party officials, formation of bands, as in the civil war years, and the slaughter of cattle. Novosibirsk reported: "the setting on fire of granaries, hay or grain, the slaughtering of horses and the wrecking of machinery belonging to party officials."[71] The GPU forwarded to the CC leaflets from the lower Volga area, a scene of a fierce peasant resistance seven years earlier:

All rise to defend your grain! Chase away tax collectors from your villages! Do not sell grain to the state for worthless pennies! Prepare yourself for struggle! Form detachments and join in the ranks under the banners of the Union of Peasant Self-Defense![72]

The party's Control Commission investigated dozens of cases of corruption of the rural party. Virtually all provincial rural cells owed money to the private sector.[73] A survey of the rural party in Saratov province showed that embezzlement of state funds was epidemic. The Committees to Aid the Poor were "dispersing funds to friends and drinking companions."[74] The CC report on the lower Volga area described:

links between party officials and anti-Soviet and kulak elements, misuse of authority for personal gain, drunkenness, patronage of alien social elements . . . drinking ties [p'ianaya smychka] between party officials and alien elements . . . They were getting money from wherever they could.[75]

In Vologda province, the Control Commission discovered the "blending of entire blocs of the soviet and party apparatus with the capitalist elite of the countryside."[76] The kulaks were taxed at a lower rate in exchange for a bribe, a phenomenon called "systematic under-taxation of kulaks." The party and the kulaks thrived together, enriching themselves at the expense of Moscow.

The ever-tougher measures against the kulaks adopted in 1928 led to ever-more ingenious ways of adaptation to the situation. In Shuiskii district, for example, the brothers Palnikov as owners of a leather factory were disenfranchised and dispossessed, their children expelled from school, and they were condemned to hard labor. The Palnikovs made a deal with the district party secretary that in the official record Palnikovs would give up the factory voluntarily, but that one brother would remain director, the other his deputy, and that their social status would be changed to employee, their children would go back to school, and they would get their civil rights back plus 40 hectares of land, listed after the factory. The party cell chair would get an undisclosed share of the factory profits in return.[77]

The overwhelming majority of party officials were comfortably set up in their provinces, and most of them learned to live well under NEP. Most party organizations in most provinces had countless financial and personal ties to the market-producing peasantry. They held shares in partnerships, rented out land, took bribes and kick-backs, loaned and invested money, and received payments for favorable decisions on allocation of resources and machinery. The rural party identified with local interests and covered up missing revenue. In other words a blending of the economic and political elites was going on in the countryside. From Moscow's point of view, the rural party was becoming an adjunct of the kulak network. There simply was no pressure from below to launch "collectivization" either from peasants or from the rural party. Stalin's decision may be seen as an attempt to stop and reverse the process in motion, the process of the withering away of the Communist Party in the countryside.

The procurement crisis of 1928 was a direct consequence of Bolshevik policies in 1926 and 1927. The chain of events can be summarized as follows. In 1923–4 the Bolsheviks practiced NEP-attuned policies. They lowered taxes, introduced real money, encouraged increases in production, and even went so far as to allow relatively free elections to rural soviets. The political fall-out was unexpected. Instead of being grateful to the party, peasants demanded more and a truly nation-wide movement to create Peasant Unions emerged. In 1925 and 1926 peasants tried to gain influence through local soviets. The prosperous peasants competed successfully with the CP for political influence and therefore they had to be removed. From this time on, the term "cultured farmer" [kul'turnyi khozyain] was slowly replaced by "kulak." Ever more loudly, the propaganda machine began to scream about the "kulak danger" in the countryside. The authorities drafted laws for deprivation of voting rights by income.

In 1926 the spiral of confrontation continued to unfold. More kulaks were disenfranchised, and more had to pay higher taxes. The prosperous peasants responded by heightened political involvement in elections, hiring poor peasants to represent them, organizing electoral blocs, and campaigning against the Communists in elections. Again official party nominees were defeated in some places, bribed in others, and threatened and blackmailed elsewhere. As a last resort peasants refused to market grain at an unfair price.[78]

The Bolsheviks were not disposed to tolerate a challenge to their political authority. The remedy was obviously to crush resistance by force and deprive peasants of any means to "sabotage" party policy. The Bolshevik mind-set was a combination of what could be called the Russian interpretation of Marxism and Russian authoritarian statism. All Communists, Stalin and Bukharin included, basically shared the goal that capitalism in the country-side was to be phased out. Given the Bolsheviks' traditional hostility to the market economy, to private enterprise, and to any kind of political independ-ence of any social group, they had to react the way they did. Drastic measures were to be applied because the Bolsheviks perceived peasant actions as acts of disobedience. Peasants were to be shown that they could not disobey the master: the socialist state. The Bolsheviks regarded peasants as essentially a source of revenue for state tasks, exactly as had the old regime. The state knew better what was good for peasants. They had to be guided to the future the state had designed for them. There is a profound continuity in the kind of attitude towards peasants held by the Tsarist and Soviet regimes.

Bolshevik–peasant interaction shows that peasants talked the language of bargaining, elections, prices, taxes, services, a discourse of a normal, modern electoral politics; the Bolsheviks talked the language of a serf owner with a whip. A challenge to authority could not go unanswered. The entire pro-duction process in agriculture was going to be taken under party control and supervision. A new Communist offensive was going to be launched to crush peasant independence. The code name for this operation was "collectiv-ization."

There hardly can be a more inappropriate term for the social and political transformation that was about to unfold than collectivization. Officially a transition was made from backward individual family farming to advanced, modern collective and socialist farming. This scheme is fundamentally flawed because peasants had collectives of all kinds in the 1920s, thriving in market conditions. There were plenty of partnerships which owned hundreds of Ford tractors; all kinds of marketing and harvesting arrangements abounded. Moreover, attempts were made to form large-scale marketing collectives and partnerships that would have represented peasants in large-scale commercial deals. Cooperatives, especially consumer cooperatives, revived in Russia after the blows they received during the civil war. It is misleading to conceptualize the change of 1928–30 as a transition from individual and backward to collective and advanced agriculture: rather it is the other way around, independent networks of collective associations were smashed, and atomized individuals without any property or rights were herded into state-run units for grain extraction, misnamed collective farms.

Was there an alternative to the Stalinist war on the peasantry, misnamed collectivization? Of course there was. The evidence is overwhelming that the long-term trends in the Russian countryside did not portend anything good for the Communist Party. Peasants were certain to continue to persist in their attempts to pay less and get more for their taxes. Unless crushed, a Peasant Union and a peasant political party were going to appear and compete with the Communists in elections. Judging by peasant demands, this party would have defended private property on land, free markets, and free prices and equal opportunities in elections. Time was on their side. With each year they accumulated more resources and experience. It would have been impossible for the Bolsheviks, without recourse to violence, to control and contain the peasants' desire to have their own marketing and bargaining organizations, collectives in a true sense of the word. The rural Communist Party was being slowly absorbed into the peasant hierarchy. It was being bribed, married, or coopted. The market economy generated wealth, modest still but growing and in the hands of people who were already campaigning against the Communists. The trends in the countryside, if left unchecked, would have posed a danger to the Communist dictatorship. The alternative to Stalinism was a market economy and a multiparty system.

Chapter 8

The proletariat against the vanguard

Official representations of workers' relations with the Communist Party in the 1920s portray unity, optimism, and revolutionary elan. The Bolsheviks' claim to legitimacy was based on their assumed role as the workers' vanguard, leading the country to socialism. Anything that failed to conform to the ideal was labeled counterrevolutionary agitation by definition. This led to interesting semantic games. Since there was not supposed to be labor unrest in a country of the victorious proletariat, strikes had to be represented as something else, most often as "counterrevolutionary provocations" of "hidden Mensheviks," White Guards, or class enemies. In confidential discourse, however, a different story emerges of workers' attitudes to NEP, the party, and socialism. The CC sent special teams to investigate troublesome situations. More steady and outspoken was the GPU. It systematically recorded protests and referred to social phenomena with surprising frankness. Strikes were referred to as strikes. Top Bolshevik leaders had to live bipolar lives between their two realities – the one represented in the official media, and the other presented in top-secret reports. Communication between the CC and the provinces, and between the CC and the GPU, is a multi-layered discourse on workers' lives, attitudes, and responses to party policy. The incongruity between propaganda representation and social reality highlights the evolution of Bolshevik labeling, the process of workers' estrangement from the party, and the causes for the demise of NEP in industry.

NEW BOSSES, OLD PROBLEMS, 1921–5

The starting point of NEP in March 1921 was marked by strikes, rallies, and violent clashes with the Bolshevik authorities, especially in Petrograd and Moscow. Workers demanded free trade and elections, an end to Cheka repression, and unrestrained labor organization and wage bargaining. With the introduction of the New Economic Policy, the only change that affected workers was the phasing out of food rationing and the slow reintroduction of money (that is prices and wages) to replace the failed coupons and labor armies. Workers still had no right to bargain for wages. Most of industry stayed nationalized. Red directors continued to run industry just as *glavki* [directorates] had earlier under War Communism. Famine still affected the lower Volga provinces. Daily and weekly Cheka reports described chaos in food supply, theft on the railroads, and "discontent in connection with the non-payment of wages in either rations or money."[1] In Moscow the number of strikes held to a steady twelve to fifteen a month, with what was called "manifestations of discontent" hovering at between fifty to seventy cases in 1922.[2] Job security was low, as most jobs required little or no training. It was easy to dismiss protesting workers and hire others.

Inefficient, bureaucratic, top-heavy Soviet enterprises had a hard time adjusting to the money economy. To survive they had to produce sellable goods or plead for a state bail-out. Most of them could not keep up with their payment obligations. Numerous enterprises found themselves operating at a loss as their products were too expensive and were not selling. Production had to be curtailed and workers laid off. This was the start of the so-called 'scissors' crisis, perhaps more accurately termed an economic crisis. The GPU informed Stalin about "a sharp deterioration of the situation in industry and collapse of production in numerous branches" which was accompanied by "late payment of wages, a sharp rise in prices, and low pay-scales for workers."[3]

In July 1923 more than 100 enterprises employing a total of some 50,000 people were on strike. In August figures totaled at some 140 enterprises and 80,000 workers.[4] In September and November the strike wave continued unabated; the GPU, hardly a pro-worker lobby in the CP, noted that it was triggered by a "further deterioration in workers' position due to confusion caused by the transition to the new currency." The GPU warned the CC of a dangerous social trend that "the number of industrial workers was declining, the frequency of strikes rising, and workers' discontent, caused by managers' excessive compensation, was increasing. As a result, the influence of anti-Soviet parties was growing."[5]

In response to a strike in Kharkov the Red director shut down the plant and called in the GPU to unmask instigators, trouble-makers, plotters, and "hidden Mensheviks." All 2,500 workers were fired and a notice, posted at the plant's gates, informed that: "Applications for rehiring were being considered on an individual basis" by a commission of the Red director, the GPU, and gubkom representatives. Little by little, the workers started to return, the trouble-makers were dismissed, and "order" was restored. The strike ended without any gains for the workers.[6] Communist trade unionists were torn between the gubkoms' demand to enforce worker compliance, and their desire to help their constituency. In some places union officials were no better than the Red directors, in others they played a constructive role.

The pattern of workers' action and Bolshevik reaction played itself out frequently in dozens of other strikes.[7] The Bolsheviks acted with the explicit purpose of rooting out the possibility of further protest. They tried to condition workers that labor protest was futile. According to GPU Deputy Chair Yagoda's report to Stalin on a strike in Donbas:

> After the end of the strike, campaigning started among the workers to free those strike instigators who had been arrested by the GPU. On November 2 the Pamanovskii mine went on strike, and the miners, numbering 5,000, walked to the township of Shakhty with the demand to free the arrested instigators. As a result, special purpose units [*ChON*] had to be deployed.[8]

Yagoda laid out everything in the open. Strike leaders were referred to as instigators of strikes, not as Black Hundred counterrevolutionaries or agents of world imperialism. Those metaphors were reserved for the public media. They had been arrested and charged with counterrevolutionary activity, even though there was nothing counterrevolutionary in demanding punctual payment of wages. Yagoda admitted that the GPU had used force to disperse workers demonstrating their solidarity with the arrested strike leaders. Yagoda and Stalin knew they were dealing with workers' protest.

The major causes of workers' discontent were remarkably similar across the expanse of Russia. First and foremost these were wage levels, late payment of wages, and the factory managers' privileges. In the report covering September–October 1923, the GPU described: "consistently late payment of wages; rude treatment of workers by factory managers, and their lavish lifestyles, which caused workers' discontent." In the Donbas "the administration was engaged in drunkenness; they set themselves up comfortably and were rude to workers." And at the Cartridge plant in Simbirsk, the antagonism "was strong between workers and high-ranking officials, who behaved tactlessly as superiors, engaged in drunkenness, and rode racing horses in plain sight of the common folks which caused sharp enmity."[9]

The Communist bosses' conduct at the factories was hardly different from that of their counterparts in the countryside. Both urban and rural elites wanted to flaunt their superior position and underscore the difference between themselves and their former social equals. Just like rural party upstarts who imitated the old master [*barin*], the urban Communist vanguard imitated the role models of the overthrown elites. In Moscow, at the Krasnyi Bogatyr' factory, the supervisor of one of the departments issued an order that workers should stand up and take their hats off when the director was passing by.[10] At many enterprises in Moscow province "workers' strong discontent was caused by factory managers appropriating bonuses for themselves."[11] At the Bryansk locomotive plant, only 30 per cent of wages for May were paid by July 1924. A series of strikes followed, countered by arrests; subsequent demands to elect a new factory committee led the latter to enlist the help of the GPU to undercut "anti-Soviet agitation."[12] Almost identical was the reaction at the Trekhgornaya textile mill in Moscow. Workers called for a meeting about low wage-scales and demanded that the GPU guarantee in advance that the workers' spokesmen would not be arrested. All 7,000 workers went on strike and all were fired. In the end almost all the workers showed up to petition for their jobs back. The management had taught them a lesson – workers could plead for a job, but not for better conditions.[13]

The strike at the locomotive plant in Sormovo, near Nizhnii Novgorod, started, like many others, over a pay dispute. Wages were two months overdue and hovered at 30 per cent of pre-war level. The management unilaterally decided to pay 10 per cent of workers' wages with state bonds. Workers demanded their full wages and went on strike. The management cut off electricity to the homes of the striking workers and threatened to fire all the workers and hire back only those who proved their political loyalty.[14] According to the GPU, the Mensheviks and Socialist Revolutionaries were "received as their own, as workers from their own milieu who spoke about the common needs."[15]

The Red directors were naturally interested in keeping their overheads low. That meant in practice that they opposed wage concessions and favored labor intensification. An underground Menshevik journal wrote: "Let's admit it, our managers are shameless capitalists." By virtue of their institutional positions, they were profoundly anti-labor: "They are shouting about the harmfulness of strikes and the necessity of abandoning the eight-hour day," and "demand an absolute managerial autocracy at the plant, limitations on the rights of trade unions, and cuts in wages." Red managers were more autocratic and less inclined to negotiate with workers than owners were before 1917; they were arrogant and stubborn in ways that were unmatched by the pre-revolutionary capitalists. "Waving their party cards, these people were attacking trade unionists, and were ready to crush anyone who dared to resist."[16]

Strike leaders argued that since NEP meant a partial restoration of capitalism, workers had to be allowed to defend their economic rights as they did in other capitalist societies. It was only natural for them to bargain for better wages, an eight-hour day, insurance boards, and so on. What they did not take into account was that, in the Bolshevik mind, "the economic struggle of the working class" was a precursor to political struggle. Allowing workers to organize in defense of economic rights would mean allowing them to organize against the Communist Party. It would mean recognizing that the Communists were not the workers' vanguard but rather new bosses who had replaced the old ones.

This reality contrasted sharply with the official representations, exacerbating workers' frustration. The glitter of the capitals under NEP was not for the workers. It was for the newly rich and for the party elite. Angry strikers circulated an underground leaflet in Sormovo:

> It is true that our country is poor. Sure – strikes bring losses. No sage has yet invented a strike that brings profits. But why do you start talking about the country's poverty only when the conversation turns to the beggarly

wages of workers? Why don't you test your oratory on a gathering in one of Nizhnii's restaurants where you will find many of your party friends. Why don't you go for a jaunt on foot and not by car along the streets of the big cities? Why don't you take a look at all those cafés, restaurants, casinos, theaters, and concert halls! Glance at Nizhnii's trade fair! Take a look! Tour the country houses [*dachas*] around Moscow; look at who lives there and how! And if, after all this, you dare to lecture the workers on sacrifices, then we can forget any talk of your honesty.[17]

Golos Rabochego [*The Workers' Voice*], an underground *samizdat* journal, characterized the system as state capitalism: "We decisively reject the notion that there is a dictatorship of the proletariat in Soviet Russia. This is the lie that fogs the minds of the workers. There is no and has never been any dictatorship of the proletariat."[18] The Red directors and gubkom bureaucrats were the new ruling class, a new bourgeoisie, pure and simple. Both sides were quite aware that workers distrusted the party, referred to the Communists as the new bosses, as "masters," a "new caste," and an array of similar names. The Voronezh gubkom wrote:

At the wood-processing factory, workers refused to vote for the Communist cell at elections, arguing that the "Communist cells always appoint their own people and do not let workers vote freely." Moreover, one worker posed a question: "Do the workers have the right to vote? If yes, then why does the cell push through its own candidates to the exclusion of all others? Why does the cell not allow workers to elect whomever they want?" Moreover, one of the speakers said that while the trade unions had used to defend workers, now they campaign for raising productivity of labor and decreased wages, whereas they themselves receive high salaries.[19]

Communist Party cells in every factory served as eyes and ears of the GPU and reported regularly and systematically on workers' attitudes. Workers realized this and coined a new nickname for them *Komishcheiki* [Com. spies] which rhymes with *Kom.iacheiki* [Com. cells].[20] Workers viewed them with suspicion and were reluctant to join. In Bryansk, for example, out of 19,198 workers, only 826 were party members.[21] Similarly, at the Putilov plant in Leningrad, only 60 out of 4,000 workers joined the party.[22] Anti-Soviet agitation was reported in favor of carting all the Communist Party bureau members out of the plant. GPU informers quoted workers as saying that "the party turned against the working class," "only careerists were in the party," and that "the power was in the hands of the kikes."[23]

Workers were not interested in what the Bolsheviks called socialist construction. In Leningrad "it was only possible to attract workers to attend meetings if their wages were on the agenda or if a concert followed the meeting." The official celebration of the May Day almost collapsed because, out of 3,300 workers at Uritsky plant, only 200 showed up.[24] With remarkable frankness, a confidential report shattered the official propaganda myth that skilled workers – "hereditary proletarians" – were the natural bearers of Communist ideology:

> In the Maltsevskii district a skilled worker has a little house and a cow. First and foremost, he cares that his wages are paid on time. He seeks peace and quiet. He is to the highest degree indifferent to the problems of the world revolution.[25]

Workers grumbled about low wages and held on to their jobs. To get drunk after work was a daily ritual for them. Trotsky's colleague Victor Serge recalled that:

> The workers escaped their miserable quarters by going to the cabarets. Housewives of the Red Putilov works section begged party committees to find a way to turn over to them a part of the salaries of their husbands. On pay-days, some drunkard proletarians lay dead drunk on the sidewalks and others reviled as you passed. I was despised as a bespectacled intellectual.[26]

Numerous accounts suggest that the workers ignored Bolshevik clubs and tended to frequent both pubs and prostitutes. When drunk, they cursed the intellectuals, Jews, and Communists. Drinking on the job was also a frequent occurrence. Alcoholism, hooliganism, fights, rape, and killings in workers' neighborhoods were topics in countless articles in the Soviet press. The GPU submitted a special report to the CC on drunkenness among workers. It was a graphic account, province by province, listing dozens of incidents, statistical calculations, and assessments. Here is a short sample of the data:

NIZHNII NOVGOROD: Workers consume alcoholic beverages directly from the bottle at the factory gate. Drunkenness is noticeable primarily among the skilled workers.

LENINGRAD: Pervasive drunkenness, particularly on pay-days. Many drunk workers are lying in the streets, dead drunk, particularly at night. Fights and gang skirmishes usually follow. At some factories drinking goes hand in hand with playing cards and prostitution.

KOSTROMA PROVINCE: During the Easter holidays a drunken free-for-all was in full swing among the workers; as a result there were many injured in drunken brawls.

THE WOOD-CUTTING FACTORY: Hooliganism – teenage workers behave themselves particularly disgustingly. Prostitution is on the rise among women workers.

PERM: During Easter pervasive drunkenness reigned supreme to the last man. Card playing, fights, and drunken brawls with the use of knife-play took place.[27]

Those familiar with workers' daily lives, culture, and habits in the years before 1913 would recognize scenes in these reports. Not much had changed in regard to the drinking habits of Russian workers. Most of the Bolshevik cultural campaigns made little impact on them. In some respects, however, Bolshevik policies made alcoholism worse. Attacks on religion, family, and marriage undermined these institutional restraints which had performed a useful function before 1913. Furthermore, under the Bolsheviks, there was no consumption incentive. If, in 1913, a skilled Russian worker might have hoped to own a house one day, especially in small industrial towns, this became virtually impossible under the Bolsheviks. A worker could never hope to own anything, least of all a house or an apartment, in the foreseeable future. Overcrowded communal apartments, if not crude barracks, with their gossip and rumors, kitchen talks, and drunken brawls – that was the lot of most workers.[28] As possessions were denounced as "bourgeois hold-overs," party members lived in houses and rode about in cars. Resentment and drinking reigned in the working-class neighborhoods.

The workers were said to be a ruling class, the government was supposed to be that of workers and peasants, and the country was said to be building socialism. Yet, in reality, workers were paid wages equal to a third of the pre-war level, often with several months' delay. They were fired for the slightest disobedience and fined or exiled for political protest. Their bosses treated them in a provocative and disdainful manner, emphasizing differences in status, income, and power. Any attempt to bargain or protest was dealt with ruthlessly by the GPU. The bosses were new but the problems in workers' lives were old.

WAS THERE AN NEP IN INDUSTRY?

The introduction of the new currency in 1923 had led to a remarkable improvement of the situation in industry, as in agriculture.[29] However, this should be seen in a proper historical context. Compared to 1921, Russian industry was in good shape in 1926. The same could not be said in comparison to 1913, largely because of the inefficiency of Bolshevik management, outdated technology, and a poorly motivated labor force. Improvement consisted of bringing a factory output up to 20 per cent to 50 per cent of 1913 levels. The Sormovo plant performed at 48 per cent output of the 1913 level in 1925, reaching only 38 per cent in the production of locomotives.[30] Only on very rare occasions did factories manage to reach 100 per cent of 1913 levels, let alone surpass those in key economic indicators.

Soviet-state heavy industry operated at a loss most of the time. The Kuzbas iron-ore industrial complex – the largest in Russia – showed a loss of 1,300,000 rubles for the 1924–5 fiscal year.[31] In Kaluga province "a number of state trusts, such as the glass factory, phosphorus mines, leather trust, and others have finished the 1926–7 fiscal year with a loss."[32] So did Sormovo locomotive plant. Economic indicators were going from bad to worse. The cost of production was rising, whereas labor productivity was not. A special commission's investigation revealed that the plant was plagued by mismanagement, poor use of resources, and an unsteady, unmotivated workforce.[33] There was a shortage of housing, discontent over low wages, and a flight of skilled workers.[34]

Like many Bolshevik confidential reports, this one identified the problems accurately. Yet it failed to indicate the real causes of the poor performance of Soviet enterprises. They were structural – to put it in ideological terms, they performed poorly because they were "socialist." In practice, "socialist" industry meant "state" industry. This meant that the management operated on the assumption that the state would not let them fail. The priority of management was not improving performance but concealing the bad performance and extracting from the state budget as much as possible for their plant. The relationship with the state was one of who could extract more for less. The very structure of Soviet industry precluded its efficiency and in fact discouraged it. Even though officially all major enterprises were organized as industrial trusts with all the attributes of economic independence (i.e. legal and fiscal status as judicial bodies in their own right), in fact they were all state property. Generating losses did not lead to bankruptcy, but instead to replacing "bad comrades" on the boards of directors with "good" ones, and allocating subsidies from the budget to correct any deficits.

At no time during NEP did Russian heavy industry perform in market conditions. One can argue that there never was any NEP in heavy industry. All enterprises in the final analysis relied on budget allocations, regardless of their profitability. The chronic unprofitability of the state metal industry was incorporated into Soviet legislation, which tried to spread the burden of inefficient enterprises across the entire economy. A 1927 decree on trusts excluded profitability as a necessary requirement of performance; the emphasis was put on fulfilling output targets set by the state.[35] In these conditions trusts had no interest in decreasing the cost of production nor in increasing efficiency because their targets would then be raised. Moreover, any profits they showed would be automatically diverted into the state budget.[36] There was no incentive to be profitable, as it implied harder work and no reward. Loss-making, state industry fulfilling a state plan was set up as early as 1926.

The second key factor for the fate of NEP was that private enterprises, mostly small, but well-run establishments, did remarkably well. This was true particularly in leather, food-processing, consumer manufacturing, and textile industries. Not only did they show profits and pay taxes designed to discriminate against the private sector, but in some cases they paid higher wages to their workers. In some provinces, such as Samara, private enterprises paid workers' wages "several times higher than at state enterprises."[37] The Bolsheviks faced an embarrassing situation. So-called "socialist industry" was failing to pay wages at enterprises they had nationalized in 1917 that were equal to the level the capitalists had paid before the war. According to the GPU: "In the majority of provinces, the average wage for workers reached barely 50 per cent of the pre-war level."[38] According to a Putilov workers' letter, smuggled out of Russia and published in an SR journal in Prague, wages of 40 rubles a month reached barely 30 per cent of the pre-war level and only 5 per cent of workers were paid up to 80 rubles a month.[39]

Wage rates showed great disparities by sector. Generally, unskilled workers were worse off under NEP than under War Communism's ration system. In Leningrad they constituted 35 per cent of the labor force and their wages were under 40 rubles a month, a meager wage to support a family.[40] In Tula the GPU report emphasized that: "Workers of low skill categories, burdened with families, received wages which did not satisfy their minimal requirements. Skilled workers were paid 55 rubles a month, and unskilled ones 25." And in Leningrad, "anti-Soviet conversations were going on among workers, pointing out that workers had shed their blood, and fought [for the revolution] and now were forced to work as in forced labor camps for 2 rubles a day. In comparison with Tsarism, nothing has improved."[41]

Leningrad had a higher than average concentration of skilled labor. In provincial industrial centers unskilled workers were worse off. In Orel textile industry wages were only 24 rubles a month, and in the food-processing industry 34 rubles a month.[42] Women textile workers in the Vladimir region were paid only 15 rubles a month. And in Sormovo the average wage of low-skilled workers was 17–19 rubles a month.[43] The social consequences of these wage-rates in the mid-1920s were that skilled workers sought employment in higher-paying private enterprises. As a result, the GPU informed the CC in 1925 that "at the majority of plants in the machine-building industry, a flight of skilled workers was under way."[44]

The Bolsheviks believed in state intervention. Their objective was to generate revenue to invest in state heavy industry. Investment capital could be generated only domestically. The policies the Bolsheviks adopted in 1926 were supposed to stimulate efficiency, savings, and investment in industry. Yet the economic consequences they unleashed led to the collapse of market mechanisms, sharp economic crisis, popular unrest, and the demise of NEP. The sequence of mounting economic woes can be reconstructed as follows: in order to generate investment capital, the Supreme Council of National Economy [VTsNKh] created an amortization fund.[45] The idea was that all branches of industry would contribute to the fund, but that heavy industry would be the primary beneficiary. Such a centralized corporative approach was supposed to demonstrate the advantages of socialism over highly particularized capitalist industry. In essence, relatively profitable textile and consumer industries subsidized heavy industry. This led to a shortage of consumer goods and a corresponding rise in prices, which in turn made the goods inaccessible to peasants. By subsidizing inefficient enterprises from the state budget and from the profits of efficient companies, the Bolsheviks encumbered the entire economy with the burdens of the most inefficient. By taxing private entrepreneurs out of existence, they were destroying consumer industry and retail trade.[46]

As of 1926, the government imposed controls over wholesale and retail prices, holding them down by decree. That in turn made economic efficiency impossible, because, under market conditions, commodity prices typically rise to a level at which production can be profitable. Yet, when the state dictated a ceiling for commodity prices, enterprises found that they could not produce profitably. In fact, they too became dependent on budget allocation to survive. Bolshevik control of market forces by decree exacerbated the crisis in industry. Abandonment of conservative monetary policy and the 1924 gold standard in 1926 was marked by sharp increases in government currency emission. That triggered a new round of inflation, price controls, budget allocations, and further entrenchment of centralized, target-production industry. As a Russian historian has put it: "In 1927–28 the national economy found itself on the threshold of total unprofitability."[47] In other words, the so-called "socialism" in industry was a consequence of Bolshevik failure to guide the economy by means of the market. The "socialist" planned industry was a cover-up for the inherent inefficiency of state industry.

The Bolshevik method of resolving the problems of Russian industry was a new offensive, a new campaign to make "socialist" industry more efficient. Production targets were raised; wages were not. Workers had to work harder to decrease the cost of production. The Bolsheviks' method to fight economic inefficiency by forcing workers to work harder for less pay undercut their purchasing power. The Nizhnii Novgorod gubkom lowered the pay-rates and increased production targets by 17 per cent in June 1925 at the Sormovo plant. As a result, unskilled workers' wages sank to 17 rubles a month, wages which "most workers never saw because they were permanently in debt to the cooperative shops."[48] A wave of strikes ripped across Nizhnii Novgorod province.

The intensification of labor campaign was combined with the forced infusion of semi-skilled Communist promotees into managerial positions. This proletarianization of management not only did not improve performance of Soviet enterprises, but probably further eroded labor relations, because it intensified hostility between the new managers, old "bourgeois" specialists, and shop-floor workers. The Bolsheviks operated on the assumption that things were bound to improve as time went on. They believed their own propaganda to the extent that difficulties were temporary, and that "social-ist" industry – that which was state-run – was superior to private. In fact the situation in industry was worsening. The Bolshevik leaders tried to squeeze more out of the peasants by taxation and more out of workers by the intensification of labor. All that the Communist leaders seemed to be able to generate were orders, demands, instructions, and target rates. The command economy was in place.

NEW RADICALISM, NEW LABELS, 1926–9

Workers' hostility to the Communists was a closely guarded state secret, a taboo, an embarrassment, and an ideological disaster. Banned from public discourse, workers' political opinions, especially those critical of the Communist Party, were systematically collected by the GPU. In August 1926, "the main factor defining workers' disposition was the decrease in wages in the main branches of industry."[49] A wave of strikes that followed was led by skilled metallists. From January to March 1927 the number of strikes fluctuated from fifty to seventy each month. What incensed the workers most was that mandated pay cuts violated existing collective agreements. The tone of workers' protests was getting more impetuous, outspoken, persistent, fearless, and openly anti-Communist.

Strikes affected all industries but especially those of mining, metal, and textiles. The new element was that Komsomol and party members often sided with their fellow workers against party superiors. Furthermore, workers began to organize unofficial associations. In Kostroma textile workers went on strike after a failure to reach agreement on production rates with the factory management. Workers were reported to be saying, "The party and the Soviet regime want to suffocate us and turn into us colonial slaves, like in India and China."[50] In the mining industry strikes were caused by a new increase in production rates and a cut in pay-scales. The situation was particularly stormy in the township of Shakhty in the Donbas. Miners complained that in order to fulfill new production targets, they had to work twelve-hour shifts. At a rally, miners shouted: "Beat the Communists and the specialists!" Several Communists were indeed assaulted. The leader of the picket lines turned out to be a Komsomol secretary.[51] In Leningrad, anti-Soviet speeches were heard at numerous factories. Rank-and-file Communists at Skorokhod factory called upon workers to vote against official CP election slates. In some cases they were defeated.

The first targets of workers' anger were the factory committees and trade unions, since these were supposed to represent the workers' economic interests. From approximately 1925 on, workers' hostility to these bodies rose steadily. In this regard the Tambov gubkom's report was typical:

> The workers' criticism of the party and its policies has shown itself most clearly in the factory committee election. Concurrently, anti-Soviet agitation (oral and written) is going on among the workers. All kinds of provocative rumors are being spread about the coming war and workers' rebellions in other cities.[52]

By 1927 the workers' rejection of factory committees and hostility to local trade union chapters and to local Communist Party cells was common knowledge in the GPU and the Central Committee. Only 10 per cent to 20 per cent of workers participated in factory committees' elections. Workers were saying that the factory committees were superfluous because they did not defend them. As one machinist at a Moscow factory put it:

> To hell with the factory committee. Why should we maintain organizations which we do not need, and which are exploiting the workers? The factory committee is but a toy in the hands of the director.[53]

The stream of reports from the provinces was overwhelming: "Sharply hostile workers' actions against trade unions have taken place in Moscow, Leningrad, and Ukraine. Communist Party election slates were defeated in numerous places."[54] More and more often references began to appear favoring independent unions, and, more importantly, a workers' unaffiliated political party [bespartiynaya partiya]. In July 1925, for example, in Kharkov at a workers' rally at the locomotive plant, a worker in a speech said that they, the workers, had to create "a party of the unaffiliated [bespartiynykh] and struggle against the Communist Party as in the old days we used to struggle against Tsarism." The speech enjoyed great success among the workers.[55]

By far the most radical component of workers were the unemployed. Losing a job for most meant serious privation and the risk of hunger and destitution, as only a third of them received any assistance.[56] To cite from a letter of the Putilov workers:

> As to how the unemployed live, it is hard to describe: they are hungry, ragged – their poverty knows no limit, their children sit in the street, right on the snow, for days on end, with their knees bare, because of holes, begging for a kopeck for bread. There is no one who gives: workers don't have much, the bourgeoisie look at them with disgust, and the commissars just ride by in automobiles. They don't care; they enjoy life.[57]

Most of the unemployed blamed Communists for their woes. At a rally of the unemployed in Moscow, speeches claimed that "the Communist Party has established its dictatorship over the working class and over the entire country," and that "Soviet power is, in fact, nothing but a system for the deceit and exploitation of workers."[58] Most disturbing, the GPU found appeals to organize rallies and unions. Such a union in Leningrad had helped to elect numerous non-Communist workers to the Leningrad soviet. At a rally of the unemployed metallists in October 1926, the GPU recorded a number of bitter statements:

> There are two classes today: the working class and Communists who have replaced the nobles and the dukes.

For the last eight years, the Communists have been fooling us [*vtirat'
ochki*]. They have done nothing for the working class.

They hire and fire whomever they please. And getting a job is only possible
through the party committee.

Enough is enough. We've got to overthrow this shameful tyranny of
Bolshevism.[59]

One speaker proposed that all the unemployed should march with their wives
and children under white flags to Smolny, "the noblemen's nest," as he put
it, and plead for jobs and bread. Another argued that unemployment had
increased because the Bolsheviks were deliberately suppressing private
enterprise, especially those employers that paid better wages than the state.
In March 1927 the GPU arrested and charged with counterrevolutionary
activity the leaders of the unemployed.

Without an institutional outlet for discontent, workers' protest in 1927
became increasingly unpredictable. The temperature of frustration at the
factories and plants rose, ready to boil over. The fall of 1928 was a period of
open defiance, spontaneous anti-Communist rallies, wild-cat strikes, assaults
on Communists, and deliberate wrecking of machinery. A new food-supply
crisis exacerbated the already tense situation. Peasants were refusing to sell
grain at a low price. The Bolsheviks chose to respond by violence. To obscure
the causes for the supply crisis, they pinned the blame on the kulaks and tried
to mobilize "class-conscious workers," as in 1918, to be sent to the
countryside to enforce the kulaks' compliance with the "proletarian dictatorship."

Yet this time the Bolsheviks had few volunteers. The workers' disposition
was definitely pro-peasant as they perceived them to be in a position similar
to their own. Peasants wanted at least a ruble a pud, that is, higher
compensation for their labor, as did the workers. A woman worker at a textile
factory in Baumanskii district in Moscow said: "There is no bread because
you have squeezed [*nazhali*] the kulaks too much."[60] At the mechanical plant
in Podolsk, a workers' rally of 7,000 resolved that "the authorities should
immediately raise the purchase price of grain from 80 kopecks to 1 ruble 80
kopecks a pud and that the agricultural tax be lowered as an incentive for
peasants to produce."[61] Such reasonable proposals were cut short as "pro-
kulak agitation."

The GPU's monthly surveys of political events are, in fact, endless lists of
protests across the country, consisting of hundreds of pages. In Moscow and
Leningrad food shortages were on everyone's mind and huge lines stood for
hours in front of bakeries. A factory committee representative warned the
party plenum in October 1928:

If the problem of food supply is not fixed quickly, we are not going to work.
Presently, a worker can be thrown out into the street for the slightest

instance of misconduct. Why then, I ask you, are you not thrown out for your mishaps? . . . Workers live now worse than pigs.[62]

Someone was responsible for the crisis, but none of the leaders were accepting responsibility. Another worker's speech at the same plenum conveys the workers' frustration well:

We are told not to panic! But don't you understand we don't have enough to eat? We are hungry. They have not delivered any rye flour for two months. Lines are 500 people long. When we go to work, we are hungry. How long is this going to last? The party leaders appoint their own people everywhere, who do not know their business. What is needed is not to appoint party members everywhere but to elect those who can work, those who are capable.[63]

Workers' solidarity with peasants and their criticism of the party fell within the range of rational responses to the dire situation at hand. Yet the fall of 1928 was distinguished by an outburst of frustration. Deprived of recourse to elections, harassed by the GPU, living under the constant threat of being fired and ending up without means of subsistence, the workers reacted by drinking and venting their rage on local Communists, Jews, and engineers.

At the gates of the Krasnokholmskaya factory No.13 in the Zamosk-vorechie district in Moscow, an unemployed worker pushed a Jewish worker to the ground. The crowd cheered him on as he beat up the Jewish worker and two other workers joined in the beating.[64]

Jews were accused of taking jobs from the Russians. Workers needed someone to blame for their misery. The Bolsheviks blamed the NEPmen, kulaks, and specialists, while the workers in turn scapegoated the Communists, specialists, and Jews.

Old Bolsheviks were shocked by the strength of anti-Semitic sentiments among workers. Lunacharsky undertook an extensive trip across the country in 1928, speaking at many factories and addressing local party cells. This is what he said at one factory in Siberia:

One peasant told me: "When the war comes, we will strangle you Communists for your taxes." Such statements, comrades, can be heard not only here but in Moscow. At the plant Krasnaya Roza, one woman worker said in response to my report on anti-Semitism: "It is shameful, comrades, that many workers at our factory, men and women, say: 'When the war comes, we will kill all the Jews and the Communists.'"[65]

Lunacharsky was appalled. A special study commissioned by the GPU on anti-Semitism among the workers concluded that even though official party policy discouraged anti-Semitism, local party officials shared anti-Semitic attitudes and in some places encouraged them.[66] It was a convenient way to channel workers' frustration away from the Communists.

In numerous instances workers' resentment of Jews and specialists led them to deliberate wreckage of machinery.

At the Novo-Bogorodskaya factory workers wanted to drive out an engineer – a Jew – so they added sawdust and sand to the oil which caused the motors to burn up.

At the AMO [the automobile works] a group of workers engaged in the systematic wrecking of the presses by throwing metal shavings into the moving parts.[67]

Workers' wreckage of machines is, of course, as old as industrialization. If a machine broke, it meant a break at state expense. Machine wreckage was a defense mechanism against the intensification of labor.

There are countless examples of factory administration and Red directors being subjected to threats and abuse at the hands of local workers. According to a GPU survey in 1929, at the Krasnoe Znamya textile factory in Moscow, an anonymous note was passed to the presidium: "If you continue to enforce discipline like this, we shall kill Director Merkulov." A woman worker added: "The factory should be cleared of the Communists. Then we shall live freely."[68] With alarm the Moscow party committee wrote at the end of 1928 about: "a number of cases of direct acts of violence directed at the representatives of the administrative-technical personnel. Threats, vigilantism [*raspravy*], violence, even the murder of foremen, specialists, and directors have taken place." The top-secret memorandum characterized all this as "terrorist atmosphere at the factories and plants."[69]

In accord with ideological requirements, worker protest had to be framed as class struggle. Thus a new set of characters entered the Soviet official lexicon: the saboteur, wrecker, terrorist, and enemy of the people, requiring exposure, unmasking, and destruction. The press was full of articles on kulak infiltration into the working class, petty bourgeois consciousness rearing its head among the workers, and the need to intensify class struggle in the course of socialist construction. The Bolsheviks blamed saboteurs, hidden enemies, and bourgeois specialists – that is everybody but themselves. The Bolsheviks needed scapegoats for rising unemployment, declining living standards, and frustration among the workers. The so-called "bourgeois specialists" could not be better for the role. They could be blamed for poor performance of "socialist" industry and accused of "sabotage." This is exactly what was done in the GPU operation which has been known ever since as the Shakhty trial.[70] A group of engineers was accused of sabotage and wrecking at a well-orchestrated show trial, an early installment in a series, as it turned out.

The Shakhty trial inflamed the already tense situation. At some factories workers silently refused to follow the orders and fulfill production targets, engaging in passive resistance. In other places they openly defied orders and subverted production targets. They appropriated Bolshevik labels and turned them against the authorities, arguing that higher production targets would inevitably cause accidents; therefore, those who set high targets were wreckers. Workers tended to project their misery upon the culprits they knew: directors, engineers, foremen, and Jews. Some workers blamed Bolshevik policies and Communist inefficiency. Consider an explanation of economic difficulties from the Borets plant in Moscow:

> They have created too many bureaus of all kinds, hence the red tape and inefficiency, which make output more expensive ... The plant does not produce much profit. And why is it that the old owner used to make a lot of dough? Now the administrative apparatus is blown out of proportion. They are careless with money.[71]

In a way this worker was explaining what was wrong with Russian state industry. A capitalist entrepreneur in the old days had done a better job in organizing production, marketing, sales, and cost-accounting than had the "socialist" management.

Russian industry was in crisis because of the structural incompatibility of NEP market economics and "socialist," that is, state owned and bureaucratized, management. Products had to sell, and they were not selling because they were too expensive. They were too expensive because the cost of production was too high. It was too high not because workers were paid too much, but because management was, by its very nature, too inefficient. Many Old Bolsheviks who thought of themselves as Marxists and reflected upon the problems of Russia's development came to the conclusion that "socialist industry" inherently failed to generate superior labor productivity, and that meant that a "socialist" revolution in Russia was doomed to failure.

The main trend in the relations between workers and the Bolshevik Party over the years of NEP did not emphasize a reforging of their alliance, nor a spontaneous revolutionary militancy among the conscious working class.[72] These were official representations mistaken for genuine reality. In GPU and gubkom reports, workers come across as apolitical folks who could not have cared less about Communist construction or any of their campaigns, least of all the production-intensification drive. They appear as crude, selfish, and heavy-drinking, aloof from the party, and downright rude to women. They spent their free time in pubs and much of their salaries on vodka.

What is important here is not whether this portrait corresponds to social reality, but that this is how the top-ranking Bolsheviks saw the workers in top-secret party–GPU communications. No doubt much of that characterization rings true to life. But, much more important, it reveals that the Bolsheviks themselves did not believe their own rhetoric. Revolutionary battalions of class-conscious proletarians, the best sons of the motherland, marching behind the party's vanguard, existed only in the imagination of Agitprop professionals. In reality the Bolsheviks pursued a tough anti-worker policy, culminating in 1929 in cutting real wages, curtailing benefits, setting up the forced-labor Gulag, and dismantling what was left of the trade unions. At the same time, the Bolsheviks created a new myth of shock worker brigades and conscious builders of socialism.[73]

Workers were unaffected by Agitrop propaganda and measured their livelihood against standards they remembered from before the war. They perceived the Bolsheviks almost exclusively as the new bosses who replaced the old ones. Since their material well-being was barely half that of the 1913 level, their skepticism about Bolshevik rule remained pronounced. From 1926 on, production-intensification campaigns radicalized workers' attitudes not in terms of class-conscious militancy but in terms of anti-establishment protest. Stalin's leadership tried to channel workers' frustration over party policies into anti-Semitism and hostility towards "bourgeois" specialists and NEPmen, but with mixed results. Workers appropriated Bolshevik official representations, in this case labels such as "wreckers," "saboteurs," "hidden enemies," and so on, but applied them against factory management and party bosses. What may come across as "revolutionary denunciation" was in fact a skillful adoption of the available means to defend economic interests. Workers' reactions to Bolshevik policy in the 1920s can be summed up as resistance.

Chapter 9

The Bolshevik old guard and the upstarts, 1924–9

Down and out and up and coming

During NEP the Bolshevik Party turned from the fighting machine of 1920 into an administrative elite. The old core of intelligentsia Bolsheviks was drowned in the sea of new recruits. From 1924 to 1926, in just two years, 800,000 new members were admitted.[1] Their views, tastes, and attitudes to the social groups they lived among determined the perceptions of numerous party organizations.[2] Some have argued that the role models the young Communists adopted and the kind of behavioral norms they practiced contributed to the rise of dictatorial culture among the Bolsheviks.[3] Studying various components of the Communist movement, be it the 25,000ers (the young workers mobilized to collectivize agriculture in 1929), the Komsomol or young party recruits, revisionist historians have found manifestations of enthusiastic revolutionary ardor and radical refutation of the past as well as the more benign political discourse of the older Bolsheviks.[4] Sheila Fitzpatrick interpreted the incorporation of hundreds of thousands of upstarts as evidence of Bolsheviks' "commitment to a proletarian identity."[5] One historian has argued that the Bolsheviks were looking for allies among the young and unskilled recruits of the Lenin levy.[6] Such observations may suggest that the imposition of the iron fist of the Stalinist dictatorship over the party and society was based on social impulses from below.[7] This idea is one of the main arguments of the "revisionist" school of thought. Young recruits are seen as propelled by revolutionary ardor ignited by the social tensions of NEP. The Bolshevik Party under NEP was becoming larger, younger, more radical, and more revolutionary, thus providing Stalin with the necessary machinery for launching his revolution from above.

The assumption that they were all young Marxist proletarians burning with desire to build socialism and worship the Great Leader is based on official iconography. The only problem with this line of reasoning is that it assumes that values, views, and cultural practices of the younger upstarts were identical with their public image.[8] When discussing Bolshevik Party development, one cannot take at face value public self-representation as if it were identical to genuinely held views. Provincial party leaders may have used revolutionary terminology in 1927–8 in their discourse with Moscow, anticipating the center's expectations, while enjoying NEP and not wanting to part with it. Radical condemnation of Trotskyites in 1927 likewise did not necessarily mean that the party members actually believed that Trotsky was a mad dog of imperialism. Such behavior might have been a political loyalty test. Even when the Bolsheviks themselves believed they meant what they were saying, public debate over policy obscured the difference in meaning. Both the Stalin supporters and the NEP defenders swore allegiance to Lenin and Leninism, saw their purpose in constructing socialism, and were committed to industrialization. The difference was in the meaning of these terms for the old guard and the new upstarts.

The purpose of the following discussion, therefore, is to outline the major trends in the development of the Communist Party, to separate public self-representation from sincerely held opinions, and differentiate between views and cultural practices publicly and privately expressed in order to pose the crucial questions: did the Communists support a new revolutionary upheaval and the abandonment of NEP in 1928? Who did? Who did not? Why?

THE NEW COMMUNISTS

Provincial party committees' reports to the CC described enormous difficulties with the recruitment drive. Many failed to fulfill the quota demanded of them. The Bryansk gubkom managed to recruit only 1,778 new members instead of the CC target of 2,000.[9] Moreover, most of the new recruits were unskilled workers. Two main reasons guided them in their choice. Almost all provincial reports suggested that the new recruits had been motivated by the "desire to get a higher-paying job and a good apartment."[10] They hoped party membership would improve their chances to escape the woes of their existence. As the CC officer, Zaslavsky, put it: "The 'Lenin levy' attracted the poorest workers because they were very sensitive as to who lived well."[11]

The second reason was that party members enjoyed a number of privileges which the unskilled workers wanted a piece of. The Bryansk gubkom frankly admitted:

> We should not close our eyes to the fact that among Leninites [Lenintsy] there are workers who entered the party in order to use it to improve their material situation. There are also those who hoped to safeguard themselves from possible lay-off and unemployment.[12]

A report from Vologda pointed out that: "The matter of material well-being dominated all other issues among them."[13] Another classified report to Stalin stated unequivocally that: "At least half of the newly admitted were those who entered fearing lay-offs. Among the skilled workers, very few enrolled."[14] When the CC officer, Zaslavsky, inquired at the Bryansk locomotive plant why this was so, he was told that the skilled workers had no interest in joining the party. Their only concerns were their family and household. As soon as the work day was over, they hurried home to get some work done in their gardens, hating it when they were required to attend meetings.

The Bolshevik mind-set would rationalize this as meaning that the skilled workers were under the influence of petty bourgeois consciousness, whereas the unskilled workers were the true proletarians attracted to the party by the appeal of its ideology. This, however, was not the impression of the CC officer. The unskilled workers hated their jobs and had no pride in their social position. Their enrollment heightened tensions with the skilled workers who viewed joining the party as joining the bosses and as betraying their "worker" identity. Zaslavsky described cases of abuse of the new recruits by older workers. Women, as usual, were the most outspoken, even in the presence of a Moscow plenipotentiary. One of them characterized the new recruits as "hooligans and drunkards."[15]

Most recruits did not understand what NEP meant. Most of them were still religious. Among female recruits (only thirty-eight in Bryansk province), all except two were illiterate. Many of them had icons in their homes. They were urged to replace them with a picture of Comrade Lenin. Many agonized over this parting with their faith and icons, as the Vladimir gubkom attested: "From all corners of the province we hear complaints that Leninites are under pressure from their families. It is difficult especially for women to overcome religiosity in themselves and members of their families."[16] From the Bolshevik perspective, the new recruits were still in the grip of bourgeois ideology.

Party authorities were also worried that many Leninites displayed a confrontational attitude towards the old guard, but the worst sin of all was that they "continued to vote against the guidelines of party authorities."

> We Leninites, they'd say, have entered the party to replace the old members who got bureaucratized. There is a clear tendency to define oneself as better than the old party guard who were ostensibly demoralized. The danger is that many among the Leninites could be influenced by any kind of demagoguery.[17]

Other recruits claimed that the Communist Party was dead without them, "the real proletarian saviors," and that the party needed them, because without them "the party would not be able to hold power."[18] The provincial officials faulted the new recruits as thinking too highly of themselves, disrespecting the old guard, disobeying guidelines, and acting independently.

The confidential message to the CC was that the coded words "conscious proletarians from the factory floor" stood for the party cadres who were unsophisticated, uneducated, and reluctant to be processed by the propaganda machine. Contrary to the claims of official propaganda that the best and the brightest, the most motivated and the skilled workers burning with revolutionary energy entered the ranks to build socialism, the poorest and the most destitute joined, primarily to obtain better material conditions, or as a substitute for unemployment insurance. The top leaders were well informed on who joined the party and why.

The recruitment drive of 1924 and 1925 profoundly changed the social fabric of the Communist Party. Some provincial organizations increased by a third or more. On paper, the recruits had impeccable credentials, either as proletarians from the factory floor or as the toiling peasants. In the judgment of the Bryansk gubkom, however, "The level of political education of the recruits was not at the required level. They were incapable of orienting themselves independently in any political and economic questions."[19] In a typical Russian province, more than half the members were barely literate, especially in agricultural provinces.

In the black earth region, south of Moscow, the Kursk province party organization boasted 3,320 Communists and 2,628 candidates after the Lenin levy in April 1924, totalling 5,948 members. Of these, only 12 had higher education, 432 had secondary education, 5,138 had primary education, and 466 had no education of any kind. Moreover, 3,384 were described as politically illiterate, implying no knowledge or understanding of the basics of Marxism–Leninism or of the current political affairs.[20] In the neighboring Orel province the CP organization had 2,902 members on January 1, 1925 (127 of whom were women); of whom 1,064 were listed as illiterate.[21]

In the neighboring Voronezh province, the gubkom also collected data on the educational level of party members; 72.2 per cent of Communists were found to be completely illiterate or semi-literate; 20 per cent had knowledge adequate for entry into a sov-party school; but only 1.9 per cent had graduated.[22] The most educated people in the Voronezh party were those who had finished Agitprop-run propaganda courses on Marxism and the party line. Another report for 1924–5 admitted that the "Communists did not read books, and did not understand them, and even if they read a newspaper it was without enthusiasm."[23] Further south in Kuban', the party committee reported that 90 per cent of their party members were politically illiterate. Only 3 per cent of party members had the skill to deliver a lecture on politics or Marxism.[24]

The profile of Communists in Vologda, another agricultural province in the north, was very similar. Over 50 per cent of party members were described as illiterate or semi-literate in a gubkom report for 1926. Of those admitted to sov-party schools, only 17 per cent actually attended classes. The prevalent attitude of rural Communists to this education was expressed by their term for it: "compulsion" [prinudilovka]. They were not interested in Marxism–Leninism or in the party line on a specific question. Ideological study was for them like performing corvée [barshchina] for the master.[25] Even in the capital itself, and even among the workers' faculty students, young Communist promotees from the factory floor, it was common to refer to the core theses of Marxism–Leninism as theology [zakon bozhii].[26]

One might expect that the educational level would be higher in the industrial provinces. In fact the Donetsk party organization in the coal-mining area of northern Ukraine was as illiterate as any other. In just one year it doubled to reach 16,585 members and 16,826 candidates (with only 2,817 women among them). Of this total membership, 65 per cent were described as politically illiterate, and 7,000 could not read or write and had no education of any kind.[27]

In the heartland of the textile industry, east of Moscow, in Ivanovo-Voznesensk province, there were 2,918 party members on January 1, 1924. Educational statistics were available on 2,885 persons: of these, 31 had higher education (that is 1 per cent); 272 had secondary education (10 per cent); 1,853 had primary education (75 per cent); and 355 had no formal education (15 per cent). A year later, on January 1, 1925, the membership increased to 5,083 with 6,156 candidates. The new members were mostly Lenin levy recruits and the vast majority were illiterate.[28]

In the neighboring industrial Nizhnii Novgorod province, the party organization numbered 16,202 on January 1, 1925, and 21,390, on April 1 that year. More than 5,000 new members were admitted during the enrollment drive on the first anniversary of Lenin's death, almost tripling the 1924 membership total. Practically all of the newcomers were politically illiterate; 4,000 were required to attend condensed versions of political literacy courses. The report added that it would have been preferable if all of them attended, but that was impossible for the lack of qualified teachers.[29] Of those who took the course, fewer than 50 per cent were able to grasp the material.[30]

In the Moscow province the party enrollment of 1925 brought 10,400 new candidates to party membership; 97.2 per cent of the newly admitted, stated the report, were politically illiterate and only 1.8 per cent had secondary or higher education. The report continued, "There is no difference as regards the educational level between the Lenin levy recruits of 1924 and those of 1925."[31]

But the Leningrad party organization showed the fastest growth rate. In the first three months of 1925 it admitted 11,284 candidates to party membership. From 84,244 members and candidates, the province organization grew in 1925 to 92,239. Of this total number, 53,854 were full party members and 38,385 were candidates. Most of them were politically illiterate and 42 per cent of them were required to go through one kind of party instruction or another.[32]

Provincial professional propagandists had to present complex subject matter to an essentially illiterate audience. They had to bring down the level of instruction to the lowest possible denominator. An assignment to Agitprop was unpopular because they did not want to teach in the required format. The Vladimir gubkom complained that Agitprop officials wanted to transfer to some other jobs.[33] Many of them felt that their skills were wasted since they had to explain Marxist theory to an audience which they knew to be incapable of comprehending it. They were often resented by their recruit-students as the latter felt belittled by the presentation. In Bryansk, for example, one of the propagandists was "a young woman, who was talking to the workers as a schoolteacher under the old regime addressed schoolchildren."[34] The recruits often made clear that they did not intend to learn anything. They already were the vanguard of the proletariat by virtue of their birth. It was the intelligentsia folks who had to learn from them because they, the real proletarians, had experienced privation on a factory floor. They defined their selection and promotion to higher social status as a birthright and as an entitlement to reject the value of old culture.

In most provinces the gubkoms set up special commissions for the work with the promotees. The job of these commissions was to identify positions and vacancies which could be filled by the party members. Gubkoms were under constant pressure to increase the percentage of party presence in all branches of administration, education, industry management, trade unions, and cooperatives. This program was officially called *kommunizatsiya* or partyization of institutions.[35] As soon as it was possible, non-party personnel were replaced by the promotees. The Voronezh gubkom, for example, reported that in just one city district 57 Leninites – that is, of the Lenin levy – were approved as suitable candidates to fill the available positions: 9 in administrative jobs, 8 in cooperatives and trade, 9 in financial institutions, 16 in local soviets, and 9 in trade unions.[36]

The Leningrad party organization provided detailed data on the process of partyization of government institutions. Those who were defined as nomenklatura or senior-level appointees [*otvetsvennye rabotniki*] had to be approved by the province committee. Their credentials and education were screened and their candidatures were approved for a specific field of government-controlled appointment. The nomenklatura appointments in Leningrad province were listed in relation to the total of the leading cadres like this:[37]

Nomenklatura appointments	Percentage of partyization
Party work	100
Propaganda	16
Trade unions	50
Courts and police	70
Industry	24
Agriculture	10

During 1925 the average percentage of partyization in the province rose from 51 per cent to 58 per cent. The ultimate goal was to reach 100 per cent in all fields: administration, industry, agriculture, and education.

The Nizhnii Novgorod gubkom boasted that out of 1,130 new party recruits in 1924, 289 were assigned to party work, 108 to work in the soviets, 548 in trade unions, and 99 in the cooperatives.[38] The Moscow provincial committee reported to the CC that by 1925 the process of promotion of proletarian cadres was proceeding according to plan. The all-city conference of administrative, soviet, and economic personnel was to develop a plan on job creation and vacancy placement of the promotees. All organizations were required to put aside a certain number of jobs for Communist promotees. The city party committee set up a special commission which conducted three city-wide conferences on the promotees' employment situation and their complaints.[39]

The provincial committees were constantly reminded to report how many new party recruits were promoted to party, soviet, trade union, and propaganda work, how many of them were of the Lenin enrollment, and what social origin and training they had. Provincial committees had to fulfill promotion targets even though this was difficult. The Gomel provincial committee, for example, wrote that:

> The task of promoting Leninites to permanent positions in administration, trade unions, and others has encountered severe difficulties due to poor education of the Leninites. But we have adopted decisive measures and 100 of them were given permanent jobs in various organizations.[40]

The enforced infusion of these recruits, the promotees [*vydvizhentsy*], into virtually all spheres of management and administration in the 1920s was a source of serious social tension in Soviet society. It brought about a collision of cultures and values inside the Bolshevik Party and in the society at large. The promotees were not adequately prepared and were unwanted wherever they were sent. High-ranking officials displayed hostility towards them. They, in turn, sensed hostility from their subordinates who regarded them as illiterate proletarian upstarts. Many of them did not know how to cope with their new responsibilities. The journal *Aktivist* commented in 1928 that the promotees

> were often completely helpless in the work they were entrusted with because these comrades arrived to a given institution or business directly from the factory floor, lacking sufficient knowledge to handle their new job. Often they were returned to where they had come from, or they returned themselves, or were put on the pay-roll but performed the simplest possible work.[41]

Satirical journals of the 1920s are full of cartoons poking fun at the promotees.

Many were not familiar with the required behavioral norms. They did not know how to address superiors and subordinates. Many were painfully aware of their lack of manners and culture. Many were the object of snide remarks and provocative statements. Many could not cope and asked to be returned to their original jobs. Some decided to hold on but hid their resentment until the time they could vent it. The new upstarts saw a constant reminder of their own incompetency in the presence of the specialists. They perceived their

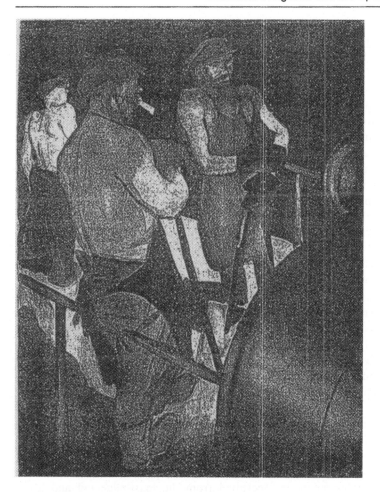

Our promotee has found himself a warm place.
You mean he's become a director?
You're kidding. He is a stoker.

Figure 9 Warm Reception
Source: *Bich* No. 16 (1927), p. 5

unwelcome reception as the arrogance of the old overthrown classes and responded in kind.

Hostility, envy, cultural clash, and false reporting are well illustrated in two reports on the integration of the promotees. A Moscow district party committee reported in 1928 that, during the previous two years, 618 promotees had been placed in administrative jobs. The CC Cadres Department [Orgraspred] investigated this report and concluded that the number of promotees taken from among the workers was insignificant, that in the apparatus of the soviet only thirty-two people had been promoted from the factory floor and that the majority of those "promoted" in fact were placed in service jobs, such as bookkeepers, financial inspectors, or sales personnel. A survey of seventy-three promotees in six institutions indicated that they "exhibited much energy in rationalizing the state apparatus and in the struggle against bureaucratization and patronage networks."[42] This meant that the promotees, fighting for their jobs, had started denouncing the specialists and the old party members as bourgeois, corrupt, and incompetent.

Hostility against the so-called "bourgeois specialists" was widespread, as were sentiments against the intelligentsia in general. This was not, of course, a manifestation of revolutionary zeal but of envy, insecurity, and ambition. Just as intense was the tension between the promotees of the 1924–5 class with the proletarian upstarts of the earlier years. Those who had made their careers in the civil war years considered themselves the backbone of the party. They felt that the party ought to be grateful to them for saving the regime. This cohort resented the illiterate upstarts of the Lenin levy who were being promoted without having served long enough. Tension in the Communist Party between its various components did not necessarily have anything to do with Trotsky or Zinoviev. There were cultural and generational frictions that had less to do with political views and more to do with social climbing and cultural incompatibility. Rivalries of various educational and social subgroups, vying for jobs, influence, and power, were becoming a disruptive factor in Communist Party politics. The easiest way to destroy rivals was with allegations of political deviancy, looking into a victim's background for links to the fallen gods.

Rapid expansion of the Communist Party and promotion of young proletarian cadres had a devastating effect. The party was transformed beyond recognition. From a party of tough commissars enforcing mobilization of the masses for the war effort and labor armies in 1920, it was turned into a network of bureaucracies recruited from the least-educated and least-prepared elements of society. The majority of the 800,000 new members could not comprehend and did not care about the debates among Old Bolsheviks in 1928. They had no opinion as to whether the theory of permanent revolution was right or wrong, or whether the Austrian Marxists' model of national autonomy was appropriate for the Soviet Union, or whether it was possible from the point of view of Marxist theory to build socialism in one country.

The majority of Communists were new people, the up and coming, who repeated what the old guard was saying – socialism, proletariat, and so on – but imbued these words with the new meanings. When the new Communists said they were building socialism, they meant that they were a part of a state administrative structure and that their job was to fulfill orders. "Construction of socialism" meant replacing the old intelligentsia and the party's old guard. It was equated in their minds with the expansion of state agencies and new opportunities. This was certainly not the understanding in 1917. A substitution of meaning that they were not conscious of had occurred.

Old Bolsheviks of all factions during the 1920s became prisoners of their own Marxist fantasy that the workers would make the party better by being representatives of the proletariat. Worker recruits turned out to be obedient instruments in the hands of the apparatus instead. They hated their worker background, thrived on the possibility of entering a privileged elite, despised the Bolshevik intelligentsia, and imitated pre-revolutionary bosses in terms of cultural practices. Proletarianization of the party, upon which Lenin had pinned so many hopes at the end of his career, turned out to be yet another utopian dream – one with dire consequences for the party in the long run.

POLITICAL OPINION

The study of political opinion in the Communist Party in the 1920s has focused on the left opposition of 1923–5, the united opposition of 1926, and the right opposition of 1928. This chronology of the Communist Party's history has become so much the standard picture that one can hardly conceptualize Communist Party politics in other terms.[43] The traditional division of political opinion in the Bolshevik Party into leftist Trotskyite, right-wing Bukharinite, and centrist Stalinist policies obscures rather than explains political currents in the CP. These ideological divisions were created by Stalin to define his agenda. In reality, rank-and-file Communists sided with the leftists on some issues, with the rightists on others, opposed all three positions on some other issues, and had no opinion on most remaining ones.

Debates among the high-ranking Bolsheviks were seldom relevant to the concerns of the comrades in the provinces. To take a political position, one had first to understand what the issues were and how taking a position affected one's interests or inclinations. In order to have a political opinion, one had to be informed about what was actually going on in the country. Very few people were. Most of the rank and file had no clue concerning even the most innocuous issues of the day. They did not know, for example, whether collective farms were performing better or worse than private ones, or whether private enterprises had higher or lower productivity in labor and wages than in the state sector; they did not know whether NEP was a success or a failure and by what criteria. Not only rank and file, but the provincial party bosses were left in the dark about the most vital economic data and events in the country. The political community was very small in Russia. Most of the educated classes were excluded from it, and most of the Communists did not comprehend it.

To make sense of the diversity of political opinion, it is useful to keep in mind economic interests and cultural values of specific Communist constituencies. Party leaders in industrial centers were guided either by a need to cover up the inefficiency of their enterprises or by their profitable cooperation with the private sector. In the countryside cooperation with the better-off peasants became the norm, as the blending of the economic and political elites got under way. Rank-and-file worker Communists formed their opinion on the basis of the social reality they faced. Clearly Trotsky's fiery critique of bureaucracy was not going to appeal to Red directors but would appeal to the rank and file. An attack on bourgeois specialists would appeal to young promotees and often not to the Red directors who needed the specialists. The upstarts' cultural profile pitted them against intelligentsia Bolsheviks of every faction.

The leftist heresy

Political preferences of the various CP groups were based on certain cultural, educational, and occupational characteristics. In the countryside leftist rhetoric was appealing to the poorer segment of Communists especially. As a report from Kuban' explained: "The minority of the party organization were most revolutionary inclined, these were the least developed members of the party."[44] At the height of NEP, they believed that the party had sold out to the kulaks, the revolution was going nowhere, the bureaucrats had seized power in the CP, and a new revolution was necessary. The key ingredients here were anti-establishment sentiment and hostility to NEP. Many of those who held such views did not know that they could be labeled Trotskyites.[45]

Trotsky's references to democratic centralism and party democracy were not appealing to that constituency.[46] These people were losing out in the conditions of NEP, hence their rejection of the party line. What they wanted most was not party democracy but the removal of the bosses from their armchairs so that they could practice "proletarian" dictatorship themselves. The Red bandits in Siberia could not part with the civil war methods and could not find a role in the conditions of peace and economic recovery. Rebelliousness and anti-establishment zeal were the key ingredients in their political thinking. Stalin was the incarnation of the establishment, yet he could tap into this constituency when he turned to drastic measures in 1928.

A counterpart to those attitudes in industry was hostility to specialists and the Red directors. The rhetoric of the failed workers' revolution was appealing to the underpaid, frustrated, and abused workers, some of them CP members. In November 1927 at a party meeting, a worker supporting Trotsky said:

Wages are hardly growing. Food is getting more expensive. Lines are everywhere. Living quarters are terrible. The party has not undertaken anything to remedy this. The CC policy encourages the growth of kulaks. The policy of repressions does not allow opposition to speak out. Everywhere decisions, prepared in advance by the apparatchiks, are being pushed through.[47]

Workers liked to hear a message that the revolution was supposed to liberate them but in fact only enslaved them, that the Red directors and the specialists were living in luxurious apartments and rode in cars, whereas the workers were consistently underpaid. The blame was assigned to party bureaucrats and to NEP as a system. As one worker in Siberia put it:

> We've got to foment a second revolution. Lenin has not finished the job. We've got to beat the hell out of the Communist Party hierarchy. In the capitalist countries workers live better. We've got to kill the specialists first.[48]

Even though these views had an appeal to some workers and rank-and-file Communists, within the CP this was a leftist heresy. At most party meetings the majority lashed out at a few oppositionists. The CC wrote:

> At every meeting speeches and comments are full of statements like this: "How long will the CC fuss over them? Why are they not expelled from the party? Imprison them! It is time to put an end to this. They do not let us work."[49]

At the height of the anti-Trotsky campaign in December 1927 and January 1928, 510 Communists were expelled from the Moscow party organization.[50] In the Bryansk province, only three oppositionists openly identified themselves as such. These were courageous people. One of them said:

> Thousands of party members have been expelled and arrested. We will not be able to build socialism in one country. You have forgotten about the world revolution. Why are you afraid to publish our platform?

Another continued: "You are bureaucrats, apparatchiks. Stalin is to blame for everything."[51] At a shoe factory party meeting in Orel province likewise a small group of courageous oppositionists denounced exploitation of workers, corruption, and privilege of the new elite. As one oppositionist said, "Many comrades do not speak here, but beyond these walls, quietly, they admit that the opposition was right."[52]

The Bolsheviks who followed politics and who were engaged emotionally in the unfolding processes in the country were a minority in the party and an insignificant minority in the urban society at large. Their anxieties and criticism, attempts to struggle and organize, should not obscure the fact that the mainstream political climate in the country was apolitical. This was particularly evident during the tenth anniversary of the October revolution in 1927. The official media unfolded a vast campaign celebrating the glorious achievements of socialist construction. Trotsky's supporters staged a counter-demonstration. Some groups organized rallies and meetings in the country-side and tried to set up printing presses and distribute literature. It may appear to have been widespread. In fact it involved no more than a few hundred Bolsheviks. The vast majority were not even aware of the incident and did not care. The general cultural climate in the country on the tenth anniversary was that of cynical mockery of the official propaganda. It was a sentiment of *déjà vu*: "We've seen it all before and we are tired of repetition." This was the spirit of numerous cartoons, articles, and jokes in the satirical journals of the time.

One article, "The Enthusiast," suggested that nobody wanted to put any effort into the empty celebrations of Red October. Instead of wasting money on posters and processions, they should have opened a school or a new department store.[53] A cartoon, titled "Bravely march the comrades," which is a line from the revolutionary song everyone knew, showed couples dancing. Fox-trot had replaced the revolutionary march, at least as a desirable pastime of the party elite.[54]

Leftist appeals could not possibly have had a large constituency among either the urban or the rural party establishment. Rural Communists were

Look: the actors are storming the Winter Palace.
And they probably charge a lot for that.

Figure 10 Materialistic Approach
Source: *Bich* No. 41 (1927), p. 11

Fox-trot is a dance fulfilling the requirements of physical culture.
Comrades, bravely keep up the step.

Figure 11 A Step to Grace
Source: *Buzutyor* No. 9 (1927), p. 12

socializing with the prosperous peasants, marrying kulaks' daughters, and taking loans from the cooperatives never meant to be repaid. In the cities a similar process was in full swing. Every gubkom had detailed information on all private enterprises, and their estimated profits. All entrepreneurs strove to have a protector among the higher-ups. Large enterprises, especially large trusts, had close links with provincial authorities. If business involved export or any contact abroad, it had to be cleared with the party authorities and the GPU.

Problems arose when private companies had to deal with competing bureaucracies. In such situations soviets rivaled gubkoms and financial scandals occasionally flared up. A rival bureaucracy would denounce its competitor, unhappy with its own share of the pie or jealous of the other's influence. As an example one can cite a scandal in Kaluga.[55] A local trust and gubkom got along very well. Someone got jealous of this cordial relationship and sent a "signal" to the center that the trust was actually a nest of counterrevolutionary specialists and former capitalists. This was the most effective way to destroy competitors, or punish those who did not deliver what was expected of them. The desired result was achieved. Once one started digging, one could always find irregularities. That meant in practice that the NEP system generated corruption, kick-backs and pay-offs. Moscow party committee admitted in December 1928:

> We have cases of moral degeneration of party members, cases of their bourgeois [*meshchanskoe*] degeneration. We have cases of bribery. Party members working in the state apparatus and in the distribution departments accept bribes. We have cases of linkage between Communists and the kulaks, and cases of systematic drinking parties of Communists with the NEPmen and bourgeois elements.[56]

The urban CP elite was closely intertwined with the leaders of private enterprise and the two elites were thriving in the conditions of NEP. According to Litvinov, a graduate of the Institute of Red Professors, and those who shared his views, NEP luxury, money, and power were destroying the party, and corruption was pervasive:

> In the economic departments, in the military and supply agencies, as well as in the diplomatic service, thieves control everything. I am sure that the percentage of thieves among the Communists employed at the Supreme Council of People's Economy, Tsentrosoyuz [Central Cooperatives Administration] and People's Commissariat of Foreign Trade is higher than 99 per cent. In those agencies everyone is a thief, beginning with the People's Commissar and ending with the simplest courier.[57]

The leftist anti-NEP rhetoric had no appeal among the vast majority of the CP apparatchiks.

The right wing deviation

In 1928 the party leadership began to shift its policies away from NEP, relying more and more on coercive collection of grain. This is known as the first steps in the unfolding drama described by Robert Conquest, a drama of dekulakization, collectivization, and famine during 1930–4.[58] Serious debate developed among the Communist Party leaders. Bukharin objected to the use of force in grain procurement. He favored retaining NEP as an economic system, and put forward an alternative plan. Its key premise was that socialism could be built by other, less violent means and that a movement towards socialized agriculture had to proceed slowly, without coercion and violence. Market-oriented farming in the countryside would remain, and only very slowly, by economic incentives, would peasants be encouraged to develop collective arrangements voluntarily, since collective agriculture was inherently superior to individual farming. According to Stephen Cohen, the right opposition represented forces in the Bolshevik Party which had come to accept the NEP system as a Leninist path to socialism, and Bukharin's ideas represented a historical alternative to the devastating collectivization launched by Stalin.[59]

Critics of this view have dismissed Bukharin's recommendations as a policy similar to Stalin's, only by more decent and less violent means. Nor was Stalin's collectivization (in fact devastation) of Russian agriculture that different from Trotsky's schemes of the early 1920s. Robert Conquest and Martin Malia have argued that differences among Trotsky, Stalin, and Bukharin on the peasant question did not amount to much. The ideology was the key to understanding Bolshevik actions.[60] All Bolsheviks shared some fundamental objectives. They all wanted to overcome private enterprise at some point. They all believed that collective forms of agriculture were objectively superior to private ones, and they all agreed that peasants had to be forced to pay for industrialization. Stalin intended to launch a new civil war in the countryside: it was to be the second revolution, as Robert Tucker put it.[61]

Pro-NEP transition to socialism à la Bukharin and anti-NEP revolutionary transition to socialism à la Stalin – this dichotomy of political opinion in the Communist Party is encountered in most reconstructions of the great overturn. The debate in the Bolshevik Party, however, was not just about the Bukharinist or Stalinist "transition to socialism," it was about the political and economic crisis in the country and about the crisis of Bolshevism as an ideology.

From the fall of 1928 onward, the center was putting pressure on local authorities to squeeze the kulaks harder, to enforce grain procurement targets and to launch dekulakization. Provincial authorities had to comply. The property of the most prosperous kulaks was being seized, often by the same people who had earlier tried to maintain good relations with them. In numerous instances the seized property was divided up by the local party cells, as is clear from this CC report to Stalin:

NORTH CAUCASUS: The compilation *svodka* of the Regional Commission points out that in the process of registry and sale of kulak property there are many abnormalities. Confiscated property was auctioned off at ridiculously low prices. Self-seeking moves and speculation by local officials was causing discontent among the peasants who say: "the prosperous are being dekulakized, but some Communists are literally robbing the peasants and becoming kulaks themselves."[62]

As a result, stated the report, the number of terrorist acts by the local population increased substantially. In August there were 77, in September 128, and in October 213, just in the north Caucasus. According to another report, "arson, the beating of Communists, and attempted murders were everyday occurrences in Tambov province."[63]

Those who advocated continuation of NEP did not consider themselves members of any opposition and resented the Stalinist leadership's attempt to pin a rightist deviation label on them. Almost every paragraph of the special report on the right deviation for 1928–9 started with the words "incomprehension of the nature of the right deviation!"

Several provincial organizations, such as Orenburg, Orel, Tashkent, Tyumen', Zlatoust', Vyatka, and many others recognized the existence of the right deviation only as an abstract theoretical concept, denied its presence in their organizations, and opposed the necessity to struggle against it.[64]

They did not support Bukharin's alternative plan of socialist construction – they hardly knew anything about it. What they stood for was the party line the way it had been practiced before the recourse to violent methods in 1928. The chairman of the Zlatoust' regional committee was quoted as saying that "the rightist deviation could exist only in Moscow. But here in Zlatoust' there was not and could not be any right-wing deviation."[65] The Urals committee admitted that everyone was denying the presence of the right deviation but at the same time defended their peasants from the excessive pressure from Moscow. The CC claimed it had "at its disposal a huge number of cases showing that the village Communist cells supported easing the pressure upon the kulaks, because they did not want to quarrel with them."[66]

Denying the existence of the right-wing deviation, numerous local Communists advocated policies which fit its definition, at least from Moscow's point of view. The CC report concluded: "We have literally an entire stratum of rural Communists who consciously oppose the party policy in the countryside."[67] This set of attitudes was expressed very well at numerous party meetings in Leningrad, where local officials complained of arbitrariness from Moscow: "The party replaces NEP with administrative methods. The party abolishes NEP. The party invents a right-wing deviation."[68]

Entire provincial organizations had to be disbanded or reorganized. The CC wrote to Stalin and Molotov in November 1929 that it "had to dissolve quite a few rural party organizations because they were not willing to conduct a decisive struggle with the kulaks."[69] Thousands were expelled or purged from the party. A special report of the Central Control Commission on the 1929 party purge admitted that local organizations were reluctant to embark upon the "cleansing" campaign, and that those who were purged were primarily expelled because of social origin, religious practices, or infrequent meeting attendance, or other non-political offenses. That meant that from the point of view of the Central Control Commission most of those holding heretical views remained in the party ranks.[70] Any attack on right-wing deviation was, in fact, an attack on the rural party and its innumerable ties to the rural community. What Stalin labeled right-wing deviation, was, in fact, the establishment's reluctance to part with NEP.

THE CRISIS OF BOLSHEVISM

The Soviet Union edged towards the chaos of another civil war under a façade called collectivization. Prices for food in the cities soared and long bread lines became places of political discussion. Discontent rose in workers' neighborhoods. Those who considered themselves the party's old guard found themselves unable to bear the unfolding drama without doing something. The years 1928 and 1929 were periods of boisterous informal discussion. Numerous student groups, university professors, and old party members formed all kinds of informal associations where they discussed politics. Some of them were so foolish that they took notes and minutes of their proceedings. Others met in the forests, as before the revolution. Still others admitted that they "gathered, discussed, and collected signatures."[71] A special report on the situation in the Leningrad party organization for 1928 stated that:

> a mood of panic was spreading among the workers and party members. There was no food in the cities and famine was coming to the countryside. Anti-Soviet conversations were commonplace in the bread lines, and the party members were afraid to defend the party line.[72]

Amid this rising tide of anxiety, discontent, and violence, Stalin celebrated his fiftieth birthday. The press exploded with laudatory articles praising Lenin's most faithful pupil and associate.[73] No doubt many of those seasoned party members raised their eyebrows: "Is this socialism? Is this Leninism? Where is the country heading?"

Any political discourse in the Soviet Union had to be expressed in terms of the procession to socialism. Anything else would have been dismissed as counterrevolutionary. One has to decode political messages expressed in the format of political correctness. Certainly many of the people who were labeled rightist deviationists – N.A. Uglanov, M.N. Riutin, V. Syrtsov, and many others – began to have doubts not only about the Stalinist course of action but about the entire enterprise of socialist construction. Evidence of this kind is

extremely difficult to obtain because those who had doubts had good reason
to keep their thoughts away from the public domain. In many cases they were
not brave enough to share their thoughts with anyone, but simply left diaries.
Some courageous individuals made public statements at party meetings,
verbalizing what was on the minds of many. Most often, however, critical
thoughts were expressed around the kitchen table.[74] Old and trusted friends
gathered for tea or a stronger drink and to discuss politics. Older-generation
Bolsheviks had to talk about politics – it was an essential feature of their
culture.[75] They had been doing this for years and needed debate. Martemyan
Riutin would write in 1932 in his famous critique of Stalinism:

> General and pointless face to face conversations about the ruinous and anti-
> Leninist character of the Stalinist leadership have become to such a degree
> universal [massovye], an almost all-embracing phenomenon, that they have
> become too repetitive and repulsive.[76]

The echoes of these conversations, reported in a variety of sources,
highlight several themes that dominated older Bolsheviks' concerns, themes
that crystallized into several widely held heretical propositions. On some
issues there was virtually universal agreement, while on others there was a
divergence of opinion. Just about everyone agreed that the party of Lenin,
the Bolshevik Party they had known in 1917, was no longer what it used to
be. The party had been usurped by Stalin and Co. Some people would put it
in stronger terms, such as "the Georgian bandit", or the "mustached one,"
and so on. The reality of the GPU dictatorship in the party was glaringly
obvious to anyone, especially after the exile of Trotsky. Those who considered themselves old-time revolutionaries and had worked under Lenin had
a hard time accepting that they no longer could express their opinions. It was
not the issues so much as the changed procedure that was a source of serious
discontent among the old ranks. These people thought of themselves as the
party elite, as the party conscience, and as the old guard which was entitled
to express opinion freely.

Echoing Bukharin, many argued that a radical departure from NEP spelled
disaster for the country's economy. Peasants were going to resist. A new civil
war in the countryside would cause peasant rebellions, devastation, and
famine, all of which would impede industrialization. Many of these gloomy
forecasts turned out to be prophetic. Defense of NEP, and critiques of Stalin
and the bureaucratization of the party did not go beyond the boundaries of
the right opposition discourse. The point, however, is that many thinking
Bolsheviks did go beyond these bounds. Their assessment of the situation can
be reconstructed in these terms: they believed that as Marxists they had to
assess the achievements of the revolution in terms of productivity of labor.
If the socialist mode of production was able to achieve a superior productivity
of labor, then the victory of the socialist revolution was feasible. Their crisis
of confidence in 1928 was rooted precisely in their realization that the

socialist sector was not characterized by superior productivity of labor. In fact those who had access to economic data knew very well that in reality the reverse was true: the private sector outperformed its "socialist" rival in all respects: productivity, workers' wages, efficiency, and innovation were higher. In agriculture it was plain for all to see that private enterprise outperformed the collective farms in all respects. The very success of NEP was predicated on the productivity of market-producing peasantry.

"What does it all add up to?" asked the Bolsheviks among themselves during those evening conversations. Some argued that a bureaucratic enterprise run by half-literate upstarts certainly could not outperform a capitalist one. They would note that enterprises run by proletarians were apparently no less exploitative of the working class. The fact that they were run by proletarians did not make them socialist. Even if all private enterprise was to be nationalized, why would a Soviet bureaucracy make the endeavor any more socialist than any other bureaucracy? Why pretend that simply because it was called "Soviet" it automatically became socialist? Socialism did not work – it was a utopia that could not outperform market forces. It meant that the experiment had not succeeded. According to Riutin, these conversations were widespread in Moscow, Leningrad, and other big cities in 1929–30. Riutin appealed to fellow party members to cease talking in the corners, stop whispering, and get up and fight as Bolsheviks.[77] For that he would wind up in a GPU camp to be shot like so many others in 1937.

By the end of NEP Bolshevism as an intellectual current was in deep crisis. Some of its older and more educated representatives came to doubt the validity of the entire project. Yet they had nowhere to go and few with whom to share their thoughts. One either had to display allegiance publicly to Comrade Stalin and the CC line, no matter what, or face the prospect of arrest by the GPU. Very few, like Riutin, found the courage to articulate their criticism of Stalin's course, knowing that arrest and imprisonment would be the price. Most others, Bukharin included, capitulated. They did not know how to justify their past actions. They did not know what to offer for the future. They had to forget how to reason independently. They learned to accept the CC line as their own. Riutin came to the conclusion in 1932 that the Leninist party had been ruined. The old guard was down and out:

> The main cohort of Lenin's comrades has been removed from the leading positions, and some of them are in prisons and exile; others have capitulated, still others, demoralized and humiliated, carry on a miserable existence, and finally some, those who have degenerated completely, have turned into loyal servants of the dictator.[78]

The bankruptcy of the socialist construction project in Russia was particularly painful since the old guard fulfilled all the recommendations Lenin had left them. The party had been proletarianized. Hundreds of thousands of workers had entered into the ranks. Instead of becoming a force for party democracy, however, the new recruits became a force of bureaucratic competition for privilege and power. The party split was avoided, exactly as Lenin had recommended: at every party gathering a new ritual demonstrated the iron unity of the party ranks behind the Central Committee. In reality, however, the Leninist recipe spelled disaster. Required public conformity made it easier to purge from the Party all those who could be labeled as opposing unity. A party split was indeed avoided, but at a price of a personal dictatorship.

Lenin's other recommendations – that the CC be enlarged and the Workers' and Peasants' Inspectorate as well as the Party Control Commission be strengthened – were all fulfilled. As a result, the CC became larger and less powerful, the Inspectorate ineffective, and the Party Control Commission controlled by the Secretariat. The dictatorship was tightened and centralized. The party belonged to the up and coming, the worker promotees, the Stalinist apparatus. Here is how Riutin explained their cooption:

> The Politburo, the Presidium of the Central Control Commission, and the province committee chairmen have turned into a gang of political crooks without any principles. They regard the party as their patrimony . . . People's Commissars, their deputies, prominent apparatchiks, editors of major newspapers, and union chairmen . . . are also ensnared by the process of degeneration. All of them, including the former workers, do not have any connection to the working people any more. They are provided for with high salaries, resorts, country houses, luxurious apartments, special, overt and covert food supply, free theaters, excellent medical care, and so on. And all this is taking place at a time when the people are being pauperized, and a semi-starvation existence is reigning over the entire country. To a certain extent, they are bribed by Stalin.[79]

Lenin's heritage was not perceived with adoration by the thinking Bolsheviks, as is customarily assumed. His New Economic Policy demonstrated the superiority of private enterprise over "socialist" production for those who wanted or were able to see. NEP revealed the superiority of capitalism and led to the strengthening of the Stalinist dictatorship. The experiment with socialist construction was doomed to failure in Russia. Riutin expressed these ideas well for many others:

> The experience of the proletarian revolution has shown us something totally unforeseen and unexpected . . . We grew up with the notion that the leadership of the party and the country under the dictatorship of the proletariat would express the will of the masses. In reality, it turned out that in the course of internal party struggle, leadership degenerated into a personal dictatorship, leading to the ruin of Soviet Power, and the party, hated by the masses, is relying primarily upon terror and provocation. This is a new phenomenon, particularly and absolutely unexpected for the party.

No matter how painful, no matter how hard, but it is necessary for all to recognize this, for all those who do not want to remain in the grip of illusions and face the fact of the total collapse of the proletarian revolution.[80]

Riutin's own solution was to fight against the Stalinist clique. His thinking revealed the profound contradiction which the older Bolsheviks faced. As a Bolshevik his instinctive desire was to call for action, yet his own analysis showed that if the party was what he described it to be, it was incapable of independent action any more. Furthermore, even if a few courageous individuals to move against Stalin were found, what would they strive to accomplish? Removing Stalin and restoring NEP would still fail to restore the fortunes of a socialist proletarian revolution in Russia. Having realized that a proletarian revolution was a utopian dream, critics like Riutin found themselves in an intellectual dead-end. The old guard was politically dead by the end of NEP, some seven years before its physical annihilation.

Assessing the development of the Russian Communist Party over the span of the 1920s, one may conclude that the party was descending deeper and deeper into self-destruction. The gap between the official imagery and reality was widening. The party continued to call itself a political party, whereas in fact it no longer was one. From a propaganda and mobilization agency in 1920 it was turning into a network of administrative and police agencies aspiring to direct economic life in the country. The true essence of the RCP, its real social composition, consisted of a hierarchical dictatorial machine, staffed by barely literate worker upstarts craving power and privilege. Many of them corrupt, unfamiliar with and uninterested in Marxism, they cheated on the Moscow bosses, and abused those below them.

The party claimed to have been Marxist–Leninist. In fact most of its members knew virtually nothing of Karl Marx's teachings and had no interest in them. The original meaning of socialism from the turn of the century implying a spiritual and economic emancipation of the exploited workers was forgotten. The Leninist heritage was defined by the Secretariat and any other opinions on what Lenin meant were phased out by the political police. The idea of building socialism degenerated into a widely held understanding that it meant fulfilling orders from above in terms of taxes, targets, production plans, or construction sites.

The RCP became an entity which claimed to be a working-class party but in fact consisted of members who had risen from a low-class milieu but resented workers. It was a party that was not really a party, claiming a false identity, and espousing a mutated ideology, hardly recognizable in comparison with its pre-revolutionary original. Many of the rank and file, many old-time thinking Bolsheviks, and certainly the top leaders knew very well that the official representations – that is, the official claims – were merely dogma which had nothing to do with reality.

Freedom to express political opinion in the party was extinct. Success and promotion were linked to politically correct opinions and obedient execution of orders from above. As a result, in a matter of a few more years, all those who had political opinions or remembered the times when they had political opinions – people like Riutin – wound up in Gulag cells, and people who thrived on not having independent political opinion and instead reiterated what was required of them, like Khrushchev, made astonishing career advances. The RCP as an organization had lost control over its own fate by the end of the 1920s. The leader-selection process, the infusion of illiterate upstarts, the dogmatization of ideology, and the personal dictatorship of the General Secretary all but predetermined its self-destruction.

Chapter 10

Conclusion

BOLSHEVIK CULTURE

The purpose of this book has been to identify major trends in the development of Russian society under the New Economic Policy during the 1920s. Most of these resulted from the Bolsheviks' interaction with various social groups. In a very nebulous way the Bolsheviks thought they were constructing socialism. Many of them wanted to believe that the party's goal was to empower workers and women, to educate the masses, to overcome religious superstition (as they would have put it), and encourage the peasantry to utilize more advanced forms of agriculture. Many Bolsheviks were convinced that they were going to make life better for the average person. The Bolshevik agenda was nothing less than that of creating a new society based on a new ideology and its corollaries – new values, rituals, beliefs, social structures, and cultural practices.

The methods the Bolsheviks chose to achieve these grand objectives were agitation, propaganda, and forcible state intervention. The missing pre-requisites for a socialist society would have to be created by resolute action of the state. This fundamentally Leninist approach was verified by the civil war years. The party became used to defining itself as an army storming fortresses. They had fought battles against the Whites and the Greens, on the transport front and on the ideological front. Any project became a campaign, with its imagery of commanders, soldiers, orders, deserters, traitors, and hidden enemies.

In contrast to internecine strife and War Communism, NEP was declared to be a temporary retreat in a Communist offensive which was going to resume some day. Communism was understood to be the final stage of the society's development, associated with a mighty state, heavy industry, a strong army, and the liberated masses following their vanguard willingly into the bright future. Socialism was not understood as a guarantee of individual liberties or self-government. In fact, the Bolsheviks themselves were not aware that they had absorbed many of the values of the pre-revolutionary Russian elite. Despite their professed internationalism they resurrected the Russian empire under new symbols; despite their professed concern for workers' liberation they displayed the same kind of patronizing attitude to workers and peasants as the Russian intelligentsia had. Despite their professed commitment to equality they reproduced a hierarchical social order in Soviet Russia. Despite their professed commitment to women's emancipation they recreated the authoritarian patterns of the past. Intellectual Bolsheviks had failed to escape the grip of cultural practices of their age. A powerful industrial state with a big army and efficient police was what the Bolsheviks were building – a state project no different from the one they had rebelled against.

The new Communist elite, upstarts from the civil war years or recruited from among the poorest strata of peasants and unskilled workers in the 1920s, were unable to abandon the values of their own authoritarian culture. When a commissar of the civil war era waved a gun at peasants and shouted: "I am your tsar and lord and I shall do with you as I please!" or when a young Communist promotee after a crash course in a party school settled comfortably in a large apartment, bought himself a car, and hired servants, we see clear evidence of subconscious reproduction of the old cultural practices. They behaved this way because this is how they understood a boss to act. They imitated the cultural norms of the old master [barin]. The culture of the new elite, despite its claims to be new and proletarian, was utterly authoritarian, and Russian without the refinement and sophistication possessed by the pre-revolutionary elite.

RECASTING SOCIETY

The New Economic Policy did not assure peace to those whom the Bolsheviks considered opponents. It was not even a truce. Communist revolutionary imagery continued to hype a violent and merciless struggle with the caricatured "enemies of the revolution:" the fat capitalist, the drunk priest, the vicious army officer, and the traitor-intellectual. The militarization of Bolshevik culture was a result of the civil war and the Communists' insecurity in Russia. They realized that they were a minority party that had come close to losing power. They were not ready to surrender political advantages to match NEP's economic concessions. The offensive continued non-stop throughout the NEP years. The Bolsheviks thought in terms of social classes and groups, not individuals. Former Mensheviks, "bourgeois" students, and SR-inclined schoolteachers were on the way out, as were others associated with the old regime. Engineers, army officers, and professors could not be removed so quickly. So the Bolshevik long-term plan was to replace the old pre-revolutionary intelligentsia as soon as new cadres were available. The NEP years were characterized by a slow displacement of the old intellectual elite, the free professions, and remnants of what was left of the old political parties.

In this process of recasting society there were essentially two key streams:

deprivees [*lishentsy*] and promotees [*vydvizhentsy*]. Some people were denied electoral rights, jobs, and freedom, while others were promoted to the positions of authority. Screenings, purges, membership drives, and propaganda campaigns were all elements of a social policy. The Bolsheviks tried to envelop society in a variety of social organizations which looked voluntary, but in fact preached Communist teaching in different ways. The purpose was to identify and involve individuals willing to serve the state and with their help involve more and more people in what the Communists called the construction of socialism. Women's departments, the Komsomol, teachers' congresses, trade unions, the League of the Godless – all these "volunteer" associations were to be transmission belts of party ideology to the masses. In power the Communists acted in exactly the same way as they had as agitators and propagandists at the turn of the century, only now they had the infrastructure of the state at their disposal in the pursuit of their objectives.

As a result, with each passing year the possibilities for non-Communist political expression narrowed. Round-ups of the political opposition became standard practice. Scrutiny of social origin became routine business. Control over what one could read, watch or listen to was widening as fast as the Bolshevik bureaucracy could manage it. The apparatus of GPU information gathering grew to be truly impressive: it processed weekly reports from every uezd, and covered virtually every public gathering, expression of discontent, and aspect of economic and political activity systematically.

The Bolsheviks changed the pace and the method of their offensive from time to time, but not the ultimate objectives. Instead of a frontal assault on the opposition parties, bourgeois intelligentsia, Church, and former professional classes, as during the civil war years, a new approach characterized the NEP years. The Bolsheviks tried to shatter these groups from within and gradually replace them with trustworthy cadres. It was low-intensity warfare, represented as the construction of socialism. The Bolsheviks were creating the infrastructure of an omnipotent state which began to penetrate into almost every corner of society.

REPRESENTATIONS

The main problem in reconstructing the history of Bolshevik interaction with society is the confusion between representations, perceptions, and social reality. The Bolsheviks represented their view of the world in Marxist–Leninist discourse, which some historians have accepted at face value. One example will suffice:

> The dictatorship of the proletariat remained the foundation of Soviet power during this period. It continued to be based upon an alliance between the working class and peasantry. That alliance had been shattered during the civil war and the dictatorship of the proletariat had become in actuality the

dictatorship of the party. NEP was designed to reforge the alliance and to rebuild the social support of the state.[1]

It is hardly possible to reforge something which had never existed. Official representations were for the most part reflections of Agitprop mythology. They endlessly repeated the saga about heroic class-conscious proletarians allied with the toiling peasantry who together were building socialism under the leadership of the Communist Party in a union of free socialist republics.

The provincial party committees likewise represented social reality in ideologically correct reports, thus conforming to the center's priorities. They wrote about hundreds of thousands of new party and Komsomol members whose hearts were burning with the desire to build socialism, tens of thousands of women attending delegate meetings, and hundreds of thousands of people of all ages flocking to the League of the Godless. Social and political life was represented as a neverending list of victories, achievements, and accomplishments. This aspect of Communist culture remained intact to the very end of the regime in 1991.

Peasants, workers, and Komsomol members also represented themselves in the official jargon of the center's discourse to promote their own agendas. A poor, unskilled, and illiterate worker who wanted to get ahead styled himself as a "conscious proletarian;" a well-to-do farmer with hired hands from the poor villagers would be a member of a "comradeship" with 50 per cent party membership in order to buy a tractor; NEPmen would do all they could to be working in "socially useful" occupations. These representations should be seen as a popular response to Bolshevik rules of engagement. These people were ready to do whatever was necessary to survive or even succeed. Official representations show how individuals, groups, and institutions presented themselves in the public sphere for political ends.

SOCIAL REALITY

To what extent did the Bolsheviks succeed in promoting new morality, values, rituals, beliefs, tastes, lifestyles, and identities within society? What elements of Communist culture were appropriated and internalized? Throughout this study we have surveyed popular attitudes on a variety of issues among virtually all social groups. Many petitions, peasant electoral instructions, letters to women's departments, workers' speeches, and resolutions found in a variety of sources are genuine voices of the people. We have encountered examples of this discourse in students' suicide letters and at Trotskyite dissidents' clandestine gatherings. They complain about reality – careerism, corruption in both plain language and Bolshevik dialect.

The people least affected by Communist propaganda were the peasants. Examination of their voting record in elections to village soviets, their resolutions [nakazy], speeches, letters, petitions, rumors, religious practices, rituals, and holidays shows remarkable resilience to Communist representations. They lived in their own cultural world quite apart from Communist visionary projections. They were relatively content with the economic arrangements of NEP, only wanting more. They wanted their own schools, self-government, family farming, and individual ownership of land. Election returns were not a matter of perceptions. Attempts to set up Peasant Unions were a fact of life, a genuine popular movement from below. Peasants' voting records, *nakazy*, letters, questions at public meetings, and actions add up to an expression of popular will: aiming to enhance their input into local government, limit taxes, and bargain over prices for their grain.

Bolshevik policy towards workers is a matter of factual record, not perceptions. It stressed making workers work harder for less pay by scaling down wages and benefits while raising production targets – all in the name of constructing socialism. The study of workers' culture, popular attitudes, and lifestyles shows a particular psychological tension caused by the gap between official representations and the miserable realities. Workers were puzzled by the contradiction between the theory that they were the ruling class and the reality that they never got their wages on time. Workers' discourse displayed tension between ordinary workers and promotees, unskilled workers and skilled, as well as hostility from the shop floor against NEPmen and Red directors. In this vein it is misleading to interpret antispecialist sentiment as an expression of revolutionary zeal. Specialists were viewed as surrogates for the factory administration and easier targets than the Red directors. Workers perceived Bolshevik policies as little different than under the old regime and openly referred to them in similar terms on numerous occasions. The workers' milieu was plagued by pervasive drunkenness and apathetic attitudes to politics. It generated the folklore of life in the barracks, dormitories, or communal apartments. From 1925 onward, workers' discontent increased, reaching its peak in 1928–9. There were no class-conscious proletarians following the party. There was instead anti-Bolshevik radicalization against lower wages and higher production rates.

The history of the Komsomol during NEP illustrates a clash between representations and reality. Styled as a transmission belt of the party and a vanguard of class-conscious youth in official propaganda, the Komsomol was in reality an organization occupied with anything but constructing socialism. In the countryside Komsomol members were hooligans bent on mischief and abuse of religious congregations. It has been suggested earlier that the underlying motivation of such behavior was not revolutionary zeal, but rebellion against authority. Such activism was perpetrated by a marginal group among rural youth, trying to use Komsomol as a way out of their rural existence.

Official praise of asceticism, collectivity, and denial of the private sphere in the-way-it-ought-to-be discourse contrasts with a reality characterized by alcoholism, sexual promiscuity, and defiance among working-class youth.

The Bolsheviks' new morality and anti-religious campaigns precipitated disrespect towards women and family life. Working-class youth rejected official propaganda guidelines and celebrated life instead with unrestrained indulgence in vodka, sex, and defiance. The new morality campaign generated not a higher proletarian, socialist morality but more lenient sexual standards and cultural practices, which were new and became what we know of as Soviet, but were contrary to the original ascetic Bolshevik intentions. The Bolsheviks reaped the consequences of their destructive preaching.

A revealing indicator of the clash between the officially proclaimed high ideals of the revolution and Soviet reality unfolded at the institutes and universities. The culture of critical thinking and questioning authority, so firmly entrenched among Russian students before the revolution, was resurrected in the 1920s. The artistic intelligentsia increasingly realized that instead of a return to normality, the NEP years were bringing about the strengthening of the Communist dictatorship. Some understood socialism as equality and justice, and Soviet power as requiring fair elections. Many interpreted socialism as something other than one-party dictatorship and political police surveillance. To the party's horror, instead of being grateful to the Bolsheviks for upward mobility, students questioned dominant policies and values. By the end of the decade it was clear that schools were not turning out class-conscious grateful cadres marching after the party no matter where it led them. The "former people," "bourgeois" professors or engineers, and old-time industrial workers had a different moral and behavioral code and different ideas of what their rights were. The rise of student dissident groups demanding free elections to the soviets, a free press, free associations, as well as their campaigning for "bourgeois" rectors and defense of academic freedoms is the most interesting cultural phenomenon of the 1920s.

The history of women in the 1920s parallels that of the students in some important ways. The Bolsheviks started out trying to mobilize the "backward female masses." Official discourse hailed the era of emancipation. Women's departments and delegate meetings preached equality and justice for oppressed women. By organizing this constituency the Bolsheviks reckoned to reap enthusiastic social support; in reality, the promise of emancipation failed to be backed up by deeds. Pay to female workers was the lowest of all categories of workers (besides children). They were the last to be hired and the first to be fired. Women in the party were the first to be purged and the last to be promoted. Sexual harassment was rampant. Rural women and worker women began to protest, demand, write letters and petitions, swamping the women's departments. From their intended function as outposts of propaganda, they turned into institutions processing complaints. The Bolsheviks admitted that their bluff had been called by phasing them out. There were only false promises, dashed hopes, and the pretense of emancipation.

Most outcomes of Bolshevik social policies and cultural campaigns in the

1920s had practical results which differed from the original plans. The Communist Party was supposed to become a proletarianized vanguard building socialism. Instead it was a conglomeration of bureaucrats – many of them corrupt, some barely literate – pursuing their own private agendas. The Komsomol was supposed to become the organizing center of the entire Soviet youth. In fact it was an institution plagued by "malaise," hooliganism, political heresies, nationalist deviations, and career climbing. Students were supposed to become the vanguard of youth. In reality, they were the vanguard of the dissident intelligentsia. Liberated women were supposed to become a grateful constituency. Instead they became increasingly articulate in their protest. Workers and peasants were expected to accept diminishing compensation and rising taxes for the sake of "constructing socialism," but failed to live up to the Bolsheviks' expectations.

None of the Bolshevik new rituals took root. Komsomol Easter and October baptism were soon forgotten. The new morality campaign degenerated into promiscuity. Communal collective living campaigns degenerated into the destruction of privacy and resulted in social tensions and problems. Religiosity was supposed to be overcome but in fact intensified by the end of the decade as a direct consequence of Bolshevik campaigns. If the Bolsheviks thought they were winning on the anti-religious front, they would not have had to resort to violence, the forcible closing of churches and the liquidation of organized religious congregations in 1929. Violence was an admission of their failure to prevail by other means. If we do not project forward, but judge the Bolshevik record during NEP years, most campaigns ended as failures. The spirit of NEP Russia was of society's resistance to its recasting by the Communist Party.

CONFIDENTIAL DISCOURSE

Confidential party discourse, until recently inaccessible, is an extremely important source for what the Bolshevik leaders knew about the society they ruled. We know now what Stalin read week after week, month after month in GPU, gubkom, and special CC reports. We know now that only thirty-three people in Russia had access to this information, mostly department chiefs of the GPU, or Politburo and CC members. As we have seen, most of these reports were compilations of raw data on election results and labor protests, as well as procurement and output statistics, education information, and evaluation of performance of local administrations.

Confidential GPU discourse is frank. It depicts Bolshevik policies, cultural practices, and popular attitudes in an undisguised manner. In contrast to local administrations' reports couched in Bolshevik jargon and rhetoric, the GPU and the CC plenipotentiaries seem to have been able to be more impolitic. Strikes and protests, dissident group activities, the malaise of the Komsomol, corruption, drunkenness, and the abuse of authority are reported systematically and regularly in those terms. Top party leaders knew that local party members were mostly illiterate and corrupt, taking bribes and hobnobbing with well-to-do peasants. They knew that voluntary associations consisted of "dead souls" and propaganda campaigns had degenerated into acts of hooliganism. They were aware that the Komsomol was a breeding ground of sexual promiscuity and ideological deviation. They also knew that many students, teachers, professors, engineers, and even army officers ridiculed Communist propaganda.

Confidential party discourse on workers makes it clear that the Bolsheviks had no illusions about the class consciousness of their proletarians supposedly marching to socialism. They were aware that most workers could not care less about socialist construction. They knew that workers were concerned about late payment of wages, the arbitrariness of Red directors, and the absence of bargaining rights they had enjoyed under capitalism. In the confidential reports workers were depicted as greedy, lazy, undisciplined, narrow-minded drunkards or petty bourgeois self-seekers.

The Bolshevik leaders knew that peasants were largely immune to Communist propaganda and were generating more wealth and political demands with every passing year. In confidential party discourse the Bolsheviks admitted that peasant leaders were more cultured than party members, knowing Soviet law, reading newspapers, forming comradeships, buying tractors, bribing party officials, and pursuing their economic interests successfully, by expanding production with every passing year. They knew that the share of Communists in rural soviets had diminished significantly in 1925, turning the CP into a marginal force there.

This privileged information did not find its way into the public sphere. The Bolsheviks never published statistics on the dwindling of their share of seats in rural soviets into single figures. Nonetheless, party leaders reacted to this information in public. The Information Department of the Central Committee processed it, and the top party leaders defined it. How exactly they interpreted the facts at hand depended on their political preferences. The party's left opposition, Zinoviev specifically, exploded with the rhetoric about the "kulak danger" in the countryside in 1925. Proponents of NEP, such as Dzerzhinsky, Sokolnikov, Bukharin, and others denied the existence of a "kulak danger" and focused on the inadequacy of local Communist cadres. Internal Bolshevik Party discourse on policy consisted of phrased politically correct representations and labels to achieve political ends. The choice of vocabulary revealed shifts in policy. During the height of NEP in 1924–5, the Bolsheviks referred to well-to-do peasants as cultured farmers [kul'turnye khoziaeva], but in 1927 they had turned into kulaks; by 1929, they were "bloodsuckers," "parasites," and "class enemies." Indeed, it would have been difficult to launch class war on cultured farmers, but it seemed more justifiable against "bourgeois parasitic elements" in the countryside.

Secret Communist communications make it quite apparent that the Communist elite was insecure. Painfully aware of its own inadequacy, it knew its grip on the country to be tenuous. As a result, an important cultural phenomenon appeared during these years: coded language. To explain workers' strikes, which were not supposed to happen in a country of the victorious proletariat, the Central Committee and the party committees resorted to labeling in the official and public discourse. Workers who went on strike were no longer workers. This noble term could no longer apply to "hirelings of the bourgeoisie" or "hidden Mensheviks." Acts of protest were labeled "sabotage" by "kulaks" on the factory floor. Women workers were "backward" and gripped by "religious superstitions." Peasants who demanded unions and the right to religious education could not simply be called peasants, but had to be identified as "kulaks," regardless of income or property. Students or engineers who criticized the Communist bureaucracy or its inadequacy were labeled as "wreckers contaminated by bourgeois consciousness." Individuals critical of the emerging system had to be defined in the terms of class struggle, as "exploiters," "parasites," "wreckers," "saboteurs," and "enemies" requiring unmasking. All these character-izations were designed to explain why social groups were not living up to the image they had in the official iconography.

SHOWDOWN

In the 1927 rural elections the Bolsheviks suffered further setbacks and cultured farmers strengthened their positions. The Bolshevik leaders acted in response to these facts. They squeezed out the private sector from the grain trade by taxation and increased disenfranchisement of those labeled "bour-geois exploitative elements." Yet these measures failed to stem the tide. With only two or three thousand Communists in a typical agricultural province, the number of kulaks typically increased every year by more than the total number of party members in the province. If left unchecked, this trend would inevitably threaten the Bolsheviks' grip on the countryside.

When peasants refused to sell grain at 60 kopecks a pud in the fall of 1927, the Bolsheviks defined it as an "offensive of the class enemy." It was not so much their Marxist ideology that guided their response as the experience of the civil war and the memory of the Green detachments. The decision to strike hard against the peasants was a product of a Bolshevik mind-set, framed by the Leninist legacy and civil war experience.

In 1928 social processes which had been unfolding throughout the 1920s confronted the Bolsheviks with a major social and political crisis. Peasants were on strike, withholding their produce from the market and demanding a fair price. Workers were in turmoil over the intensification of labor and falling wages, blaming the Red directors and specialists. Students campaigned for fair elections and academic freedom. Women workers demanded equal pay and an end to sexual harassment in the work-place, leading strikes at numerous factories and vociferous opposition in village soviets. Workers, peasants, students, teachers, professors, women, and religious community leaders all articulated their ideas, demands, and petitions on how to improve the situation. All these manifestations of civic activism were signs that the society had recovered from the blows of the civil war. There was no popular activism for a Stalinist revolution from above; if anything it was against Bolshevik policies and practices. NEP was generating a healthy society incompatible with the Communist Party dictatorship. If peasants had received a fair price and a Peasant Union; workers had been allowed an unaffiliated party and free trade unions; women had received equal pay and respect; and students, teachers, and professors had been granted their academic freedoms, Russia would have continued to evolve towards a normal country. It would have been a triumph of civil society. The alternative to Stalinism would have been a multiparty system and a market economy.

The party leaders perceived these interests as a challenge that could not go unanswered. From the Bolshevik point of view, it was a society in crisis. Seen from this perspective, Stalin's revolution from above was a move to stop the processes unfolding in NEP Russia. Peasants had to be herded into state-controlled units, which would be misnamed collective farms, to provide for the extraction of grain and workers' wrath had to be redirected against specialists and the Jews. They had to be forced to work harder and demand less. Women were going to be forced to obey their superiors without delegate meetings or departments. Students, teachers, and professors were going to be purged repeatedly until they learned the correct party line. Enemies in the party were going to be unmasked and banished.

The break with NEP had little to do with the wishes of the party rank and file or the wishes of any other social group. It was instead a preemptive strike of the central party–state apparatus against the perceived threat of a new economic union between the pro-NEP local party officialdom and prosperous rural and urban entrepreneurs. It was just as much a strike at the party, which was, in effect, an autonomous local elite tied to the peasantry, as it was a blow against entrepreneurial peasantry. It was a policy designed to strengthen the center's control over the provinces and their provincial party cliques and sources of revenue, both in agriculture and industry. It was an admission of failure to generate voluntary social support. It was a new war on society to preserve the dictatorship. It was a matter of constructing a centralized state, to be represented as "constructing socialism."

THE CULTURE OF SOVIETISM

As Russia entered the 1930s, everyone had to accept the official myth that the country was approaching socialism and everyone loved Comrade Stalin, the greatest leader of all mankind. The GPU was to force people to act as if they believed that official representations were reality: that they lived in a society of happy workers and collective farmers overfulfilling the plan with joy. People voted as they were supposed to, condemned the "mad Trotskyite dogs," and praised the genius of Comrade Stalin. Some withdrew from public life or artistic endeavors into private concerns. Many others committed suicide, or crawled on their knees to plead for forgiveness for their past mistakes, like Pyatakov, Bukharin, Kamenev, and Zinoviev. They adopted official rhetoric in order to pass political loyalty tests. They learned to say the right things and began to separate their public personas from private ones. Thus the culture of Sovietism was formed: thinking one thing but saying something else. Its key feature was parading at every opportunity the official Communist representations as if they were one's own.

Within narrow circles of friends, unofficial and un-Soviet culture persisted during the late 1920s and into the 1930s. Songs, jokes, and stories circulated which ridiculed the idiocy of official representations. We know now that Stalin knew that peasants hated him, that workers made derogatory jokes about him, and that the Old Bolsheviks grumbled around kitchen tables, while praising him at party meetings. Stalin referred to this as double-dealing to be unmasked. His response was the purge, meaning not just dismissal, but imprisonment or execution.

This public display of loyalty and private grumbling reached the very top of the Communist Party itself. Only a few like Martimian Riutin dared to make public what everyone knew anyway: that Stalin's clique had usurped power from the party, that socialism had turned out not to be what the revolutionaries dreamed of, and that everyone pretended that the country was marching to socialism. According to Riutin, everyone knew that everyone around them was pretending but feared to admit it except to trusted friends. The most striking examples were the thoughts of and conversations among Old Bolsheviks about the fate of the revolution, the cause of socialism, and the nature of political order in Russia at the end of the decade. In that discourse they admitted that things were not what they appeared to be: the Communist Party was not a Leninist vanguard building socialism, but a Stalinist bureaucratic machine, staffed by semi-literate upstarts who had replaced the Old Bolsheviks. Stalin's war on peasants, represented as building socialism, was nothing but an imposition of a new serfdom. The Old Bolsheviks' discourse is fascinating not only because it has a truthful ring to it, but because it outlived the Old Bolsheviks. This discourse among trusted friends about how bad things really were became an essential part of Soviet culture.

We have, therefore, examined three levels of Soviet discourse: official propaganda representations celebrating victories and exposing enemies in the public sphere, a flow of critical assessments in the confidential communications of the political police, often resorting to labeling, and private critical conversations around the "kitchen table" and in *samizdat*. In the 1930s the fear of the police was so pervasive that the third level disappeared almost entirely. People were afraid to share their private thoughts even with their closest friends. After Stalin, the private sphere would revive somewhat and dissident voices would sound louder from year to year. In Brezhnev's times, the repetition of the party dogmas devoid of meaning became ritualized until finally the empty shell of Marxism–Leninism was cast aside as a useless Agitprop relic in 1991. Stalin's revolution from above in the last years of the 1920s brought the Bolsheviks six decades of power before society dislodged them again from their hegemonic political dictatorship.

Notes

Complete bibliographic information on cited books is in the bibliography.

Unless otherwise indicated the archival materials cited are from the former Central Party Archive, currently called RTsKhIDNI – Russian Center for the Preservation and Study of the Documents of Modern History in Moscow. To avoid repetition, the number of Fond and Opis' are indicated only if different from the preceding note.

INTRODUCTION: REVOLUTIONARY IDENTITY

1 For the most eloquent presentation of this view, see Stephen Cohen, *Bukharin and the Bolshevik Revolution* and "Bolshevism and Stalinism" in Robert Tucker, ed., *Stalinism*, and Moshe Lewin, *Russian Peasants and Soviet Power.*
2 J. Bowlt, *Russian Art of the Avant-garde* and John Milner, *Vladimir Tatlin and the Russian Avant-garde*; Camilla Gray, *The Great Experiment: Russian Art 1863–1922.*
3 For pioneering studies, see Richard Pipes, *Russia under the Bolshevik Regime*, esp. ch. 6 "Culture as Propaganda," pp. 282–387; Peter Kenez, *The Birth of the Propaganda State*; Brandon Taylor, *Art and Literature under the Bolsheviks*, Vol. 1: *The Crisis of Renewal 1917–1924*; Richard Stites, *Revolutionary Dreams.*
4 Nadezhda Mandelshtam, *Hope against Hope. A Memoir*, p. 168.
5 Robert Darnton, *Great Cat Massacre and Other Episodes in French Cultural History*; Simon Schama, *Citizens. A Chronicle of the French Revolution.*
6 Roger Chartier, *Forms and Meanings, Cultural History: Between Practices and Representations*, and *On the Edge of the Cliff: History, Language and Practices.*
7 For the latest eloquent defense of this view, see Martin Malia, *The Soviet Tragedy.*
8 Of the enormous literature on the Russian revolutionary movement, one can single out Terence Emmons, *The Formation of Political Parties*, Abraham Ascher, *The Revolution of 1905*, and Richard Pipes, *Struve. Liberal on the Left.*
9 Jane Burbank, *Intelligentsia and Revolution.*
10 Norman Naimark, *Terrorists and Social Democrats.*
11 Beate Fieseler, *Frauen auf dem Weg in die Russischen Sozialdemokratie, 1890–1917.*
12 John Keep, *The Rise of Social Democracy in Russia.*
13 For the classic in the field, see Franco Venturi, *Roots of Revolution.*
14 Manfred Hildermeier: *Die Sozialrevolutionäre Partei Russlands.*
15 Anna Geifman, *Thou Shalt Kill.*

16 Vladimir Brovkin, *The Mensheviks after October*.
17 See, for example, John Biggart, "Anti-Leninist Bolshevism. The Forward Group of the RSDRP," *Canadian Slavonic Papers* 23 (June 1981), pp. 134–53.
18 See "Lenin and the Origins of Bolshevism," in Richard Pipes, *The Russian Revolution*, pp. 341–85.
19 Neil Harding, *Lenin's Political Thought*, Alfred G. Meyer, *Leninism*, and Leonard Schapiro and Peter Reddaway, *Lenin: The Man, The Theorist, The Leader. A Reappraisal*.
20 See, for example, David Mandel, *The Petrograd Workers*.
21 For an excellent discussion of alternatives in 1917, see Vladimir Buldakov, "The October Revolution: Seventy-Five Years On," *European History Quarterly* 22:4 (October 1992), pp. 497–517.
22 T.H. Rigby, *Lenin's Government. Sovnarkom*.
23 For detailed discussion see Vladimir Brovkin, *Behind the Front Lines of the Civil War*.
24 Philip Pomper, *Lenin, Trotsky, Stalin*.
25 Katerina Clark, *Petersburg, Crucible of Cultural Revolution*. See also, for example, Hugh Hudson Jr., *Blueprints and Blood*.
26 Boris Grois, *The Total Art of Stalinism*.
27 Jay Leida, *Kino. A History of the Russian and Soviet Film*, p. 251.
28 Chistina Lodder, *Russian Constructivism*.
29 Richard Stites discusses the demise of the avant-garde in *Revolutionary Dreams*. See also Matthew Cullerne Brown, *Art under Stalin* and Hans Günter, ed., *Culture of the Stalin Period*.
30 Igor Golomstock, *Totalitarian Art*.
31 Christopher Read, *Culture and Power in Revolutionary Russia*.
32 Peter Kenez, *Cinema and Soviet Society*, Dmitry Shlapentokh and Vladimir Shlapentokh, *Soviet Cinematography*.
33 For a Soviet collection of materials on propaganda, see I.M. Bibikova and N.I. Levchanko, eds, *Agitatsionno Massovoe iskusstvo. Oformlenie prazdnenstv*.
34 Lynn Mally, *Culture of the Future*, Stephen White, *Bolshevik Poster*.

1 EXTRACTING SOCIALLY ALIEN ELEMENTS

1 For some new evidence, see Richard Pipes, *Unknown Lenin*.
2 *Obzory GPU*, F.17, Op. 87, Doc. 177.
3 Yagoda, To: Biuro Sekretariata, *Smeta GPU* (6 September, 1923) Op. 84, Doc. 587, p. 83.
4 Tula Gubkom, To: CC "Otchet Tulskogo Gubkoma" (January 1925) Op. 16, Doc. 1377, p. 33.
5 A.M. Gam, A.S. Masal'skaia, I.N. Selezneva, "Deportatsiya inakomysliashchikh v 1922 Godu," *Kentavr* No. 5 (1993), pp. 75–90.
6 "Lenin Orders Deportations," *New York Times* (15 June, 1992), p. A11.
7 A.M. Gam, *et al.*, "Deportatsiya," p. 87.
8 Ibid., p. 88.
9 "Vybory v Sovet i SD partiya", *Sotsialisticheskii Vestnik* (21 September, 1922).
10 "Kto boitsya, a kto net, iz pis'ma" (4 May, 1921) p. 13; "Dni nashei zhizni. Pis'mo iz Moskvy" (17 April, 1921) p. 8; "Sekretnye osvedomiteli v Men'shevistskikh organizatsiyakh" (5 August, 1921), all in *Sotsialisticheskii Vestnik*, and "Rezoliutsiya TsKa o provokatsiyakh" in *Iz Partii* No. 2 (February 1923), p. 46.
11 "Khronika sobytii," *Iz Partii* No. 4 (1923), p. 13.

12 "Pod gradom udarov," *Sotsial Demokrat* No. 5 (May 1923), p. 7.

13 Boris Dvinov, *Ot legal'nosti k podpol'yu*, p. 142.

14 CC, To: all Gubkoms, "Tsirkuliar TsKa RKP(b) o merakh bor'by s men-shevikami" (October 1923) Op. 184, Doc. 467, p. 282.

15 GPU Info. Dept, To: Comrade Stalin (31 August, 1923) Op. 87, Doc. 177, p. 2.

16 Ibid. (1 July–15 September, 1923)

17 For a list of underground periodicals, see "Na Postu," *Sotsialisticheskii Vestnik* No. 19 (4 October, 1922), p. 8, Berlin.

18 Zam.Pred. OGPU, Yagoda, To: Mekhlis, Stalin's Secretariat, "Kratkii Obzor Polit-Ekonom. Sostoyaniya Respubliki" (15 September–1 November, 1923) Op. 87, Doc. 177, p. 5.

19 Ibid. (February 1924), p. 18.

20 Andre Liebich, *From the Other Shore. Russian Social Democracy after 1921*.

21 S.V. Medvedev, "Zayavlenie v TsKa RKP(b)" (1924) Op. 84, Doc. 587, p. 95.

22 Yagoda, To: Mekhlis, Stalin's Secretariat, "Kratkii Obzor ..." (February 1924), Op. 87, Doc. 177, p. 17.

23 Numerous instances are cited in "TsKa: Ko vsem chlenam partii, ko vsem mestnym organizatsiyam," *Iz Partii* No. 4 (May 1923).

24 *Khronika presledovanii v Sovetskoi Rossii* No. 2 (Berlin 1923). See also Raphail Abramowitsch: *Die Politischen Gefangenen in der Sowjetunion*.

25 See the full text in English in Brovkin, ed., *Dear Comrades*, Doc. 42, p. 237

26 Spence, *Boris Savinkov. Renegade on the Left*.

27 Shchetinov, *Krushenie melko-burzhuaznoi kontr-revoliutsii v Sovetskoi Rossii*.

28 For a recent collection of documents, see Felshtinsky, *VCHK – GPU: dokumenty i materialy*.

29 John Curtiss, *The Russian Church and the Soviet State 1917–1930*, p. 129; Rene Füllop Miller, *The Mind and Face of Bolshevism*, pp. 249–50; also Sergius Troitsky, "The Living Church," in William Emhardt, ed., *Religion in Soviet Russia* pp. 303–33.

30 D. Pospielovsky, *The Russian Church and the Soviet Regime, 1917–1982*.

31 Gregory Freeze, "Counter-reformation in Russian Orthodoxy: Popular Response to Religious Innovation, 1922–1925," *Slavic Review* 54:2 (1995), pp. 305–39.

32 For an account of church politics surrounding convocation of the sobor implying a strong connection of the renovationists with the GPU, see Richard J. Cooke, *Religion in Russia under the Soviets*, pp. 157–67.

33 Nachalnik Shestogo Otdeleniya Sekretnogo Otdela GPU, Tuchkov [Chief of the sixth department of the Secret Department of the GPU], To: Zam Pred. OGPU Tov. Menzhinsky [Deputy Chief of the GPU], "Doklad Nachal'nika Shestogo Otdeleniya Sekretnogo Otdela OGPU O Prodelannoi Rabote Po Tserkovnikam i Sektam v Proshlom 1923 Godu" (24 February, 1924) F.17, Op. 187. Doc. 176. (Hereafter *Doklad*.)

34 On the confiscation, see a recent detailed study by Jonathan Daily, "'Storming the Last Citadel': The Bolshevik Assault on the Church, 1922," in Brovkin, ed., *The Bolsheviks in Russian Society*, pp. 235–70.

35 *Doklad*, p. 2.

36 Ibid., p. 3.

37 Ibid., p. 3.

38 Ibid., p. 4.

39 Ibid., p. 5.

40 Ibid., p. 9.

41 Ibid., p. 9.

42 See: Dmitry Pospielovsky, "The Renovationist Schism in the Russian Orthodox

Church," *Russian History/Histoire Russe* Vol. 9 No. 2–3 (1982), pp. 285–308, esp. pp. 306–7.

43 "Doklad o prodelannoi rabote po vydvoreniyu byvshikh pomeshchikov iz Tul'skoi gubernii," in *Materialy GPU* (January 1925–November 1925) F. 17, Op. 87, Doc. 199.

44 A.I. Dobkin, "Lishentsy 1918–1936," in *Zven'ya: istoricheskii. al'manakh*, Vol. 12 (Moscow–St. Petersburg 1992), 608 note 36; *Sovetskoe stroitel'stvo* 5 (1930): 10; Ibid., 6 (1930): 12–13.

45 For analysis, see Vyacheslav V. Ivanov and Felix Y. Roziner, eds, *The Concise Encyclopedia of Soviet Civilization* (New York, NY: Henry Holt & Co: forthcoming). See also David Brandenberger, "*Lishentsy*: Class Enemies in a Classless Society."

46 M. Rzhevusskii, "Nalogovoe bremya v SSSR," *Ekonomicheskoe obozrenie* 5 (1927): 156–86; *Svod Ukazov RSFSR*, 1925, no. 39, art. 275; *Svod Ukazov RSFSR*, 1926, no. 56, art. 433; *Svod Zakonov SSSR*, 1926, no. 44, art. 312; *Svod Zakonov SSSR*, 1927, no. 58, art. 580.

47 *Svod Zakonov SSSR*, 1936, no. 1, art. 2.

48 *3-aia sessiya TsIK SSSR, 4-go sozyva* (1928): 243–44, cited in E.H. Carr and R.W. Davies, *Foundations of a Planned Economy, 1926–1929*, Vol. 2, pp. 276.

49 Walter Duranty, *I Write as I Please* (1935), p. 277.

50 "Doklad o prodelannoi rabote po vydvoreniyu byvshikh pomeshchikov iz Tul'skoi gubernii," in *Materialy GPU* (January 1925–November 1925) F. 17, Op. 87, Doc. 199.

51 Eugene Lyons, *Assignment in Utopia*, p. 176.

52 For greater detail, see David Brandenberger, "*Lishentsy*: Class Enemies in a Classless Society"; Walter Duranty, *Duranty Reports Russia*, p. 385.

53 William White, *These Russians*, pp. 66–7.

54 Duranty, *Duranty Reports Russia*, p. 28.

55 Tobenkin, *Stalin's Ladder: War and Peace in the Soviet Union*, p. 145.

56 Ibid., pp. 140–1.

57 Golfo Alexopoulous, "The Ritual Lament: A Narrative of Rehabilitation in the 1920s and 1930s," AAASS Convention, Washington DC, October 1995.

58 Tobenkin, *Stalin's Ladder*, p. 145.

2 THE CULTURE OF THE NEW ELITE, 1921–5: ASCETIC KNIGHTS AND DRINKING PALS

1 Stalin's biographers have described NEP as a contest between political figures. See L.D. Trotsky, *My Life* and *Kratkii kurs istorii VKP(b)*: See also R.C. Tucker, *Stalin as Revolutionary*, pp. 254–67; L.D. Trotsky, *Stalin: An Appraisal of the Man and His Influence*; A. Antonov-Ovseenko, *Portret tirana*; I. Deutscher, *Stalin*; R.H. McNeal, *Stalin: Man and Ruler*; A. Ulam, *Stalin: The Man and His Era*; D. Volkogonov, *Triumf i tragediya*; S. Cohen, *Bukharin and the Bolshevik Revolution*.

2 According to some, the conflict at the top reflected disagreements over policy throughout society. See Carr, *Interregnum*; A. Erlich, *The Soviet Industrialization Debate*; M. Lewin, *Political Undercurrents in Soviet Economic Debates*; R. Day, *Leon Trotsky and the Politics of Economic Isolation*; B. Knei-Paz, *The Social and Political Thought of Leon Trotsky*.

3 Debate and factionalism are in E. Acton, *Rethinking the Russian Revolution*; R.V. Daniels, "Evolution of Leadership Selection in the Central Committee, 1917–1927," in W.M. Pintner and D.K. Rowney, eds, *Russian Officialdom*; J.

Ali, "Aspects of the RKP(b) Secretariat, March 1919 to April 1922," *Soviet Studies* 3 (1974).

4 On links between Stalinism and Leninism, see M. Fainsod, *How Russia is Ruled*; N. Harding, *Lenin's Political Thought*; J. Keep, *The Rise of Social Democracy in Russia*; R.H. McNeal, *The Bolshevik Tradition*; A. Ulam, *The Bolsheviks*; R. Pipes, *Russia under the Bolshevik Regime*.

5 Chase sees the same tendancy, but attributes the division of party and people to the party's commitment to NEP's unpopular economic retreat. *Chase, Workers, Society and the Soviet State.*

6 Iu.O. Martov to S.D. Shchupak (20 June, 1920) Document No. 35 in Brovkin, ed., *Dear Comrades*, p. 210.

7 Molotov To: All Gubkoms: "O borbe s izlishesvami i o prestupnom ispol'zovanii sluzhebnogo polozheniia" (12 October, 1923) F. 17, Op. 84, Doc. 467, p. 2.

8 Carr points this out in *The Interregnum, 1924–26*, Vol. 1, chapter 3.

9 Molotov, To: All Gubkoms "O borbe s izlishesvami . . .," p. 2.

10 *Desyatyi S'ezd RKP(b) Mart 1921 goda. Stenograficheskii Otchet*, p. 229.

11 GPU Deputy Chair Yagoda To: Mekhlis, Comrade Stalin's secretariat "Obzor Politiko-ekonomicheskogo sostoyaniya" (15 September–1 November, 1923) Op. 87, Doc. 177, p. 5.

12 TsKa. *Gubernskie obsledovaniia* (1926) Op. 67, Doc. 317, p. 166.

13 "Doklad o rabote yacheiki tekstil'shchikov. Fabrika Profintern" (1925) Op. 16, Doc. 95, p. 258.

14 Bryansk Gubkom, To: CC Info. Dept. "Operativnaya Svodka" (15 June–1 July, 1925) Doc. 73, p. 70.

15 MK, Agitrop, "Svodka No.3. Voprosy podannye na sobraniyakh goroda Moskvy" (1925) Op. 16, Doc. 553, p. 107.

16 Samara Gubkom, To: CC, *Informatsionnyi Otchet* (April–June, 1925) Doc. 692, p. 143.

17 *Krokodil*, October 1929.

18 Tula Gubkom, "Svodka No. 8" (February 1925) in *Otchety Gubkoma* Doc. 1377, p. 63.

19 Votkinsk Gubkom, "Direktivnoe Pismo" (1928) Op. 67, Doc. 318, p. 124.

20 Sekretar' Tambovskogo Gubkoma, To: Biuro Sekretariata RKP(b) "Polit. pis'mo za mai, iiun' 1924," F.17, Op. 84, Doc. 741, p. 19.

21 CC Info. Dept. "Ezhednevnaya Polit. Svodka, No.75" (11 February, 1925)" F.17, Op. 84, Doc. 910.

22 *Otchety Tul'skogo Gubkoma* (1925) svodka No. 19, Op. 16, Doc. 1377, p. 84.

23 "O boleznennykh yavleniyakh v partorganizatsii," (10 August, 1925) Op. 84, Doc. 917.

24 "Materialy Inform. otdela OGPU po krestianstvu Tambovskoi gubernii," (December 1924–January 1925) Op. 84, Doc. 858, p. 3.

25 Ibid., p. 4.

26 "O boleznennykh yavleniyakh v partorganizatsii" (10 August, 1925) Op. 84, Doc. 917, p. 53.

27 Ibid.

28 "Materialy Inform. otdela OGPU po krestianstvu Tambovskoi gubernii," Doc. 858, p. 2.

29 Otvetstvennyi Sekretar' Tambovskogo GK, Birn, To: Inform. Otdel Tska RKP(b) (25 May, 1925) "Politicheskoe sostoyanie gubernii za yanvar' – mart 1925," Doc. 741, p. 134.

30 GPU, "Obzor politicheskogo i ekonomicheskogo sostoyaniya SSSR" (21 March, 1924) Op. 87, Doc. 177, p. 7.

31 Kamen'kovich, pomoshnik sekretarya, Inform. otdel TsKa, To: Vsem Sekretaryam

TsKa RKP(b) and To: Inform. otdel OGPU and to: Comrade Kaganovich, "Vypiska iz Inform doklada Tambovskogo Otdela OGPU" (1924) Op. 184, Doc. 741, p. 42.

32 "Materialy Inform. otdela OGPU po krestianstvu Tambovskoi gubernii," Doc. 858, p. 4.
33 Vyatka Gubkom, To: CC Info. Dept. *Dopolnitel'nyi Otchet o rabote sredi Lenprizyva* (1924) Op. 16, Doc. 161, p. 55.
34 "Doklady rabochikh otpusknikov Putilovskogo zavoda," in Leningrad Gubkom: *Otchety* (July–September 1925) Doc. 767, p. 228.
35 CC Info. Dept, "Spravka o nalichii nenormalnykh yavlenii v Vologodskoi partiinoi organizatsii" (1929) Op. 67, Doc. 317, p. 143.
36 Leningrad Obkom, To: CC Info. Dept. *Zakrytoe Pis'mo* (1928) Op. 67, Doc. 440.
37 Vyatka Gubkom, To: CC Info. Dept. "Otchet Gubkoma" (July–September 1924) Op. 16, Doc. 161, p. 1.
38 Samara Gubkom, To: CC *Informatsionnyi Otchet* (January–March 1925) Doc. 692, p. 24.
39 Central Control Commission: *Kratkii Otchet TsKK o chistke rukovodyashchego sostava Vologodskoi Gubernskoi partiinoi organizatsii i* F. 17, Op. 67, Doc. 317, p. 143.
40 Bryansk Gubkom: "Tsirkuliar no.1" (2 February, 1924) Op. 16, Doc. 72. p. 79.
41 Ibid. To: CC, "Otchet Gubkoma" (1924) Doc. 69, p. 2.
42 Kursk Gubkom, To: CC, "Otchet Gubkoma," (May–June 1924) Doc. 519, p. 10.
43 Kostroma Gubkom, "Polozhenie ob individualakh" Doc. 488, p. 136.
44 Don Okruzhkom, To: CC, "Informatsionnyi Otchet Donskogo okruzhnogo komiteta" (January–March 1925) Doc. 939, p. 62.
45 Vladimir Gubkom, To: CC, "Otchet" (1924) Doc. 90, p. 100.
46 Gomel Gubkom, To: CC, "Otchet" (22 October, 1924) Doc. 175, p. 24.
47 Vladimir Gubkom, To: CC, "Otchet" (1924) Doc. 90, p. 102.
48 Ibid., p. 104.
49 Ibid., p. 105; Orel Gubkom, To: CC, "Otchet Gubkoma, 1925" Doc. 624, pp. 73–6.
50 Ibid., p. 102.
51 Ibid., p. 103.
52 Vladimir Gubkom, To: CC, "Otchet" (1924) Doc. 90, p. 103.
53 Leningrad Obkom, To: CC, "Otchet" (July–September 1925) Doc. 767, p. 92.
54 "Desyatiletie boriby. Vnutripartiinaya oppozitsiya v RKP(b) v period voennogo kommunizma i Nepa," in V.V. Zhuravlev, *et al.* eds, *Vlasti i Oppozitsiya,* pp. 90–131 (see p. 114).
55 "Manifest Rabochei Gruppy RKP(b)" (May 1923) in Op. 84, Doc. 420, p. 73.
56 Molotov, To: Vsem Gubkomam (8 May, 1923) F. 17, Op. 84, Doc. 467.
57 Victor Serge, "Vignettes of NEP," in Steinberg, ed., *Verdict of Three Decades,* pp. 124–53 (see p. 137).
58 Ibid., p. 148.
59 I.I. Litvinov, "Ptitsegonstvo nadoelo dosmerti," Iz Dnevnika 1922, in *Neizvestnaya Rossiia XX Vek,* Vol. 4 (Moscow: Mosgorarkhiv, 1993), pp. 81–140 (see p. 88).
60 Ibid., p. 116.
61 Ibid., p. 93.

3 BOLSHEVIK ACTIONS AND PEASANTS' REACTIONS, 1921–5: FACE THE VILLAGE, FACE DEFEAT

1 V. Brovkin, *Behind the Front Lines of the Civil War.*
2 S. Fitzpatrick, *Stalin's Peasants,* p. 3.

3 Richard Day, "Preobrazhensky and the Theory of the Transition Period," *Soviet Studies* 27:2 (April 1975), pp. 196–219. For key documents of the "Left" opposition, see Y. Felshtinsky, ed., *Arkhiv Trotskogo*. For a discussion of agrarian debates, see L.H. Siegelbaum, *Soviet State and Society between Revolutions*, pp. 137–9. See also M. Malia, *Comprendre la Révolution russe*, pp. 175–7.

4 See a collection of "Gos. Inform. Svodki, Informatsionnogo otdela Vecheka" with the name list in F. 17, Op. 87, Doc. 176.

5 F. 17, Op. 84, Doc. 196

6 "Gosinformsvodka, Informatsionnogo otdela Vecheka" (11 January, 1922) F. 17, Op. 87, Doc. 176, p. 2.

7 "Ezhednevnaya Informatsionnaya Svodka Transportnogo otdela Vecheka" (16 January, 1922) Ibid., p. 9.

8 GPU Deputy Chair, Yagoda, To: Mekhlis, Stalin's Secretariat, "Obzor politicheskogo i ekonomicheskogo sostoyaniya" (15 September–1 November, 1923) F. 17, Op. 87, Doc. 177, ibid., p. 5.

9 Richard Pipes, *Russia under the Bolshevik Regime*, p. 374.

10 Zam. Pred. OGPU Trilisser, Nachalnik Inform. Otdela OGPU Alekseev, "Obzor polit. sostoyaniya SSSR" (July 1926) F. 17, Op. 87, Doc. 200a, p. 8.

11 CC Information Department Deputy Chair Bisyarin, To: Vsem chlenam Politbiuro i Orgbiuro i tovarishchu Molotovu, "Materialy o poyavlenii antagonizma mezhdu krestianstvom i rabochim klassom" (1925) F. 17, Op. 84, Doc. 916, p. 5.

12 Yagoda, To: Mekhlis, Stalin's Secretariat, "Obzor politicheskogo i ekonomicheskogo sostoyaniya" (15 September–1 November, 1923) F. 17, Op. 87, Doc. 177.

13 Bisyarin, To: Molotov "Materialy o poyavlenii antagonizma . . ."(1925) F. 17, Op. 84, Doc. 916, p. 5.

14 Birn, Tambov, To: Politburo, *Politpis'mo.* (25 February, 1925) Doc. 741, p. 50.

15 Shirankov, [Military Academy cadet] To: Nachalnik i Kommissar Artelliriiskoi akademii *Raport* (21 June, 1925) Op. 84, Doc. 741, p. 150.

16 Trilisser, and Alekseev, "Obzor polit. sostoyaniya SSSR" (July 1926) Op. 87, Doc. 200a, Prilozhenie.

17 Ibid. (September 1926) Doc. 200a, Prilozhenie No. 4.

18 Ibid. (August 1926) Doc. 200a, p. 7.

19 "Svodka No. 15 materialov inform otdela OGPU o politicheskom sostoyanii i ekonomicheskom rassloenii derevni" (26 April–7 May, 1925) Op. 84, Doc. 916.

20 Bisyarin, To: Politburo and Molotov, "Materialy o poyavlenii antagonizma . . ." (1925) Op. 84, Doc. 916, p. 5.

21 "Obzor polit. sostoyaniya SSSR" (October 1926) F. 17, Op. 87, Doc. 200a.

22 Kaganovich, To: Molotov, "Vyderzhki iz polit. svodok OGPU," Item: "Mysli bespartiinogo krestianina" Op. 84, Doc. 858.

23 Orekhovo-Zuevo GPU, To: OGPU Secret Dept. Chief, "Perechen' voprosov na volostnykh i uezdnykh s'ezdakh sovetov" (26 January, 1926) Op. 87, Doc. 199.

24 OGPU, To: CC, "Krestianskie soyuzy" (April 1925) Op. 87, Doc. 199, Prilozhenie No.2.

25 To: RCP(b) CC, "Perevybory v sovety" (March 1925) F. 17, Op. 16, Doc.175, p. 169

26 MK, To: CC Info. Dept. "Polit. svodka po zapiskam" (November–December 1925) F. 17, Op. 16, Doc. 553, p. 199.

27 OGPU, "Obzor polit. sostoyaniya SSSR" (August 1926) Op. 87, Doc. 200a.

28 Ibid. (November 1926) Doc. 200a.

29 OGPU, To: CC, "Krestianskie soyuzy" (April 1925) Doc. 199, Prilozhenie No. 2.

30 Bisyarin, To: Politburo, "Materialy o poyavlenii antagonizma . . ." (1925) Op. 84, Doc. 916.

31 CC Info. Dept., "Ezhednevnaya politicheskaya svodka" (21 January, 1925) Op. 84, Doc. 910.
32 *Otchety Tul'skogo Gubkoma* Svodka No. 1 (1925) Op. 16, Doc. 1377, p. 11.
33 Bisyarin, To: Politburo, "Materialy o poyavlenii antagonizma ..." (1925) Op. 84, Doc. 916.
34 *Otchety Tul'skogo Gubkoma* Svodka No. 3 (1925) Op. 16, Doc. 1377, p. 33.
35 Voronezh Gubkom, To: Org. Biuro TsKa, *Otchet* (1924–5) Doc. 125, p. 50.
36 To: Secretary of VTsIK Comrade Kiselev, Siberia, Altai, Op. 67, Doc. 365, p. 6.
37 See V. Brovkin: *Behind the Front Lines of the Civil War*, chs 10 and 11.
38 OGPU, To: CC, "Krestianskie Soyuzy" (April 1925) Op. 87, Doc. 199.
39 Karpusha, "Vpechatleniya ot provedennoi predvybornoi kampanii," Op. 16, Doc. 175, p. 42.
40 OGPU, "Informatsionnaya svodka, Vypiska" (March 1925) F. 17, Op. 84, Doc. 916.
41 OGPU, To: CC, "Krestianskie Soyuzy" (April 1925) Op. 87, Doc. 199.
42 OGPU, "Informatsionnaia svodka, Vypiska" (March 1925) F. 17 Op. 84, Doc. 916.
43 The preceding examples are from OGPU, To: CC, "Krestianskie Soyuzy", p. 8.
44 Zam. Nach. Sekret. Chasti, Samara GPU, Chernitsky, To: Nach. Sekret Otdela OGPU (24 January, 1925), "Dokladnaya Zapiska" Op. 87, Doc. 199.
45 OGPU, "Informatsionnaya svodka" No. 42 (August 1925) Doc. 196.
46 OGPU Info. Dept., To: (There follows the list of eleven persons who were authorized to read this top secret document, see discussion below); "Svodka No. 15 materialov o politicheskom sostoyanii i ekonomicheskom rassloenii derevni" (26 April–7 May, 1925) Op. 84, Doc. 916.
47 Bisyarin, To: Politburo, "Materialy o poyavlenii antagonizma ..." (1925) Op. 84, Doc. 916, p. 10.
48 OGPU Info. Dept., "Svodka No. 15 materialov o politicheskom sostoyanii i ekonomicheskom rassloenii derevni" (26 April–7 May, 1925) Doc. 916.
49 Bisyarin, To: Politburo, "Materialy o poyavlenii antagonizma ..." (1925), p. 13.
50 Ibid.
51 Ibid., p. 8.
52 GPU, "Obzor politicheskogo sostoyaniya SSSR" (January 1927) Op. 84, Doc. 201.
53 CC Info. Dept., "Ezhednevnaya politicheskaya svodka" (27 January, 1925) Doc. 910, p. 1.
54 Voronezh Gubkom: *Otchet* (1 December, 1924–1 October, 1925) F. 17, Op. 16, Doc. 129.
55 *Otchety Tul'skogo Gubkoma* Svodka No. 1 (1925) Op. 16, Doc. 1377, p. 16.
56 Vyatka, *Otchety Gubkoma* (1924) Doc. 161, p. 58.
57 Voronezh Gubkom, To: Org. Biuro TsKa, *Otchet* (1924–5) Doc. 125, pp. 5–6.
58 Orel, *Otchety Gubkoma* (1924) Doc. 624, p. 162.
59 Kursk, *Otchet Gubkoma* (May–June 1924) Doc. 519.
60 *Otchety Vladimirskogo Gubkoma* (May 1924) Doc. 90, p. 187.
61 *Otchet Samarskogo Gubkoma* Doc. 692.
62 Ibid., pp. 42–3.
63 Ibid.
64 Ibid.
65 "Doklad o Volostnykh konferentsiyakh" (1925) Doc. 175, pp. 30–2.
66 *Perevybory v sovety* (Gomel: March 1925) Doc. 175, p. 165.
67 Ibid.
68 Upolnomochennyi po vyboram Churovacheskoi volosti Gomelskoi gubernii, To: CC RCP(b) *Perevybory v sovety* (March 1925) Doc. 175.

69 OGPU, "Informatsionnaya svodka" (July 1925) Op. 87, Doc. 196.
70 *Otchety Tul'skogo Gubkoma* Svodka No. 3 (1925), Doc. 1377, p. 33.
71 *Informatsionnye Otchety Samarskogo Gubkoma* (January–March 1925) Doc. 692, pp. 42–3.
72 MK, To: Orgraspred, "Informatsionnaya svodka" (1925) Doc. 583, p. 90.
73 Gubkom Secretary Kryukov, Voronezh Gubkom, "Otchetnost'" (October–December 1924–1925) Doc. 129, p. 110.
74 *Otchet Vladimirskogo Gubkoma* (October–November 1924) Doc. 90, p. 200.
75 Secretary, Tambov Gubkom, Birn, To: CC, "Politicheskoe sostoyanie gubernii" (January–March 1925) Op. 87, Doc. 196, p. 134.
76 *Otchety Gomel'skogo Gubkoma* (1925) Op. 16, Doc. 175, p. 12.
77 CC Info. Dept. To: Comrade Stalin, "Spravka po voprosu o kazachestve" (November 30, 1925) Op. 84, Doc. 909, p. 35.
78 All the above-cited data on election returns is in *Informatsionnyi Otchet Donskogo Okruzhnogo Komiteta* (January–March 1925) F. 17, Op. 16, Doc. 939.
79 Kubansko-Chernomorskaya oblast, *Otchet* (Spring 1925) Doc. 951, p. 47.
80 Ibid., p. 69.
81 Ibid., p. 100.
82 GPU, "Obzor Polit. Sostoyaniya SSSR" (March 1925) Vypiska, Op. 84, Doc. 916.
83 To: Secretary of VTsIK, Kiselev, F. 17, Op. 67, Doc. 366, p. 9.
84 CC Info. Dept. To: Comrade Stalin, "Spravka po voprosu o kazachestve," (November 30, 1925) F. 17, Op. 84, Doc. 909, p. 35.

4 PROPAGANDA AND POPULAR BELIEF

1 The new name was Upravlenie Agitatsii i Propagandy TsKa VKP(b), for the list of departments and activity of subdepartments, see F. 17, Op. 125.
2 Kommissiia Po Rukovodstvu Gazetnoi Informatsiyei, F. 17, Op. 60, Agitprop, Doc. 439. On newspaper publishing, see: Kenez *The Birth of the Propaganda State*, pp. 226–9.
3 "Vypiska iz protokola zasedaniia TsKa RKP(b) 22 March 1922," in Narkompros papers, F. 17, Op. 84, Doc. 419, p. 23.
4 "Vsem chlenam Politbiuro," F. 17, Op. 84, Doc. 419.
5 "Billiuten' Kommissii Orgbiuro TsKa Po Nabliudeniyu nad Chastnym Knizhnym Rynkom," F. 17, Op. 60, Agitprop, Doc. 178, pp. 7–10.
6 For the most insightful discussion of cinema and its reception, see Jay Leida, *Kino: A History of the Russian-Soviet Film*, esp. pp. 155–70.
7 Glavnyi Repertuarnyi Komitet, "K proizvodstvennomu planu Kinosektsii," F. 17, Op. 60, Doc. 753, p. 1.
8 See also *Protokoly Zasedanii Foto-Kino Kommissii pri APO TsKa* (1924) Op. 60, Doc. 528.
9 Glavnyi Repertuarnyi Komitet, "K proizvodstvennomu planu Kinosektsii," F. 17, Op. 60, Doc. 753, p. 1.
10 Ibid., p. 237.
11 "Doklad za 1924 god" (October 1924–March 1925) F. 17, Op. 60, Doc. 753, p. 257.
12 Lebedev-Polianskii, Zav. Glavlita, "Vsem gublitam" (1925) Op. 60, Doc. 753, p. 237.
13 Pochpskii Uezd Party Committee, To: Bryansk Gubkom, "Plan raboty" (Summer 1924) Op. 16, Doc. 69, p. 85.
14 Kenez, *The Birth of the Propaganda State*, pp. 134–5.

15 Stites, *Revolutionary Dreams*, pp. 97–101.
16 Kursk Gubkom, "Otchet" (June 1924) F. 17, Op. 16, Doc. 519, p. 77.
17 On posters, see White, *The Bolshevik Poster* and Guerman, *The Art of the October Revolution*.
18 Holmes, *The Kremlin and the Schoolhouse*.
19 *Protokoly zasedanii kollegii Agitpropotdela TsKa RKP(b)* (January–April 1923) F. 17, Op. 60, Doc. 408.
20 Bryansk Gubkom, "Otchet" (June 1924) Op. 16, Doc. 69, p. 23.
21 Vladimir Gubkom, "Otchet" (November 1924) Doc. 90, p. 189.
22 Fitzpatrick, *Education and Social Mobility*, p. 98.
23 Ibid., p. 32.
24 Fitzpatrick, "The Soft Line on Culture and Its Enemies," in *The Cultural Front*, pp. 91–115 (see pp. 100–2).
25 Peter Konecny, "Chaos on Campus: The 1924 Student *Proverka* in Leningrad," *Europe-Asia Studies* 46:4 (1994), pp. 617–35.
26 Voronezh Gubkom, "Informatsionnyi otchet Voronezhskoi organizatsii RKP(b)" (May–June 1924) F. 17, Op. 16, Doc. 129, p. 6.
27 Nizhnii Novgorod Gubkom, To: CC "Otchet" (1924) Doc. 584, p. 5.
28 Agitprop, To: Stalin, "Proekt Ustava Kommunisticheskogo universiteta," F. 17, Op. 84, Doc. 419, p. 72
29 CC, To: Vsem Gubkomam, "O prieme v vuzy," Doc. 467.
30 Fitzpatrick, *The Commissariat of Enlightenment*; John Hatch, "The Politics of Mass Culture: Workers, Communists and Proletkult in the Development of Workers' Clubs," *Russian History/Histoire Russe* Vol. 13: 2–3 (1986), pp. 119–48.
31 Bryansk Gubkom, "Otchet raboty Propgruppy TsKa" (April 1925) F. 17, Op. 16, Doc. 73, p. 26.
32 "Doklad Otvetstvennogo instruktora Zaslavskogo, Obsledovanie Bryanskogo Zavoda," Doc. 72, p. 12.
33 See Jeffrey Brooks, "Studies of the Reader in the 1920s," *Russian History/Histoire Russe*, Vol. 9: 2–3 (1982), pp. 187–203.
34 "Doklad . . . Zaslavskogo," F. 17, Op. 16, Doc. 72, p. 12.
35 *Otchet Donskogo Komiteta* (1925) Doc. 939, p. 132.
36 On illiteracy see Pethybridge, *Social Prelude to Stalinism*, pp. 132–56.
37 Gomel Gubkom, "Otchet" (1925) F. 17, Op. 16, Doc. 175, p. 130.
38 Kursk Gubkom, "Otchet" (June 1924) Doc. 519, p. 54.
39 Samara Gubkom, "Informatsionnyi Otchet" (March 1925) Doc. 692, p. 105.
40 *Otchety Tul'skogo Gubkoma*, Svodka No. 3 (1925) Doc. 1377, p. 32.
41 Vyatka Gubkom, *Otchety Gubkoma* (1924) Doc. 161, p. 125.
42 Vladimir Gubkom, "Otchet" (November 1924) Doc. 90, p. 185.
43 Voronezh Gubkom, "Otchet" (August 1924) Doc. 129, p. 31.
44 Gomel Gubkom, "Novozybkovskii uezd. Perevybory v sovety" (March 1925) Doc. 175, p. 162.
45 Gomel Gubkom: "Vpechatleniya o provedennoi otchetnoi kampanii. Selo Deniskovichi. Preniya po dokladu VTsIKa," Doc. 175, p. 42.
46 Voronezh Gubkom, To: Orgbiuro, "Otchet 1924–1925," Doc. 125, p. 10.
47 S. Grachev, 25 September, 1927, in *Materialy Saratovskogo Gubkoma*, F. 17, Op. 69, Doc. 310, p. 64.
48 On rural readers see Regine Robin, "Popular Literature of the 1920s: Russian Peasants as Readers," in Fitzpatrick *et al.*, eds, *Russia in the Era of NEP*, pp. 253–68.
49 Gomel Gubkom: Zav. ONO, Korolev, "Vpechatleniya ot provedennoi kampanii perevyborov v selsovety," F. 17, Op. 16, Doc. 175, p. 48.

50 Kursk Gubkom, "Otchet" (May–June 1924) Doc. 519, p. 77.
51 Gomel Gubkom, "Novozybkovskii uezd" (March 1925) Doc. 175, p. 162.
52 "Doklad ob obsledovanii yacheiki RKP," Kostroma (November 1925) Doc. 488, p. 175.
53 Leningrad Gubkom, "Otchet" (April 1925) Doc. 766, p. 74.
54 Orel Gubkom, "Otchet" (1925) Doc. 624, p. 73.
55 Stites, *Russian Popular Culture*, pp. 47–9.
56 GPU, *Obzor politicheskogo polozheniya* (1927) F. 17, Op. 87, Doc. 201.
57 On foreign films, see Kenez, *Cinema and Soviet Society*, pp. 73–5
58 For Agitprop documents and directives, see "Tezisy, svodki po anti-religioznoi propagande," F. 17, Op. 60, Doc. 438.
59 For conference resolutions in English, see Appendix 1 in Hecker, *Religion and Communism*, pp. 275–89.
60 "Stenogramma anti-religioznogo soveshchaniia pri Agitprope TsKa, 1926," F. 17, Op. 60, Agitprop, Doc. 791, p. 32.
61 Ibid., p. 52.
62 "Krestiane i anti-religioznaya propaganda," *Antireligioznik*, n.1 (1924), Moscow, p. 11.
63 "Stenogramma . . ." F. 17, Op. 60, Doc. 791, p. 181.
64 Bryansk Gubkom "Otchet za 6 mesyatsev" (1924) F. 17, Op. 16, Doc. 69, p. 159.
65 "Zadachi i metody raboty sredi krestian," *Antireligioznik*, no.2 (1926), p. 27.
66 Helmut Altrichter, "Insoluble Conflicts: Village Life between Revolution and Collectivization," in Fitzpatrick, *et al.*, eds, *Russia in the Era of NEP*, p. 201.
67 Bryansk Gubkom, "Plan raboty Agitpropa," F. 17, Op. 16, Doc. 69, p. 43.
68 Bryansk Gubkom, "Sostoyanie Bryanskoi organizatsii" (September 1925) Doc. 73, p. 39.
69 Info. Dept. CC VLKSM, "Svodka o anti-religioznoi propagande" (July 1925) F. 1, Op. 23, Doc. 392, p. 18. KA.
70 "Doklad ob obsledovanii yacheiki RKP Vvedenskoi volosti" (November 1925) F. 17, Op. 16, Doc. 488, p. 174.
71 "Stenogramma . . ." F. 17, Op. 60, Doc. 791, p. 181.
72 Stites called it "Rituals of a counterfaith," in *Revolutionary Dreams*, pp. 109–10.
73 Vladimir Gubkom, "Otchet" (May 1924) F. 17, Op. 16, Doc. 90, p. 31.
74 Kursk Gubkom, "Otchet" (May–June 1924) Doc. 519, p. 57.
75 Orel Gubkom, "Otchet" (1925) Doc. 624, p. 76.
76 Voronezh Gubkom, "Otchet 1924–1925," Doc. 125, p. 98.
77 Spinka, *Christianity Confronts Communism*, esp. "Communism Strikes Hard," pp. 81–119 (see p. 109).
78 Lunacharsky, *Khristianstvo ili Kommunizm*.
79 "Nauka i religiya," *Biulleteni Literatury i Zhizni*, No. 3–4 (1923), p. 64.
80 "Disputy tserkovnikov," Ibid., No. 2 (1923) p. 63.
81 TsKa VLKSM, To: Vsem Gubkomam, "Ob anti-religioznoi propagande v rozhdestvenskie prazniki," F. 1, Op. 23, Doc. 392, p. 4.
82 *Antireligioznik*, No. 2 (1926) p. 4.
83 Lewin: "Popular Religion in 20th Century Russia," in *The Making of the Soviet System*, pp. 52–72.
84 Berdiaev, "Communism and Christianity," in *Origin of Communism*, pp. 158–89 (see p. 172). On tenacity of popular belief, see also Timasheff, *Religion in Soviet Russia*, pp. 58–95.
85 Pascal, *The Religion of the Russian People*, p. 14.
86 Voronezh Gubkom, "Otchet " (August 1924) F. 17, Op. 16, Doc. 129, p. 30.
87 Information on Orel province is in this report from Kursk province GPU Chief

Studitov, "Doklad o sostoyanii derevni po Kurskoi gubernii," F. 17, Op. 84, Doc. 858, p. 13.

88 Voronezh Gubkom, "Otchet " (June 1924) F. 17, Op. 16, Doc. 129, p. 4.
89 Secretary, Tambov Gubkom, Birn, To: Biuro Secretariata TsKa, "Polit. Pis'mo za mai, iiun, 1924," F. 17, Op. 87, Doc. 196.
90 Gomel Gubkom, To: CC, "Otchet" (1925) F. 17, Op. 16, Doc. 175, p. 10.
91 For a study of aspects of rumor as fantasy, legend, or misunderstanding, see Kapferer: *Rumors. Uses, Interpretations, and Images*, pp. 27, 29, 33.
92 OGPU, "Informatsionnaya svodka" (July 1925) F. 17, Op. 87, Doc. 196.
93 From. CC Info. Dept., To: Comrade Stalin, "Spravka po voprosu o kazachestve" (30 November, 1925) F. 17, Op. 84, Doc. 909.
94 OGPU, "Informatsionnaya svodka, Vypiska" (March 1925) Doc. 916.
95 Ibid., p. 27.
96 Ibid., p. 15.
97 CC Info. Dept, "Spravka o Golode" (22 May, 1925) Doc. 741, p. 132.
98 OGPU, "Inform. svodki v sviazi s konchinoi Lenina," F. 17, Doc. 708.
99 OGPU Info. Dept, "Spetsial'nye svodki o sostoyanii respubliki" (4 February, 1924) Doc. 708.
100 Ibid., p. 25.
101 Ibid.
102 *Otchety Tul'skogo Gubkoma*, Svodka No. 3 (1925) F. 17, Op.16, Doc. 1377, p. 36.
103 Ibid., p. 24.
104 OGPU Info. Dept, "Spetsial'nye svodki o sostoyanii respubliki" (4 February, 1924) F. 17, Op. 84, Doc. 708.
105 Ibid.
106 Bryansk Gubkom, "Otchet" (November 1924) F. 17, Op. 16, Doc. 69. p. 148
107 Arkhipenko, Kubano-Chernomorskaya oblasti, To: CC "Otchet" (1925) Doc. 951, p. 51.
108 Tula, "Otchety" (January 1925) Doc. 1377, p. 16.
109 Info. Dept. CC VLKSM, "Ezhemesiachnaya svodka" (15 September–15 October, 1925) F. 1, Op. 23, Doc. 302, pp. 14. KA.
110 Orel Gubkom, "Otchet" (1925) F. 17, Op. 16, Doc. 624, p. 38.
111 Samara Gubkom, "Informatsionnyi Otchet" (April–June 1925) Doc. 692, p. 139.
112 Gregory Freeze, "Counter-reformation in Russian Orthodoxy: Popular Response to Religious Innovation, 1922–1925," *Slavic Review* 54:2 (1995), p. 321.
113 Pascal, *The Religion of the Russian People*, p. 21.
114 *Otchet Donskogo Komiteta* (1925) F. 17, Op. 16, Doc. 939, p. 36.
115 Vladimir Gubkom, To: CC "Otchet" (May 1924) Doc. 90, p. 31.
116 Arkhipenko, Kubano-Chernomorskaya oblasti, To: CC, "Otchet" (1925) Doc. 951, p. 112.
117 S. Grachev, *Materialy Saratovskogo Gubkoma* 25 September, 1927 F. 17, Op. 69, Doc. 310, p. 44.
118 "Doklad ob obsledovanii yacheiki RKP" (November 1925) Doc. 488, p. 193.
119 "Stenogramma . . ." F. 17, Op. 60, Doc. 791.
120 Harper, *Making Bolsheviks*, p. 37.
121 According to one source, 1,440 churches were closed in 1929 alone: Wilhelm De Vries, *Kirche und Staat in der Sowjetunion*, p. 14.

5 THE KOMSOMOL AND YOUTH: A TRANSMISSION BELT THAT SNAPPED

1 Voronezh Gubkom, "Otchet Voronezhskoi organizatsii" (August 1924) F. 17, Op. 16, Doc. 129, p. 173.

2 Ibid. (May–June 1924), p. 60.

3 CC KSM, To: CC RCP(b) and TsKK, "Dokladnaya Zapiska o boleznennykh yavleniyakh v Komsomole" (1927) F. 17, Op. 69, Doc. 126, p. 120.

4 Vyatka Gubkom, To: All Uezdkoms, "Komsomol" (7 September, 1925) Op. 16, Doc. 164, p. 98.

5 Fisher, *Pattern for Soviet Youth*, p. 32.

6 Isabel Tirado, "The Komsomol and Young Peasants: The Dilemma of Rural Expansion, 1921–1925," *Slavic Review* 52:3 (Fall 1993), pp. 460–76.

7 CC KSM, To: CC RCP(b) and TsKK, "Dokladnaya Zapiska . . ." (1927) F. 17, Op. 69, Doc. 126, p. 120.

8 "Svodka o sostoyanii soyuza po Sibiri (April 1925)," in *Ezhemesyachnye svodki po regionam* F. 1. Op. 23, Doc. 302, p. 4. KA.

9 "Sostoyanie Verkhne-Seredskogo kollektiva KSM" (November 1926) F. 17, Op. 69, Doc. 127, p. 14.

10 CC KSM Info. Dept. Chief Shastin, *Ezhemesyachnaya svodka* (November 1925) F. 1, Op. 23, Doc. 302, p. 6. KA.

11 Samara gubkom, *Informatsionnyi Otchet* (March 1925) F. 17. Op. 16, Doc. 692, p. 98.

12 Yemel'ianov, Secretary of Local information of the CC Info. Dept., "Materialy k dokladu o chastichnoi kassatsii vyborov selsovetov" Doc. 175, pp. 35–40.

13 CC KSM "Rost obshchestvenno-politicheskoi aktivnosti molodezhi, 1927" F. 1, Op. 23, Doc. 495, p. 138. KA.

14 OGPU Info. Dept., To: Comrade Kaganovich, "Otnoshenie krest'ian k RKSM i RKP," F. 17, Op. 84, Doc. 741, pp. 42–3.

15 Isabel Tirado, "The Revolution, Young Peasants, and the Komsomol's Antireligious Campaigns," *Canadian-American Slavic Studies* 26:1 (1992), pp. 97–117.

16 Informator CC Teterin, in "Svodka o sostoianii soyuza" (May 1925) in *Ezhemesyachnye Svodki TsKa* F. 1, Op. 23, Doc. 302, p. 5. KA.

17 Ibid. (15 September–15 October, 1925), p. 12.

18 Ibid. (November 1925), p. 6.

19 "Materialy k dokladu TsKa VLKSM v partkomissiyu TsKK o boleznennykh yavleniyakh v Komsomole i bor'be s nimi" (1928) [only 28 copies made] Doc. 821, p. 7. KA.

20 Kostroma Gubkom, "Doklad ob obsledovanii volosti," F. 17, Op. 16, Doc. 488, p. 192.

21 CC Info. Dept., To: Comrade Molotov (March 1925) F.1, Op. 23, Doc. 298, p. 1. KA.

22 "Antikommunisticheskie organizatsii molodezhi. Sibir," in *Spravki GPU o deyatelnosti antikommunisticheskikh organizatsii*, Doc. 298, p. 36. KA.

23 Leningrad GK VLKSM, "Antikommunisticheskie organizatsii molodezhi i rabota religioznykh sekt," Doc. 518, p. 64. KA.

24 "Informatsionnaya spravka o nastroenii molodezhi i Komsomol'tsev" (15 August 1927) Doc. 681, p. 16. KA.

25 CC KSM, To: CC RCP(b) and TsKK: "Dokladnaya Zapiska . . ." (1927) F. 17, Op. 69, Doc. 126, p. 118.

26 "Doklady rabochikh otpusknikov Putilovskogo zavoda," in *Otchety Leningradskogo Obkoma* (July–September 1925) Op. 16, Doc. 767, p. 244.

27 MK KSM, To: CC RCP(b), "Boleznennye yavleniia v organizatsii" (Moscow 1926) Op. 69, Doc. 126, p. 12.

28 "Doklad o sostoyanii fabrichno-zavodskikh yacheek RKSM," in Bryansk gubkom, *Operativnaya Svodka* (15 June–1 July, 1925) Op. 16, Doc. 73, p. 131.

29 CC KSM, To: CC RCP(b) and TsKK: "Dokladnaya Zapiska . . ." Op. 69, Doc. 126, p. 120.

30 "Doklad o sostoyanii fabrichno-zavodskikh yacheek RKSM," in Bryansk gubkom, *Operativnaya Svodka* (15 June–1 July, 1925) Op. 16, Doc. 73, p. 120.

31 *Otchety Leningradskogo Obkoma* (July–September 1925) Doc. 767, p. 244.

32 Bryansk Gubkom, *Operativnaya Svodka* (15 June–1 July, 1925) Doc. 73, p. 120.

33 GPU, To: CC *Dokladnaya zapiska o pianstve sredi rabochikh* (August 1925) Op. 87, Doc. 199.

34 MK KSM, To: CC RCP(b), "Boleznennye yavleniia v organizatsii," (Moscow 1926) Op. 69, Doc. 126, p. 49.

35 Komitet Krasnoi Presni, To: MK, "Obsledovanie yacheiki Rabochei Gazety" (Moscow 1926) Doc. 126.

36 CC KSM, "Massovaya Kul'turno-bytovaya rabota Komsomola" (1927) F. 1, Op. 23, Doc. 584, p. 13. KA.

37 Bryansk Gubkom, *Operativnaya Svodka* (15 June–1 July, 1925) F. 17, Op. 16, Doc. 73, p. 131.

38 Ibid.

39 Ibid., p. 132.

40 Peter Gooderham, "The Komsomol and Worker Youth: The Inculcation of 'Communist Values' in Leningrad during NEP," *Soviet Studies* 34:4 (October 1982), pp. 506–28 (see p. 515).

41 Lunacharsky, *Vpadochrye Nastroeniya Molodezhi. Yeseninshchina*, pp. 56–7.

42 CC KSM, "Ob usilenii massovoi kulturnoi raboty VLKSM v sviazi s rostom pianstva i khuliganstva v srede molodezhi," F. 17, Op. 69, Doc. 126, p. 145.

43 Stites, *Russian Popular Culture*, p. 51.

44 Lynn Mally, "The Rise and Fall of the Soviet Youth Theater TRAM," *Slavic Review* 51:3 (1992), pp. 411–30 (here, p. 418).

45 Anne E. Gorsuch, "Flappers and Foxtrotters. Soviet Youth in the 'Roaring Twenties,'" *The Carl Beck Papers in Russian and East European Studies* No. 1102, p. 3, and Gorsuch, "Soviet Youth and the Politics of Popular Culture during NEP," *Social History* 17:2 (May 1992), pp. 189–201.

46 Starr, *Red and Hot. The Fate of Jazz in the Soviet Union.*

47 Sheila Fitzpatrick, "Sex and Revolution: An Examination of Literary and Statistical Data on the Mores of Soviet Students in the 1920s," *Journal of Modern History* 50:3 (1978), pp. 252–78.

48 CC KSM, To: Stalin, *O sostoianii i rabote RLKSM* F. 1, Op. 23, Doc. 296, p. 3. KA.

49 MK KSM, To: CC RCP(b), "Boleznennye yavleniia v organizatsii" (Moscow 1926) F. 17, Op. 69, Doc. 126, p. 43.

50 CC VLKSM, Info. Dept., *O metodakh raboty sredi devushek* (1925) F. 1, Op. 23, Doc. 391, p. 61. KA.

51 Ibid., p. 28.

52 Voronezh Gubkom, "Otchet, 1924–25" F. 17, Op. 16, Doc. 125, p. 116.

53 CC KSM, "Devushka i Komsomol" (1926) F.1, Op. 23, Doc. 391, pp. 10–20. KA.

54 Ibid., p. 49.

55 Chernomorskii Okruzhkom, To: CC KSM, "Svodka" (December 1925) Doc. 302, p. 8. KA.

56 MK KSM, To: CC RCP(b), "Boleznennye yavleniia . . ." (1926) F. 17, Op. 69, Doc. 126, p. 10.

57 CC Info. Dept. VKP(b), "Sostoyanie RKSM i partiinoe rukovodstvo Komsomolom" (February 1926) F. 1, Op. 23, Doc. 488, p. 16. KA.

58 CC KSM, Info. Dept, "Iz Pis'ma Simbirskogo VK" (1927), Doc. 584, p. 16. KA.

59 Ibid., p. 17.

60 Victor Serge, "Vignettes of NEP," in Steinberg, ed., *Verdict of Three Decades*, p. 150.
61 CC KSM, "Devushka i Komsomol" (1926) F. 1, Op. 23, Doc. 391, p. 45. KA.
62 "Boleznennye yavleniya v shkole" (1928) Doc. 821, p. 41. KA.
63 Ul'yanovsk gubkom, To: CC KSM, "Ezhemesyachnaia svodka" (15 September–15 October, 1925) Doc. 302, p. 12. KA.
64 CC KSM, To: CC RCP(b), *Bytovye Boleznennye Yavleniia v Komsomole i Borba s Nimi* (June 1926) Doc. 495, p. 104. KA.
65 CC VLKSM, *Massovaya, Kul'turno-bytovaya rabota VLKSM* (1927) Doc. 584, p. 17. KA.
66 Eric Naiman, "The Case of Chubarov Alley: Collective Rape, Utopian Desire and the Mentality of NEP," *Russian History/Histoire Russe* 17:1 (spring 1990), pp. 1–30 (see p. 12).
67 MK KSM, To: CC RCP(b), "Boleznennye yavleniia . . ." (1926) F. 17, Op. 69, Doc. 126, p. 9. KA.
68 Ibid., p. 12.
69 CC KSM, "Boleznennye yavleniia v Komsomole" (Moscow 1927) Doc. 126, p. 107. KA.
70 CC KSM, "Informatsionnaya spravka o nastroeniyakh molodezhi i Komsomol'tsev" (15 August 1927) Doc. 681, pp. 10–15. KA.
71 CC KSM, "Massovaya kul'turno-bytovaya rabota Komsomola" (1927) Doc. 584, p. 4. KA.
72 MK KSM, To: CC RCP(b), "Boleznennye . . ." (1926) F. 17, Op. 69, Doc. 126, p. 5.
73 Ibid.
74 Ibid., p. 9.
75 Cherepovets GPU, "Memorandum No. 121 politkontrolya" (June 1925) F. 1, Op. 23, Doc. 298. KA.
76 MK KSM, To: CC RCP(b), "Boleznennye . . ." (1926) F. 17, Op. 69, Doc. 126, p. 7.
77 From CC KSM, To: Orgraspred, "O Boleznennykh yavleniiakh v Komsomole i nedostatkakh partiinogo rukovodstva" (1927) Doc. 682, p. 168.
78 Ibid.
79 CC KSM, "O Boleznennykh yavleniiakh . . ." Doc. 126, p. 117.
80 Ibid.
81 Kubokrug, To: CC KSM, "Ob antisemitizme sredi molodezhi" (November 1927) F. 1, Op. 23, Doc. 664, p. 75. KA.
82 CC VLKSM, "O boleznennykh yavleniiakh v Komsomole i nedostatkakh partiinogo rukovodstva Komsomol'skoi raboti" [1927] Doc. 661, p. 35. KA.
83 "Vozzvanie 'Russkii Komsomolets,'" in *Spravki Tska* Doc. 664. KA.
84 CC LKSMU, "Antikommunisticheskie organizatsii" (August 1925) Doc. 298, p. 3. KA.
85 Ibid.
86 "Spravka o politicheskikh nastroeniyakh Komsomol'tsev i rabochei molodezhi," Doc. 664, p. 74. KA.
87 CC KSM, To: CC RCP(b), "Boleznennye iavleniya . . ." (1927) F. 17, Op. 69, Doc. 126, p. 117.
88 CC KSM, "O boleznennykh yavleniyakh v Komsomole" (18 July, 1927) F. 1, Op. 23, Doc. 661, p. 13. KA.
89 MK KSM, To: Moscow gubkom, *Kratkii otchet* (February 1926–February 1927) Doc. 681. p. 5. KA.
90 To: CC RCP(b) (7 November 1927), in *Spravki TsKa o negativnykh yavleniiakh,*

oppozitsionnykh vystupleniyakh i antikommunisticheskikh organizatsiyakh, Doc.
664, p. 55. KA.

91 "Materialy k dokladu TsKa VLKSM v partkommissiyu TsKK o boleznennykh
yavleniiakh v Komsomole i bor'be s nimi" (1928) Doc. 821, p. 22. KA.

92 "Rabfakovtsy i studenchestvo," *Novaya Rossiya* No. 1 (Petrograd 1922), p. 51.

93 "Informatsionnyi Otchet Donskogo okruzhkoma" (January–April 1925) F. 17,
Op. 16, Doc. 939, p. 62.

94 "Doklad ob obsledovanii partraboty v Leningradskikh Vuzakh" (April–May
1926) F. 17, Op. 69, Doc. 128, p. 59.

95 Ibid.

96 N. Meshcheryakov, "Predel skorbi" (December 1922) F. 17, Op. 84, Doc. 419.

97 Sheila Fitzpatrick, "Sex and Revolution: An Examination of Literary and
Statistical Data on the Mores of Soviet Students in the 1920s," *Journal of
Modern History* 50 (June 1978), pp. 253–78.

98 Stites, *Popular Culture*, p. 62.

99 Lunacharsky, *Upadochnye Nastroeniya Sredi Molodezhi. Yeseninshchina*, p. 92.

100 Letters to *Komsomol'skaya Pravda* in "Spravki Informatsionnogo Otdela Tska
o kul'turno-bytovoi rabote" (1926) F. 1, Op. 23, Doc. 584, p. 18. KA.

101 Ibid., p. 20.

102 MK KSM, To: CC RCP(b) "Boleznennye ..." (1926) F. 17, Op. 69, Doc.
126, p. 27.

103 Ibid., p. 40.

104 Ibid., p. 50.

105 Peter Konecny, "Revolution and Rebellion: Students in Soviet Institutes of
Higher Education, 1921–1928," *Canadian Journal of History* 27:3 (1992),
pp. 451–73.

106 MK KSM, To: CC RCP(b), "Boleznennye ..." (1926) F. 17, Op. 69, Doc.
126, p. 60.

107 CC KSM, To: CC RCP, *Organizatsionnaya svodka* No. 8 (18 July, 1927) F. 1,
Op. 23, Doc. 661, p. 25. KA.

108 Moskovskaya Studencheskaya Organizatsiya Partii Levykh Sotsialistov Revo-
liutsionerov, To: Studenchestvu Vuzov i Rabfakov, *Otkrytoe Pismo* (1926) in
Spravki TsKa Doc. 664, pp. 30–40. KA.

109 "Boleznennye yavleniia v shkole (1928)" Doc. 821, p. 41. KA.

110 GPU, "Obzor politicheskogo sostoyaniya SSSR" (February 1927) F. 17, Op.
87, Doc. 201.

111 Ibid.

112 "Doklad ob obsledovanii partraboty v Leningradskikh Vuzakh" (April–May
1926) F. 17, Op. 69, Doc. 128, pp. 44–5.

113 Ibid., pp. 50–2.

114 Ibid., p. 53.

115 Ibid., pp. 60–3.

116 Voronezh Gubkom, "Otchet Gubkoma" (1924–25) F. 17, Op. 16, Doc. 125,
p. 116.

117 Peter Gooderham, "The Komsomol and Worker Youth: The Inculcation of
'Communist Values' in Leningrad during NEP," *Soviet Studies* 34:4 (October
1982) pp. 506–28.

6 WOMEN: FALSE PROMISES, DASHED HOPES
AND THE PRETENSE OF EMANCIPATION

1 Elizabeth Waters, "The Female Form in Soviet Political Iconography," in
Clements, *et al.*, eds, *Russia's Women*, p. 232; R. McNeal, "The Early Decrees

of Zhenotdel," in Yedlin, ed. *Women in Eastern Europe and the Soviet Union*, p. 76; B. Farnsworth, "Communist Feminism: Its Synthesis and Demise," in C. Berkin and C. Lovett, eds, *Women, War and Revolution*, pp. 145–65; and Stites, *The Women's Liberation Movement in Russia*, p. 345.

2 Elwood, *Inessa Armand*, p. 242.

3 Farnsworth, *Aleksandra Kolontai*.

4 Smidovich, "Doklady o rabote Zhenotdela, 1923," F. 17, Op. 10, Doc. 98.

5 Stites, "Zhenotdel: Bolshevism and Russian Women, 1917–1930," *Russian History/Histoire Russe*, Vol. 3, part 2 (1976), pp. 174–94, and "Equality, Freedom and Justice: Women and Men in the Russian Revolution, 1917–1930" (Research Paper No 67, Jerusalem: The Hebrew University of Jerusalem, 1988), p. 6; and Alix Holt, "Marxism and Women's Opression: Bolshevik Theory and Practice in the 1920s," in T. Yedlin, ed., *Women . . .*, p. 104.

6 Christine Worobec, "Victims or Actors? Russian Peasant Women and Patriarchy," in Kingston-Mann and Mixter, eds, *Peasant Economy. Culture and Politics*.

7 "Village Women Experience the Revolution," in Farnsworth and Viola, eds, *Russian Peasant Women*, pp. 145–66; Victoria Bonnell, "The Representation of Women in Early Soviet Political Art," *The Russian Review* 50 (91):270, and "The Peasant Woman in Stalinist Political Art of the 1930s," *American Historical Review* 98:1 (1993), p. 64.

8 "Obzor rezul'tatov i rosta raboty sredi rabotnits i krestianok, 1923," in "Obzory raboty zhenskikh delegatskikh sobranii," F. 17, Op. 10, Doc. 104, p. 23.

9 Voronezh gubkom, "Otchet Voronezhskoi organizatsii" (May–June 1924) F. 17, Op. 16, Doc. 129, p. 53.

10 Vladimir Gubkom, "Otchet o rabote sredi rabotnits i krestianok Vladimirskoi gubernii" (March 1925) Doc. 90, p. 215.

11 Kursk Gubkom, "Doklad o rabote zhenotdela" Doc. 519, p. 80.

12 Zhenotdel, To: Voronezh Gubkom, "Otchet zhenotdela" (June 1924) Doc. 129.

13 Vladimir Gubkom, "Otchet" (November 1924) Doc. 90, p. 200.

14 Voronezh: "Otchet Zhenotdela" (December 1924) Doc. 129.

15 Voronezh Gubkom, To: CC "Otchet" (August 1924) Doc. 129, p. 57.

16 Ibid. (December 1924) Doc. 488, p. 110.

17 Vladimir Gubkom, "Otchet" (November 1924) Doc. 90, p. 200.

18 Kubansko-Chernomorskaia oblast, To: CC "Otchet Gubkoma" (1925) Doc. 951, pp. 80–85.

19 Kursk Gubkom, "Doklad o rabote zhenotdela" Doc. 519, p. 80.

20 "Doklad ob obsledovanii " (November 1925) Doc. 488, p. 117.

21 Orgraspred MK, "Informatsionnaya svodka Moskovskii Uezd" (1925) Doc. 553 p. 89.

22 Inform Podotdel TsKa RKSM, "Svodki o rabote sredi devushek," (April 1925–January 1926) F. 1, Op. 23, Doc. 391, p. 15–17. KA.

23 Fedotiv, Zav.org.instruktor, To: Volynskii gubkom (29 April, 1925), in "O rabote sredi devushek," Doc. 391, p. 17. KA.

24 Gomel Gubkom, "Novozybkovkii uezd" (March 1925) F. 17, Op.16, Doc. 175, p. 162.

25 TsKa VLKSM, "Devushka i Komsomol. Obzor, Svodka po metarialam Org. Otdela TsKa. Vyatskaia guberniia," F. 1, Op. 23, Doc. 391, p. 50. KA.

26 TsKa VLKSM, ibid., "Voronezhskaia guberniia," p. 41.

27 Isabel Tirado, "The Village Voice: Women's Views of Themselves and Their World in Russian *Chastushki* of the 1920s," *The Carl Beck Papers* No. 1008 (1993).

28 TsKa VLKSM, "Ezhemesyachnye svodki" (15 September–15 October, 1925) from Severo-Dvinskii gubkom, "Otchet" F. 1, Op. 23, Doc. 302, p. 12. KA.
29 "Materialy k dokladu TsKa VLKSM v partkomissiyu TsKK o boleznennykh yavleniyakh" (1928) Doc. 821, p. 10. KA.
30 TsKa VLKSM, To: Orgraspred, "Soveshchanie aktiva *Komsomol'skoi Pravdy* (January 1929)" F. 17, Op. 69, Doc. 682, p. 61.
31 "Milent'evskaya volost," in *Gubernskie obsledovaniya TsKa* (1926) F. 17, Op. 67, Doc. 317, p. 36.
32 "Otchety Tul'skogo Gubkoma, Svodka No. 11" (February 1925) F. 17, Op. 16, Doc. 1377, p. 84.
33 B. Clements, "Impact of the Civil War on Women and Family Relations," in D. Koenker, ed., *Party State and Society in the Russian Civil War*, pp. 105–23; B. Farnsworth, "Bolshevik Alternatives and the Soviet Family, the 1926 Marriage Law Debate," in D. Atkinson, *et al.*, eds, *Women in Russia*; Goldman, *Women, The State and Revolution*.
34 "Milent'evskaya volost," in *Gubernskie obsledovaniia TsKa*, p. 36.
35 Zhenotdel Shadrinskogo Ukoma (Ekaterinburg province 1923), *Otchet*, in *Obzory raboty Zhenskikh delegatskikh sobranii*, F. 17, Op. 10, Doc. 104, p. 27.
36 Barbara E. Clements, "Baba and Bolshevik: Russian Women and Revolutionary Change," *Soviet Union/Union Soviétique*, Vol. 12, part 2 (1985), pp. 161–84.
37 Bryansk Gubkom, "Otchet" (April 1924) F. 17, Op. 16, Doc. 69, p. 5.
38 "Doklady rabochikh otpusknikov, 1925" Doc. 767, p. 228.
39 Kubansko-Chernomorskaia oblast, "Otchet" (1925) Doc. 951, p. 90.
40 Smith, *Woman in Soviet Russia*, p. 26.
41 Ivanovo-Voznesensk gubkom, "Otchet za 1925" F. 17, Op. 16, Doc. 337, p. 68.
42 "Doklad Zaslavskogo" Doc. 72, pp. 12–15.
43 Zav. Gub. Zhenotdelom, Smeliakova, "Otchet o rabote sredi rabotnits i krestianok Vladimirskoi Gubernii" (January–March 1925) Doc. 90, p. 215.
44 Untitled leaflet in *Otchety Nizhegorodskogo Gubkoma* (April–June 1925) Doc. 584, p. 36.
45 "Svodka No. 1. O Rabote sredi zhenzhin. Itogi perevyborov delegatskikh sobranii" F. 17, Op. 69, Doc. 555, p. 31.
46 Ibid., p. 33.
47 Kubansko-Chernomorskaia oblast, "Otchet Gubkoma" F.17, Op. 16. Doc. 951, p. 79.
48 "Zakrytoe pis'mo MK" (1926) F. 17, Op. 67, Doc. 444, p. 3.
49 *Otchety Orlovskogo Gubkoma* (1925) F. 17, Op.16, Doc. 624, p. 95.
50 Diane Koenker, "Men Against Women on the Shop Floor in Early Soviet Russia: Gender and Class in the Socialist Workplace," *American Historical Review* 100:5 (December 1995), p. 1449; and "Sostoyanie Bryanskoi organizatsii" (September 1925) F. 17, Op. 16, Doc. 73, p. 39.
51 Ivanovo-Voznesensk Gubkom, "Otchet za 1925," Doc. 337, p. 67.
52 Artiukhina, Chair, Women's Department, To: Orgbiuro, "O plane verbovki v partiyu rabotnits" (1928) F. 17, Op. 69, Doc. 285, p. 115.
53 "Otchety Votkinskogo Obkoma" (1928–9) F. 17, Op. 67, Doc. 318, p. 105.
54 "Zakrytoe pis'mo Leningradskogo Obkoma" Doc. 440, p. 170.
55 "O Rabote sredi zhenzhin. Itogi perevyborov delegatskikh sobranii" F. 17, Op. 69, Doc. 555, p. 21.
56 Kazantzakis, *Russia . . .*, p. 191.
57 Ibid., p. 89.
58 TsKa VLKSM, "Obzor o rabote Komsomola sredi devushek" (1928) F. 1, Op. 23, Doc. 863. KA.

59 "Byt rabochei molodezhi" (15 June–1 July, 1925) F. 17, Op. 16, Doc. 73. p. 131.
60 Anne E. Gorsuch, "Flappers and Foxtrotters. Soviet Youth in the 'Roaring Twenties'," *Carl Beck Papers in Russian and East European Studies* No. 1102, p. 17.
61 TsKa VLKSM, "Obzor o rabote Komsomola sredi devushek" (1928) F. 1, Op. 23, Doc. 863, p. 14. KA.
62 "Soveshchanie aktiva *Komsomol'skoi Pravdy*" (1929) F. 17, Op. 69, Doc. 682, p. 85.
63 Anne E. Gorsuch, "Flappers and Foxtrotters," p. 14.
64 Molotov, To: All Gubkoms 12 October, 1923. "O borbe s izlishesvami i o prestupnom ispol'zovanii sluzhebnogo polozheniia" F. 17, Op. 84, Doc. 467, p. 2.
65 Orgraspred. MK, "Inform. Svodka, obzor zhizni yacheek" (1925) F. 17, Op. 16, Doc. 553, p. 32.
66 Bryansk Gubkom, "Otchet" (June 1924) F. 17, Op. 16, Doc. 69, p. 43.
67 From Kuban' Gubkom, "Doklad o predvaritel'nykh itogakh proverki neproizvodstvennykh yacheek" F. 17, Op. 16, Doc. 95, p. 278.
68 Instruktor Sedov, "Materialy obsledovaniya" (April 1927) F. 17, Op. 69, Doc. 310, p. 102.
69 Ibid.
70 "Nado krichat' chtoby uslyshali. Iz doklada gubsoyuza," in *Obzory raboty Zhenskikh delegatskikh sobranii* F. 17, Op. 10, Doc. 104, p. 124.
71 N. Alekseeva, To: Donbas Zhenotdel, Doc. 104.
72 Artiukhina, To: Orgbiuro, "O plane verbovki ..." (1928) F. 17, Op. 69, Doc. 285, p. 115.
73 Ibid., p. 116.
74 Zam.Zav. Stat. Otdel TsKa Vizel, "Svodka po voprosam raboty sredi zhenshchin" F. 17, Op. 69, Doc. 555, p. 11.

7 TOWARDS SHOWDOWN IN THE COUNTRYSIDE, 1926–8

1 "Doklad tovarishcha Yakovleva na MK," in MK (November 1925) F. 17, Op. 16, Doc. 553, p. 199.
2 Ibid.
3 *Otchety Leningradskogo Obkoma* (1925) Doc. 766, p. 37.
4 *Otchety Samarskogo Gubkoma* (March 1925) Doc. 692, p. 45.
5 *Otchety Tul'skogo Gubkoma*, Svodka No. 7 (1925) Doc. 1377, p. 53.
6 OGPU, "Obzor polit. sostoyaniya SSSR" (July 1926) F. 17, Op. 87, Doc. 200a.
7 *Otchety Tul'skogo Gubkoma*, Svodka No. 6 (1925) Op. 16, Doc. 1377, p. 47.
8 Sibirskii kraikom, "O Sostoianii derevenskikh partiinykh organizatsii i polozhenii krestyan" Doc. 1040, p. 149.
9 Kubansko-Chernomorskaya oblast, "Rezul'taty part.proverki" Doc. 951, p. 202.
10 *Otchety Tul'skogo Gubkoma*, Svodka No. 5 (1925) Doc. 1377, p. 43.
11 Info. Dept. CC RCP, To: Comrade Stalin, "Svodka naibolee kharakternykh voprosov na partiinykh konferentsiiakh" (1925) F. 17, Op. 84, Doc. 909.
12 OGPU, "Informatsionnaya svodka," No. 45 (August 1925) F. 17, Op. 87, Doc. 196.
13 CC RCP, To: Comrade Stalin, "Ezhednevnaya svodka" (15 February, 1925) F. 17, Op. 84, Doc. 910.
14 Sibirskii kraikom, "O Sostoianii derevenskikh partiinykh organizatsii i polozhenii krestian" F. 17, Op. 16, Doc. 1040, p. 147.
15 Ibid., p. 161.

16 OGPU, "Informatsionnaya svodka" (August 1925) No. 43, Section "Siberia," F. 17, Op. 87, Doc. 196.
17 Ibid., Svodka No. 45.
18 Ibid., Svodka No. 43.
19 Ibid., Svodka No. 42.
20 Ibid.
21 Ibid.
22 Ibid.
23 "Dokladnaya zapiska" (1925) in *Otchety Gomelskogo Gubkoma* Doc. 175.
24 *Otchety Leningradskogo Gubkoma* (1925) F. 17, Op. 16, Doc. 766, p. 253.
25 Tovstukha, To: Stalin, "Obzor polit. sostoyaniya SSSR" (July 1926) Prilozhenie 1, F. 17, Op. 87, Doc. 200a, p. 3.
26 Ibid.
27 Ibid.
28 Ibid., p. 8.
29 Ibid.
30 Ibid. Prilozhenie No. 1, p. 8.
31 Ibid. (December 1926), p. 15.
32 Ibid.
33 Ibid. (November 1926).
34 Ibid. (August 1926), Prilozhenie No. 3, p. 7.
35 Ibid. (September 1926) Prilozhenie No. 6, p. 7.
36 OGPU, To: CC, Subject, "Krestianskie Soyuzy" (April 1925) Doc. 199, Prilozhenie No. 4 (March 1925)
37 Ibid. Prilozhenie No. 2.
38 Ibid. Prilozhenie No. 4.
39 Info. Dept. CC RCP, "Spravka o Golode po Materialam GPU" (May 1925) F. 17, Op. 84, Doc. 741, p. 131.
40 *Otchety Tul'skogo Gubkoma*, Svodka No. 3 (1925) F. 17, Op. 16, Doc. 1377, p. 44.
41 OGPU, "Obzor polit. sostoyaniya v SSSR" (March 1925) F. 17, Op. 84, Doc. 916, p. 8.
42 OGPU, "Informatsionnye svodki, No. 51 and 53" (October 1925) Op. 87, Doc. 196.
43 OGPU, "Obzor polit. sostoyaniya SSSR" (August 1926) Prilozhenie No. 3, "Banditizm" Doc. 200a, p. 7.
44 Ibid. (November 1926).
45 T. Levichev, "O lishenii izbiratel'nykh prav," *Sovetskoe stroitel'stvo* 11 (1928), pp. 99–101.
46 Zam. Pred. OGPU Yagoda, "Obzor Polit. sostoyaniya SSSR" (March 1927) F. 17, Op. 87, Doc. 201, p. 4.
47 Ibid. (February 1927), p. 6.
48 Vserossiiskii Tsentral'nyi Ispolnitel'nyi Komitet, *Vybory v Sovety v Dia-grammakh* (Moscow: VTsIK 1927), p. 18.
49 "Sostoyanie raboty v derevne. Novosibirskii okrug" (9 March, 1927) F. 17, Op. 69, Doc. 310, p. 18.
50 "Zakon o lishenii izbiratel'nykh prav i narusheniyakh ego na praktike," *Sovetskoe stroitel'stvo* No. 5 (46) (May 1930), p. 3.
51 GPU Deputy Chair Yagoda, "Obzor Polit. sostoyaniya SSSR" (February 1927) F. 17, Op. 87, Doc. 201, p. 10.
52 Ibid.
53 OGPU, "Vybory sel'sovetov" (1927) Prilozhenie No. 4, item No. 99, Doc. 201.

54 "Sostoyanie raboty v derevne. Novosibirskii okrug" (9 March, 1927) F. 17, Op. 69, Doc. 310, p. 9.
55 GPU Deputy Chair Yagoda, "Obzor . . ." (March 1927) Op. 87, Doc. 201, p. 9.
56 Ibid., p. 10.
57 Ibid.
58 OGPU, "Vybory sel'sovetov" (1927) Prilozhenie No. 4, item No. 90, Doc. 201.
59 Instruktor Sedov, Saratov gubkom, To: Org. Raspred, Subject, *Materialy Saratovskogo Gubkoma* (1927) F. 17, Op. 69, Doc. 310.
60 Yagoda, "Obzor . . ." (March 1927) Op. 87, Doc. 201.
61 Ibid. (January 1927), p. 12.
62 Ibid. (March 1927)
63 OGPU, "Vybory sel'sovetov" (1927) Prilozhenie No. 4, item No. 96, Doc. 201.
64 Yagoda, "Obzor . . ." (March 1927) Doc. 201.
65 Ibid., p. 10
66 OGPU, "Vybory sel'sovetov" (1927) Prilozhenie No. 5, items No. 1–15, Doc. 201.
67 Ibid.
68 Strel'tsov, "O polozhenii v Vologodskoi organizatsii" (August 1929) F. 17, Op. 67, Doc. 317, p. 189.
69 Votkinsk obkom, To: Zavodskaya part. organizatsiia, "Direktivnoe Pis'mo" Doc. 318, p. 124.
70 *Obzory GPU 1923–24* Op. 87, Doc. 177, p. 8.
71 "Sostoyanie raboty v derevne. Novosibirskii okrug (9 March, 1927)" Op. 69, Doc. 310, p. 9.
72 CC Info. Dept, "Spravka o boleznennykh yavleniiakh v Ust' medvedskoi i Mikhailovskom raione Nizhne-Volzhskogo kraya" Op. 67, Doc. 451, p. 54.
73 "Spravka ob usilenii kulatskoi aktivnosti," Doc. 366.
74 S. Grachev (25 September, 1927), To: Saratov gubkom, in *Materialy Saratovskogo Gubkoma* Op. 69, Doc. 310, p. 37.
75 CC Info. Dept., "Spravka o boleznennykh yavleniiakh v Ust' medvedskoi . . ." Op. 67, Doc. 451, p. 54.
76 CC Info. Dept., Roshal', To: CC, subject, "Spravka o nalichii nenormal'nykh yavlenii v Vologodskoi partiinoi organizatsii" Doc. 317, p. 143.
77 Strel'tsov, "O polozhenii v Vologodskoi organizatsii" (August 1929) Doc. 317, p. 194.
78 Davies: *The Socialist Offensive*, p. 39.

8 THE PROLETARIAT AGAINST THE VANGUARD

1 "Ezhednevnaya Informatsionnaya svodka. Transportnogo otdela Vecheka" (16 January, 1922) F. 17, Op. 87, Doc. 176, p. 10.
2 "Politsostoyanie goroda Moskvy i Moskovskoi gubernii" (November–December 1922) Doc. 176, pp. 1–5.
3 Unshlikht GPU Info. Dept., To: Stalin, *Obzor* (17 July, 1923) and (31 August, 1923) Doc. 177.
4 GPU Deputy Chair Yagoda, To: Comrade Stalin's Secretariat, Comrade Mekhlis, *Kratkii Obzor Polit-ekonomicheskogo polozheniya respubliki* (1 July–15 September, 1923) Doc. 177.
5 Ibid.
6 *Iskorka* No. 7 (Yekaterinoslav: 25 May, 1922), Nicolaevsky Collection, series 6, Hoover Institution, Stanford, California.

7 Pethybridge, *One Step Backwards, Two Steps Forward*, pp. 269–89. On strikes in Smolensk, see William Rosenberg, "Smolensk in the 1920s. Party–Worker Relations," *Russian Review* No. 2 (1977), pp. 125–50.

8 GPU Deputy Chair Yagoda, To: Stalin's Secretariat, *Obzor Polit-ekonomicheskogo sostoyaniya* (15 September–1 November, 1923) F. 17, Op. 87, Doc. 177, p. 5.

9 Ibid.

10 GPU Info. Dept., To: CC, *Obzor Polit. sostoyaniya* (October 1923) Op. 84, Doc. 468, p. 67.

11 Ibid.

12 Bryansk Gubkom, To: CC *Otchet* (May–June 1924) Op. 16, Doc. 69.

13 Yagoda, To: Stalin's Secretariat, Comrade Mekhlis, *Kratkii Obzor* ... (1 July–15 September, 1923) Op. 87, Doc. 177.

14 "Sormovskaya stachka i ee itogi," *Golos Rabochego* No. 1 (September 1923), Nicolaevsky Collection, series 6.

15 Yagoda, To: Stalin's Secretariat, *Obzor Polit-ekonomicheskogo sostoyaniya* (15 September–1 November, 1923) F. 17, Op. 87, Doc. 177, pp. 5–6.

16 "Rabochii klass i Sotsial Demokratiia," *Sotsial Demokrat* No. 1 (February 1923) and "RKP," *Sotsial Demokrat* No. 2, Nicolaevsky Collection, series 6.

17 "Sormovskaia stachka i ee itogi," *Golos Rabochego* No. 1 (September 1923).

18 "Nash Put'," and "Kapitalizm, bol'sheviki i my," *Sotsial Demokrat* No. 8 (August 1923), Nicolaevsky Collection, series 6.

19 Voronezh Gubkom, To: CC, "Otchetnost" (October–December 1924) F. 17, Op. 16, Doc. 129, p. 95.

20 *Iskorka* No. 7 (Yekaterinoslav: 25 May, 1922) Nicolaevsky Collection, series 6.

21 "Otchet o rabote Prop. gruppy TsKa" (February–April 1925) F. 17, Op. 16, Doc. 73, p. 26.

22 "Pismo rabochikh," *Revoliutsionnaya Rossiya* No. 43 (Prague: June 1925), p. 23.

23 GPU, To: Stalin, *Obzor Polit. sostoyaniya SSSR* (August 1926) section, "Workers" F. 17, Op. 87, Doc. 200a, p. 4.

24 Leningrad Gubkom: "Obzory s krupnykh predpriyatii Leningrada," Op. 69, Doc. 43, p. 4.

25 Otvetstvennyi Instruktor Zaslavskii, To: Stalin, Molotov, Kuibyshev (Sovershenno sekretno), "O Leninskom sostave" Op. 16, Doc. 72, p. 27.

26 Serge, "Vignettes of NEP," in *Verdict of Three Decades*, p. 149.

27 GPU, To: CC, "Dokladnaya zapiska o pianstve sredi rabochikh" (21 August, 1925) F. 17, Op. 87, Doc. 199.

28 On culture of communal apartments, see Boym, *Common Places*, pp. 121–68.

29 *Fabrichno-zavodskaya promyshlennost' Soyuza SSR za 1927–28 i 1928–29*; Kviring, *Ocherki razvitiya promyshlennosti SSSR 1917–1927*; and Samuel A. Oppenheim, "Between Right and Left. G.Ya. Sokol'nikov and the Development of the Soviet State, 1921–1929," *Slavic Review* 48:4, pp. 593–613.

30 Nizhegorodskii Gubkom, To: CC, "Otchet" (April–June 1925) F. 17, Op. 16, Doc. 584, p. 48.

31 CC Info. Dept. Deputy Chief Dvinskii, To: CC, "Spravka ob otdel'nykh momentakh v sostoyanii i rabote Kuznetskoi okruzhnoi partorganizatsii" (18 June, 1928) Op. 67, Doc. 367, p. 103.

32 "Obzor o sostoyanii i rabote Kaluzhskoi gubernskoi partiinoi organizatsii" (July 1928) Doc. 436, p. 15.

33 "Programma obsledovaniya Nizhegorodskoi Organizatsii" (1928) Op. 16, Doc. 345, p. 9.

34 Nizhegorodskii gubkom, To: CC, "Otchet" (April–June 1925) Doc. 584, p. 50.
35 L.A. Neretina, "Reorganizatsiya gosudarstvennoi promyshlennosti v 1921–25 godakh. Printsipy i tendentsii razvitiia," in Davis, *et al.*, eds, *NEP. Priobreteniya i Poteri*, pp. 75–87 (here, p. 84).
36 I.A. Isaev, "NEP – rynochnaya perspektiva," in Davis *et al.*, eds, p. 98.
37 Samara gubkom, To: CC, "Informatsionnyi Otchet" (April–June 1925) F. 17, Op. 16, Doc. 692, p. 105.
38 Unshlikht, To: Stalin (31 August, 1923) Op. 87, Doc. 177, p. 2
39 "Pismo rabochikh," *Revolyutsionnaya Rossiya* No. 43 (Prague: June 1925), p. 23.
40 Leningrad Gubkom, To: CC, "Informatsionnyi Otchet" (April 1925) F. 17, Op. 16, Doc. 766, p. 18.
41 GPU, To: CC, *Informatsionnaya Svodka No. 37* (14–21 July, 1925) Op. 87, Doc. 196.
42 Orel Gubkom, To: CC, "Otchet" (January–April 1925) Op. 16, Doc. 624, p. 109.
43 Nizhegorodskii Gubkom, To: CC, "Otchet" (April–June 1925) Doc. 584, p. 131.
44 GPU, To: CC, *Informatsionnaya Svodka No.42* (August 1925) Op. 87, Doc. 196.
45 Andrea Graziosi, "'Building the First System of State Industry in History.' Piatakov's VSNKh and the Crisis of the NEP 1923–1926," *Cahiers du Monde Russe et Soviétique* 32:4 (October–December 1991), pp. 539–80 (see p. 554).
46 Ball, *Russia's Last Capitalists: The Nepmen*, pp. 72–6.
47 Yu. P. Bokarev, "Denezhnaya politika serediny 20kh godov," in Davies, *et al.*, eds, *NEP*, pp. 113 and 118.
48 "Vypiska iz sekretnogo protokola Nizhegorodskogo Gubkoma" (12 June, 1925), in *Otchety Nizhegorodskogo Gubkoma* F. 17, Op. 16, Doc. 584, p. 137.
49 GPU, To: Stalin, *Obzor Politsostoyaniya SSSR* (August 1926) section, "Workers" Op. 87, Doc. 200a, p. 4.
50 GPU Deputy Chair Yagoda and Info. Dept. Chief Alekseev, To: Stalin, *Obzor Politsostoyaniya SSSR* (May 1927) section, "Workers" Doc. 201, p. 3.
51 Ibid. (March 1927).
52 Tambov City Committee Secretary Birn, To: CC Secretary Bubnov and CC Info. Dept., "Politicheskoe sostoyanie gubernii" (January–March 1925) (25 May, 1925) Op. 84, Doc. 741, p. 134.
53 GPU, To: Stalin, *Obzor Politsostoyaniya SSSR* (January–March 1927) section, "Politnastroenie rabochikh" Op. 87, Doc. 201, pp. 3–4.
54 Ibid., p. 4.
55 GPU, To: CC, *Informatsionnaya Svodka No. 38* (July 1925) Doc. 196.
56 On unemployment, see Ward, *Russia's Cotton Workers and the New Economic Policy*, pp. 134–40.
57 "Pismo rabochikh," in *Revolyutsionnaya Rossiya* No. 43 (Prague: June 1925), p. 24.
58 GPU, To: Stalin, *Obzor Politsostoyaniya SSSR* (May 1927) section, "Workers" F. 17, Op. 87, Doc. 201, p. 8.
59 Ibid. (October 1926) Doc. 200a
60 MK, To: CC, "Zakrytoe Informatsionnoe pis'mo" (29 December, 1928) Op. 67, Doc. 444, pp. 8–9.
61 GPU, To: Orgraspred CC, "Kulatskaya vylazka na Podol'skom mekhanicheskom zavode," Doc. 444.
62 MK, To: Orgraspred CC, "Informatsionnaya spravka o prodovol'stvennom polozhenii Moskvy i gubernii i o nastroeniyakh v sviazi s prodovol'stvennymi zatrudneniiami" [On food supply in Moscow and popular attitudes in connection with food supply difficulties] (15 October, 1928), Ibid., p. 8.
63 Ibid.

64 MK, To: CC, "Zakrytoe Informatsionnoe pis'mo" (29 December, 1928) Op. 67, Doc. 444, pp. 6–7.
65 Lunacharsky, To: Kiselyov in CEC (no year, most likely 1928) Doc. 365, p. 58.
66 MK, To: CC Info. Dept. Prilozhenie No. 4, "Nastroenie rabochikh v raione" [Krasnaya Presnya district] Doc. 446, pp. 50–2.
67 MK, To: CC, "Zakrytoe Informatsionnnoe pis'mo" (29 December, 1928) Doc. 444, p. 4.
68 MK, To: CC, "Informatsionnoe soobshchenie o nastroenii rabochikh v svyazi s ratsionalizatsiei i sokrashcheniem rabochei sily" (15 April, 1929) Doc. 444, pp. 1–2.
69 Ibid., pp. 6–7.
70 Bailes: *Technology and Society under Lenin and Stalin*, pp. 74–88; Lambert: *The Technical Intelligentsia and the Soviet State*, pp. 39–40
71 MK, To: CC Info. Dept. Prilozhenie No. 4, "Nastroenie rabochikh v raione" Op. 67, Doc. 446, p. 47.
72 Chase, *Workers, Society, and the Soviet State. Labor and Life in Moscow, 1918–1929*, p. 299; also Siegelbaum: *Soviet State and Society between Revolutions*, p. 106, and Kuromiya, *Stalin's Industrial Revolution. Politics and Workers, 1928–1932*, p. 21.
73 Andrea Graziosi, "Stalin's Antiworker Workerism, 1924–1931," *International Review of Social History* 40 (1995), pp. 234–7.

9 THE BOLSHEVIK OLD GUARD AND THE UPSTARTS, 1924–9: DOWN AND OUT AND UP AND COMING

1 Politburo Postanovlenie, "O regulirovanii rosta partii" (13 October, 1927) F. 17, Op. 69, Doc. 285, p. 67.
2 The "Lenin levy's" impact on the Communist Party is detailed in T.H. Rigby, *Communist Party Membership in the USSR*, pp. 115–17. William Rosenberg considers the question in "Smolensk in the 1920s: Party–Worker Relations and the 'Vanguard' Problem," *Russian Review* 2 (1977), as does Sheila Fitzpatrick in "The problem of class identity in NEP society," in Fitzpatrick *et al.*, eds, *Russia in the Era of NEP*. See also M. Lewin, "The Social Background of Stalinism," in R. Tucker, ed., *Stalinism*, and Pethybridge, *One Step Backwards, Two Steps Forward*, and *The Social Prelude to Stalinism*.
3 On the cadres' training to obey, see Gill, *The Origins of the Stalinist Political System*; T. H. Rigby, "The Origins of the Nomenklatura System," in I. Auerbach, *et al.*, eds, *Felder und Vorfelder russischer Geschichte*; Service, *The Bolshevik Party in Revolution*; S. Blank, "Soviet Institutional Development during NEP: A Prelude to Stalinism," *Russian History* 2–3 (1982). On the low cultural level of the party and corruption, see Getty, *The Origins of the Great Purges*.
4 See the controversial Viola, *Best Sons of the Fatherland*. There is a discussion of an ideological "proletarian mandate" for Stalin in the late 1920s in Merridale, *Moscow Politics and the Rise of Stalin*, pp. 220–1.
5 Fitzpatrick, *The Russian Revolution*, p. 97.
6 John B. Hatch, "The 'Lenin Levy' and the Social Origins of Stalinism. Workers and the Communist Party in Moscow, 1921–1928," *Slavic Review* 48:4 (Winter 1989), pp. 558–78.
7 For the most eloquent summary of this school of thought, see Sheila Fitzpatrick, "New Perspectives on Stalinism," *The Russian Review* 45:4, (1986), pp. 357–75.

8 Sheila Fitzpatrick discusses the assumed identities in "The Problem of Class Identity in NEP Society," in Fitzpatrick, *et al.*, eds, *Russia in the Era of NEP*, pp. 12–33 (here, p. 28).
9 Instruktor N. Volynsky, "Obsledovanie Lenprizyva Bryanskoi gubernii, 1924" F. 17, Op. 16, Doc. 72, p. 25.
10 Vladimir gubkom, To: CC Info. Dept., "Otchet za iiun', iiul', avgust 1924" Doc. 90, p. 173.
11 Otvetstvennyi Instruktor Zaslavskii, "Doklad. Obsledovanie Bryanskogo zavoda," Doc. 72.
12 Bryansk gubkom, To: CC, "Otchet Gubkoma" (May–June 1924) Doc. 69, p. 34.
13 Instruktor TsKa Magidov, "Materialy obsledovaniya TsKa" (1926) Op. 67, Doc. 317, p. 15.
14 To: CC RCP, To: Stalin, Molotov, Kuybyshev. Sovershenno sekretno, "O Lensostave" Op. 16, Doc. 72, p. 26.
15 Zaslavskii, "Doklad . . ." section "Predstavleniya Lenintsev" Doc. 72, pp. 3, 5, 6.
16 Vladimir gubkom, To: CC Info. Dept., "Otchet 1924" Doc. 90, p. 85.
17 Bryansk gubkom, To: CC, "Otchet Gubkoma" (May–June 1924) Doc. 69, p. 34 and *Otchet Za Shest Mesiatsev* (1924) Doc. 69, p. 117.
18 Zaslavskii, "Doklad . . ." section, "Predstavleniia Lenintsev" Doc. 69, pp. 10–11.
19 Bryansk Gubkom, *Otchet Za Shest Mesiatsev* (1924).
20 Kursk Gubkom, To: CC, *Otchet Gubkoma May–June 1924* Doc. 519, p. 65.
21 Orel Gubkom, To: CC, *Otchety Gubkoma* (1925) Doc. 624, p. 73.
22 Voronezh Gubkom, To: CC Info. Dept., "Otchet" (October–December 1924) Doc. 129, p. 110.
23 Voronezh Gubkom, To: CC Org. Biuro, "Otchet 1924–1925" Doc. 125, p. 5.
24 Kubansko-Chernomorskaya oblast', To: CC, *Otchet 1925* Doc. 951, p. 69.
25 Instruktor TsKa Magidov, "Materialy obsledovaniya TsKa" (1926) Op. 67, Doc. 317, pp. 10–11.
26 I.I. Litvinov, "Ptitsegonstvo nadoelo dosmerti," Iz Dnevnika 1922 in *Neizvestnaya Rossiia XX Vek* Vol. 4, p. 91.
27 *Informatsionnyi Otchet Donetskogo Gubkoma* (January–March 1925) F. 17, Op. 16, Doc. 1049, p. 2.
28 Ivanovo-Voznesensk Gubkom, To: CC, *Otchet* (October–December 1924) Doc. 335, p. 17.
29 Nizhnii Novgorod Gubkom, To: CC, *Otchet* (April 1925) Doc. 584.
30 "Vypiska iz sekretnogo protokola Nizhnegorodskogo Gubkoma" (12 June, 1925) Doc. 584, p. 157.
31 MK, To: CC, "Info. otchet o vydvizhenii, 1925" Doc. 553, p. 279.
32 Leningrad Gubkom, *Otchety* (April 1925) Doc. 766, p. 18.
33 Vladimir Gubkom, To: CC Info. Dept., "Otchet: Oktiabr, Noiabr' 1924" Doc. 90, p. 187.
34 CC RCP, To: Stalin, Molotov, Kuybyshev, "O Lensostave" Doc. 72, p. 26.
35 Ivanovo-Voznesensk Gubkom, To: CC, "Otchet gubkoma" (October–December 1924) Doc. 335, p. 41.
36 Voronezh Gubkom, To: CC, "Informatsionnyi Otchet organizatsii RKP(b)" (May–June 1924) Doc. 129, p. 32.
37 Leningrad Gubkom, To: CC, "Otchet gubkoma" (July–September 1925) Doc. 767, p. 41.
38 Nizhnii Novgorod Gubkom, To: CC, "Otchet" (1924) Doc. 584, p. 8.
39 MK, To: CC, "O vydvizhenii" (1925) Doc. 553, p. 280.
40 Gomel Gubkom, To: CC, "Otchet" (22 October, 1924), Doc. 175, p. 24.

41 *Aktivist* No. 21 (Moscow: 1928).
42 "Raskhozhdeniya mezhdu otchetom paikoma i zapiskoi orgraspreda Tska" F. 17, Op. 67, Doc. 445.
43 This approach has been adopted, for example, by such modern authors as Chris Ward in *Stalin's Russia*. On Stalin's rise see Carr, *Socialism in One Country, 1924–26*, Vol. 1, pp. 155–6, 162; Cohen, *Bukharin*, ch. 9; Carr, *The Interregnum, 1923–1924*; Daniels, *The Conscience of the Revolution*; Fainsod, *How Russia is Ruled*; Narkiewicz, *The Making of the Soviet State Apparatus*; Schapiro, *The Communist Party of the Soviet Union* and *The Origins of Communist Autocracy*.
44 Kubansko-Chernomorskaia oblast', To: CC, *Otchet* (1925) F. 17, Op. 16, Doc. 951, p. 52.
45 See, for example, CC Info. Dept., "Obsuzhdenie mestnymi organizatsiyami vnutripartiinogo polozheniya v sviazi s vystupleniyami liderov oppozitsii v oktiabre 1926 goda" Op. 69, Doc. 271, p. 38.
46 On Trotsky's "Thermidorean reaction" see his *Stalin*, p. 393, and particularly *My Life* and *The Revolution Betrayed*. Another early witness's testimony is Milovan Djilas, *The New Class*. Further analysis is provided in M. Krygier, "'Bureaucracy' in Trotsky's analysis of Stalinism," in Sawer, ed., *Socialism and the New Class*; D.W. Lovell, *Trotsky's Analysis of Soviet Bureaucratization*; R.H. McNeal, "Trotskyist interpretations of Stalinism," in Tucker, ed., *Stalinism*.
47 "Otchet o provedennoi rabote v Ryazanskoi gubernii" (November 1927) Doc. 270, p. 128.
48 "Spravka ob otdel'nykh momentakh v sostoyanii i rabote Kuznetskoi okruzhnoi partiinoi organizatsii" (18 June, 1927) Op. 67, Doc. 367.
49 "Otchet o provedennoi rabote v Ryazanskoi gubernii" (November 1927) Op. 69, Doc. 270, p. 131.
50 Vtoroi plenum MK VKP(B) (31 January–2 February, 1928) Op. 67, Doc. 444, p. 35.
51 "Doklad o diskussii po voprosam 15 s'ezda. Bryansk, Bezhitsa" (19 November, 1927) Op. 69, Doc. 270, p. 93.
52 "Doklad o rabote Orlovskoi gruppy preds'ezdovskoi diskussii" (Fall 1927) Doc. 270, p. 120.
53 *Bich* No. 41 (Moscow: October 1927), p. 11.
54 "Smelo Tovarishchi v nogu," *Buzuter* No. 9 (Moscow: February 1927), p. 12.
55 Kaluga gubkom, To: CC, "Obzor sostoyaniya Kaluzhskoi gubernskoi partiinoi organizatsii" (July 1928) F. 17, Op. 67, Doc. 436, pp. 16–17.
56 MK, To: CC, "Zakrytoe informatsionnoe pis'mo" (29 December, 1928) Doc. 444, p. 10.
57 I.I. Litvinov, "Ptitsegonstvo nadoelo dosmerti," Iz Dnevnika 1922 in *Neizvestnaya Rossiia XX Vek*, Vol. 4, p. 96.
58 Conquest, *The Harvest of Sorrow*.
59 Stephen Cohen, "Bolshevism and Stalinism," in Tucker, ed., *Stalinism*, pp. 3–30.
60 Conquest, *The Harvest of Sorrow*; Malia, *The Soviet Tragedy*, pp. 192–3.
61 Tucker, *Stalin in Power*, pp. 89–91.
62 CC Info. Dept., To: Stalin, "Informatsionnaya svodka" (21 November, 1929) F. 17, Op. 69, Doc. 696, p. 20.
63 Tambov, To: Comrade Kaganovich (January 1929) Doc. 699.
64 CC Info. Dept., "Spravka o pravoi opasnosti" (December 1928–January 1929) Doc. 672, p. 3.
65 Ibid.
66 Ibid., p. 7.
67 Ibid., p. 8.

68   Ibid., p. 2.
69   Severnyi Kavkaz, To: CC Info. Dept., Stalin, Molotov, Kaganovich, Svodka No. 34 (November 1929), "O khode khlebozagotovok" Op. 69, Doc. 696, p. 32.
70   TsKK: "O proverke i chistke partii za oktiabr 1929 goda" Doc. 680, p. 1.
71   Leningrad Control Commission Chairman Desov, "Otchet 1927" Op. 67, Doc. 440.
72   "Nekotorye vyderzhki iz svodki LK" Doc. 440.
73   See *Pravda* (21 December, 1929)
74   See, for example, the case of Ya. S. Tseitlin, a Komsomol leader in *Izvestiya TsKa* No. 1 (1990), p. 50.
75   Adam Ulam noted this perceptively in his *Stalin: The Man and His Era*, p. 271.
76   Martemyan Riutin, *Na Koleni Ne Vstanu*, p. 243.
77   Ibid.
78   Ibid., p. 117.
79   Ibid., p. 226.
80   Ibid., p. 238.

10 CONCLUSION

1   Viola, *Best Sons of the Fatherland*, p. 17

Bibliography

Abramowitsch, Raphail, *Die Politischen Gefangenen in der Sowjetunion*. Berlin: J.H.W. Dietz Nachf. G.m.b.H., 1930.

Acton, Edward, *Rethinking the Russian Revolution*. London, New York: E. Arnold N.Y. (in the US distributed by Routledge), 1990.

Altrichter, Helmut, *Die Bauern von Tver. Vom Leben auf dem russischen Dorfe zwischen Revolution und Kollektivierung*. München: Oldenbourg, 1984.

Antonov-Ovseenko, Anton, *Portret tirana. The Time of Stalin. Portrait of a Tyranny*. New York: Harper Colophon Books, 1981.

Ascher, Abraham, *The Revolution of 1905*. Stanford, CA.: Stanford University Press, 1992.

Atkinson, Dorothy, Dallin, Alexander and Lapidus, Gail, eds, *Women in Russia*. Stanford, CA.: Stanford University Press, 1977.

Auerbach, I. *et al.*, eds, *Felder und Vorfelder russischier Geschichte: Studien zu Ehren von Peter Scheibert*. Friburg: Rombach, 1985.

Aves, Jonathan, *Workers against Lenin: Labour Protest and the Bolshevik Dictatorship*. London, New York: Tauris Academic Studies, 1996.

Bailes, Kendall E., *Technology and Society under Lenin and Stalin. Origins of the Soviet Technical Intelligentsia, 1917–1941*. Princeton, N.J.: Princeton University Press, 1978.

Ball, Alan M., *Russia's Last Capitalists: The Nepmen, 1921–1929*. Berkeley, London: University of California Press, 1987.

Benjamin, Walter, *Moscow Diary*. Cambridge, Mass.: Harvard University Press, 1986.

Berdiaev, Nicholas, *Origin of Communism*. Ann Arbor, MI.: University of Michigan Press, 1984.

Berelovitch, Wladimir, *La Soviétisation de l'école russe 1917–1931*. Lausanne: L'age d'Homme, 1990.

Berkin, Carol R. and Lovett, Clara M., eds, *Women, War and Revolution*. New York, London: Holmes and Meier, 1980.

Bibikova, I. M. and Levchanko, N.I., eds, *Agitatsionno Massovoe iskusstvo. Oformlenie prazdnevstv*. Moscow: Iskustvo, 1984.

Bowlt, John E., ed., *Russian Art of the Avant Garde: Theory and Criticism 1902–1934*. New York: Viking, 1976.

Boym, Svetlana, *Common Places: Mythologies of Everyday Life in Russia*. Cambridge, Mass.: Harvard University Press, 1994.

Brovkin, Vladimir, *Behind the Front Lines of the Civil War. Political Parties and Social Movements in Russia*. Princeton, N.J.: Princeton University Press, 1994.

—— *The Mensheviks after October. Socialist Opposition and the Rise of the Bolshevik Dictatorship*. Ithaca, N.Y.: Cornell University Press, 1987.

—— ed., *Dear Comrades*. Stanford, CA.: Hoover Institution Press, 1991.

—— ed., *The Bolsheviks in Russian Society. Revolution and Civil Wars*. New Haven and London: Yale University Press, 1997.

Brown, Matthew Cullerne, *Art under Stalin*. New York: Holmes & Meier, 1991.

Burbank, Jane, *Intelligentsia and Revolution. Russian Views of Bolshevism 1917–1922*. Oxford, New York, Toronto: Oxford University Press, 1986.

Carr, E.H., *The Interregnum, 1923–1924*. New York, London: Macmillan, 1958.

—— *Socialism in One Country, 1924–1926*. New York, London: Macmillan, 1958–64.

Carr, E.H. and Davies, R.W., *Foundations of a Planned Economy, 1926–1929*, Vol. 2. London: Macmillan, 1969.

Chartier, Roger, *Forms and Meanings. Texts, Performances, and Audiences from Codex to Computer*. Philadelphia: University of Pennsylvania Press, 1995.

—— *Cultural History: Between Practices and Representations*. Ithaca, N.Y.: Cornell University Press, 1988.

—— *On the Edge of the Cliff: History, Language and Practices*. Baltimore: Johns Hopkins University Press, 1997.

Chase, William J., *Workers, Society, and the Soviet State: Labor and Life in Moscow, 1918–1929*. Urbana, Ill.: University of Illinois Press, 1987.

Clark, Katerina, *Petersburg, Crucible of Cultural Revolution*. Cambridge, Mass.: Harvard University Press, 1995.

Clements, Barbara, Engel, Barbara Alpern and Worobec, Christine D., eds, *Russia's Women. Accommodation, Resistance, Transformation*. Berkeley, CA.: University of California Press, 1991.

Cohen, Stephen F., *Bukharin and the Bolshevik Revolution: A Political Biography 1888–1938*. New York: Knopf, 1973.

Conquest, Robert, *The Harvest of Sorrow: Soviet Collectivization and the Terror-Famine*. New York: Oxford University Press, 1987.

Cooke, Catherine, *Russian Avant-garde: Theories of Art, Architecture and the City*. London: Academy Editions, 1995.

Cooke, Richard J., *Religion in Russia under the Soviets*. New York, Cincinnati: The Abingdon Press, 1924.

Curtiss, John S., *The Russian Church and the Soviet State 1917–1930*. Boston: Little, Brown & Co., 1953.

Daniels, Robert V., *The Conscience of the Revolution: Communist Opposition in Soviet Russia*. Cambridge, Mass.: Harvard University Press, 1960.

Darnton, Robert, *The Great Cat Massacre and Other Episodes in French Cultural History*. New York: Basic Books, 1984.

Davies, R.W., *The Socialist Offensive: The Collectivization of Soviet Agriculture 1929–30*. Cambridge, Mass.: Harvard University Press, 1980.

Davies, R.W., Dmitrenko, V.P., Mau, V.A., *et al.*, eds, *NEP. Priobreteniya i Poteri*. Moscow: Nauka, 1994.

Day, Richard, *Leon Trotsky and the Politics of Economic Isolation*. Cambridge: Cambridge University Press, 1973.

Deutscher, Isaac, *Stalin: A Political Biography*. New York: Oxford University Press, 1967.

De Vries, Wilhelm, *Kirche und Staat in der Sowjetunion*. München: Verlag Anton Pustet, 1959.

Djilas, Milovan, *The New Class: An Analysis of the Communist System*. New York: Praeger, 1957.

Duranty, Walter, *I Write as I Please*. New York: Simon & Schuster, 1935.

—— *Duranty Reports Russia*. New York: Simon & Schuster, 1934.

Dvinov, Boris, *Ot legal'nosti k podpol'iu*. New York: Inter-University Menshevik Project, 1962.

Edmonson, Linda, ed., *Women and Society in Russia and the Soviet Union*. New York: Cambridge University Press, 1992.

Elwood, R.C., *Inessa Armand. Revolutionary and Feminist*. Cambridge: Cambridge University Press, 1992.

Emhardt, William Chauncey, ed., *Religion in Soviet Russia*. London: Mowbray, 1929.

Emmons, Terence, *The Formation of Political Parties and the First National Elections in Russia*. Cambridge, Mass.: Harvard University Press, 1988.

Erlich, Alexander, *The Soviet Industrialization Debate, 1924–1928*. Cambridge, Mass.: Harvard University Press, 1960.

Fainsod, Merle, *How Russia Is Ruled*. Cambridge, Mass.: Harvard University Press, 1953.

Farnsworth, Beatrice, *Aleksandra Kolontai. Socialism, Feminism and the Bolshevik Revolution*. Stanford, CA.: Stanford University Press, 1980.

Farnsworth, Beatrice and Viola, Lynne, eds, *Russian Peasant Women*. New York, Oxford: Oxford University Press, 1992.

Felshtinsky, Yurii, ed., *Arkhiv Trotskogo Kommunisticheskaia oppozitsiya v SSSR*, 4 volumes. Moscow: Terra, 1990.

—— *VCHK – GPU: Dokumenty i materialy*. Moscow: Izd. gumanitarnoi literatury, 1995.

Fieseler, Beate, *Frauen auf dem Weg in die russischen Sozialdemokratie, 1890–1917*. Stuttgart: F. Steiner, 1995.

Figes, Orlando, *A People's Tragedy. A History of the Russian Revolution*. New York: Viking, 1997.

Fisher, Ralph Talcott, Jr., *Pattern for Soviet Youth*. New York: Columbia University Press, 1959.

Fitzpatrick, Sheila, *The Commissariat of Enlightenment: Soviet Organization of Education and the Arts under Lunacharsky, October 1917–1921*. Cambridge: Cambridge University Press, 1970.

—— *The Russian Revolution 1917–1932*. Oxford, New York: Oxford University Press, 1982.

—— *The Cultural Front. Power and Culture in Revolutionary Russia*. Ithaca, N.Y.: Cornell University Press, 1992.

—— *Stalin's Peasants. Resistance and Survival in the Russian Village after Collectivization*. New York, Oxford: Oxford University Press, 1994.

—— ed., *Cultural Revolution in Russia, 1928–1931*. Bloomington: Indiana University Press, 1978.

—— ed., *Education and Social Mobility in the Soviet Union, 1921–1934*. Cambridge: Cambridge University Press, 1979.

Fitzpatrick, Sheila, Rabinowitch, Alexander, and Stites, Richard, eds, *Russia in the Era of NEP. Explorations in Soviet Society and Culture*. Bloomington: Indiana University Press, 1991.

Frierson, Cathy, *Peasant Icons. Representations of Rural People in Late 19th Century Russia*. New York, Oxford: Oxford University Press, 1993.

Geifman, Anna, *Thou Shalt Kill. Revolutionary Terrorism in Russia 1894–1917*. Princeton, N.J.: Princeton University Press, 1994.

Getty, J. Arch, *The Origins of the Great Purges: The Soviet Communist Party Reconsidered, 1933–38*. London, New York: Cambridge University Press, 1985.

Gill, Graeme, *The Origins of the Stalinist Political System*. Cambridge: Cambridge University Press, 1990.

Gleason, Abbott, *et al.*, eds, *Bolshevik Culture: Experiment and Order in the Russian Revolution*. Bloomington: Indiana University Press, 1985.

Glickman, Rose, *Russian Factory Women. Workplace and Society 1880–1914.* Berkeley, CA.: University of California Press, 1984.

Goldman, Wendy, *Women, the State and Revolution: Soviet Family Policy and Social Life, 1917–1936.* New York: Cambridge University Press, 1993.

Golomstock, Igor, *Totalitarian Art.* New York: Icon editions (US edition), Harper-Collins, 1990.

Gorsuch, Anne E., *Enthusiasts, Bohemians and Delinquents: Soviet Youth Culture, 1921–1928.* Ann Arbor, MI.: UMI Dissertation Services, 1995.

Graham, Loren, *The Soviet Academy of Sciences and the Communist Party, 1927–1932.* Princeton, N.J.: Princeton University Press, 1967.

Gray, Camilla, *The Great Experiment: Russian Art 1863–1922.* London: Thames and Hudson, 1962.

Graziosi, Andrea, *The Great Soviet Peasant War: Bolsheviks and Peasants, 1917–1933.* Cambridge, Mass.: Harvard University Press, 1996.

Grois, Boris, *The Total Art of Stalinism. Avant-garde, Aesthetic Dictatorship and beyond.* Princeton, N.J.: Princeton University Press, 1992.

Guerman, Mikhail, *The Art of the October Revolution.* New York: Harry N. Abrams inc. Publishers, 1979.

Günter, Hans, ed., *Culture of the Stalin Period.* New York: St. Martin's Press, 1990.

Gurvich, G.S., *Istoriia sovetskoi konstitutsii.* Moscow: Politizdat, 1923.

Harding, Neil, *Lenin's Political Thought.* New York: St. Martin's Press, 1978.

Harper, Samuel N., *Making Bolsheviks.* Chicago, Ill.: University of Chicago Press, 1931.

Hecker, Julius F., *Religion and Communism. A Study of Religion and Atheism in Soviet Russia.* London: Chapman and Hall, 1933.

Hildermeier, Manfred, *Die Sozialrevolutionäre Partei Russlands.* Köln, Wien: Bohlau, 1978.

Hindus, Maurice, *Broken Earth.* New York: New York International Publishers, 1926.

Holmes, Larry, *The Kremlin and the Schoolhouse: Reforming Education in Soviet Russia.* Bloomington: Indiana University Press, 1991.

Hudson, Hugh, Jr., *Blueprints and Blood. The Sovietization of Soviet Architecture 1917–1937.* Princeton, N.J.: Princeton University Press, 1994.

Hughes, James, *Stalin, Siberia, and the Crisis of the New Economic Policy.* New York: Cambridge University Press, 1991.

Huszar, George B., *The Intellectuals.* London: n.p., 1960.

Isham, Heyward, ed., *Remaking Russia. Voices from within.* Armonk, N.Y.: M.E. Sharpe, 1995.

Kagarlitsky, Boris, *The Thinking Red? Intellectuals and the Soviet State, 1917 to the Present.* New York: Verso, 1988.

Kapferer, Jean-Noel, *Rumors. Uses, Interpretations, and Images.* New Brunswick, N.J., and London: Transactions, 1990.

Kautsky, Karl, *Bolshevism v Tupike.* Paris: Sotsialisticheskiy Vestnik, 1930.

Kazantzakis, Nikos, *Russia: A Chronicle of Three Journeys in the Aftermath of the Revolution.* Berkeley, CA.: Creative Arts Book, 1989.

Keep, John, *The Rise of Social Democracy in Russia.* Oxford: Clarendon Press, 1963.

Kenez, Peter, *The Birth of the Propaganda State. Soviet Methods of Mass Mobilization.* Cambridge, London, New York: Cambridge University Press, 1985.

—— *Cinema and Soviet Society 1917–1953.* New York: Cambridge University Press, 1992.

Kingston-Mann, Esther and Mixter, Timothy, eds, *Peasant Economy. Culture and Politics, 1800–1921.* Princeton, N.J.: Princeton University Press, 1991.

Klinghoffer, Arthur Jay, *Red Apocalypse. The Religious Evolution of Soviet Communism.* Lanham, MD.: University Press of America, 1996.

Knei-Paz, Baruch, *The Social and Political Thought of Leon Trotsky*. Oxford: Clarendon Press, 1978.

Koenker, Diane, *et al.*, eds, *Party, State and Society in the Russian Civil War*. Bloomington: Indiana University Press, 1988.

Kratkii Kurs istorii VKP (b). Moscow: Pilitizdat, 1938.

Kuromiya, Hiroaki, *Stalin's Industrial Revolution. Politics and Workers, 1928–1932*. New York, New Rochelle, Sydney: Cambridge University Press, 1988.

Kvashonkin, A.V., *et al.*, eds, *Bolshevistskoe rukovodstvo: Perepiska, 1912–1927*. Moscow: Rospen, 1996.

Kviring, Em., *Ocherki razvitiya promyshlennosti SSSR 1917–1927*. Moscow: Gosizdat, 1929.

Lambert, Nicholas, *The Technical Intelligentsia and the Soviet State. A Study of Soviet Managers and Technicians, 1928–1935*. London: Macmillan, 1979.

Leida, Jay, *Kino: A History of the Russian-Soviet Film*. Princeton, N.J.: Princeton University Press, 1983.

Lewin, Moshe, *Political Undercurrents in Soviet Economic Debates from Bukharin to the Modern Reformers*. Princeton, N.J.: Princeton University Press, 1974.

—— *Russian Peasants and Soviet Power. A Study of Collectivization*. New York: W.W. Norton, 1975.

—— *The Making of the Soviet System. Essays in the Social History of Interwar Russia*. New York, N.Y.: Pantheon, 1985.

Liebich, Andre, *From the Other Shore. Russian Social Democracy after 1921*. Cambridge, Mass.: Harvard University Press, 1997.

Lih, Lars, ed., *Stalin's Letters to Molotov*. New Haven and London: Yale University Press, 1996.

Lodder, Christina, *Russian Constructivism*. New Haven, Conn.: Yale University Press, 1983.

Lovell, David W., *Trotsky's Analysis of Soviet Bureaucratization*. London, Dover, N.H.: Croom Helm, 1985.

Lunacharsky, Anatoliy, *Khristianstvo ili Kommunizm. Disput s Mitropolitom Vedenskim*. Moscow: n.p., 1925.

—— *Upadochnye Nastroeniya Sredi Molodezhi. Yeseninshchina*. Moscow: Izdatel'stvo Kommunisticheskoi Akademii, 1927.

Lyons, Eugene, *Assignment in Utopia*. New York: Harcourt, Brace and Company, 1937.

McNeal, Robert H., *The Bolshevik Tradition: Lenin, Stalin, Khrushchev*. Engelwood Cliffs, N.J.: Prentice Hall, 1963.

—— *Stalin: Man and Ruler*. New York: New York University Press, 1988.

Malia, Martin, *Comprendre la révolution russe*. Paris: Editions du Seuil, 1980.

—— *The Soviet Tragedy. A History of Socialism in Russia, 1917–1991*. New York, London, Toronto: The Free Press, 1994.

Mally, Lynn, *Culture of the Future. The Proletkult Movement in Revolutionary Russia*. Berkeley, CA., Oxford: University of California Press, 1990.

Mandel, David, *The Petrograd Workers and the Soviet Seizure of Power*. New York: St Martin's Press, 1984.

Mandelshtam, Nadezhda, *Hope against Hope. A Memoir*. New York: Atheneum, 1983.

Merridale, Catherine, *Moscow Politics and the Rise of Stalin: The Communist Party in the Capital, 1925–1932*. New York: St Martin's Press, 1990.

Meyer, Alfred G., *Leninism*. Boulder, Col., London: Westview Press, 1986.

Miller, Rene Füllop, *The Mind and Face of Bolshevism*. New York: Knopf, 1929.

Milner, John, *Vladimir Tatlin and the Russian Avante-garde*. New Haven, Conn.: Yale University Press, 1983.

Nahirny, Vladimir C., *The Russian Intelligentsia: From Torment to Silence*. New Brunswick, N.J.: Transaction Books, 1983.

Naiman, Eric, *Sex in Public. The Incarnation of Early Soviet Ideology*. Princeton, N.J.: Princeton University Press, 1997.

Naimark, Norman, *Terrorists and Social Democrats: The Russian Revolutionary Movement under Alexander III*. Cambridge, Mass.: Harvard University Press, 1983.

Narkiewicz, Olga A., *The Making of the Soviet State Apparatus*. Manchester: Manchester University Press, 1970.

Pascal, Pierre, *The Religion of the Russian People*. London, Oxford: Mowbrays, 1976.

Pethybridge, Roger, *The Social Prelude to Stalinism*. London: Macmillan, 1974.

—— *One Step Backwards, Two Steps Forward. Soviet Society and Politics in the New Economic Policy*. Oxford: Clarendon Press, 1990.

Pintner, Walter M. and Rowney, D.K., eds, *Russian Officialdom. The Bureaucratization of Russian Society from the 17th to the 20th Century*. Chapel Hill, N.C.: University of North Carolina Press, 1980.

Pipes, Richard, *Struve. Liberal on the Left*. Cambridge, Mass.: Harvard University Press, 1970.

—— *The Russian Revolution*. New York: Knopf, 1990.

—— *Russia under the Bolshevik Regime*. New York: Knopf, 1993.

—— ed., *Unknown Lenin. From the Secret Archive*. New Haven, London: Yale University Press, 1996.

Platforma RSDRP. Paris: Sotsialisticheskii Vestnik, 1924.

Pomper, Philip, *Lenin, Trotsky, Stalin. The Intelligentsia and Power*. New York: Columbia University Press, 1990.

Pospielovsky, Dmitry, *The Russian Church and the Soviet Regime, 1917–1982*. 2 volumes. Crestwood, N.J.: St. Vladimir Seminary Press, 1984.

Read, Christopher, *Culture and Power in Revolutionary Russia: The Intelligentsia and the Transition from Tsarism to Communism*. Basingstoke: Macmillan, 1990.

—— *From Tsar to Soviets. The Russian People and Their Revolution 1917–1921*. Oxford: Oxford University Press, 1996.

Rees, E.A., *The Birth of Stalinism: The Rise and Fall of the Workers' and Peasants' Inspectorate, 1920–1934*. New York: St Martin's Press, 1987.

Reiman, Michael, *Die Geburt des Stalinismus. Die UdSSR am Vorabend der "Zweiten Revolution"*. Frankfurt/Main: Europäische Verlag, 1979.

Rigby, T.H., *Communist Party Membership in the USSR, 1917–1967*. Princeton, N.J.: Princeton University Press, 1968.

—— *Lenin's Government. Sovnarkom*. Cambridge, New York: Cambridge University Press, 1979.

Riutin, Martemyan, *Na Koleni Ne Vstanu*. Moscow: Politizdat, 1992.

Rosenberg, William, ed., *Bolshevik Visions. First Phase of the Cultural Revolution in Soviet Russia*. Ann Arbor, MI.: Ardis, 1984.

Sawer, Marian, ed., *Socialism and the New Class: Towards the Analysis of Structural Inequality within Socialist Societies*. Bedford Park, South Australia: Australian Political Studies Association, 1978.

Schama, Simon, *Citizens. A Chronicle of the French Revolution*. New York: Knopf, 1989.

Schapiro, Leonard, *The Origins of Communist Autocracy: Political Opposition in the Soviet State: First Phase, 1917–1922*. New York: Praeger, 1965.

—— *The Communist Party of the Soviet Union*. New York: Vintage, 1970.

Schapiro, Leonard and Reddaway, Peter, *Lenin: The Man, The Theorist, The Leader. A Reappraisal*. London: Pall Mall Press, 1967.

Service, Robert, *The Bolshevik Party in Revolution: A Study in Organizational Change*. New York: Barnes & Noble, 1979.

—— *The Russian Revolution, 1900–1927*. Atlantic Highlands, N.J.: Humanities Press International, 1986.

Shchetinov, Yurii, *Krushenie melko-burzhuaznoi kontr-revoliutsii v Sovetskoi Rossii*. Moscow: Izd. Moskovskogo universiteta, 1984.

Shlapentokh Dmitry and Shlapentokh, Vladimir, *Soviet Cinematography 1918–1991*. New York: Aldine de Gruyter, 1993.

—— *Ideological Conflict and Social Reality*. New York: Aldine de Gruyter, 1993.

Siegelbaum, Lewis H., *Soviet State and Society between Revolutions, 1918–1929*. Cambridge: Cambridge University Press, 1992.

—— *Making Workers Soviet: Power, Class and Identity*. Ithaca, N.Y.: Cornell University Press, 1994.

Smith, Jessica, *Woman in Soviet Russia*. New York: Vanguard Press, 1928.

Spence, Richard, *Boris Savinkov. Renegade on the Left*. Boulder, Col.: East European Monographs, 1991.

Spinka, Matthew, *Christianity Confronts Communism*. New York, London: Harper and Brothers, 1936.

Starr, S. Frederick, *Red and Hot. The Fate of Jazz in the Soviet Union, 1917–1991*. New York: Limelight Editions, 1994.

—— *Melnikov: Solo Architect in a Mass Society*. Princeton, N.J.: Princeton University Press, 1978.

Steinberg, Julien, ed., *Verdict of Three Decades*. New York: Duel, Sloan and Pearce, 1950.

Stites, Richard, *The Women's Liberation Movement in Russia*. Princeton, N.J.: Princeton University Press, 1978.

—— *Revolutionary Dreams. Utopian Vision and Experimental Life in the Russian Revolution*. New York, Oxford: Oxford University Press, 1989.

—— *Russian Popular Culture. Entertainment and Society since 1900*. Cambridge: Cambridge University Press, 1992.

Taylor, Brandon, *Art and Literature under the Bolsheviks*, Vol. 1: *The Crisis of Renewal 1917–1924*. London, Concord, Mass.: Pluto Press, 1991.

Timasheff, Nicholas S., *Religion in Soviet Russia 1917–1942*. London: Sheed & Ward, 1943.

Tobenkin, Elias, *Stalin's Ladder: War and Peace in the Soviet Union*. New York: Minton, Balch & Co., 1933.

Trotsky, Leon, *Stalin: An Appraisal of the Man and His Influence*. New York: Stein & Day, 1967.

—— *My Life*. New York: Pathfinder, 1970.

—— *The Revolution Betrayed: What is the Soviet Union and Where is it Going?* New York: Pathfinder, 1972.

Tucker, Robert, *Stalin as Revolutionary: A Study in History and Personality 1879–1929*. New York: W.W. Norton, 1973.

—— *Stalin in Power. The Revolution from Above, 1928–1941*. New York, London: W.W. Norton, 1992.

—— ed., *Stalinism. Essays in Historical Interpretation*. New York, London: W.W. Norton, 1977.

Ulam, Adam B., *The Bolsheviks. The Intellectual and Political History of the Triumph of Communism in Russia*. New York: Macmillan, 1965.

—— *Stalin: The Man and His Era*. Boston: Beacon Press, 1989.

Venturi, Franco, *Roots of Revolution. A History of the Populist and Socialist Movement in 19th Century Russia*. New York: Knopf, 1960.

Viola, Lynn, *Best Sons of the Fatherland: Workers in the Vanguard of Collectivization*. Oxford: Oxford University Press, 1987.

Volkogonov, Dmitrii, *Triumf i tragediya. Politicheskii Portret I.V. Stalina v dvukh knigakh*. Moscow: Agenstvo Pechati i Novosti, 1989.

Ward, Chris, *Russia's Cotton Workers and the New Economic Policy*. Cambridge, New York: Cambridge University Press, 1990.

—— *Stalin's Russia*. London, New York: Routledge, Edward Arnold: 1993.

Weiss, Evelyn, *Russische Avantgarde 1910–1930*. Köln: Sammlung Ludvig, 1986.

White, Stephen, *The Bolshevik Poster*. New Haven, London: Yale University Press, 1988.

White, William C., *These Russians*. New York: Charles Scribner's Sons, 1931.

Wilson, Janey R., ed., *Architectural Drawings of the Russian Avant-Garde*. New York: Museum of Modern Art, 1990.

Wood, Elizabeth, *The Baba and the Comrade: Gender and Politics in Revolutionary Russia*. Bloomington: Indiana University Press, 1997.

Yakovlev, A.N., ed., *Reabilitatsiia. Politicheskie Protsessy 30–50-kh Godov*. Moscow: Politizdat, 1991.

Yedlin, Tova, ed., *Women in Eastern Europe and the Soviet Union*. New York: Praeger, 1980.

Youngblood, Denise, *Movies for the Masses: Popular Cinema and Soviet Society in the 1920s*. New York: Cambridge University Pres, 1992.

Zhadova, Larisa A., *Malevich: Suprematism and Revolution in Russian Art 1910–1930*. New York: Thames & Hudson, 1982.

Zhuravlev, V.V., *et al.*, eds, *Vlast i Oppozitsiya. Rossiiskii Politicheskii Protsess XX stoletiya*. Moscow: Rospen, 1995.

Zinoviev, Grigorii, *Ob Antisovetskikh partiiakh i techeniiakh*. Moscow: Gosizdat, 1922.

Index